Early Childhood Parenting Skills

A Program Manual for the Mental Health Professional

Richard R. Abidin

PAR Psychological Assessment Resources, Inc.

Dedication

I would like to dedicate this manual to Mary Abidin, the mother of our four children, and to my children and grandchildren for the opportunity to learn from them.

Special Thanks

I would like to express special thanks to Suzanne Button, who diligently helped in bringing this manual to fruition. Her contributions were manifold: Her editorial assistance helped clarify my thinking and improved the readability of the document; the chapters she wrote for this manual are valuable additions; and, most importantly, the process of our interaction made the task of writing easier and more enjoyable.

I would also like to express my thanks and appreciation to the many parents who have, over the years, shared with me their experience of being a parent. These individuals have taught me that this manual is only a starting point, a structure, to begin the process of helping parents. Those who aspire to help parents develop successful early childhood parenting skills must respect the differences among parents and work flexibly to meet or accommodate their special needs.

PAR Psychological Assessment Resources, Inc./P.O. Box 998/Odessa, FL 33556/Toll-Free 1-800-331-TEST

9 8 7 6 5 4 3 2 1   Reorder #RO-3343   Printed in the U.S.A.

Table of Contents

Preface v

Introduction to the Manual vii

Section I: Getting Started—Some Background Issues 1

Chapter 1: Using the Early Childhood Parenting Skills Program 3

Chapter 2: Working With Nontraditional Families
(by Suzanne Button) 9

Chapter 3: Evaluating Outcomes of Parenting Skills Programs 19

Section II: The Program Sessions and Modules 31

Chapter 4: Learning Successful Parenting Skills: An Introduction 33
    Session 1: Building a Group Identity by Sharing 33

Chapter 5: Developing the Child's Working Model of Self 37
    Session 2: I Am Worthwhile, I Am Lovable * 38
    Session 3: I Am Competent, I Am Responsible * 51

Chapter 6: Evaluating the Parent-Child Relationship 65
    Session 4: Recognizing Positive and Negative Cues 65

Chapter 7: Building Your Relationship With Your Child 79
    Session 5: Communicating Love and Acceptance 79
    Session 6: Learning to Recognize Your Child's Feelings Through
        Reflective Listening 88
    Session 6A: Reflective Listening – Review and Practice (Optional) 104
    Session 7: Sharing Yourself 108
    Session 8: Building a Relationship – Review and Practice of Three Techniques 121

Chapter 8: Providing Discipline 123
    Session 9: Discipline in the Parent-Child Relationship * 123

Chapter 9: Managing Children's Behavior 135
    Session 10: Who Owns the Problem? – Resolving Conflicts 136
    Session 11: Using Behavior Modification Principles (With or Without
        Audiovisual Presentation) 147
    Session 12: Consequences That Increase and Decrease Behavior –
        Selecting Behaviors to Change 160

Session 13: Recording Behavior and Setting Consequences 169

Session 14: Using Behavior Modification Principles With Appropriate Reinforcers....181

Session 15: Using the Behavioral Modification Method on Yourself 195

Chapter 10: Managing Your Feelings...201

Session 16: The ABCs of Understanding Emotions 202

Session 17: Applying the ABC Model to Your Interactions With Your Child.................213

Session 18: Parent to Parent Interactions: Controlling Your Emotions 219

Session 19: Managing Emotions in Your Parenting Partnership 239

Section III: Single Session Lectures or Workshops* 245

Session 20: Optimizing Your Child's Development — Ages 0-48 Months
    (by Suzanne Button)...247

Session 21: Special Education and Your Legal Rights
    (by Suzanne Button)...257

Session 22: Helping Your Child With Schoolwork
    (by Richard R. Abidin and Suzanne Button) 269

Session 23: Communicating Effectively With Your Child's Teachers
    (by Richard R. Abidin and Suzanne Button) 283

Session 24: Empowering Your Family to Meet Goals — Effective Use of
    Social Supports
    (by Suzanne Button)...291

Section IV: Annotated Bibliography of Recommended Readings 301

*May be used as a single session lecture or workshop or in combination with any other program module or short course.

Preface

For centuries, people of diverse racial and religious backgrounds have struggled to create a good life for themselves and their children. Men and women have developed and applied advanced technology to conquer disease, mass-produce goods, and travel through space. These achievements could not have come about without man's recognition of the importance of education and training. Through education, men and women have developed the skills necessary to meet advanced technological goals.

Until recently, however, little training was available to prepare men and women for raising children effectively. In this area—possibly the most important human activity—we have failed to recognize the urgent need for education, training, and skills development. In most societies, individuals must be trained and licensed to practice medicine, to teach, or even to repair plumbing. No requirements beyond biological ones exist, however, for the practice of parenting. The idea of licensing parents is clearly absurd, but something must be done to better prepare men and women for the task of raising children.

We might ask why so little has been done to help men and women develop their child-rearing knowledge and skills. The development of parenting training has been complicated by such factors as the notion of a natural "mothering instinct," fear of outside interference in private family matters, diverse cultural traditions, and different value systems. Professionals concerned with children and parenting have complicated matters by presenting their particular suggestions as the "right way" to parent.

Each of these "right ways" grew out of a specific set of assumptions and values, described how children should develop, and dictated how they should be managed. Guidelines for parenting presented in this fashion are limited in their usefulness to the average parent, probably because they fail to separate theoretical assumptions from the practical, everyday reality of raising children. Although theoretical knowledge of child development is important, parents need training in practical skills that they can apply with their individual children in their own "unique" situations.

Mental health professionals recognize that maladjusted and unproductive human beings generally see themselves as having limited choices and limited means by which to achieve their goals. Effective intervention takes place when an individual develops the knowledge and skills necessary to meet his or her goals or is able to clarify or adjust those goals so that they *can* be achieved. Effective intervention for parents, then, should provide a wide range of necessary and effective developmental knowledge and parenting skills.

Parents do not report that they wanted to raise an unhappy, maladjusted, and ineffective child; yet, many such children exist today. Professionals who work with families report that many parents have little insight into their own values and assumptions regarding parenting, as well as little access to alternative means of managing and developing desirable and effective behavior in their children. Serious problems in the positive adjustment of children are often related to gross knowledge and skill deficiencies in their parents.

We know that other factors, such as poverty and physical disability, can contribute to poor development and adjustment in childhood. We also know that children are sturdy, adaptive creatures, who, if reared effectively, can cope with and often overcome socioeconomic and physical disadvantage. Children of parents, whether rich or poor, who are unschooled and unskilled in parenting, often develop into unhappy, maladjusted, and ineffective human beings. Parents must be given the opportunity to develop the knowledge and specific skills necessary to rear their children effectively in whatever environment they may find themselves.

The following set of Early Childhood Parenting Skills Sessions was developed as a way to organize currently available knowledge into a program for basic parenting skills training. By identifying important areas of knowledge from various professions concerned with children and their development and specifying parenting skills to implement that knowledge, this program provides one opportunity for parents to both learn and practice important parenting skills. The author embarked on the task of developing these sessions as an interface between theoretical knowledge of child development and the everyday, practical reality of raising children. The sessions are based on a review of professional literature, discussions with hundreds of parents, interviews with over 50 leading authorities on child development, and the author's own clinical experience in this field.

The ideas and skills presented in these sessions do not represent the "right way" or the "only way" to foster the healthy development of children. Rather, the sessions attempt to provide parents with the insight and skills necessary to reach their own parenting goals. Ideas and skills are presented with a deep respect for the integrity of the family and the ideas and goals of individual parents. Each parent must feel free to accept, reject, or selectively implement any of the skills presented in these sessions.

Richard R. Abidin, Jr., EdD
Curry Programs in Clinical and School Psychology
University of Virginia
March 1996

Introduction to the Manual

This manual was developed to encourage a wide range of individuals to become involved in the process of educating parents in the skills of parenting. Professionals from a wide range of disciplines encounter parents in need of support and guidance as they attempt to fulfill the role of parent. Although the manual is structured to provide a curriculum for group instruction, the concepts and skills are equally applicable to one-on-one consultations with parents. Professionals who work with parents of young children should find the substance of this manual useful in a number of settings.

Professional qualifications for the appropriate use of this Parenting Skills Program include a number of different disciplines. Most commonly, they will be psychologists, professional counselors, social workers, nurse practitioners, early childhood educators, ministers, or psychiatrists. Regardless of the discipline, the professional needs three sets of qualifications:

1. Substantive academic background is the first major requirement. An understanding of early child development, family psychology, and interpersonal psychology is essential. The supplementary readings provided in each section of this manual are designed to reinforce those areas in the professional's academic background.

2. Appropriate values and attitudes are the second major requirement. Professionals need to be aware of the values and attitudes they possess and express through their actions. They need to value parents' efforts and recognize that parenting is difficult, given all of life's demands, and the fact that some children ,for a variety of different reasons, make the task extraordinarily difficult. Although the care of the child is the focus of parenting, the child is not to be valued above the parent. In point of fact, valuing and supporting the parent is the professional's focus and immediate concern. Section II of this manual describes the importance of the parents' own values and actions in influencing their child's self-concept. In similar fashion, the professional needs to work with parents in ways that do not destroy the parents' confidence or suggest, in any way, that they are incompetent as parents.

    An attitude of respect for the parents' strengths, despite any shortcomings, is essential to creating a supportive learning environment. Individuals who avail themselves of the services of professional parent educators/consultants often will hold beliefs that are at odds with what is being taught. The professional must not seek to convert, but rather to obtain a fair hearing for the ideas and a reasonable trial of the parenting approaches presented. Ultimately, parents must decide for themselves what they should do, and they must not feel demeaned because they cannot fully accept the skills as presented.

3. Interpersonal skills are the third major requirement. The professionals who are most likely to read this manual are members of service professions that require reasonable interpersonal skills such as empathic listening (tracking both the

affect and the content of parents' communication. Therefore, these basic skills will be presumed. The primary point to be emphasized is that the professional needs to continuously interact with parents in ways that foster the development of a positive parenting self-concept. The parents who participate in this program will be taught the importance of interacting with their children in ways that help the children develop a working model of themselves as "loveable and worthwhile" individuals who are "competent and responsible" for their behavior (Sessions 2 and 3). Thus, professionals are challenged to behave in ways that would meet the same standards they would teach, and expect of, parents.

The content of the Early Childhood Parenting Skills Program is designed to address the relationship issues and the developmental issues that are recognized as being essential to an "ideal" broad-based program (Barclay & Houts, 1995). The Professional Manual is organized into four major sections. Each section is designed for a different purpose but, taken as a whole, they should help achieve the overall goal of the manual: to provide professionals with background and structure that facilitates their work with parents of young children.

Section I consists of three chapters which provide information that will be useful to the professional before the parent education or consultation actually begins. Chapter 1, "Using the Early Childhood Parenting Skills Program," describes the basic structure and process used in the training sessions and presents different options for using the 19 individual sessions in sequences or modules of instruction. Chapter 2, "Working With Nontraditional Families," is designed to sensitize the professional to parenting issues relating to nontraditional families. These issues often require some adaptation on the part of the professional with regard to language, content, or the process of interaction. The professional is encouraged to make use of the annotated bibliography in Section IV of this manual. This bibliography contains a number of resources that will strengthen the professional's background in relation to nontraditional families or families with specialized circumstances. Chapter 3, "Evaluating Outcomes of Parenting Skills Programs," provides the professional with both a structure and rationale for designing an evaluation and information on specific measures and approaches that have been found useful in the evaluation of parenting skills program outcomes.

Section II contains the 19 sessions that form the substantive core of the Early Childhood Parenting Skills Program. It is important to emphasize that the professional is free to use these sessions in a flexible manner, choosing the sessions that best meet his or her specific needs. A professional who wanted to focus on helping parents to become aware of the importance of the child's developing self-concept might only use Sessions 1 to 3. Or those same three sessions could be used in combination with Sessions 10 to 14, which focus on managing children's behavior using behavioral principles. Sessions 2, 3, and 9 may be used as single-session lecture/workshops or in combination with any other program module. The substance of the Early Childhood Parenting Skills Program is drawn from four general areas of psychology: self-concept theory, relationship and humanistic communications, behavioral principles, and cognitive psychology. The professional who practices in an integrated, eclectic manner will be very comfortable with this manual; others will be challenged to integrate these new approaches into their current practice.

Section III provides five different lecture/workshops that are designed as single-session presentations to parents in community groups (e.g., PTA meetings, church groups, service organizations, etc.). Presentations of this sort often stimulate referrals to the professional as well as the formation of parenting skills groups in the community.

Section IV contains an annotated bibliography which, as was mentioned earlier, may help to fill in any gaps in the professional's background. This bibliography is also contained in the Parents' Workbook, and it may be a useful tool for the professional in guiding parents' extracurricular reading.

The Early Childhood Parenting Skills Program is presented with the hope that it will be useful to professionals who are interested in supporting the efforts of parents to learn effective parenting skills. Success with this Program does not depend on the specific discipline or the level of education of the professional user. The program has been used successfully by individuals with a doctoral degree and graduate students. Professionals will modify and customize the program to fit their own individual style and the needs of the parents with whom they interact.

Section I

Getting Started –
Some Background Issues

1 Using the Early Childhood Parenting Skills Program

Introduction

The Parenting Skills Program may be employed by a wide range of professionals who work with parents and children. Two major skills are required of mental health professionals who wish to teach parenting skills using this Program. First, they should have an open and democratic leadership style. Second, they must be able to communicate both acceptance of and respect for the efforts of parents involved in the Program. Parents' efforts to raise their children as happy, effective people may not always be constructive, but they will be genuine and well meant.

The sessions presented in this program integrate a wide range of educational strategies and theoretical orientations. Client-centered humanistic psychology, rational-emotive psychology, and behavioral psychology are all heavily represented. No one set of strategies—for adults or for children—should be presented as being more important than another. All must be presented in an atmosphere of openness and respect for alternative strategies, and parents must be encouraged to employ these strategies in an honest and flexible fashion. If a child notices changes in his or her own reactions or behaviors (or those of the parents), the parents should be encouraged to provide the child with an honest explanation for these changes.

This Program does not present a totally novel method or rationale for parenting or child management. Rather, it is an effort to draw together both common knowledge and knowledge that is currently available in the field of behavioral science. The Program development was based on a number of assumptions about its implementation and about the attitude of the professional toward the parents involved. First, we assume that there is no "one correct way" to raise children and that no one school of psychology, theory, or technique can provide the total answer.

Throughout the Program, we draw concepts from different schools of psychological thought. Some of these concepts may seem contradictory; such contradictions are likely to be resolved if you, as the Parenting Skills professional, maintain an attitude of respect toward your own efforts and those of the parents with whom you interact. Above all, you must remember that, no matter what parents are currently doing with their children, they are doing their best—with the knowledge and skills currently available to them—to raise happy, productive children. Parents typically believe, based on what little knowledge about child development they may have, that their actions are in their child's best interests.

Further, you must understand that the difference between success or lack of success in parenting is often a matter of *frequency* and *intensity*. The unsuccessful parent often uses many of the same parenting skills as the successful parent; however, the successful parent employs these effective skills more consistently and more confidently.

The most essential attitude for the Parenting Skills professional is one of respect. You must have a genuine respect for parents, and this respect must be reflected in your nondefensive response to parents who challenge the content of a particular session or the methods of intervention proposed. Here again, a democratic leadership style will facilitate parents' acceptance and their acquisition of the skills being taught.

Structuring the Individual Training Sessions

Most of the Program sessions require 1½ to 2 hours and are composed of three major activities:

- Review and share the home practice experiences from the previous session (20 - 30 minutes).

- Present the new topic(s) (40 minutes).

- Discuss what the ideas presented in the new topic mean to each parent and introduce the home practice assignment (20 - 30 minutes).

Review and Sharing of the Home Practice Experiences

This section is an essential means of feedback between you and the parents. This is your opportunity to find out how well the parents understood the previous session topic and to clarify any miscommunication or misunderstanding.

This section also gives parents an opportunity to see that other parents are also trying new strategies and ideas, being challenged, and experiencing frustration. Sharing experiences and feelings will have a strong, positive impact in motivating the parents. Different parents react differently: Some respond to encouragement and challenge; some may work harder in order to compete with other parents. In the author's experience, failure to share home practice experiences often leads to a relatively passive parental response to that session and, ultimately, to the entire Program.

Presenting the New Topic

The structure provided in this manual will help the inexperienced mental health professional to implement the Program successfully. With time, you will become less dependent on the specific words presented in this manual, and each session will be embellished with your own personal style. Flexibility is encouraged as long as the objectives for each session are achieved. A straight lecture style may tend to discourage parents from participating in the sessions, because this type of group process becomes highly leader-oriented; the opportunity for parental reaction and spontaneous response is minimized. You can use the lecture style to cover the main content points of a session; this usually works best when the main points are covered in about 15 minutes. Supplemental points or issues can then be addressed during the open discussion period that follows.

A common and effective way to cover each session's content is to present the content ideas in combination with specific questions to parents regarding the related experiences they have had with their own children. When presenting material in this fashion, you must pay careful attention to nonverbal cues. Are the parents understanding the new material? Are their reactions negative or positive? If you sense an uncertain response in the parents, you might well stop the lecture to address this concern:

> **"Some of you may be having doubts about what you are hearing,"** or **"I get the sense that some of you might not be getting *what* I am saying because of *how* I am saying it. Maybe I could clear it up by answering some of your questions at this point."**

Comments like these are important in two ways: They help to ensure comprehension of the material, and they maintain the environment of mutual respect between you and the parents. Understanding of the material presented and mutual respect among the group participants are both essential elements for an effective group session.

Dealing with parental resistance to content. If an open discussion of parents' objections to specific Program content does not alleviate their resistance to the new ideas you are presenting, you may wish to handle that resistance differently. For example, parents may continue to question, challenge, or object to the two "major keys" to raising a well-adjusted child (or to any of the other new ideas presented in a session). When dealing with this type of resistance, keep the following points in mind. They are designed to help parents understand how this Program will be useful to them on a practical, day-to-day level.

One important dimension of parents' involvement and commitment to this program is their belief that what they are learning will lead to important results in terms of *their own child's* development and future functioning. As the professional, you must be sensitive to any signs that parents are not seeing the connection between the material you are presenting and their own child's future success. You need to help parents see how the two major keys on which the Program is based and the parenting skills they are learning will help them to achieve three primary and universal parenting goals.

First, all parents would like to be able to influence and manage their child's behavior in ways that don't involve the use of force. Second, parents hope that their child will develop a respect for, and ultimately adopt, many of the parents' own values. Finally, parents hope that their child will become a responsible adolescent (and then an adult) who is not overly influenced by peers or other individuals or groups outside of the family. Parents want their children to learn how to be in control of their own behavior.

Parental influence. We must recognize that, when children are young, their primary source of knowledge about themselves and the world around them is the relationship they have with their parents. As children get older and expand their range of experience with others, day-to-day parental influence decreases. We now know, however, that children who were raised with love and respect develop similar patterns of thinking and feeling, which then guide their actions and reactions later in life.

Initially, a young child's size and dependency give the parent enormous power and control, both physically and psychologically. The physical power lasts for a relatively short period, however, and parents who depend on physical control to raise and influence a child are ultimately doomed to failure. The sooner a parent weans himself or herself from that approach to child management, the faster that parent will develop more successful and enduring patterns of influence on the child's future behavior. Parents need to understand that, although the pain of physical punishment stops, the child's negative feelings of rejection and of being unacceptable endure. If a child sees his or her parent as a consistent source of love and acceptance who really understands how the child feels and thinks, then that child will be more willing to accept parental direction and influence.

Shared family values. At the same time that most children allow parents to influence their overt behaviors, children who are raised by sensitive parents are also more willing and more able to understand and respect their parents' values. By interacting with their parents and communicating with them about what to do and what not to do, these children learn and adopt their parents' values, attitudes, and approaches to others. Certainly, during adolescence and young adulthood, every individual will reexamine these learned values and attitudes. This is a natural and expected part of human development. The important point here is that the reference point and benchmark of an individual's sense of self-worth will be his or her learned family values instead of some other (external) value system. In contrast, when a child has feelings of rejection and a sense of not being worthwhile or competent as a result of interactions with his or her parent(s), the starting point for that child in adolescence and young adulthood will be a search for values other than those learned within the family.

Resistance to external influence. The child's sense of self provides the foundation for resistance to influences from peers and popular culture. When a child has experienced parental communication that fosters feelings of being worthwhile and competent, he or she is less vulnerable to the need for respect and approval from others. Self-respect and the certain knowledge of love and respect from parents and family create the security and objectivity a child needs to evaluate both the motives and values of others and the likely outcome of a given set of behaviors that are encouraged or modeled by individuals outside the family. Children whose parents guided them to exercise their own judgment about thousands of choices early in life and then respected the child's decisions will be more inclined to make their own decisions and to expect the same kind of respect for those decisions from others.

Clearly, a parent can neither lay out the course of a child's life nor prevent all problems from occurring. Parents can, however, act in ways that exert influence on their child—both now and in the future. The parenting skills presented in this training Program are designed to assist parents in exerting positive influence on their children that, in turn, facilitates the child's future development.

Discussing the ideas presented. Helping parents connect the material presented in the session with their individual family situations requires the greatest degree of professional skill and empathy. Parents may feel shaky in their understanding of the new material, and this may heighten their fear of appearing foolish. You can help by recognizing and encouraging candor and genuine efforts toward understanding. Try to suspend judgment of the parents' efforts; use reflective listening, and pay attention to parents' feelings as well as to their actual words. Respond to legitimate requests for clarification of concepts or information, and encourage discussion of individual or group struggles with new ideas.

Avoid responding to parental requests for judgment (approval or disapproval) of their efforts or proposed plans of action. In responding to such requests, it is most constructive if the "Helpful Praise" and "Helpful Criticism" responses taught in Session 2 are modeled for parents.

Planning the Program to Meet Your Needs

The 19 Program sessions may be presented in their entirety, or materials may be combined and organized into one of three specially tailored short courses:

Basic Course (19-20 Sessions)

Professionals who use the basic Program contained in the first 19 sessions will note that the skills taught in one session are useful in the succeeding sessions. The fact that each session is presented separately does not mean that the ideas and skills presented are not interrelated and complementary. Parents should be encouraged to think about how the communication and relationship-building skills taught in Sessions 1 through 8 (with or without the optional review session that follows Session 6) relate to the behavior modification principles presented in Sessions 11 through 15 and to the material on managing feelings presented in Sessions 16 through 19.

Short Course 1 (7 Sessions)

Objectives:

1. To sensitize parents to the impact of their own behavior on their child's developing self-concept.

2. To provide parents with a set of skills that will help them manage their feelings toward their children and their spouses.

Sessions to be presented: 1, 2, 3, 16, 17, 18, and 19.

Short Course 2 (10-11 Sessions)

Objectives:

1. To sensitize parents to the impact of their own behavior on their child's developing self-concept.

2. To provide parents with the means to evaluate their individual relationship with their own child.

3. To provide parents with the skills needed to build and maintain a positive relationship with their own child.

4. To provide parents with the skills needed to identify ownership of problems and to resolve conflicts as they arise.

5. To provide parents with a conceptual framework for understanding discipline as a learning tool and for guiding their own disciplinary actions.

Sessions to be presented: 1, 2, 3, 4, 5, 6 (with optional review session following), 7, 8, 9, and 10.

Short Course 3 (10 Sessions)

Objectives:

1. To sensitize parents to the impact of their own behavior on their child's developing self-concept.

2. To alert parents to the potential effects of alternative forms of discipline.

3. To teach parents the skills required to successfully employ appropriate principles of behavior modification.

Sessions to be presented: 1, 2, 3, 9, 10, 11, 12, 13, 14, and 15.

Special Lectures and Single-Session Workshops

In addition to the three specially designed short courses, you may find a number of the session topics in this manual useful for single-meeting lecture/presentations to public groups. Sessions that fit well within this framework include the following:

2. Developing the Child's Working Model of Self, Part 1: I Am Worthwhile— I Am Lovable

3. Developing the Child's Working Model of Self, Part 2: I Am Competent, I Am Responsible

9. Discipline in the Parent-Child Relationship

20. Optimizing Your Child's Development – Ages 0-48 Months

21. Special Education and Your Legal Rights

22. Helping Your Child With Schoolwork

23. Communicating Effectively With Your Child's Teachers

24. Empowering Your Family to Meet Goals – Effective Use of Social Supports

In addition, the annotated bibliography at the end of this manual provides additional resources to broaden your own knowledge of child development and parenting. This list of recommended readings will also prove helpful to parents who have a specific problem they would like to explore in greater depth or to parents who are interested in strengthening and expanding the skills they learn through this Program.

2 Working With Nontraditional Families

by Suzanne Button

Introduction

The traditional nuclear family—a family with married, opposite-gender parents and their biological children—is fast becoming a "minority" in the United States. Census data from 1991 indicate that almost one third of all children in the U.S. live with one parent, that the number of unmarried couples who live together and have children has steadily increased over the past 20 years, and that the number of families in which both partners work and care for their children continues to rise (Saluter, 1992). Apparently, many individuals are constructing alternative family forms that reflect their values, accommodate their lifestyles, and permit more cooperation between partners, extended family members, and friends (Eiduson, Kornfein, Zimmerman, & Weisner, 1988).

Nontraditional families, then, are families that have adopted family structures and functioning styles that do not reflect those of the traditional, nuclear unit. Examples of nontraditional family styles include single-parent families in which a mother or father raises the child alone, two-parent families in which the father is the primary caregiver, gay- or lesbian-parented families, families with nonbiological (adopted or foster) children, families of divorce and remarriage, and families in which nonimmediate family members raise the children of blood relatives. In all of these families, individuals live, love, and work together, and function according to their economic need and their personal and political choice.

Given the rising prevalence of nontraditional family lifestyles, it is highly likely that the parent educator will have an opportunity to work with many parents whose families function in a nonnuclear, alternative fashion. It is important, then, that the educator come to understand nontraditional families and respect their competencies, their values, and their commitment to caring for their children. In this chapter, we will briefly present various nontraditional family styles and provide suggestions for working with and understanding nonnuclear families.

Nontraditional Family Styles

Each of the nontraditional family categories discussed in this chapter includes a wide range of functioning styles, role-assignments, strengths, and weaknesses (Eiduson et al., 1988). Rather than approaching nontraditional families from a deficit model (i.e., a focus on what is missing from these families), the professional must explore the ways that these alternative and varied forms of family life are adaptive, competent, and ultimately successful. It is important to be aware of the difficulties inherent in choosing a nonnuclear family style without losing sight of the fact that most nontraditional families function successfully and raise well-adjusted children (Gottfried & Gottfried, 1994). When taking an informed, respectful, and competence-based approach, the professional is more likely to achieve a working relationship with nontraditional parents based on trust.

Single-Parent Families

Various events can lead to the creation of a single-parent family. Death, separation, divorce, and out-of-wedlock pregnancy all lead to family reorganization and can result in children being raised by one parent. In about 88% of single-parent families, the children live with their mothers; but an increasing number of children live with their fathers after a family reorganizes (Gottfried & Gottfried, 1994).

Many people believe that single-parent families are not as healthy as two-parent families, and that children raised by only one parent are at serious psychological risk. Not all research supports these beliefs. In many studies, single-parent families who are not living in poverty raise children who function in all areas as well as their two-parented counterparts (Combrinck-Graham, 1989).

However, some areas of family functioning often are affected negatively by the absence or unavailability of a parent. Because family members take on new roles and responsibilities while attempting to cope with the situation that led to the loss of a parent, they often feel overwhelmed, angry, depressed, or all three, during the early stages of family reorganization. Research suggests, however, that these are temporary difficulties that will decrease as roles are successfully negotiated and emotional difficulties begin to be resolved.

The financial repercussions of single parenting, however, are not so readily resolved. In the U.S., the total income for single-mother families is about one third lower, on average, than that of two-parent families. This is due to two factors: (a) Two-parent families have greater earning capacity than one-parent families, and (b) women earn lower average salaries than men. Consequently, children in most single-mother families live in economically disadvantaged circumstances, and single-mother families must contend with the stressors that are inherent in such circumstances (Laosa, 1988).

As in any other type of family, successful functioning in a single-parent family is dependent on a variety of factors. Lindblad-Goldberg (1989) suggests that several areas in single-parent families should be developed or strengthened, or both, as they are indicators of successful adaptation to the stressors discussed earlier. Areas for potential professional intervention include the single parent's ability to adapt to changing circumstances and to solve problems that arise, the family's available sources of social support, family members' abilities to take on new roles and responsibilities as the need arises, and the caregivers' belief in their own strengths and abilities. Finally, the financial resources of the single-parent family can be bolstered by contacting appropriate local agencies, taking steps to obtain child support, and helping family members find work.

Families After Divorce/Stepfamilies

In the U.S., one out of every two marriages will end in divorce, and about one third of all children will experience divorce in their families (Saluter, 1992). Eventually, about 80% of adults who divorce remarry, and their children become members of a combined family (Papernow, 1994). Divorce and eventual remarriage are long-term, developmental family processes that involve many stages of adjustment, readjustment, and challenge for parent and child alike. Divorcing parents often need support as they cope with the stressors inherent in the initial family breakup, the negotiation of two family homes, and the development of new relationships in stepfamilies.

During the breakup of a family, individual family members are likely to experience considerable sadness, anger, guilt, and anxiety (Hetherington & Arasteh, 1988). These emotions may be so strong that they interfere with a parent's functioning at work or with a child's social and academic functioning. In addition, the intense turmoil involved in the initial breakup sometimes leads parents to increase their use of controlled substances for some time (Teybur, 1992). This period of emotional upheaval can last for more than 2 years, and all family members need considerable support—from helping professionals and from their social support networks—as they cope with this difficult time. It is important to remember that strong emotions are normal during this stage and that the turmoil settles down eventually. Parents must be encouraged to make support plans for themselves and their children during this phase, to plan their breakup carefully for the benefit of their children, and to find healthy channels for expressing the negative emotions they are feeling.

When the emotional chaos of the initial breakup phase settles down, families begin the business of adopting new lifestyles, reorganizing family roles, and adjusting to parents' separate living arrangements (Teybur, 1992). During this phase, parents experiment with their new identities by going to school, changing jobs, or starting new relationships. This transition phase is a trial-and-error period, which can be exciting for parents but extremely stressful for children. Parents must be encouraged to provide stability and predictability for their children as they expand their own lifestyles and identities. By keeping as many things as possible from changing (e.g., school, babysitter, friends, schedules), parents can reassure their children that their lives are structured, safe, and relatively predictable. In addition, parents should understand that the manner in which they both negotiate custody, visitation, and support will strongly affect the family's adjustment to the divorce. Parents must learn to negotiate positively with the ex-partner to minimize their children's exposure to conflict around family reorganization. A positive parenting partnership will provide security for the children and set the stage for long-term, positive adjustment in the family.

As the family adjusts to its new lifestyle, a period of stability arises. Parents settle into their new identities, stable patterns of custody or visitation are established, and children begin to feel more secure as their lives become more and more predictable (Teybur, 1992). During this stable phase, parents often settle into a serious romantic relationship that can lead to the formation of a stepfamily. As the stepfamily begins to form, a new developmental process takes shape (Papernow, 1994).

In the initial stages after remarriage, most stepfamily members retain the emotional ties, belief systems, and behavioral patterns that they established in their family of origin (Combrinck-Graham, 1989). Still, the newly-married parents hope they will be able to form a loving, stable family that will heal the pain of divorce. Papernow (1994) suggests that this belief is largely based on fantasy and that the first developmental challenge for stepfamilies is the experience of conflict and negative emotion that arise as the families are formed. Children experience anger, sadness, and confusion as a new adult enters the family; ex-partners feel afraid they are being replaced in their children's lives.

These difficult emotions begin to settle down as the stepfamily enters a stage of awareness (Papernow, 1994). Family members—particularly parents—begin to understand that conflict and negative emotion are normal processes in the formation of a new family; fantasies are given up in favor of more realistic family goals. During this time, family members should be supported as they acknowledge and name difficult feelings, give up old fantasies, and form new relationships and new family structures. If the family members understand that they are experiencing normal, developmental processes, they are more likely to negotiate those processes successfully (Combrinck-Graham, 1989).

As the initial conflicts resolve, stepfamily members begin to negotiate their new relationships more actively. New households establish family rules, partners solidify their relationships in the face of challenges from the children, and children begin to form friendly, nonparental relationships with their stepparents (Papernow, 1994). Conflict during this time is likely to revolve around practical issues such as household chores, bedtimes, and discipline. During this period, the helping professional can assist couples as they solidify their relationship; help stepparents learn to enter their stepchild's life in a nonthreatening, nonparental fashion; and facilitate the successful negotiation of household rules.

As the new family decides on and settles into family rules, new relationships, and stable living arrangements, family members begin to enjoy each other and to build more intimate, solid relationships. The stepparent may begin to move into a more parental role; stepchildren are more likely to accept this movement and may even welcome it. Negotiation is still necessary, but the family has developed more effective, stable patterns for decision-making and conflict resolution. As the family enters this final, increasingly stable stage, they will have mourned the loss of past relationships, developed realistic expectations, formed solid parenting partnerships and stepfamily relationships, and developed cooperation between the two households (Visher & Visher, 1988).

In working with remarried families, the professional must keep these normative developmental processes in mind. Family members can be supported as they learn to discuss and resolve difficult emotions in their attempt to negotiate new roles and new rules. By giving plenty of positive feedback, teaching problem-solving skills, facilitating conflict resolution, and helping families develop practical solutions to everyday problems, the professional can help stepfamilies with their positive development (Combrinck-Graham, 1989; Papernow, 1994).

Gay- or Lesbian-Parented Families

Although reliable figures are not currently available, current estimates suggest that between 4 and 14 million children in the U.S. are living with gay or lesbian parents (Patterson, 1995a). These parents may be single, or they may have same-sex partners. Gay- and lesbian-parented families result when partners bring children from a previous marriage, when individuals choose to adopt, or when parents conceive a child through donor insemination. Lesbian mothers often give birth to their children; gay fathers may conceive their children with a single female friend, a lesbian couple, or a surrogate mother. Because these families form in such diverse ways, children with lesbian or gay parents are being raised in various—and often strikingly adaptive—parenting/family arrangements and styles. Before making assumptions about working with these families, the professional must understand the individual family style involved.

Unfortunately, the same prejudices and hostilities that face lesbian and gay individuals in our country also plague their families. The psychological health of the parents, the quality of life they provide for their children, and the nature of their commitment to their families have all been questioned by individuals and institutions with assumptions based on faulty, stereotypical beliefs about gays and lesbians (Bozett, 1987; Gottfried & Gottfried, 1994). Many gay- and lesbian-parented families cope with hostility from the legal system, a lack of support from biological family members, and antigay bigotry from the community at large (Patterson, 1995a).

As Patterson points out in her 1995 review of the literature, the scientific study of gay- and lesbian-parented families has begun to negate this hostility and bigotry. Like their heterosexual counterparts, lesbian mothers and gay fathers exhibit varying degrees of psychological health, which reflect their histories, their biological predispositions, and their current available resources (Gottfried & Gottfried, 1994). Lesbian mothers and heterosexual mothers display more similarity than differences in parenting attitudes and ability; gay fathers and heterosexual fathers may struggle with the same lack of experience in, and socialization for, parenting (Gottfried & Gottfried, 1994; Patterson, 1995a).

The assumption that a child parented by a lesbian mother or a gay father will be at greater risk for developmental or psychological problems has also been negated in the literature. Children of gay and lesbian parents do not "grow up gay." Rather, they exhibit a rate of homosexuality similar to that of the heterosexual-parented population (Gottfried & Gottfried, 1995). These children exhibit the same rate of behavioral problems, psychiatric disturbance, and quality of peer relationships and social functioning as do their heterosexual-parented peers (Patterson, 1995b). Children parented by gay or lesbian parents do, however, worry about being stigmatized as a result of their parent's sexual orientation (Gottfried & Gottfried, 1994).

Families headed up by gay men and lesbians exhibit considerable strengths. Household and child care activities are shared more equally and more satisfactorily between same-sex partners; same-sex partners also report greater satisfaction with their couple relationships than do their heterosexual counterparts (Patterson, 1995a). Although the unique nature of their family situations may be challenging to gay- and lesbian-parented families, their ability to adapt to child rearing by utilizing a variety of sources of support (family, friends, partners, and the gay/lesbian community) may be more than adequate to meet these challenges.

Working with gay- and lesbian-parented families, then, should be based on the same principles of respect, curiosity, and strength-development that inform work with any other family. The professional should base his or her evaluation of family difficulties on individual strengths and weaknesses and should examine his or her own biases if they get in the way of this competence-based approach. In addition, the professional must remain aware of the biases and bigotry that face these families, helping families learn to cope with and combat the negative reactions they may face in their communities.

Adoptive Families

Approximately 2% of all children in the U.S. have been relinquished by their biological parents and, subsequently, adopted. Like all families, adoptive families come from a variety of cultural and ethnic groups and socioeconomic strata; they present a range of strengths, weaknesses, struggles, and styles of functioning (Brodzinsky & Schechter, 1990). Most children adopted in this country are born here; a small, but increasing, percentage are adopted overseas and brought to the U.S. (Combrinck-Graham, 1989). Children are placed for adoption because of death, poverty, choice, or lack of ability to parent. Parents who adopt may do so out of free choice, because they cannot conceive biological children, or because they have been asked by a friend or relative to take responsibility for a child. In any case, adoption involves the loss and subsequent gain of a child, and adoptive families often struggle with the emotions that naturally result from such a powerful experience (Reitz & Watson, 1992).

The literature on adoption suggests that adopted children are over-represented in clinical settings due to their increased developmental risk (Combrinck-Graham, 1989). Many adoptees are born prematurely or without the benefit of prenatal care; some struggle with issues of abandonment as a result of being placed for adoption (Reitz & Watson, 1992). It is important to remember, however, that about 77% of all adoptions result in a stable adoptive family and a well-adjusted adopted child (Combrinck-Graham, 1989). Despite the discouraging information in the literature, the professional must focus on the strengths of a presenting adoptive family and help the family to cope with adoption stress by rallying those strengths.

A review of the sizeable literature on adoption is beyond the scope of this chapter. Intervention with adoptive families must be designed to fit the particular developmental stage in which the family is struggling, the cultural issues involved in coping with adoption, and the personal resources of the family members involved. The professional should familiarize himself or herself with the individual issues presented by an adoptive family before working with that family and must carefully evaluate the family's individual strengths and weaknesses (Reitz & Watson, 1992).

Regardless of their particular presentation, most adoptive families seeking professional assistance will be struggling with the intense—but normal—emotions that accompany the experience of adoption. Adoptive parents may feel inadequate, frightened of losing their child, tentative about parenting, or torn by their child's behavioral difficulties (Reitz & Watson, 1992). Adopted children are likely to feel abandoned and rejected by their biological parent, to be curious about their lost parents, and to experience developmental disruption if adopted after age 5 (Brodzinsky & Schechter, 1990). Although many of these emotions can be frightening to family members, they must be named and expressed before they can be resolved (Reitz & Watson, 1992).

Throughout the adoption literature, families that successfully cope with adoption exhibit a tendency to talk openly about the emotions and experiences which surround the adoption (Brodzinsky & Schechter, 1990). The helping professional, then, is encouraged to acknowledge that adoption is quite different from a biological birth and that the emotions experienced by the family are a logical result of such an experience (Combrinck-Graham, 1989). Families can be taught or encouraged, or both, to avoid secrecy and to discuss the adoption process openly. By modeling and maintaining an open, respectful, and normalizing stance, the professional can support adoptive families as they face a variety of developmental and family issues (Reitz & Watson, 1992).

In this chapter, we have introduced some commonly-encountered nontraditional family styles. The information presented here is by no means exhaustive. The professional may work with nonmarried couples raising children together, with families whose fathers are the primary caregivers, with parents who raise their children in a communal setting, with nonbiological foster families, or with families in which nonimmediate biological relatives (e.g., grandparents, siblings) raise another family member's children. In addition, many families will present a combination of these nontraditional styles and will function with a combination of the strengths and stressors involved in each style. It is the professional's job to communicate with these families respectfully and openly in order to learn about and support them in their *individual* strengths and struggles.

It is also the professional's responsibility to challenge his or her own biases by continuing to learn about nontraditional families. The information presented here is a good beginning, but the professional may wish to consult the references and recommended readings listed at the end of this chapter for more comprehensive coverage of these issues. By combining curiosity and respect for individual families with a solid understanding of the literature regarding nontraditional families, the professional will become a more effective advocate and helper for such families.

References

Bozett, F. W. (1987). *Gay and lesbian parents*. New York: Praeger.

Brodzinsky, D. M., & Schechter, M. D. (Eds.). (1990). *The psychology of adoption*. New York: Oxford University Press.

Combrinck-Graham, L. (Ed.). (1989). *Children in family contexts: Perspectives on treatment*. New York: Guilford.

Eiduson, B. T., Kornfein, M., Zimmerman, I. L., & Weisner, T. S. (1988). Comparative socialization practices in traditional and alternative families. In G. E. Handel (Ed.), *Childhood socialization* (pp. 73-101). New York: Aldine De Gruyter.

Gottfried, A. E., & Gottfried, A. W. (1994). *Redefining families: Implications for children's development*. New York: Plenum.

Hetherington, E. M., & Arasteh, J. D. (Eds.). (1988). *Impact of divorce, single parenting, and stepparenting on children*. Hillsdale, NJ: Erlbaum.

Laosa, L. M. (1988). Ethnicity and single parenting in the United States. In E. M. Hetherington & J. D. Arasteh (Eds.), *Impact of divorce, single parenting, and stepparenting on children* (pp. 23-49). Hillsdale, NJ: Erlbaum.

Lindblad-Goldberg, M. (1989). Successful minority single-parent families. In L. Combrinck-Graham (Ed.), *Children in family contexts: Perspectives on treatment* (pp. 116-134). New York: Guilford.

Papernow, P. L. (1994). *Becoming a stepfamily: Patterns of development in remarried families*. San Francisco: Jossey-Bass.

Patterson, C. J. (1995a). Lesbian mothers, gay fathers, and their children. In A. R. D'Augelli & C. J. Patterson (Eds.), *Lesbian, gay, and bisexual identities over the lifespan: Psychological perspectives* (pp. 262-290). New York: Oxford University Press.

Patterson, C. J. (1995b). Families of the lesbian baby boom: Parents' division of labor and children's adjustment. *Developmental Psychology, 31*, 115-123.

Reitz, M., & Watson, K. W. (1992). *Adoption and the family system: Strategies for treatment*. New York: Guilford.

Saluter, A. F. (1992). *Marital status and living arrangements: March 1991* (U.S. Bureau of the Census, Current Population Reports, Series P-20, No. 461), Washington, DC: U.S. Government Printing Office.

Teyber, E. (1992). *Helping children cope with divorce*. New York: Lexington Books.

Visher, E., & Visher, J. (1988). *Old loyalties, new ties: Therapeutic strategies with stepfamilies*. New York: Brunner Mazel.

Recommended Readings

Bartholet, E. (1993). *Family bonds: Adoption and the politics of parenting*. Boston: Houghton Mifflin.

Beer, W. R. (1989). *Strangers in the house: The world of stepsiblings and half-siblings*. New Brunswick, NJ: Transaction.

Copper, B., Ehrensaft, D., Ferguson, A., Hill Collins, P., Lindsey, K., & Van Gelder, L. (1994). Part VB.: Valuing alternative families. In A. M. Jaggar (Ed.), *Living with contradictions: Controversies in feminist social ethics* (pp. 430-471). Boulder, CO: Westview Press.

Fanshel, D., Finch, S. J., & Grundy, J. F. (1990). *Foster children in a life course perspective*. New York: Columbia University Press.

Flaks, D. K., Ficher, I., Masterpaqua, F., & Joseph, G. (1995). Lesbians choosing motherhood: A comparative study of lesbian and heterosexual parents and their children. *Developmental Psychology, 31*, 105-114.

Kaufman, T. S. (1993). *The combined family: A guide to creating successful step-relationships*. New York: Plenum.

Maluccio, A. N., & Sinanoglu, P. A. (Eds.). (1981). *The challenge of partnership: Working with parents of children in foster care*. New York: Child Welfare League of America.

Pollack, S., & Vaughn, J. (1987). *Politics of the heart: A lesbian parenting anthology*. Ithaca, NY: Firebrand.

Walsh, W. M. (1992). Twenty major issues in remarriage families. *Journal of Counseling and Development, 70*, 709-715.

3 Evaluating Outcomes of Parenting Skills Programs

Introduction

This manual provides the professional with a variety of educational programs designed to enhance the parenting skills of parents of preschool and early-elementary-school-aged children. The content of the Early Childhood Parenting Skills Program is consistent with the recommendations of Barclay and Houts (1995) with regard to an "ideal broad-based program" (page 223). Each set of skills is designed to enhance the quality of the parent-child interaction and the functioning of the parenting system in general. The most important question relative to these programs and to any other parenting education program is whether they work? There is often a need for the parent educator to document (for a variety of third parties such as funding agencies, school systems, mental health boards, etc.) the effectiveness of the services provided to parents. This chapter is designed to provide the professional with an overview of the issues involved in program evaluation. Recommendations are made for measures that have been shown to be sensitive to any behavioral and attitudinal changes in parents that have occurred as a result of parent education programs.

Evaluation of parenting skills programs is an important, but complex, task. Some of the key issues in designing a relevant, efficient, and valid method of assessing the outcomes for parenting programs will be addressed. The first task for professionals is to determine what parenting skills outcomes they want to achieve and to specify both the specific and the global changes they hope will occur in the parents. Further, it is important to define these outcomes in terms of short-term and long-term effects. Figure 1 presents a model designed to facilitate the conceptualization and definition of goals.

	Short-Term	Long-Term
Specific Goals		
Global Goals		

Figure 1. Model for defining parent education goals.

To illustrate the model, let's assume that a helping professional decides to teach the two keys to healthy personality development in children (Developing the Child's Working Model of Self, Sessions 2 & 3) and the relationship building section of the

Program (Sessions 5-8). Using the chart in Figure 1 as a guide, what outcomes might be expected in each cell for the sessions selected?

- Specific Goals/Short Term—The parent will understand the two keys to the child's working model of self and will also know and be able to describe the techniques that are useful in building a relationship with the child. The parent will more frequently listen to and observe the child's activities without intruding.

- Specific Goals/Long Term—The parent will use the two keys to the child's working model of self in interactions with the child. The parent will more often stay near the child but will not intrude in the child's activities unless it is essential to protect the child. The parent will use the relationship-building techniques in interactions with the child (i.e., "reflective listening" and "sharing themselves").

- Global Goals/Short Term—The parent will see his or her child as more acceptable and enjoy being around the child. The parent will express positive feelings and approval toward the child more often. The parent will perceive the child as less stress producing and will, therefore, be less stressed in his or her role as parent.

- Global Goals/Long Term—The parent will develop a more respectful attitude toward the child and the child's abilities. The parent will become more encouraging of the child's independence and sense of competence. The parent will develop a greater sense of attachment to the child and an enhanced sense of competence about his or her own role as parent. The parent will be more comfortable and relaxed in interactions with the child.

	Short-Term	Long-Term
Specific Goals	1. Know and understand two keys to child's working model of self. 2. Know and describe technique for building parent-child relationship. 3. Listen to and observe child without intruding.	1. Use two keys to working model of self. 2. Stay near the child without intruding. 3. Use relationship building techniques.
Global Goals	1. See child as acceptable. 2. Express positive feelings and approval. 3. Be less stressed.	1. Be more respectful. 2. Encourage independence. 3. Feel more competent, comfortable, and relaxed in interactions.

Figure 2. Example of completed model for defining parent education goals for Sessions 2 and 3 and Sessions 5-8.

Having specified these goals, the next task of the parent educator will be to find a method to measure the attainment of these goals. Four major approaches to the assessment of parent outcomes that can be used with the above model will be considered. It should be noted that the types of changes or goals specified in each of the four quadrants of the model may be assessed by one or more of the four approaches. The use of multiple assessment approaches enhances the validity of the findings and facilitates interpretation of the results. For example, if a program is evaluated by only a behavioral observation scale, the findings may be criticized in that the parents may have learned to show the professional a specific behavior without changing their actual attitude or view of the child. Likewise, if a parent report measure is used, the opposite criticism may be rendered: the parents may be telling the professional what they *think* they do or what they think the professional wants to hear, but their behavior hasn't actually changed. The use of different types of measures reinforces the believability of measured changes and clarifies the nature of the changes achieved.

The issue of the timing of outcome assessments must also be considered. Should the assessment occur immediately following the learning, or should it occur 1 week, 3 months, or 1 year later? The timing issue is important in relation to being able to demonstrate both the fact that learning occurred and the relative stability of that learning. The short time frame may indicate that the learning occurred, but that learning may have been ephemeral with no long-term effects. Measurement that occurs a year later may reveal little difference between groups due to the intervening education or parenting experiences among the groups or to the adaptation of the learned behavior or attitudes by the parent to meet the needs of a developing child. From an instructional perspective, outcome assessments that occur 1 week to 1 month later are usually sufficient to demonstrate that learning occurred. Assessment that occurs 3 to 6 months later is likely to demonstrate that the parent perceives the importance of the learning and is motivated to maintain and use that learning. The longer time period allows for a clearer indication of the impact of the parent's learnings on the child's behavior.

To increase the acceptability of the results of the outcome evaluation, it is important to employ some premeasures. One can, to some extent, infer the impact of the training program by measuring the functioning of an untreated comparison group. This inference, however, assumes initial comparability of the two groups and the fact that the comparison group was not subjected to unknown experiences that might have altered functioning. The pre–post assessment design allows for the reasonable conclusion that the program taught the parents something and also creates the possibility of detecting changes in parent or child functioning.

Recommendations for instruments that would be useful to assess various outcomes will be presented along with some discussion of collateral issues relative to their use. A discussion of how some of these measures could be used to assess the goals presented in Figure 2 will be provided at the end of this chapter.

Outcome Evaluation

Four major approaches to the assessment of outcome will be discussed: Knowledge Examinations, Observations of Behavior, Self-Report Measures, and Ratings.

Knowledge Examinations

Knowledge Examinations are designed to determine how much of the information taught in the sessions the parent participants remember. These tests are generally not standardized, but they are written and designed by the professional in relation to the specific content of the sessions. First, the professional lists the specific knowledge that is taught in each session. Once this is accomplished, the test should be content and face valid (i.e., the questions asked will be directly related to the information that was taught in the class). The next step is to determine the format of the questions (i.e., true-false, multiple choice, fill in the blanks, or essay). For the sake of simplicity and the reliability of scoring, true-false or multiple choice questions are preferred. As a rule of thumb, between 5 and 10 questions per session are recommended. The next step is to administer the test to two or three parents with backgrounds similar to the parents who will participate in the sessions to determine if they understand what the questions are asking. Ideally, they should be available to tell the professional what they think each question is asking. With this feedback, revisions are made to questions that do not communicate clearly prior to their use in the evaluation. This is an important step, because the parent's performance on an evaluation should reflect his or her knowledge, unimpaired by a question that doesn't communicate well.

Knowledge Examinations serve well as a means of assessing specific information in relation to both the short-term and long-term goals of the parent education program. They do not, however, work well to assess global outcomes such as changes in attitude or values. From this consideration of Knowledge Examinations alone, it becomes apparent that no single measurement approach will be effective for the assessment of the four quadrants of the model presented in Figure 1. Each professional will need to decide which and how many of the quadrants to assess in evaluating the outcomes of the parent education program. Clearly, the more goals and quadrants to be assessed, the more measures and the more different types of assessment approaches will need to be employed. As the professional begins the process of selecting measures, it will immediately become apparent that compromises need to be made; in reality, a professional often will have to accept less than an ideal and fully comprehensive assessment of outcomes. Prior to reaching a decision on the particular goals to be assessed and the methods to be employed, the professional may need to step back and ask some basic questions about the goals of this particular parent education program. The types of questions that should be considered include the following: How, if at all, will the parents' knowledge of parenting and attitudes about themselves and their child change? Will the program lead the parents to change their behaviors towards their child and others? Will anything learned in the sessions cause problems for the parents in their relationships with their spouses or others in the family system? This last issue is raised because, all too often, well-intentioned helping professionals will cause a parent to reorder knowledge, values, and skills, which will then disrupt other elements of the parenting system. This issue is particularly acute in situations where only one parent is involved in the parent education program but other adults are also responsible for parenting and child care. All too often, the parent will see the new ways as the "right way," and this may lead to conflict with the other caregiver(s). Both the professional and the involved parent need to be sensitive to this issue and to develop a means of addressing it. Having the other caregiver review the home practice assignments with the participating parent is often helpful in closing this gap.

Observations of Behavior

The observation of parent-child interaction is the most time consuming and costly method of assessing outcomes of parent education programs. The great strength and value of this method is that, by assessing the parent-child interaction, one can determine directly whether the parent has incorporated the session content into his or her behavioral repertoire and whether the skills that were taught can be spontaneously displayed. All other methods of outcome assessment require an inference regarding the connection between the acquired knowledge and skill and the use of that knowledge and skill in the parenting process.

The decision to use observation as the method of choice for assessing the outcomes of the training requires a number of decisions, not the least of which is the particular parent-child observation system to be used. Four preliminary issues must be addressed before selecting an observation system:

1. What situational context or activity involving the parent and child might best reveal what was learned (e.g., playing together, eating together, working on a project)? The primary issue here is that any activity selected should create an opportunity for the skills that were taught to be displayed. For example, if you are concerned about how a parent handles limit setting, a free play activity might be less appropriate than a situation in which the parent must teach the child to do something or get the child to do a specific set of behaviors (e.g., stop playing and clean up the toys).

   Part of the issue of the observational context is whether the observation should be structured or more spontaneous. Completely natural observations are desirable in one way, in that they may facilitate generalization of behavior to other contexts. The problem is that only a limited amount of time is usually available for observation, and the variability of natural contexts and situations may destroy the reliability of the measure. In nonstructured contexts, you cannot control what will happen; other people enter the scene, a phone rings, or parent and child are engaged in an activity that doesn't call for the specific learned skills to be displayed.

   For the most part, it is recommended that a structured task or context be created that calls for use of the specific skills that were taught. This can be accomplished most successfully in the training setting, but it may also occur in the home situation with proper structure and planning.

2. The level of behavior you are interested in assessing must be determined (i.e., how specific or molecular versus how molar is the behavior you are interested in assessing). Molecular behavior would include such specific behaviors as eye contact, gentle touch, smiles, and so forth. At the molar level, the style of parent-child interaction is characterized as rejecting, controlling, affectionate, or the like. Molar judgments are generally based on a combination of specific behaviors and judgments as to the quality of interactions that occur in a stream of behavior.

3. Three basic types of data may be collected under the rubric of observational data. They array themselves along a continuum from specific behavioral counts (of the frequency of a behavior), to binary checklists that record the simple occurrence of the behavior during a given interval, to molar ratings of dimensions of behavior about which the observer makes guided qualitative judgments.

4. The professional needs to define or specify the behaviors to be observed. This may be accomplished by either creating a specialized behavior observation system that matches the goals of the parent education sessions or by selecting an existing parent-child observation system.

Existing Observation Systems

The following three existing observation systems were designed to assess parent-child interaction during early childhood. They have been selected from among the dozens of available systems based on relative ease of use, available validity research, and relevance to the goals of the Early Child Parenting Skills Program. The three systems represent the three types of data collection methods: Behavioral Counts, Binary Checklists, and Rating Scales.

Behavioral Count. The Dyadic Parent-child Interaction Coding System (DPICS; Robinson & Eyberg, 1981) has been successfully used in a number of program evaluation and research projects designed to assess parent-child interactions (Robinson & Eyberg, 1981; Eyberg & Robinson, 1982). This system is appropriate for use with both normal and behavior problem children ages 2 to 8 years who come from low- and middle-class families. The observations are designed to occur on two occasions, during which there are two 5-minute play sessions. The play sessions are structured such that one is directed by the child and the other by the parent. The behaviors which are counted include parent direction, praise, positive and negative contact, questions, child compliance, and positive and negative behaviors. The manual for the DPICS contains all necessary information about how to use the system in a valid and reliable manner.[1]

Binary Checklist. The Home Observation for the Measurement of the Environment (HOME; Caldwell, 1972), and the HOME Inventory (Bradley, Caldwell, Brishy, & Magee, 1992) have been used extensively in a wide range of

---

[1]The DPICS may be obtained from Social and Behavioral Sciences Documents, Select Press, P.O. Box 9838, San Rafael, CA 94912. Request the Dyadic Parent-child Interaction Coding System Psychological Document 13, 24 (MS #2582).

studies designed to evaluate the effectiveness of parent education and intervention programs. Although the scale was originally designed to assess the quality of a child's home environment, it provides a range of items that allow for the observational assessment of important parent-child interactional behavior. The HOME and the HOME Inventory should be administered in the parent's home. They may be used with mother-child dyads from infancy through pre-adolescence. Items are scored in a simple *yes* or *no* format; the scale assesses a variety of behaviors related to parent-child interactions, including responsivity, stimulation of child's language, and the like.[2]

Rating Scale. Maternal Behavior Rating Scale (MBRS; Mahoney, Finger, & Powell, 1985). Although originally developed for use with parents of mentally retarded children, the MBRS assesses a number of important parenting behaviors with regard to preschool children in general (Mahoney, Powell, & Finger, 1986). The ratings are obtained from 10-minute direct or videotaped observations of dyadic free play between parent and child using a standard set of toys. Although the professional educator may need to adapt the context for the ratings, the rating categories and descriptions of the dimensions should prove very useful. The dimensions of parental behavior rated include expressiveness, warmth, directiveness, effectiveness, and sensitivity to child state.

The MBRS is a global 7-item rating scale designed to assess the quality of maternal interactive behavior with young children. The rating may be completed by anyone who has had an opportunity to observe the mother in interaction with her child. Parents and other family members may rate each other's behaviors. This measure is under development, and shows promise as a quick method of assessing maternal behavior.[3]

Self-Report Measures

The strengths and weaknesses of self-report measures must be considered in relation to their use in any specific evaluation effort. First, the appropriateness of each self-report measure to the goals of the program needs to be determined. Second, the validity of the measure for the purpose under consideration should be established in the literature. The strengths of self-report measures lie primarily in the ease of data collection and scoring, the relatively low cost, and the ability to cover a wide range of parenting issues in a short period of time. The principal weakness of self-report measures is the possibility that the parent will respond to each item based on what appears to be the socially desirable answer (i.e., the parent will say the "right thing"). Thus, positive results obtained in postprogram administrations of self-report measures may be a function of social response bias. The relation between parents' self-reports and changes in their parenting attitudes and behaviors may not be unequivocally established. In selecting a self-report measure, it is important to determine whether

[2]The HOME and the HOME Inventory may be obtained from Betty Caldwell, Center for Research on Teaching and Learning, University of Arkansas, Little Rock, AR 72204.

[3]The MBRS may be obtained from Gerald Mahoney, School of Education, University of Michigan, Ann Arbor, MI 48109.

the research literature has established an association between scores on the measure and specific parenting behaviors. Four self-report measures which have wide applicability as pre- and postmeasures of important parenting outcomes are presented here. These measures are grouped into two categories: Parent Functioning and Family Functioning.

Parent Functioning. The Parenting Stress Index (PSI; Abidin, 1995a) was designed to assess the potential for dysfunctional parenting and problematic child development. It has been used as an evaluation and diagnostic measure in a wide range of parent education and intervention programs. The test items are in a multiple-choice format and are divided into two global domains: Child Characteristics and Parent/Situational Characteristics. The PSI subscales provide for the assessment of a relatively broad range of important parenting outcome variables. Within the Child Domain, four subscales cover parental perception of the child's behavioral characteristics, and two subscales relate to the parent's perception of the quality of the parent-child interaction. The Parent Domain subscales assess parenting variables that have an established connection to positive or dysfunctional parenting (e.g., sense of competence, depression, attachment to child, social isolation, restriction of role, relationship with child's other parent). A software version of the PSI (PSI3 *Plus*; Abidin, 1995b) permits on-screen administration, scoring, and report generation for individual clinical diagnostic assessment, as well as the overall assessment of group outcomes. The major strength of the PSI is the extensive research base that establishes its validity. Most importantly, the predictive and current validity of the PSI scores have been demonstrated in a number of studies involving observed behavior of individual parents. The PSI Professional Manual (Abidin, 1995a) provides information on its statistical characteristics, interpretation of its scales, and its extensive research base. The PSI is available in a number of languages. It requires a fifth-grade reading level, but it may also be administered by reading the questions aloud to a group of parents. No special training is required beyond familiarity with the test administration section of the manual. The PSI may be administered in 20-25 minutes.[4]

Family Functioning. The Family Adaptability and Cohesion Evaluation Scale (FACES III; Olson, Portner, & Lavee, 1985) is part of a series of family inventories. It was developed to assess two important aspects of family functioning throughout the family life cycle. The FACES III subscales assess the two major dimensions (Adaptability and Cohesion) of the circumplex model of family functioning (Olson, 1986). FACES III has been used in hundreds of research projects evaluating both intervention outcomes and family functioning. The respondent is asked to decide for each of 20 statements how frequently, on a scale of 1 (*almost never*) to 5 (*almost always*), the described behavior occurs in his or her family. Sample statements include the following: Rules change in our family, Children have a say in their discipline, Family members feel very close to each other. The norms for the FACES include 2,453 respondents, and the scale is psychometrically sound. Factor analysis

---

[4]Print and software versions of the PSI are available from Psychological Assessment Resources, Inc., P.O. Box 998, Odessa, FL 33556 (1-800-331-8378).

supports the two subscales of Adaptability and Cohesion as independent dimensions. Importantly, the subscales display minimal correlations to measures of social desirability, suggesting that the respondents' self-reports are not biased by the tendency to present themselves in a favorable light. Reliability of the scales is acceptable (Cohesion, $r = 0.77$; Adaptability, $r = 0.62$).[5]

The Parent As A Teacher Inventory (PAAT; Strom & Johnson, 1978; Strom, 1993) was designed to assess a parent's values and attitudes toward the child. Parents express their feelings and standards regarding their ability to guide their child's behavior in ways that will facilitate the child's development. The questionnaire requests that parents respond to 50 statements along a 4-point continuum ranging from *strong no* to *strong yes*. Sample items include the following: Wants child to talk more than self, Lets child experiment with problem solving, and Comfortable playing with child. The scale is applicable to parents of children ages 2 to 12 years. The inventory yields five separate scales that are relevant to the nature and quality of the parent-child interaction: Creativity (stimulation of creative and independent action on the part of the child), Control (extent of parental control), Play (creation of play opportunities), Frustration (frustration with interactions), and Teaching (ability to facilitate child's learning). The PAAT has been validated in relation to both general measures of child development, and specific observed parenting behavior. The PAAT requires a fifth-grade reading level; it may be administered individually or in groups by relatively inexperienced individuals in 20-30 minutes. One strength of the PAAT is that it is available in a number of different languages. Although the PAAT has relatively limited normative data available, its primary use in assessing change within the specific treatment group would not require norms.[6]

Ratings

Rating scales are characterized by the fact that the rater's attention is focused on specific behaviors or interactions. The rater's task is not to evaluate the meaning of the behavior or interaction, but rather the frequency of its occurrence. The focus on specific behavior and the absence of a global interpretation increases the reliability of the measure and allows for raters who have not had extensive training. The problem of many behavioral rating systems is that they focus on a narrow band of behaviors and may not reflect changes that are created by a broadly focused training program. Parents, like many other individuals, often learn skills that they apply in only some situations or in relation to only some specific child behaviors. Ratings that target specific behaviors must be focused on situations in which those behaviors are likely to occur.

The Eyberg Child Behavior Inventory (ECBI; Robinson, Ross, & Eyberg, 1977) is a parent report scale designed to assess 36 of the most common behavioral problems

---

[5]FACES III is available from Family Social Science, 290 McNeal Hall, University of Minnesota, St. Paul, MN 55108.

[6]The PAAT may be obtained from Robert Strom, Office of Parent Development International, Division of Psychology in Education, Arizona State University, Tempe, AZ 85287 *or* from Scholastic Testing Service, 480 Meyer Road, Bensenville, IL 60106-1617.

of young children. The parent is asked to rate the child's behavior in relation to each item along a 7-point continuum from *never occurs* to *always occurs*; this yields an Intensity Score. Additionally, the parent is asked to respond *yes* or *no* regarding whether the particular behavior is a problem; the sum of the number of items defined as a problem is the Problem Score. The dual response method allows for the determination of how troubling a given child's behavior is to the parent. Thus, it is possible for a parent to endorse the item "Dawdles in getting dressed" as a 7 (*always occurs*) and yet also respond that it is not a problem. The ECBI has a good normative base and is a psychometrically sound instrument. Alpha, split half, and test-retest reliability for both the Intensity Score and the Problem Score range from .86-.98. For complete information on the statistical characteristics of this instrument, refer to the ECBI manual (Eyberg, 1992). The ECBI has been shown to be sensitive to intervention effects and should be useful in monitoring changes in children's behaviors as well as parents' perceptions of whether the child's behavior is a problem.[7]

Development of an Evaluation Protocol

The following evaluation protocol was designed to assess the goals defined in Figure 2 for the two keys to healthy personality development in children (Sessions 2 and 3) and the relationship building sessions (Sessions 5-8) of the Early Childhood Parenting Skills Program. These sections of the Program involve a mixture of specific behavioral skills and attitudinal changes that center around the nature of the communication between parent and child. Given the fact that this selection of parenting skills will be taught in only 6 sessions, only short-term goals will be addressed.

The information to be used in the evaluation will be gathered using a pre- and post-model involving observations and parental self-report questionnaires. The observations will be collected during a 5-minute child-directed play session followed by a 5-minute parent-directed play session on the day the parents register for the parenting skills sessions. The post-assessment would occur during a wrap-up and completion session at the end of the training.

The DPICS will be used with one modification: Praise and criticism will be tallied only when the parent employs the method of praise and criticism taught in the program. "Listening for feelings" and "sharing yourself," along with all other positive parenting behaviors, will be tallied under the positive contact and positive behavior categories of the DPICS. All other behavior will be coded as directed in the DPICS manual. During both the pre- and post-session observations, the parents will be provided the same five developmentally appropriate toys for use in the play session.

The self-report questionnaires will include the PSI and the ECBI; 30 minutes should be allowed for their completion. If this is not possible, the questionnaires may be given to the parents in stamped, self-addressed envelopes for later return. Completing the forms on site is the preferred method. During the sign-up and wrap-up sessions and while the parents are completing the questionnaire, child care will

---

[7]The ECBI may be obtained from Psychological Assessment Resources, Inc. Call Toll-Free 1-800-331-TEST (8378).

need to be provided. The parent-child dyads can be taken to the setting for the play observation during the initial sign-up session and during a general socializing and play time following the wrap-up session. Approximately 2 hours will be needed on each occasion, depending on the size of the group.

The three measures to be used in this assessment are all directly related to the short-term specific and global goals presented in Figure 2. The DPICS will allow for the assessment of changes in the parent's way of interacting with the child. The targeted behaviors of this coding system, with the minor suggested changes, tailor the measure to the behavioral objectives of the parenting skills training program. It may be desirable to make further refinements or to simplify the coding system after a trial run, especially if other parenting skills are to be taught. The PSI will facilitate assessment of both specific and global goals and will help answer the following questions: Are there changes in how stress-producing the parents perceive their child to be? Are parents less distressed by the role of being a parent? Do parents find the child more positively reinforcing? Do they feel closer to their child? These and other parent-related perceptions may be assessed by the PSI. The ECBI provides a means of determining whether changes have occurred in the number of common behavior problems exhibited by the child or whether the parent is less distressed by these behaviors. Often, as a function of the skills taught in the sessions, the parent will develop more realistic expectations regarding the child's behavior. Thus, while the child may or may not change the frequency of certain common child behaviors, parents will often be less bothered by those behaviors. The ECBI is sensitive to this important change in parental functioning.

Additional Measures of Parenting Behaviors, Attitudes, and Child Functioning

The following resources are available in most university libraries. Each contains descriptions and critiques of measures that are applicable to a specific area of parenting and provides information about obtaining each measure.

Bailey, D. B., & Simeonsson, R. J. (1988). *Family assessment in early intervention*. Columbus, OH: Merrill Publishing.

Jacob, T., & Tennenbaum, D. L. (1988). *Family assessment: Rationale, methods, and future directions*. New York: Plenum.

Touliator, J., Perlmutter, B., & Straus, M. (Eds.). (1990). *Handbook of family measurement techniques*. Newbury Park, CA: Sage.

Buros Institute of Mental Measurements. (1994). *Mental measurement yearbooks*. Lincoln: University of Nebraska.

Educational Testing Service. (1996), *Test collection*. Princeton, NJ: Author.

Pro-ed. (1996). *Test critiques*. Austin, TX: Author.

References

Abidin, R. R. (1995a). *Parenting Stress Index: Professional manual* (3rd ed.). Odessa, FL: Psychological Assessment Resources.

Abidin, R. R. (1995b). Parenting Stress Index (PSI3 Plus) [Computer software]. Odessa, FL: Psychological Assessment Resources

Barclay, D. R., & Houts, A. C. (1995). Parenting Skills: A review and developmental analysis of training content. In W. O'Donahue & L. Krasner (Eds.), *Handbook of psychological skills training: Clinical techniques and applications* (pp. 195-228). Boston: Allyn & Bacon.

Bradley, R., Caldwell, B. M., Brishy, J., & Magee, M. (1992). *The HOME Inventory: A new scale for families of pre- and early adolescent children with abilities*. Little Rock: University of Arkansas Center for Research on Teaching and Learning.

Caldwell, B. (1972). *Home Observation for the Measurement of the Environment*. Little Rock: University of Arkansas Center for Research on Teaching and Learning.

Eyberg, S. (1992). Parent and teacher behavior inventories for the assessment of conduct problem behaviors in children. In L. VandeCreek, S. Knapp, & T. L. Jackson (Eds.), *Innovations in clinical practice: A source book* (Vol. 11, pp. 261-270). Sarasota, FL: Professional Resource Press.

Eyberg, S. M., & Robinson, E.A. (1982). Parent-child interaction training: Effects on family functioning. *Journal of Clinical Child Psychology*, *11*, 130-137.

Mahoney, G., Finger, I., & Powell, A. (1985). Relationship of maternal behavioral style to the development of organically impaired mentally retarded infants. *American Journal of Mental Deficiency*, *90*, 296-302.

Mahoney, G., Powell, A., & Finger, I. (1986). The maternal behavior rating scale. *Topics in Early Childhood Special Education*, *6*, 44-55.

Olson, D. H. (1986). Circumplex model VII: Validation studies and FACES III. *Family Process*, *25*, 337-351.

Olson, D. H., Portner, J., & Lavee, Y. (1985). Family Adaptability and Cohesion Evaluation Scale III. In D. H. Olson, H. I. McCubbin, H. Barnes, A. Larsen, M. Muxen, & M. Wilson (Eds.), *Family inventories in a natural survey of families across the family life cycle* (pp. 69-81). St. Paul: University of Minnesota Family Social Service.

Robinson, E. A., & Eyberg, S. M. (1981). The Dyadic Parent-child Interaction Coding System: Standardization and validation. *Journal of Consulting and Clinical Psychology*, *49*, 245-250.

Robinson, E., Ross, A. W., & Eyberg, S. M. (1977, August). *The standardization of the Eyberg Child Behavior Inventory*. Paper presented at the annual meeting of the American Psychological Association, San Francisco.

Strom, R. (1993). *Revised Parent As a Teacher Inventory*. Bensenville, IL: Scholastic Testing Service.

Strom, R., & Johnson, A. (1978). Assessment for parent education. *Journal of Experimental Education*, *47*, 9.

Section II

The Program Sessions and Modules

4 Learning Successful Parenting Skills: An Introduction

Session 1

Building a Group Identity by Sharing

Introduction

The first session of your parent education program will probably involve a number of basic administrative matters. However, it is also important that some sense of group identity be formed during this session. In future sessions, parents will share their struggles to learn and practice new child-rearing skills. The more accepted and secure the group members feel, the easier it will be for them to fully participate in those sessions. A growing sense of group identity will facilitate that acceptance and security for all the group members.

During this session (and the following two sessions), you, as the professional, must focus on facilitating group identity, communicating acceptance to every parent, and tuning in to the degree of threat experienced by each individual in the group. As parents develop trust and confidence in you, they will become more open to the ideas and skills you are presenting. You can encourage the parents' trust by relaxing, sharing your own experience whenever this is appropriate, and accepting parents' contributions without expressing judgment or criticism.

This may seem like a difficult task when a parent's behavior seems to be particularly harmful to the child. However, you must remember that few parents will engage in behavior they know will hurt their child. Destructive behavior patterns occur because the parent has no alternative method of handling the situation. Parents are more likely to succeed in the Early Childhood Parenting Skills Program (and to learn the alternative methods they need) when they feel that their reactions and comments are accepted, without judgment, by the professional.

The three exercises described in this chapter may be used during this first session to "break the ice" and to help the group begin to form a sense of identity. Only you, the professional, can determine how appropriate each exercise will be for the particular group of parents.

Group Size. The ideal group size is 6 to 20. With smaller groups, you will have to maintain a more active monitoring role, because the experience may become more intense than is recommended.

Physical Setting. Group members can sit facing each other in a circle or around a large conference table. Because sharing is essential to the success of the group, parents should not sit in rows during any of the sessions of this Early Childhood Parenting Skills Program.

Session Objectives

1 To develop empathy, trust, and comfort among members of the group.

2 To help parents begin to interact with one another.

 ## Materials

Pencils

Pad of paper

Schedule

● Exercise 1 (20 - 25 minutes)

● Exercise 2 (20 - 25 minutes)

● Exercise 3 (optional) 20 - 25 minutes

● Discussion of the home practice assignment (10 minutes)

Special Notes for the Mental Health Professional

You must provide a comfortable balance between authoritative and democratic leadership. Be prepared to refocus group discussion on personal feelings (to prevent intellectualizing), but there is no need for you to enter the process as long as the group is working at a personal, feeling level. You should also be ready to intervene gently and tactfully if one member of the group is taking up more than his or her share of the discussion time.

Setting the Tone

Prepare by explaining that the group will engage in two sharing exercises. The purpose of these exercised is to share experiences and feelings—without intellectualizing the discussion. Mention that it is important for the group to share *feelings and experiences* and not judgments and opinions. When it seems appropriate, you may briefly discuss the idea that exchanging memories, experiences, and feelings often helps people to feel warmth and closeness for each other. These feelings help people to relax and feel good about their situation. Being relaxed and comfortable often encourages people to pay closer attention to their situation and to learn more easily.

Exercise 1

All participants are given a piece of paper and a pencil. They are asked to write down one thing that concerns them most about being in a group like this one. All the slips of paper are folded and mixed up in a bowl. Then, each group member draws one slip of paper, reads it aloud, and talks about how he or she would feel if this was his or her own concern. *(Note: Parents who draw the slips of paper they wrote should return them to the bowl and draw again.)* Other members of the group may also respond to the concern after the parent who drew that paper has finished discussing it. Be sure you monitor the pace of the discussion so that all of the slips of paper can be read within the allotted time. Encourage discussion by asking whether anyone has any other feelings or reactions. Ask the other group members how they would feel if this was their concern. When the exercise is completed, collect and destroy the slips of paper without comment and in full view of all the participants.

Exercise 2

Pass out new slips of paper. This time, ask group members to write down a brief description of a happy or an unhappy event from their own childhood. Again, fold the slips and mix them up in a bowl. Group members are asked to draw a slip (not their own) and explain how it would feel that have that childhood experience. Encourage discussion by asking participants how that experience would have affected them. Other questions might include: "What do you think the child was thinking or feeling at the time? Why would this event be important to a child? What else could this child have been thinking or feeling? In this exercise, you are trying to help parents get in touch with the feelings they experienced as children. This will help them to take a child's perspective. And the exercise also helps the participants build a group identity through sharing. At the end of the exercise, collect and destroy the slips of paper without comment.

Exercise 3

Ask parents to briefly describe (on a slip of paper) something their child did that they found particularly bothersome or upsetting. Parents should simply describe what the child did or said and where the behavior took place, and not why it bothered them. Again, mix the slips in a bowl. Each parent draws a slip of paper, reads it aloud, and then explains why the behavior would be bothersome. If the parent says he or she doesn't think the behavior would be a bother, ask the parent to imagine why it might bother someone else. Then ask the other group members to express their thoughts. This exercise allows the group members to do some risk taking—without having to fully own their reactions or reveal their individual concerns. It is an important first step toward sharing reactions and concerns, and it will help the group transition into open disclosure and full ownership of concerns and feelings. At the end of the exercise, remember to collect and destroy all slips of paper without comment.

Discussion of the Home Practice Assignments

(The purpose and importance of the weekly home practice assignment must be reviewed with the group along the following lines.)

As a part of the parenting sessions, I will be asking you to complete a weekly home practice assignment. Each assignment is described in your Workbook. Generally, the assignments contain four parts:

1. A review of the main ideas presented in the session.

2. Practical examples of the ideas and skills we discussed in the session.

3. Practice exercises to help you remember and think about the skills

4. An assignment that gives you a framework for practicing those skills with your child.

Completing the weekly home practice assignments is as important as attending the sessions. Working on the assignments will remind you to use the skills you are learning. Only with practice will these ideas and skills become a natural part of the way you interact with your child. Home practice is also the way you learn to identify any problems or barriers to using the new set of skills in your own family. Each week, I will invite members of the group to share their experiences and reactions to the home practice assignment. You will always be free to share or not to share. In my experience, as the program progresses parents become increasingly interested in sharing their own experiences and asking for suggestions about how to use the skills more effectively. But again, whether you share is always your choice.

5 Developing the Child's Working Model of Self

Introduction to Sessions 2-3

Sessions 2 and 3 focus on issues related to the child's developing self-concept. The self-concept is one of the most important determinants of behavior. It consists of all the thoughts and feelings people have about who they are, what they believe in, what they can or cannot do, and anything else that makes them unique and separate individuals (Neisser, 1993).

A person who has a good self-concept feels worthwhile, capable, and important; one who has a poor self-concept feels inadequate, incompetent, and unimportant. Feelings like these will affect how individuals interact with others and how they perform the tasks required for daily living (Quandt, 1984; Wyman, Cowen, Work, & Kerley, 1993). Because it has so much influence on a child's success (or failure), it is important for parents to learn about the importance of a good self-concept and how their own behaviors will influence the development of their own child's self-concept.

Most researchers agree that self-concept is learned through repeated interaction with significant others over long periods of time (Cicchetti & Beeghly, 1990; Wylie, 1979). As significant others communicate their approval or disapproval of a child's characteristics, abilities, and accomplishments, the child learns a view of himself or herself as important or unimportant, competent or incompetent, valued or devalued (Blechman & Culhane, 1993; Neisser, 1993). Collectively, these experiences help to form the child's working model of self. Because parents are the first (and among the most important) of the significant individuals in a child's environment, they need to understand the way their reactions to their children will influence how the children come to feel about themselves.

For purposes of discussion, the child's working model of self (self-concept) has been broken down into two major belief systems. These components are presented (in Sessions 2 and 3) as the two basic ways of understanding interactions between parent and child and their effect on the child's developing self-concept. Understanding these two major belief systems will help parents determine whether specific interactions with their child will add to or detract from their child's positive working model of self.

I Am Worthwhile, I Am Lovable

Introduction

The first major belief system is "I am worthwhile, I am lovable." During the earliest mother-infant interactions, children begin to develop a sense of being secure and being loved. The experience of being valued by the primary caregiver (and by other family members) lays the foundation for a positive model of self and, as a result, for the quality of future social interactions (Baumrind, 1991). Through interactions with parents and significant others, the child develops an internal picture of both self and others. This picture functions as a guide, or template, for future interactions with people outside the family (Crittenden, 1990; George & Solomon, 1989) and can enable the child to better meet the challenges and expectations he or she encounters throughout life (Kagan, 1984). Children who feel loved and valued will learn to love and value themselves and others. By contrast, the inability to love and value oneself often leads to a lifetime of maladaptive social behavior, which is characterized by an inability to trust others or to form stable relationships.

Parents provide security and communicate love for their children in many ways. They provide food, clothing, shelter, safety, and discipline. Parents respond to the emotional needs of their children and offer their children opportunities for learning and growth. *Among the various ways parents communicate their love is by creating an organized and reciprocal social environment.* Such an environment is of major importance, because it helps children to feel secure and loved.

Every interaction between parent and child offers the opportunity to express love and caring, both verbally and nonverbally. A parent's gestures, facial expressions, body language, and words can all help a child to feel loved and secure. Likewise, as the developing child begins to express feelings and desires, it is important that the parent learn to recognize and understand what the child is feeling and communicating.

The experience of being understood by a parent and of having one's needs met is the very core of love. From such experiences, the child's sense of emotional and physical security develops. Thus, whether or not a child develops a sense of being worthwhile and lovable depends not only on what a parent does to and for the child, but also on the parent's ability to understand what the child is feeling and trying to communicate.

Recognition of the importance of reciprocity in relationships with children is a primary goal in both working models of self (Sessions 2 and 3). Parents must develop an understanding that what a child thinks and believes is just as important as what a parent does to and for the child. Therefore, parents must learn to be sensitive and open to communication from their child, so that they will understand the impact of their own behavior on that child (Sameroff, 1991; Tronick, 1982).

Although parents love their children, the children are all too often unsure or ambivalent about how their parents feel about them. Children need to be told, in ways that make it clear, that their parents love them. Whereas children need regular praise and encouragement in order to learn that they are worthwhile human beings (Adler, 1971), they sometimes need criticism and discipline as well. But love and acceptance can be communicated along with the criticism. Haim Ginott (1965) talks about helpful praise and criticism as they are presented in this session. The session includes ways that a parent can praise and criticize a child's *behavior* without making the child feel unloved or devalued as a person.

In summary. A child's feelings about himself or herself (self-concept) and internal pictures of the surrounding world are learned through repeated interaction with significant individuals, beginning with the earliest interactions with the mother. Parents communicate feelings about their children in many ways, both verbal and nonverbal. These communications teach children how to feel about themselves. It is important that parents become aware of their influence on the child's self-concept and learn ways to communicate that will increase their child's positive feelings about self, enabling the child to move through life in a competent and successfully adaptive manner.

Special Notes for the Mental Health Professional

You may encounter some difficulty with two of the exercises in this session. Some parents may be reluctant to participate in the Mirror Exercise. This self-confronting experience comes very early in the Program, and it is likely to elicit anxiety from some or all of the group members. You must be prepared to deal with that anxiety, but also to urge every parent to participate in this valuable and insightful exercise. The Mirror Exercise will evoke interesting discussion about the possible disparity between what is communicated verbally and what is communicated nonverbally (through gestures and facial expressions).

Your explanations of the concepts of helpful praise and constructive criticism may confuse some group members. Use the self-concept diagram provided in Figure 3 (as well as any other visual or verbal aids you may find helpful) to emphasize the two-part structure of helpful praise and the three-part structure of helpful criticism. It will also be helpful if you model these techniques in your own communications with the parents.

Emphasize to the parents that completion of the workbook home practice assignment for each session is very important to the success of this Parenting Skills Program. Completion of home practice assignments allows parents to participate actively in the review discussion at the beginning of each new session and provides additional practical opportunities for parents to implement the skills they are learning in the Program.

You must remain sensitive to the motivation and skills of each group member. Writing ability, reading comprehension, and attitudes toward the session topic will vary, and these differences should be considered when assigning home practice. You may need to modify some assignments according to the abilities, motivation, and individual attitudes within a particular group. If necessary, you should provide some incentive for completion of assignments, as home practice is such an integral part of the skills to be learned in the Program.

One problem frequently encountered in parent education programs is that only one parent attends the class. This tends to limit the transmission of information and skills into the total parenting and family system; it can also become a source of tension within that system.

Tensions can arise when an outside authority is seen as influencing, or even controlling, events inside the family. They may also occur as the parents or caregivers grow apart in terms of their knowledge of parenting skills and approaches to parenting. The following suggestions are made in an effort to address these problems:

1. If you and the group are comfortable with the idea, parents without partners might audiotape the lecture/discussion portion of the session.

2. You might encourage parents to discuss the session with their caregiving partners, have the absent caregivers read the Review Summary of the session in the Workbook, and (if the participating parents are comfortable with the idea) have the nonparticipant partners review their responses to the home practice assignments.

3. You might encourage parents to bring to the sessions their partners' questions or concerns about what is being learned and the effect of the program on the child or on the family dynamics.

As you become more sensitive to these important issues, you will develop successful ways to address them. The important concept here is to find a way to involve the absent partners actively in the Program. Hopefully, this will avert problems at home at the same time and enhance the motivation of the participant parents.

Session Objectives

1 To present the first major key to raising an effective, happy, and loving child: whenever possible, the things a parent does to, with, and for the child should help that child learn that he or she is worthwhile and lovable.

2 To demonstrate how a parent's verbal and nonverbal behaviors affect the child's developing self-concept.

3 To illustrate different methods for praising and criticizing children's behavior. "Helpful praise" and "helpful criticism" are presented as two communication methods that increase the child's security and help the child maintain a positive self-concept.

Sequence

- Lecture/Discussion (30 - 40 minutes)
- General discussion (30 - 40 minutes)
- Discussion of the home practice assignment (10 - 20 minutes)

Materials

Blackboard (or large marking board)

Chalk (or markers)

Eraser

3 Table-top mirrors

Written instructions for the Mirror Exercise

Lecture/Discussion

Belief Systems and the Self-Concept

The ideas I will be presenting during this session and the next are called belief systems. Belief systems are the child's ideas about what kind of person he or she is. Psychologists, psychiatrists, educators, and successful parents have learned that children who develop positive beliefs about themselves are happier, more successful, and easier to get along with. Understanding and using these ideas will help you to raise a confident, capable, and loving child.

The first belief system we want our parenting to develop in our child is the idea of being a worthwhile and lovable person. *(Write the words "worthwhile" and "lovable" on the board.)*

Every belief or idea that a child has about himself or herself is learned. These feelings *(point to the words on the board)* are also learned, and they form one of the two major parts of the child's self-concept. *(Complete the diagram shown in Figure 3 on the board.)*

When I say that beliefs are learned, I mean that, just as children learn to talk or read or play a game, children learn who they are by the things people do and say to them.

In some ways, parents and other people around the child are like mirrors. When the child does something, the parent's reactions to that action—their words and the expressions on their faces—reveal what they think about the child. Because parents are the source of all good things, things like food, warmth, and affection, children cannot survive without their parents when they are very young. When their parents act angry or annoyed, rather than risk being rejected or abandoned by the parents, children will respond as though there is something wrong or bad about themselves. If the parent is angry, yells, or is physically rough with a child repeatedly, the child will begin to learn that he or she is always doing something wrong, and is, therefore, not worthwhile or lovable.

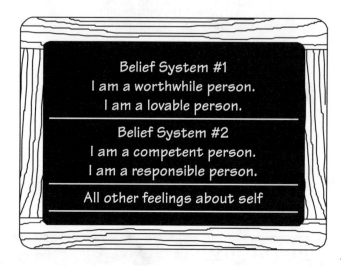

Figure 3. A diagram of the child's self-concept.

Q Why do you think it's important for a child to learn that he or she is a worthwhile and lovable *person? (Pause for parents' response, then summarize these responses on the board.)*

Yes, these are all reasons why we must help our children develop this important belief. People who don't believe that they are worthwhile or lovable are often depressed and tired, and they have a hard time accomplishing anything. Many adults today are depressed because they do not believe that they are worthwhile and lovable. Let me give you an example. Listen to the words of a 19-year-old woman suffering from depression. She is talking to her therapist about her job and her coworkers. Pay particular attention to what she says about her beliefs about herself.

Patient: "Mary tries to be friendly and helpful, but I just don't have the energy to go for a walk during lunch hour."

Therapist: "What do you do?"

Patient: "Well, I just hang around the office and try to finish my work. I'm not as fast as the other word processors. They're really good. *(Long pause.)* I don't understand why Mary tries to help. All I do is get in the way, and I'm no fun to be with. She's probably just a good person who feels sorry for me. *(Tears.)* God, why am I so rotten at making friends with people?"

Another important reason for helping your child to feel worthwhile and lovable is that, until your child feels worthwhile and lovable, he or she will not be able to give love or to help other people feel worthwhile.

Q If your child can't do these things, what do you think his or her relationships with you and others will be like? *(Pause for parents' response. Write their responses on the board and summarize them, using the parents' own words.)*

You all seem to appreciate how important this key to a healthy self-concept really is. Now I'm going to turn down the lights. I want you to close your eyes and imagine that you are a little child again. Think back to when you were between the ages of 2 and 6. Imagine that you're back in your house and your mother is talking to you. Listen carefully while I give you some examples of the things that parents might say to children. Pay attention to how you—the child—feel. Remember, you are the child being spoken to, and you need to get in touch with how you feel about what is being communicated.

1. *(Dramatically and sarcastically)* **"You just don't care about anyone but yourself! You know I was saving that cookie for your sister. You are mean and selfish!"**

Q How would you feel and think about yourself if the parent you loved talked to you like that? *(Pause for parents' response. Praise and restate parents' response, pointing out how the person's feelings could affect his or her positive self-concept.)*

2. *(Concerned and interested)* **"Alex, I know you like to use my pots and pans, and I like to share them with you. But you must tell me when you want to use them, so I won't waste time looking for them."**

Q How would you feel and think about yourself if the parent you loved talked to you like that? *(Pause for parents' response. Praise and restate parents' response, pointing out how the person's feelings could affect his or her positive self-concept.)*

These examples were designed to show the effect that our words may be having on our children. Our words can affect our children at the moment they are spoken, but they can also affect our children's long-term beliefs in themselves as worthwhile and lovable individuals. Note that, in both cases, the parent expressed disapproval of the child's behavior. What was said, however, was different in two important ways. The second communication did not attack the child's character and, most importantly, it provided the child with guidance on how to handle that specific situation in the future.

Now I would like you to take turns going to the back of the room, where I have set up three mirrors. You should go three at a time, with each of you sitting at your own mirror. When you get there, read the instructions next to the mirror silently. Please don't talk while you are there or after you come back to your seat. Just read and follow the directions while sitting in front of your mirror.

While the groups of three are doing the Mirror Exercise, the rest of you can be thinking about the ways you communicate praise and criticism to your own child. Don't turn around until it's your turn to go back to the mirror. While you are waiting your turn, please write some notes to yourself that describe two different interactions with your child: First one in which you were proud of your child's behavior, and several in which you were disappointed or upset by your child's behavior. You will need your notes later when we discuss praising and criticizing children's behavior.

Please be seated. Look into the mirror and do the two things described below. Please do not rush through this exercise, because it is important that you think about what you are seeing. Try to remember how this exercise feels so you can talk about it later.

1. Imagine that you are talking to your child without saying a word. Use your face to let the child know that you are proud and love him or her. If you need to, imagine that your child just gave you a present that he or she worked very hard to make.

2. This time, use your face to show your child that you are annoyed or angry. If you need to, you can imagine that you just walked into your garage and found your child with his or her new clothes covered with paint.

Figure 4. Written instructions for the Mirror Exercise.

Q Now that you have all had a turn at the mirror, why do you think I asked you to do this exercise? *(Restate parents' response. Praise and elaborate as follows.)*

All of the things you mentioned are true. Most importantly, I want you to remember that you communicate with your children by how you look as much as you communicate by what you say. Parents often find it harder to communicate their pride and love than their annoyance and anger. This tells us something. Things that we do frequently feel easy and comfortable, but things we don't do very often feel strange and uncomfortable. If you found it hard to communicate pride and love without words, then you know something important you can do to help your child feel more worthwhile and lovable. You can practice showing love and pride in your face.

Praise and Criticism That Are Not Destructive

We know that, when we communicate with our children, they will listen to our words while they are watching our faces. It is important to use words and facial expressions that let your children know that you love and respect them, even when they have done something you don't agree with. Now we're going to look at the "do's" and "don'ts" of talking to your child. The "do's" will help your child develop the belief that he or she is worthwhile and lovable. The "don'ts" might get in the way of your child developing that positive working model of self.

When you are talking with your child, it is important to give praise. Sometimes you will also have to give criticism. Both are important, and both should be handled properly.

Helpful Praise. To begin with, it is important that you learn to praise your child's efforts and accomplishments without judging the whole person as "good." When you say things to your child like "You are such a good boy" or "You are always so honest," you can actually create a feeling of guilt in your child. The child cannot accept praise like that, because he or she knows it is not true, that it is phony. Your child knows that he or she is sometimes not good and not always honest. Praise that is helpful is praise that describes *exactly what your child did that was so pleasing. (Write the following illustration on the board.)*

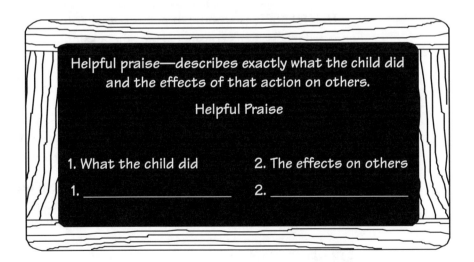

Figure 5. An illustration of helpful praise.

For example, John helped his mom clean the house before company came—without her asking. Let's use this example to look at the difference between unhelpful and helpful praise.

First the unhelpful praise:

"John, you are such a good boy. You are always so helpful and thoughtful. I am proud of you, and I know I can always depend on you."

Now, the helpful praise:

"John, I really appreciate your helping me dust the furniture. When you help like that I feel great, and it gives me extra time to get ready."

(Fill in the blanks on the board as shown in Figure 6.)

Figure 6. An illustration of specific helpful praise.

Helpful praise is specific. It points out what John did and how that action affected others. Let's consider some other examples. Tell me if these examples of praise are helpful or unhelpful.

1. **"I appreciate your helping me finish your room by tucking in the blanket on your bed."** *(Helpful Praise)*

Q Is this helpful praise? *(Pause for parents' response. Review the components of helpful praise by filling in the blanks on the board.)*

2. **"Karen, you always work so hard to help me. I know I can always depend on you."** *(Unhelpful Praise) (Pause for parents' response. Ask parents to tell you what's missing.)*

Q Is this helpful praise? *(Pause for parents' response.)*

3. **"Karen, I appreciate your helping me finish your room by tucking in the blanket on your bed. I really like it when your room is neat."** *(Pause for parents to respond that it is helpful.)*

(Use the following examples if the group needs additional practice. For each example, ask whether the praise was helpful. If the praise was not helpful, ask parents to suggest some alternatives.)

4. **"Our yard looks great with all the leaves raked. Thank you for helping me pick up the piles of leaves."** *(Helpful Praise)*

5. **"I really enjoyed watching your school play. You spoke your lines loud and clear. I heard every word."** *(Helpful Praise)*

6. **"Jim, I'm glad you were a good boy while I was gone."** *(Unhelpful Praise)*

7. **To Molly, who has just brought home a report card with all A's: "Oh Molly, you always make me so proud. I know I can depend on you."** *(Unhelpful Praise)*

8. **"Jeff, you wrote a very neat homework paper. It was very easy for me to check."** *(Helpful Praise)*

9. **"You did a great job. Thanks for always being my good helper."** *(Unhelpful Praise)*

10. **Next, we have a mother on the telephone. She hangs up and says to her 4 year-old: "You are such a good girl. You are always so quiet."**

Q Is this helpful praise? *(If the parents recognize this as an example of unhelpful praise, ask the follow-up question.)*

Q What would be helpful praise in this situation? *(Parents should respond with something like, "Thank you for being quiet while I was on the telephone. That way, I can hear the other person better.")*

(If there is time, request some other examples of helpful praise from parents. Ask parents to pick out the two components of helpful praise in their own examples, and add several of these examples to the list on the board. Then write the diagram shown in Figure 7 on the board.)

It is important to remember that, for children older than about 7 years, it is better to ask the child to decide what else he or she could have done, rather than just have the parent decide for the child the way I have it written here. *(Note: This modification to the helpful criticism model is designed to accommodate a child's level of development and problem-solving ability. It has two other benefits: It communicates respect for and confidence in the child's own problem-solving ability, and it allows the parent an opportunity to clarify the motive behind the child's behavior, which is often not quite what the parent assumed.)*

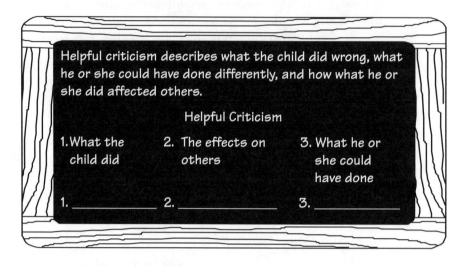

Figure 7. A diagram of the three components of helpful criticism.

Let me give you a few examples:

1. **Mark, age 5, takes a toy away from his little brother. Dad steps in and says, "When you will not share any of your toys with your brother, you can't expect him to share any with you."**

2. **Another father, faced with the same situation, steps in and says, "Mark, you are being selfish. You have no right to steal someone else's things. If I catch you stealing again, you are going to get it!"**

Q Which father is using helpful criticism? *(Parents should say the first father.)*

Q Why is the first remark helpful and the second one not? *(Pause for parents' response. Diagram the first example on the board, demonstrating the three components.)*

Here is another example:

3. **"Rachel, I asked you not to go outside after your bath. You are such a messy girl! Your clothes are all dirty, and we have to change them. Now we're going to be late for your doctor's appointment this morning."**

Q Is this helpful or unhelpful criticism? *(Parents should respond that it is unhelpful.)*

Q How might this parent express helpful criticism to Rachel? *(Parent should respond with these ideas: "Rachel, I asked you not to go outside after your bath. Now your clothes are dirty and we will have to change them before we go to the doctor's. I really don't like to rush to get to the doctor's. Next time, play inside as I asked you to.")*

Here's another example of unhelpful criticism:

4. **"Johnny, you broke the glass because you were a bad boy. You didn't listen to Daddy. He told you three times not to play with it, and you broke it on purpose."**

Q How might you give some helpful criticism to Johnny? *(Parents' responses should be accepted and reinforced. Helpful criticism might be: "Johnny, the glass broke because it was too heavy to carry with one hand. That was an important glass for Daddy, and I'm sad that we won't have it for him to use. Now you see why Daddy told you to put it down or use two hands to carry it.")*

Here are some more examples of unhelpful criticism.

5. **"I can't stand that fussing anymore. Please go to your room and play. I really have a bad headache now."**

6. **"I told you that window would get broken if you played ball so close to the house. What do I have to do to make you listen to me, give you a beating? Are you stupid?"**

7. **"See what happened because you didn't stop fighting? Your brother is crying, and that plant is broken. You should know better than to fight with your brother."**

These examples show that parents can praise and criticize their children in ways that are helpful or harmful. Helpful ways don't tear down the child or make the child feel that he or she is a bad person. But the child will still learn from that helpful criticism.

In some of the later sessions, we will work on how to talk to your children so they will feel that they can communicate openly with you. Learning and practicing these new ways of talking to children will do two things for you: They will help you to build a closer relationship with your child, and they will help you to teach your child that he or she is a worthwhile and lovable person.

You should remember from this session that the first major key to developing a well-adjusted, competent, and loving child is that you, as a parent, must continually ask yourself the following question when interacting with your child: *"Will what I am doing now make my child believe he or she is worthwhile and lovable?"*

Certainly you won't be able to keep this question in your mind all the time. Sometimes you might be angry, and you won't want to ask yourself such a question. But, if you keep this question in mind most of the time, the positive approach will become familiar to you after a while. It will begin to guide your behavior, and you will make big steps toward ensuring the future success and happiness of your child.

General Discussion

Q Think about what we did and talked about today. Does anyone have any questions or reactions?

(Pause for parents' response. Keep an expectant look on your face as you look at the group. Handle parents' reactions with the following attitude: "Yes, it is difficult/strange. There are problems with any new idea, but if you follow through, I know you will find this one helpful to you and your child in the long run." Help parents explore how their children will react and when would be good times to try these new parenting skills.)

Q Would anyone be willing to share an experience with your own child in which you think helpful praise or helpful criticism would have been useful?

(Pause and allow the parents some time to form a response. Help parents formulate their responses so they communicate helpful praise and helpful criticism. Refer to the diagrams on the board. Try to talk about as many of their responses as possible. As the parents hear about different ways to give helpful praise and helpful criticism, they will feel more comfortable about giving their own examples and about using these concepts at home.)

Discussion of the Home Practice Assignment

(At the end of the general discussion, give the parents directions and information concerning their Workbooks and the home practice assignments. This would be a good time to raise the issue of involving the nonparticipating, caregiving partner in the educational process. You may want to review the issues raised earlier in the "Special Notes for the Mental Health Professional" section.)

Before we finish, I want to talk a bit about your Workbooks and the weekly home practice assignments they contain. During each of our sessions, we will discuss some ideas concerning our children and our roles as parents. Some of these ideas may be new to you, and some of the skills we talk about may be difficult to learn. The Workbooks give you an opportunity to think about and practice these new ideas and skills. That is why the home practice assignments are a must—if you want to get the full benefit from our sessions. I'll start each new session by reviewing the home practice assignment from the previous session. It will be helpful to the whole group if each of you can share your particular reactions to, and experiences with, the home practice assignment.

I Am Competent, I Am Responsible

Introduction

The second major key to a child's working model of self is the child's belief that he or she is competent and responsible. We have seen how children learn they are lovable and worthwhile through interaction with their parents and other significant people in their lives. Children learn that they are competent and responsible in the same way. A child's feelings of competence and sense of responsibility influence his or her behavior just like the beliefs about self-worth do (Blechman, Tinsley, Corella, & McEnroe, 1985).

White (1959) emphasized the central importance of a belief in one's own competence to the development of a healthy and functional personality. A sense of personal efficacy is recognized as one of the core human motivations. White postulated that "effectance motivation," like all basic drives of the individual, can be influenced by experience. Through interaction with their environment, children develop either a "feeling of efficacy" or a sense of marginal competence. Without a sense of efficacy, a child's belief that effort and persistence will result in achieving a goal is diminished. Bandura (1990) concluded his review of the research on nonability determinants of competence by expressing the practical implications of a positive sense of competence:

> Thus, individuals who believe themselves to be inefficacious are likely to effect little change even in environments that provide many opportunities. Conversely, those who have a strong sense of efficacy, through ingenuity and perseverance, figure out ways of exercising some manner of control in environments containing limited opportunities and many constraints. (p. 337)

Masterpasqua (1989) goes beyond the conclusions of Bandura and asserts that the individual's sense of competence—the belief that he or she can cope with and master problems—is central to and predictive of good mental health.

A child who feels competent believes that he or she has sufficient skill, knowledge, or experience to cope with persons, tasks, and situations in an appropriate and adequate manner (Sternberg & Kolligan, 1990). At the moment of birth, an infant possesses certain competencies: developing language, taking actions that cause responsive behavior in others, and acting on his or her environment to get a response. For example, an infant's abilities to cuddle with a caregiver and to gaze into the caregiver's eyes are efficient tools for building a quality attachment between them (Stern, 1985). As the infant discovers the ability to elicit the caregiver's response, that infant begins to learn that he or she has the capacity to influence the surrounding world in an effective or competent manner (Sternberg, 1990). Throughout the early development years, the child continues to build on this sense of competence through physical and social interactions with the environment. He or she develops competency in motor skills, mental skills, language skills, and interpersonal and social skills.

As a child masters these skills, he or she receives positive feedback from self and from significant others about the worth of these skills and about the child's ability to master them. This feedback becomes the foundation for the child's future accomplishments (Baumrind, 1993). Children who have disabilities that interfere with their performance are particularly vulnerable to impairment of their sense of competency. Enhancing the child's self-concept relative to competence and mastery is challenging, but it may be effectively accomplished (Jones, 1992). Believing in his or her own competence will allow the child to approach new challenges willingly. If this sense of competence is strong, the child will try harder and persist longer when faced with new and challenging tasks (Sternberg, 1990).

Adequate preparation for life also requires a sense of responsibility. This sense of responsibility goes hand in hand with the sense of competence. As a child begins to try new experiences and learn new things, the child finds that he or she is capable of causing both good and bad things to happen. The child learns that he or she is responsible for certain events. When this knowledge of responsibility is accompanied by a belief in his or her own competence, the child begins to recognize that behavior *and* the results of that behavior are both under his or her own control.

Many parents believe that they must teach responsibility to their children by punishing and rewarding various behaviors (Dinkmeyer & McKay, 1973). On the contrary, responsibility must be given to the child in such a way that he or she learns to handle it without damage to feelings of self-worth and competence. As the child repeatedly experiences the natural consequences of behavior—without the threat of harsh punishment—he or she will learn to accept responsibility by linking the action with its result or consequence.

Some parents feel that they should perform certain tasks for their child, because they can accomplish the tasks more quickly or effectively. Parents may feel that they need to protect their child from the failure and frustration inherent in "trial and error" learning. By continually jumping in to perform challenging tasks for a child, the parent is limiting that child's opportunities to learn competence and responsibility. It is important that parents learn to strike a healthy balance between abandoning their child to tasks and situations that are beyond the child's coping ability and allowing the child to struggle while learning to cope with new problems or tasks.

The child must also learn that he or she can fail at a task (or do something wrong) without the threat or experience of parental rejection. The experience of failure and the need to try again using a new approach are essential in the dual process of learning to be competent and responsible. Parents must support this learning process by allowing "failure" to occur under their supervision. When a child's action is wrong—in the sense that it violates a social norm or expectation—the child needs to learn the impact of that behavior on others. The communication between parent and child should highlight both the choice the child has made, and the opportunity to make a different choice. This new choice might include a new course of action, as well as making restitution to the offended or injured party.

In the final analysis, the development of a sense of competence and responsibility takes place in the context of a parent—child relationship in which the child is allowed to make choices and act, secure in the knowledge that the parent will give only the help or correction that is absolutely necessary for the child to solve the problem. The child must also be sure that this help will be offered without any threat of rejection or loss of love.

In Summary. Competence and responsibility form the second major belief system in a child's working model of self. Children learn that they are competent by mastering developmental tasks and by receiving positive feedback regarding that mastery. Children acquire a sense of responsibility by experiencing the natural consequences of their own actions. If this experience occurs in an environment that is loving, accepting, respectful, and supportive, children will learn that they are responsible for their behavior. They will also learn to willingly perform socially appropriate behaviors without parental pressure.

Special Notes for the Mental Health Professional

Allow ample time to review and discuss the home practice from Session 2. Parents should be encouraged to offer their own responses to the home practice activities and to raise any questions they may have had about the assignments. Reinforce and encourage discussion so that group members feel that this part of the session is just as important as learning new material. Parents' understanding of the information presented in Session 2 is critical to their learning the concepts presented in this session.

The second half of this session can present some difficulties. You will demonstrate four parental behaviors that will foster the development of competence and responsibility in children:

1. A noninteracting, noninterfering presence and acceptance of a child's efforts to face new tasks or situations.

2. Use of helpful praise and helpful criticism.

3. Altering a situation to help a child cope with it.

4. Helping the child experience the natural and logical consequences of his or her own behavior.

Parents often object to the noninteracting, noninterfering method of helping a child face new tasks or situations. Many parents see themselves as teachers, and the idea of allowing their child to make mistakes or to do something in a less-than-effective way is upsetting to them. Be sensitive to parents' objections, but be prepared to deal with them constructively. One particularly effective way of dealing with these objections is to help the parents become aware of how the child might feel in a given situation. Specifically, ask the parents to imagine how they would think or feel if their own parents were correcting them or showing them a "better" way to do something. It is important to help parents learn that they may think they are helping, but they may actually be sending negative messages to the child: that the child has failed again, that the child cannot do anything right, or that the child is incompetent. There is no question that parental correction and instruction are necessary and helpful, but the appropriate kind and frequency of parental correction and feedback must be clearly understood.

Session Objectives

1. To demonstrate that it is important for children to develop a sense of competence; to show parents how their interactions with their child can influence that development.

2. To teach parents how they can help their children to feel competent and in control of their behavior and the results of that behavior.

3. To teach parents how they can help their children accept responsibility by allowing them to experience and recognize the natural consequences of their own actions.

Sequence

● Review and sharing of home practice (10 - 15 minutes)

● Lecture/Discussion (30 - 40 minutes)

● General discussion (30 - 40 minutes)

● Discussion of the home practice assignment (5 minutes)

 ## Materials

Blackboard (or large marking board)

Chalk (or markers)

Eraser

Review and Sharing of Home Practice Experiences

Last session we discussed the first key to your child's working model of self—"I am worthwhile, I am lovable." We talked about some ways to communicate love and acceptance as well as criticism. We called these helpful praise and helpful criticism. *(Put the diagram of helpful praise used in Session 2 on the board. Review the two components of helpful praise and the three components of helpful criticism.)*

Q Who would like to share their home practice experience with the group?

(Pause, wait for a volunteer. If no one comes forth in 10-15 seconds, urge parents to respond by explaining that sharing ideas and experiences is one of the best ways to help ourselves and each other, because hearing how other parents do things gives us new ideas and perspectives for our own situations. If parents still resist, talk about the feelings that might be keeping them from sharing—embarrassment, fear of looking foolish, etc.—and then try again. Use the diagram on the board to discuss the examples provided by the parents.)

Competence and the Self-Concept

Today we are going to discuss the second major belief system that forms your child's working model of self: "I am competent, I am responsible." Understanding this second major key to a positive self-concept will help you to facilitate your child's happy and successful development. The first element in this belief is competence. In order to become successful and happy, your child must learn to believe that he or she is competent. Psychological research has shown that individuals who believe they are competent will be more satisfied with themselves, will try harder and longer to solve problems, and will be more willing to try new things. People who feel competent are often more willing to learn; they believe that they are capable of changing their world—or part of it. Because they feel capable of taking effective action, such individuals are more resistant to depression and anxiety. When your child feels competent, he or she will get higher grades in school and will be more likely to accept responsibility for actions taken at home and at school.

(Write the word "competence" on the board.)

Q What does competence mean to you? When and where does it show itself?

(Abbreviate parents' responses and write them on the board. Make sure to point out the following idea: We develop our sense of competence from everything we do—social activity, conversation, reading and other school work, play, getting around, helping ourselves, creative activity, etc.)

Now, fortunately or unfortunately, children learn and develop a sense of themselves as good players, talkers, or readers from how well they actually do these things; but they also pay attention to how they feel about their ability to do things well. Their experience of doing things well and their feelings of competence or incompetence come together to form their overall belief about whether or not they are competent.

Q How do you think a child who feels *competent* will behave in the following situations:

1. **Meeting a new neighbor.** *(Pause for parents' response; encourage parents to be concrete and specific, to model posture, behavior, and words.)*

   Yes, the child who feels competent would probably go up, introduce himself or herself, and make friends.

2. **Becoming involved in the class play.** *(Pause for parents' response.)*

   Yes, that child would probably work hard to get a part and aim for the most important part possible.

3. **Being sent to the store to buy something.** *(Pause for parents' response.)*

   Yes, the child might see the trip to the store as a way to show how grown up he or she can be. He or she would really enjoy the parent's recognition of that maturity.

4. **Being left with a baby sitter.** *(Pause for parents' response.)*

   Yes. The child would see the babysitter as someone to have fun with and learn things from. The child would want to do things with the sitter and get the sitter to do things for him or her.

Q Now, how do you think a child who feels *incompetent* will behave in the same situations?

1. **Meeting a new neighbor.** *(Pause for parents' response. Summarize and reflect the responses of the group.)*

2. **Becoming involved in the class play.** *(Pause for parents' response. Summarize and reflect the responses of the group.)*

3. **Being sent to the store to buy something.** *(Pause for parents' response. Summarize and reflect the responses of the group.)*

4. **Being left with a baby sitter.** *(Pause for parents' response. Summarize and reflect the responses of the group.)*

Okay. We've talked about the idea that a sense of competence is part of the second major key to raising a successful and happy child. You can see that a child's belief in his or her own competence or incompetence will affect just about everything that child does. Which child would you prefer—a competent one or an incompetent one? *(Pause.)*

How you deal with your child in a thousand everyday situations will determine the difference. You won't always be able to handle situations so that they will help your child to feel competent. But, if you keep the competence key in mind just 51% of the time, you can make a real difference in your child's life. You should try to ask yourself, as often as you can, *"How will what I am doing affect my child's sense of competence. Will it make my child believe he or she is competent or incompetent?"*

We have the basic ideas; now let's examine them more closely so you can see how you can put this idea to work with your child on a day-to-day basis.

There are two ways you can help your child develop a sense of competence: First, you can reinforce and encourage the child's efforts to try different things, and second, you can make the child's world—your home—easier for someone that age to deal with. Let's thing about these ideas one at a time.

Reinforcement and encouragement mean appreciating what your child accomplishes—without focusing on the elements of the behavior that are not successful. For example, when Christina begins to use a spoon, her mother could reinforce her efforts with comments like, "What a big girl—you are feeding yourself!" This reinforcement and encouragement is given despite the fact that the spoon is being held wrong, with half of the food ending up on Christina's cheeks and chin. On the other hand, the child's mother could say, "No Christina, you're holding that wrong. Look, do it like Mommy. Careful now, you're making a mess!" But Christina's mother would be telling Christina that her behavior is not acceptable and that she is not doing very well. Let's consider some other examples.

> **Sally's father was watching her paint a picture. He noticed that Sally was about to use purple paint to color a boy's hair, so he said, "No, Sally. Who ever heard of someone with purple hair? Use black or brown to color the boy's hair."**

Q What was Sally's father telling her? *(Pause for parents' response.)*

Yes. Her father was saying that he did not like the way she was painting her picture, that she wasn't doing it right. Here is another example:

> **John's mother sent him to the store to buy a loaf of bread. When he came back empty-handed she said, "John, why can't you ever do what I ask you to? I have to do everything myself. What a pain!"**

Q What was John's mother telling him about his competence? *(Pause for parents' response.)*

Exactly. John's mother was saying that he was not competent and that she would have to do everything herself in order to get things done right. Now think about this example.

> **Three-year-old Robin is having a birthday party. Her mom is in the living room with all the guests, and she sees Robin coming around the corner holding a plate of cookies. One of the cookies drops to the floor, so Mom jumps up and rushes over to take the plate away from Robin. She says, "Here Robin, I'll take that. You might spill them. Go play with your friends. I'll pass out the cookies."**

Q What do you think the mother in this story was teaching her daughter about her competence? *(Pause for parents' response.)*

From Robin's point of view, it probably seemed like her mother was saying that she could not be trusted to handle that situation—that she was not competent.

Q How might Robin's mother respond in order to help Robin develop a sense of competence? *(Pause for parents' response. If parents are slow to respond, you can provide the following examples of constructive responses.)*

  1. She might have stayed where she was and given Robin a big smile, full of approval and pride.

2. She could have said, "Thank you for helping, Robin. It's nice to have someone who can help me."

Q Now, if Robin's mother responded in one of these last two ways, what might have been the risk? *(Pause for parents' response.)*

More cookies might have spilled, but this risk seems minor when compared with the potential step forward for Robin in terms of her sense of competence and personal pride. If you look at situations like this one in light of your child's personal development, instead of worrying about how to get a specific task done efficiently, you will probably find that you prefer to do what will help your child develop a stronger sense of competence. Saving a cookie or two doesn't seem as important as giving your child another opportunity to feel competent and accepted.

Let me describe another situation, and then see if you can provide a response that would reinforce and encourage this child, building his sense of competence.

Billy, age 6, is working in the basement of his house. His father hears the pounding of a hammer and comes down to see what is happening. In the basement, Dad sees nails all over the floor and Billy working on a lopsided box with all four sides of different lengths. The sides don't exactly fit together, and bent nails are sticking out of the wood.

Q What might Billy's father say if he wanted to help Billy develop a sense of competence? *(Pause for parents' response. If parents don't come up with constructive examples, you can provide the following examples of constructive responses.)*

1. He might just stand there and smile with an interested look on his face.

2. He could smile and say, "What are you making Billy?" Billy could tell him, and Dad could say, "It sure looks hard to make. Let me know when it's done." Dad could then walk away.

Q What are the risks here? *(Pause for parents' response.)*

True, Billy could cut his hand or hit his finger with the hammer. But, it might be worth a small cut or bruise for Billy to have the sense of pride and competence that comes from doing something yourself.

It may seem like these ideas don't make sense, because we all know that children do need advice and instruction. Some parents give their child too many instructions on a given day. As a rule of thumb, when you instruct your child, try not to give more than one set of instructions every 10 minutes. You should always express your instructions as suggestions or questions. In this case, Billy's father could have given him one suggestion. For example, Billy's dad could have said, "Billy, do you think putting the box in the vise would make it easier to work on?"

Q Do you have any questions or reactions to this type of response? *(Pause for parents' response. Discuss parents' concerns.)*

Now let's consider how you can manage your child's world—your home—and your child's behavior in a way that helps to develop a sense of competence.

Your home is your child's world, especially when your child is young. There are many things you can do in this world to increase your child's sense of competence. For example, you can try to arrange things so your child can meet some of his or her own needs and responsibilities. This means taking your child's size, strength, and muscle coordination into account. Here are some examples of changes that parents can make to encourage competence and independence in their child:

1. Put a small bench in the bathroom so your child can get his or her own glass of water.

2. Attach big tags to zippers so your child can open and close them easily.

3. Sew (or pin) corners on the foot ends of your child's top sheet and blanket, so your child can make his or her own bed more easily.

4. Instead of using small drawers or high shelves, put a large box or container of toys in your child's room so your child can get the toys out and put them away.

Q What are some things you could do to make it easer for your child to act competently and independently at home? *(Pause for parents' response.)*

Before we move on to the idea of responsibility and logical consequences of behavior, let's go over what's been said so far. It is important that you help your child feel capable of handling the tasks and situations he or she encounters. After your child experiences feelings of competence in daily activities a number of times, he or she will be able to face handling new situations with confidence. In time, your child will see himself or herself as competent. This sense of competence will support your child's positive self-concept.

Lecture/Discussion

Responsibility and Logical Consequences

Now let's move on to the second part of this belief system: "I am competent, I am *responsible*." In order to feel competent, a child must learn to be responsible. This means that the child must be willing to accept responsibility for his or her own actions. Parents can help their children learn that they are competent and that there are logical consequences of their behavior. These consequences—whether positive or negative, acceptable or unacceptable—are the result of the child's own actions. As children learn to accept the consequences of their behavior, they will learn to change their behavior when they want to change the consequences. Let's talk about some examples of consequences that are very likely to teach responsibility.

Three-year-old Tim was playing outside and stepped into a mud puddle. His shoes and clothes got wet and muddy. He came into the house to ask for some dry clothes. When he asked if he could go back outside to play, his shoes were still wet. In a very matter-of-fact and calm manner his mother said, "I'm sorry, Tim. You can't go back outside, because your shoes are still all wet."

Notice that Tim's mother pointed out the consequence of his own behavior, teaching Tim about his responsibility. She did not say, "No, you were bad, and you got your shoes wet." She didn't feel she had to give Tim a lecture about how he might catch a cold or about being careless and getting all wet. Tim could see that what he did—getting himself and his shoes all wet—led to his having to stay indoors. Because he probably doesn't like the consequence, he is more likely to learn not to get his shoes wet in the future.

This seems like a simple thing to do, but you may find it hard to put into practice. Lots of parents are used to punishing "bad behavior" by getting angry, yelling, or scolding. But there's another good thing about letting children learn responsibility through consequences; letting Tim see that he can't play outside because of his own actions helps to keep his mother from getting upset. When he doesn't have to respond to an emotionally upset mother, Tim can better see that he is the one responsible—both for his actions and for their consequences.

If you want to help your child learn to accept responsibility for behavior, you must be careful to point out logical consequences in a way that has no nasty overtones. Many people react aggressively to irresponsible behavior, as if to say, "I've got you now!" It is important to point out both *negative* and *positive* consequences to your child, and it is best if you can point out more positive consequences than negative. Here's an example of pointing out the positive consequences of a child's behavior:

A mother is admiring a picture that her child has just finished in a coloring book. Mom says something like, "You worked slowly and carefully on this picture, and it looks neat and pretty."

You see that this mother has pointed out the positive results of the child's behavior—a picture that looks neat and pretty. Here's another example:

Gary comes home from school with a big smile and excitedly tells his mother that he got the highest score on a spelling assignment. He says, "Look, Mom, the teacher even wrote 'Excellent' on my paper!" His mom looks at his paper with pride and says, "That's great, Gary. You studied hard for that test last night, and got an excellent mark. You should be really proud of yourself."

Gary's mother has pointed out the consequence of his behavior. He studied hard, and his hard work resulted in a high grade. Gary deserves to feel proud of his own work His mother let him know that his pride in himself is what's important, and he doesn't have to worry about making his mother proud.

Now, here's an example of a parent pointing out a negative consequence:

Amy and her father decide to go out in the yard to play ball. Amy's dad asks, "Where is the ball, Amy?" Amy shrugs her shoulders and says, "I can't find it." Amy's father says, "I guess you didn't put your ball back in the toy box. Now we can't find it, so we can't play ball."

Notice that the father has pointed out Amy's actions and the consequences of those actions.

Q What was the behavior that led to the consequence Amy's dad pointed out? *(Pause for parents to respond that the behavior was not putting the ball back in the toy box.)*

Q What was the consequence of not putting the ball away? *(Pause for parents to respond that the consequence was not being able to find it and not being able to play.)*

Exactly. The father showed Amy that her behavior—not putting the ball away—led to the consequence of not being able to find the ball when they wanted to play. Amy's father demonstrated to her that she is responsible for her behavior and for the consequences of that behavior.

You can't escape all the conflicts you might have with your children. You can, however, help them to see that they are responsible for their actions, because their behavior brings about logical results. By pointing out these consequences in a calm and supportive way, you can avoid becoming angry and upset. You can help your child learn responsibility and increase your child's sense of competence at the same time. Try to remember to ask yourself, "How will what I am doing or saying affect my child's awareness of the consequences of his or her behavior? Will what I'm doing or saying help my child accept responsibility for his or her actions?"

General Discussion

Q Does anyone have any questions or reactions about this two-part key to your child's working model of self: I am competent, I am responsible? Can anyone think of a way you might put these ideas to use at home? *(Pause for parents' response.)*

Discussion of the Home Practice Assignment

This week I would like you to consider the ideas we've talked about today. You can work on the home practice assignment at different times during the coming week. But don't try to do the whole assignment at one sitting, because each part of the assignment will act as a reminder for you to use these ideas with your child. All new behaviors are learned best when you have to think about them and practice them often. Remember to bring your workbooks next time. We'll start by reviewing the home practice from this session.

References

Adler, M. (1971). *A parent's manual.* Springfield, IL: Charles C. Thomas.

Bandura, A. (1990). Conclusion: Reflections on nonability determinants of competence. In R. J. Sternberg & J. Kolligan (Eds.), *Competence considered* (pp. 315-340). New Haven, CT: Yale University Press.

Baumrind, D. (1991). The influence of parenting style on adolescent competence and substance abuse. *Journal of Early Adolescence, 11,* 56-94.

Baumrind, D. (1993). The average expectable environment is not good enough: A response to Scarr. *Child Development, 64,* 1299-1317.

Blechman, E. A., & Culhane, S. E. (1993). Early adolescence and the development of aggression, depression, coping, and competence. *Journal of Early Adolescence, 13,* 361-382.

Blechman, E. A., Tinsley, B., Corella, E. T., & McEnroe, M. J. (1985). Childhood competence and behavior problems. *Journal of Abnormal Psychology, 94,* 70-77.

Cicchetti, D., & Beeghly, M. (1990). Perspectives on the study of the self in transition. In D. Cicchetti & M. Beeghly (Eds.), *The self in transition: Infancy to childhood (pp. 1-16).* Chicago: University of Chicago Press.

Crittenden, P. M. (1990). Internal representational models of attachment relationships. *Infant Mental Health Journal, 11,* 259-277.

Elkind, D. (1990). Introduction: Changing conceptions of competence. In R. J. Sternberg & J. Kolligan (Eds.), *Competence considered* (pp. 1-10). New Haven: Yale University Press.

George, C., & Solomon, J. (1989). Internal working models of caregiving and security of attachment at age six. *Infant Mental Health Journal, 10,* 222-237.

Ginott, H. (1965). *Between parent and child.* New York: Hearst Corporation.

Gordon, T. (1989). *Teaching children self-discipline.* New York: Times Books/ Random House.

Jones, C. J. (1992). *Enhancing self-concepts and achievement of mildly handicapped students: Learning disabled, mildly mentally retarded, behavior disordered.* Springfield, IL: Charles C. Thomas.

Kagan, J. (1984). *The nature of the child.* New York: Basic Books.

Masterpasqua, F. (1989). A competence paradigm for psychological practice. *American Psychologist, 44,* 1366-1371.

Neisser, U. (1993). *The perceived self: Ecological and interpersonal sources of self-knowledge.* New York: Cambridge University Press.

Phillips, D. A., & Zimmerman, M. (1990). The developmental course of perceived competence and incompetence among competent children. In R. J. Sternberg & J. Kolligan (Eds.), *Competence considered* (pp. 41-66). New Haven: Yale University Press.

Quandt, I., & Selznick, R. (1984). *Self-concept and reading.* Newark, DE: International Reading Association.

Sameroff, A. J. (1991). *Relationship disturbances in early childhood: A developmental approach.* New York: Basic Books.

Stern, D. N. (1985). *The interpersonal world of the infant.* New York: Basic Books..

Tronick, E. (1982). *Social interchange in infancy: Affect, cognition, and communication.* Baltimore, MD: University Park Press.

White, R. (1959). Motivation reconsidered: The concept of competence. *Psychological Review, 66,* 297-333.

Wylie, R. C. (1979). *The self-concept: Theory and research on selected topics (Rev. ed., Vol. 2).* Lincoln: University of Nebraska Press.

Wyman, P. A., Cowen, E. L., Work, W. C., & Kerley, J. H. (1993). The role of children's future expectations in self-system functioning and adjustment to life stress: A prospective study of urban at-risk children. *Development and Psychopathology, 5,* 649-661.

6 Evaluating the Parent-Child Relationship

Session 4

Recognizing Positive and Negative Cues

Introduction

The first part of this session introduces the ideas of effectiveness and power in child management. Parents who believe that they must be forceful and firm with their children may have difficulty making a distinction between these new ideas and their former ideas about how to make their children behave. Do your best to avoid a debate about the virtues of forceful versus "permissive" approaches to handling children. Emphasize that effectiveness is more important than the logical merits of any one parenting strategy. By focusing on effectiveness, you can help parents realize that there are a number of effective and ineffective ways to interact with children in every circumstance.

It is also important to stress that the effectiveness of any strategy will depend on the quality of the ongoing parent-child relationship. You will find the analogy of a savings account (presented as part of this session) a useful way to explain the differences between positive and negative parent-child relations.

The second portion of this session is designed to help parents recognize signs or cues that indicate whether their ongoing relationship with their child is positive or negative. Encourage parents to suggest cues from their own relationships instead of relying solely on the examples provided. Parents may be reluctant to respond because of embarrassment or fear of appearing inadequate. It may be especially difficult for them to share their own negative relationship cues. This is a good time for you to share your personal experiences—particularly any negative ones—to help parents feel more comfortable about examining their own relationships with their children.

One important cue to a positive relationship is the open expression of feelings between parent and child. Parents will probably find it easy to accept the idea that the expression of pleasant, positive feelings indicates a good relationship. It may be difficult, however, for them to understand how the open expression of hostility, anger, or other negative feelings can also be a positive sign. You should point out that open communication of feelings and freedom of expression—regardless of the content of that expression—are the positive aspects of the expression of negative feelings. You must emphasize that even when parents do not agree with or approve of what their child says, they must let the child know that he or she is loved and accepted enough to express his or her feelings freely. Let parents know that later sessions will include specific skills for dealing with negative communications more effectively. For now, the most important thing is for the parent to be able to accept such negative communications as honest experiences of how the child is feeling at that moment.

It is often useful to parents for you to discuss their expectations with regard to their child's compliance with their directions in the context of the latency of children's compliance responses in general. Research (e.g., Kochanska & Aksan, 1995; Kuczynski, 1992; Kuczynski & Kochanska, 1990) suggests that, in normal families, children's noncompliance to an initial directive from a parent is often as high as 40-50%. Clearly, noncompliance occurs too often to be considered primarily a childhood dysfunction.

In Summary. The primary focus of this session is to help parents to understand the direct connection between the quality of the parent-child relationship and the amount of power or force the parent must use to ensure the child's compliance and cooperation. The weaker or more negative the relationship, the more force will be required.

Session Objectives

1 To help parents realize that their effectiveness in guiding their child's behavior depends on the quality of their relationship with that child.

2 To demonstrate the concepts of *effectiveness* and *power* as they relate to child management techniques; to teach parents to analyze their own child management methods in terms of these concepts.

3 To help parents assess the quality of their ongoing relationships with their own children.

Sequence

● Review and sharing of home practice from Session 3 (5 - 10 minutes)
● Lecture/Discussion (50 - 70 minutes)
  – Lecture on effectiveness and the use of force in the parent-child relationship (10 - 15 minutes)
  – Group discussion of the signs or cues of a positive relationship (15 - 20 minutes)
  – Lecture on the signs or cues of a negative relationship (10 - 15 minutes)
  – Group discussion of examples provided by the mental health professional and members of the group (15 - 20 minutes)
● General discussion on evaluating the parenting relationship (15 - 20 minutes)
● Discussion of the home practice assignment (5 minutes)

Materials

Blackboard (or large marking board)

Chalk (or markers)

Eraser

Handout: Examples of Parent-Child Relationship Situations

Review and Sharing of Home Practice Experiences

Q What were some of your reactions to the home practice assignment from Session 3? *(Pause for parents' response. All parents should get a chance to speak and share their home practice experiences.)*

Lecture/Discussion

Effectiveness and Power in Child Management

In most of the remaining sessions we will be talking about skills parents can use when managing their children's behavior. This is an important part of parenting, and parents often worry about the strategies or techniques they use to guide and discipline their children. It's easy to know whether or not a child management technique has been helpful, but it can be really difficult to figure out *why* that technique was helpful or not helpful. Let's look at some examples of techniques for managing children's behavior problems.

Billy, who is 6 years old, and his younger brother Jimmy are playing in their bedroom. Their parents are trying to watch television in the living room, but they are getting annoyed because the boys are so loud. The noise gets louder and louder. Finally, Dad rushes into the room and tells the boys to quit being noisy or he will spank them and send them to bed. Dad goes back to the living room. The boys are quiet for a few minutes, but soon the noise is as loud and distracting as it was before.

Let's look at another approach to handling the same problem.

The boys are being very loud. Dad walks into the room and says, "What are you boys playing?" Billy says, "Jimmy is a ghost and he's trying to catch me." "Sounds like fun, guys. But your mother and I are trying to watch the news, and we can't hear because it's so noisy in here." "We'll try to be quieter." Dad returns to the living room and the boys are quieter.

We can all tell which technique worked and which didn't, but it is more important to talk about why. What is the difference between the two approaches? Well, in the first example, the father was unable to get the boys to stay quieter. Threatening them did work for a few minutes, but they were soon making as much noise as they were before their father yelled at them.

This approach was not very effective. In the second example, after Dad explained the situation to the boys, they got quieter—and stayed that way. The second approach, then, was very effective.

Another way the two examples differed was in the amount of force the father used. Threatening the boys with physical punishment is a strategy that involves using a great deal of force. Explaining to the boys how their behavior is interfering with what you want to do is a strategy that involves very little force. Now, whenever one person wants another person to do something, a certain amount of force is involved. The amount of force can be high or it can be low. For example, when a mugger threatens to shoot you if you don't hand over your wallet, he's using a very high degree of force. If your spouse says he or she would rather not go to a movie tonight but will go if you really want to, the amount of force is very low.

Listen to this example, and think about the amount of force being used and whether the parenting strategies are effective.

Mom and Dad are relaxing in the living room, and their daughter Becky is listening to tapes in her room. Becky has the volume turned very high, and it is really annoying her parents. Mom goes to Becky and says, "Becky, I just can't relax when your music is so loud. It hurts my ears, and I feel myself getting angry." Becky turns down the music for a few minutes, then turns it up again. Finally, Dad walks into the room, pulls out the plug, and puts the tape player up on a shelf in the closet where Becky cannot reach it. He says, "Now maybe you'll learn to listen when we ask you to do something!" Becky gets very angry and begins to shout, "I hate you!" She keeps shouting for about 10 minutes, and no one feels relaxed.

Q How do Mom's and Dad's approaches differ from each other in force and effectiveness? *(Pause for parents' response.)*

Yes. Mom's approach was low in force and low in effectiveness, whereas Dad's approach was high in force, but still low in effectiveness.

Force and effectiveness are two very important issues to consider when deciding how you will guide your child's behavior. Effectiveness is an easy concept to understand—we all want to be effective in guiding our children. The issue of force is a little less clear. To understand why force is so important, we need to consider how the use of force affects parent-child relationships.

Lecture/Discussion

The Relationship Savings Account

Think about your relationship with your own child as if it were a kind of savings account. Sharing feelings of good will, appreciation, respect, and love with your child is like putting money into that savings account. When conflicts arise, some positive feelings are withdrawn from the account to deal with the situation. Sometimes, it seems like children have stopped looking to their parents for guidance and support. It seems as though all the good feelings have been withdrawn from the account over time, and the parent-child relationship is bankrupt. There are no good feelings left to help resolve conflicts and keep the positive aspects of the relationship going. *(If needed, you can diagram the savings account analogy shown in Figure 8 on the board.)*

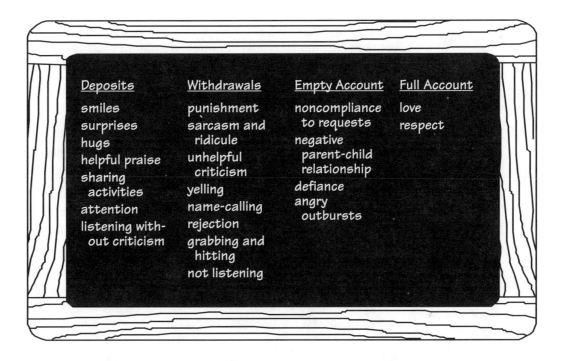

Deposits	Withdrawals	Empty Account	Full Account
smiles	punishment	noncompliance to requests	love
surprises	sarcasm and ridicule	negative parent-child relationship	respect
hugs	unhelpful criticism		
helpful praise	yelling	defiance	
sharing activities	name-calling	angry outbursts	
attention	rejection		
listening without criticism	grabbing and hitting		
	not listening		

Figure 8. The relationship savings account.

Let's look at some examples of the consequences of positive and negative parent-child relationships.

Sally and her mother really get along well. They enjoy each other's company and respect each other's feelings. One day, Sally's mother was planning to have some of her friends over for dinner. She was having trouble getting everything done, so she said to Sally, "I'm afraid I won't be ready when my friends get here." Sally said, "I'll do the dishes. Will that help?"

Mrs. Bradwell and her daughter Karen don't seem to get along very well. One afternoon, Mrs. Bradwell said, "Karen, will you help me with the dishes so I can get the house cleaned up before my friends get here?" Karen answered, "I'll be right there." Ten minutes later, Karen still had not started to help with the dishes.

Both mothers tried to get their daughters to help. They both used low-force techniques, but these low-force methods only work when there is love and respect in the relationship account. Sally's mother could draw on the affection and mutual respect in her relationship with Sally. When the account is bankrupt, as it was for Mrs. Bradwell and Karen, it is impossible to draw from it when using low-force techniques. *(Talk about these examples in the context of the savings account diagram to further illustrate the analogy, if needed.)*

Both mothers used the same technique. One mom was effective, one was not. Why? Because of a difference in the *quality* of the two parent-child relationships. And this is the important point: The effectiveness of any technique for managing and guiding your child's behavior will depend upon the quality of the relationship between you and your child. The more affection and respect you have invested in your relationship with your child, the more effective you will be in managing your child's behavior.

This is why force is such an important issue to consider. Using force to manage your children is like taking money out of your relationship savings account. The more force you use, the greater the cost to your relationship with your child. In fact, the amount of force used in any parent-child relationship is one way of measuring how positive or negative that relationship is.

Remember, the most important goal in child management is effectiveness. There are certainly times when it's necessary to use force and power, and most parents will occasionally find themselves disciplining their children by using force and power. But it's important not to draw from your relationship savings account too often; using high force on a regular basis might bankrupt that account of positive feelings.

Q Are there any reactions, comments, or questions about what I've said so far? *(Entertain questions. When all questions have been addressed, begin the discussion of how children show their parents love and respect.)*

Q What are some of the ways your children signal to you that they care about you, respect you, or are happy that you are their parents? *(Pause for parents' response. If responses are not forthcoming in about 30 seconds, supply an example like the one that follows.)*

My little girl shows me her coloring work and then tells me, "It's for you." She thinks I am someone she can share her accomplishments with. Can you think of some other examples?

(Get as many examples from the parents as you can, and list them on the board. The list might include examples of the following categories: child demonstrates affection verbally or nonverbally, child shows concern for the parent's feelings either verbally or through behavior, child expresses themes of parent-child warmth through play, child seeks parent's assistance with

difficult tasks, child shares accomplishments with parent, child models parent behavior. Supply examples from the above categories that the parents don't mention. You may also have an opportunity here to emphasize that different parental values will influence whether the parent sees a child's behavior as positive or negative.)

As you can see, there are lots of different ways that young children let you know they care about you. Of course, each child develops his or her own ways of letting the parents know that he or she values their relationship. If you can learn to tune in to your child's expressions of affection and respect, you have one way of *knowing* that your relationship is positive.

Q Who is willing to share a way that your child expresses affection? *(Pause for parents' response.)*

There are also ways to tell if your relationship is negative, or bankrupt. First, I'll to describe some of the signs that your relationship with your child might be in danger of bankruptcy. Then we'll look at some examples of parent-child interaction so you can learn how to identify the signs of bankruptcy in each example. Our goal is learning to assess the quality of your relationship with your own child. There are five basic signs of trouble in the parent-child relationship:

(Write the first sign of trouble shown in Figure 9a on the board.)

Figure 9a. Signs of trouble in a parent-child relationship.

Of course, this could also mean that you have not tuned in to the messages of affection your child is actually sending.

(Add the second sign of trouble to the list on the board.)

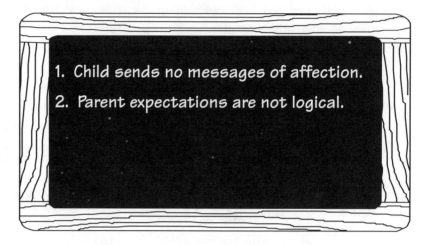

Figure 9b. Signs of trouble in a parent-child relationship.

The second indication of trouble is if the messages you send to your self—the things you tell yourself about situations—are not logical; then you may find that you often see your child as being a problem. For example, you may tell yourself, "People should always put the cap back on the toothpaste tube." You may allow yourself to get angry if your child forgets to do this. But this means you will probably often be angry with your child, because children often forget these sorts of things. If you frequently experience negative emotions concerning your child's behavior, your relationship may be in trouble.

(Add the third sign of trouble to the list.)

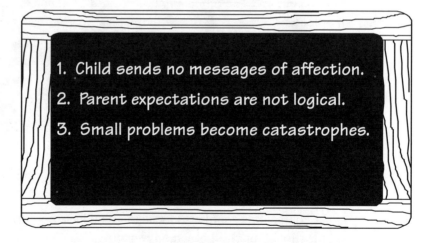

Figure 9c. Signs of trouble in a parent-child relationship.

A third sign of trouble is when minor problems become major catastrophes. This is a real indication that your relationship with your child is failing. If a lost pair of mittens sets off a parent-child squabble that lasts for hours or days, and the incident is brought up again and again, the parent-child relationship is definitely in trouble. Of course, this can work both ways. Your child can turn a small disappointment into evidence that the whole world is against him or her.

(Add the fourth sign of trouble to the list.)

Figure 9d. Signs of trouble in a parent-child relationship.

The fourth sign of relationship problems involves the way you talk to your child. Some types of communication are destructive to a positive parent-child relationship. For example, Stuart is pretending to bake a cake, and his father tells him that he is a sissy. Father's name-calling tells Stuart that he is not accepted, and this loosens the bonds of affection between them. Name-calling is a good example of destructive communication. Other examples are sarcasm, lecturing, threatening, shaming, and blaming. Destructive communications are any communications that attack the child's sense of self-worth and competence; these communications damage the child's positive self-concept.

(Add the fifth sign of trouble to the list.)

Figure 9e. Signs of trouble in a parent-child relationship.

The fifth sign of parent-child relationship problems is the frequent use of high-force strategies to deal with children.

As I mentioned earlier, when there is love and respect in the relationship savings account, good feelings can be drawn from that account to influence your child's behavior. When your child cares for you and cares about your feelings, you have a powerful, effective, and low-force method of influencing the child's behavior. Because your child wants to maintain a good relationship with you, his or her behavior will be influenced by your feelings. The child will continue to do things that he or she knows will please you and avoid doing things that won't please you. A positive parent-child relationship allows issues to be handled by low-force methods; and low-force methods reinforce a child's sense of personal responsibility.

Q Does anyone have some thoughts about these five signs of relationship problems that you would like to share? *(Pause for parents' response.)*

Okay. Here are some examples of situations that contain cues or signals about the quality of the particular parent-child relationships. *(Pass out a handout describing the following 10 parent-child situations.)*

I'll read each situation, and then, I'd like you to tell me how positive or negative the parent-child relationship seems, and what cue or signal helped you to decide. Assume that the pattern of behavior in each example characterizes that particular parent-child relationship. *(Read each situation aloud.)*

1. **Beth is playing with her dolls. The mother doll says to the baby doll, "Would you like to go to the park, honey?" The baby doll answers, "Oh yes!"** *(Guide the group discussion. This child's expression of positive feelings through play is a sign of a positive relationship.)*

2. **"If I hear that one more time, I'm sending you back to bed without supper."** *(This use of force is a negative sign.)*

3. **Mary says, "When I get big, I want to be a mother. That would be neat."** *(This is a positive sign, because Mary sees being a mother as a positive role.)*

4. **Katie forgot to put her bike on the porch. Her father says, "I guess you don't know how to take care of your bike. I'm putting it in the garage. You can't ride it for 2 weeks."** *(Severe punishment for a minor transgression is a sign of a negative relationship.)*

5. **Billy, age 5, tells his mother that he hates her. His mom spanks him, saying, "You don't talk to me like that, you brat. You ever smart-mouth me again, and you won't sit down for a week."** *(There are three negative signs here: Mother is punishing Billy for expressing important feelings, teaching him not to share feelings; she is also using excessive force and name-calling.)*

6. **Sara asks her father, "Is it all right if I tell you something?" Father says, "Sure." Sara tells her father, "I don't like Benjamin."** *(This communication has both positive and negative signs. Sara does share her feelings with her father, but she asks first because she is not sure that she can.)*

7. **Scott, who is 10 years old, is sucking his thumb. His mother tells him, "Take your thumb out of your mouth. Only babies suck their thumbs."** *(This is a negative sign—Scott's mother is shaming him, attacking his sense of being worthwhile.)*

8. **Tony has had a bad day. He forgot his lunch, got in a fight at school, and had to stay inside during recess. He comes home from school, goes straight to his room, and stays there until it is time for supper.** *(This is a negative sign—Tony can't share bad feelings with his mother; she shows no interest in his sad behavior.)*

9. **Amy says to her father, "Daddy, can ghosts fly through the wall at night?"** *(This is a positive sign—Amy is tentatively sharing her feelings of fear with her father.)*

10. **Shelly comes home from school and tells her mother, "I hate that fat old teacher. I wish I didn't have to go to school."** *(This is a positive sign—Shelly can share her unpleasant feelings with her mother.)*

General Discussion

Let's talk about some signals that tell us when things are going well or going not so well in our relationships with our own children. *(This is a good time to share an example of negativity in your relationship with your own child or other personal experience.)*

Would anyone like to share a positive or negative signal with the group? *(Pause for parents' response.)*

Discussion of the Home Practice Assignment

During the coming week, try to tune into these positive and negative signals between you and your child. Look for signs which tell you how strong your relationship is. When you notice these signs, write them down on a piece of paper. Bring your examples to our next session, so we can discuss them. Remember, all relationships have both positive and negative signs. It is important that you write down examples of *both* kinds. One thing I have learned is that when parents share some specific positive and negative relationship signs they have noticed, all the group members become more aware and more sensitive to both their own feelings and their children's feelings. This awareness has a positive effect: It motivates parents to work on making their parenting skills more effective. For that reason, your home practice assignment for this session is important to all of us.

References

Kochanska, G., & Aksan, N. (1995). Mother-child mutually positive affect, the quality of child compliance to requests and prohibitions, and maternal control as correlates of early internalization. *Child Development*, 66, 236-254.

Kuczynski, L. (1992). The concept of compliance in childrearing interaction. In J. M. A. Jansen & J. R. M. Gerris (Eds.), *Child rearing: Influence on prosocial and moral development* (pp. 125-144). Amsterdam, The Netherlands: Swets & Zeitlinger.

Kuczynski, L., & Kochanska, G. (1990). Development of children's noncompliance strategies from toddlerhood to age 5. *Developmental Psychology*, 26, 398-408.

Examples of Parent-Child Relationship Situations

1. Beth is playing with her dolls. The mother doll says to the baby doll, "Would you like to go to the park, honey?" The baby doll answers, "Oh yes!"

2. "If I hear that one more time, I'm sending you back to bed without supper."

3. Mary says, "When I get big, I want to be a mother. That would be neat."

4. Katie forgot to put her bike on the porch. Her father says, "I guess you don't know how to take care of your bike. I'm putting it in the garage. You can't ride it for 2 weeks."

5. Billy, age 5, tells his mother that he hates her. His mom spanks him, saying, "You don't talk to me like that, you brat. You ever smart-mouth me again, and you won't sit down for a week."

6. Sara asks her father, "Is it all right if I tell you something?" Father says, "Sure." Sara tells her father, "I don't like Benjamin."

7. Scott, who is 10 years old, is sucking his thumb. His mother tells him, "Take your thumb out of your mouth. Only babies suck their thumbs."

8. Tony has had a bad day. He forgot his lunch, got in a fight at school, and had to stay inside during recess. He comes home from school, goes straight to his room, and stays there until it is time for supper.

9. Amy says to her father, "Daddy, can ghosts fly through the wall at night?"

10. Shelly comes home from school and tells her mother, "I hate that fat old teacher. I wish I didn't have to go to school."

PAR Psychological Assessment Resources, Inc./P.O. Box 998/Odessa, FL 33556/Toll-Free 1-800-331-TEST

7 Building Your Relationship With Your Child

Session 5 — Communicating Love and Acceptance

Introduction

The important point in this lesson is that it is not enough for parents to love and accept their child. They must demonstrate that love and acceptance in all interactions with the child. Whether the child is being praised or scolded, the parent must actively demonstrate love and acceptance. Emphasize that this requires active steps as opposed to the passive (and false) assumption that children know they are loved because all parents love their children.

Special Notes for the Mental Health Professional

This session will introduce six methods of communicating love and acceptance. Of these six, the idea that parents should join in a child's activity when invited and that they should allow the child to be the leader and direct their participation seems to be the most difficult concept for parents to understand and accept. Help the parents explore their feelings about reversing roles with their children. Allow plenty of time to discuss this issue. Many parents feel threatened by the idea of giving their child an opportunity to be in control and of being, themselves placed in a submissive role. You might open the discussion with this point, giving the group members an opportunity to air their feelings on the subject.

You can also help by modeling this idea to the group. Look for an opportunity to place yourself in a submissive position with various members of the group. By acknowledging a parent's individual expertise and knowledge or by allowing a parent to explain or reexplain a concept to the group, you allow that parent to take a leadership role within the group. It is important to point out that, although there may be some activities that are potentially harmful to a child's well-being in which a parent should intervene, there are countless opportunities for parents to allow their child to assume a leadership role in relation to the parent.

Session Objectives

1 To convey the importance of the quality of the parent-child relationship in terms of love and acceptance.

2 To teach parents six ways to communicate love and acceptance to their child.

Sequence

● Review and sharing of home practice (10 - 15 minutes)

● Lecture/Discussion (30 - 35 minutes)

● General discussion (25 - 35 minutes)

● Discussion of the home practice assignment (5 - 10 minutes)

Materials

Blackboard (or large marking board)

Chalk (or markers)

Eraser

Pencils and note cards for each parent

Review and Sharing of Home Practice Experiences

Q Who would like to share the results of their home practice assignment?

Q Did anyone have any specific problems or reactions to the assignment? *(Encourage everyone to share home practice experiences, but take care not to pressure parents. This must be a voluntary act.)*

Lecture/Discussion

The Quality of the Parent-Child Relationship

How do our children know that we love them? That we like them? That we accept them? There are many ways to answer these questions, and we'll focus on some of these answers today.

We all know that parents are expected to love their children. But when you read the newspaper, you have to wonder about the parent-child relationships in some homes. You read about kids running away, getting into trouble, harming their families, and so on. I don't believe that the parents of those children don't love their kids. I've never met a parent who didn't love and care about his or her children. But I wonder if these kids *really knew* that their parents loved and accepted them.

If I asked you right now, "How could you let your children know that you love them," you would probably give me the obvious answer: You would simply tell them—"I love you."

But, it probably won't surprise you to hear that telling your child is not enough. Merely saying, "I love you" is not enough for us as married partners or as parents. All of us need to *experience* acceptance in order to know that they are loved. Our kids are no exception. Let me give you an example.

Imagine a young boy, Eugene, who just brought home a terrific report card. His mom and dad find it easy to show their acceptance of Eugene's good work. Then their older son, Gary, walks in and anxiously hands over a report card with some not-so-terrific grades. How can Mom and Dad show their concern about Gary's poor grades while, at the same time, accepting him as worthwhile and competent? I hope this doesn't sound too hard to do. Here's what the conversation might sound like:

Gary walks into the room with his eyes down and a sort of scared look on his face. He hands his report card to his parents and says, "I don't feel so great. Look what I got in math and science." Mom says, "Well, let's take a look. But, before I open this up, I want you to know something. I'm more concerned that you're feeling so upset about your grades. Can we sit down and talk about that first?"

This scene could also be handled without using words. Mom or Dad could simply give Gary a hug and allow him to feel comforted. Either way, Gary needs to feel love by knowing he is accepted when times are bad as well as when times are good.

There are six basic ways that you can show this kind of love and acceptance to your children:

1. First, you can simply tell them. You can say that you love them. I said earlier that this was probably an obvious thing to do for most parents. But, let's take a closer look at this communication. Sometimes it seems like children hear more about how they should not act or what they should not do than they hear about how much we love and appreciate them. Telling our children we love them may be an obvious idea. Still, we often forget to express our love and appreciation directly to our children.

2. There is another way that you can show love and acceptance that has nothing to do with words. You can communicate through gestures and actions. There are several ways you can use gestures and actions to communicate love and acceptance of your children. Remember when Gary anxiously handed over his report card? I suggested that his mom or dad could have given him a hug. That's a good example of communicating love and acceptance through action. *Touching is a very powerful way of showing our feelings—especially feelings of love and acceptance.* To the preschool or early elementary school-aged child, briefly hugging with an arm around the shoulder, gently stroking the child's head, and holding the child's hand all communicate love and acceptance. These actions are important,

because they help to build closeness into the parent-child relationship. Remember last session when we talked about the "savings account" of positive feelings? Well, this is an example of how positive feelings can be deposited into the relationship savings account. Those positive feelings can be helpful when times get rougher. Touching is an important and necessary experience for a young child. It is just as necessary as feeding and clothing the child. You may need to use touch differently as your child gets older, but it will always be important.

3. There is another powerful way to share feelings of love and acceptance without words. It may sound strange at first, but it is very real and very useful. This method is to stay out of your child's activities. When you join in your child's activities, you often send an unintended message that goes something like this: "Without me to help you, your activity probably won't go very well." When you watch your child play or work on something *without helping* you are actually showing love and acceptance. You are saying, in an indirect way, "I accept you and what you do, and I am interested in you." In short, by not always playing the part of the master teacher who has to tell the child what to do and how to do it, you show love and acceptance by giving your child the freedom to do things his or her own way. All people, especially children, appreciate having the freedom to try, and to fail, and then to try again. Of course, there are times when you must interfere—when your child is endangering self or others. Most of the time, however, it is really okay to let your child try things, even if he or she isn't doing it exactly the way you would. It's really hard to sit back and watch when your child is having trouble. It is a natural impulse to jump in and help. Sometimes, though, children need to struggle with a task, and even fail at it, so they can figure out for themselves how to do the task a better way. Sometimes you can help best by staying out of your child's activities.

4. The fourth way of showing acceptance of your children is like talking, but not exactly. When you listen to people talk on the telephone, you often hear them saying, "Uh huh," "Yeah," "Hmm," or "Okay." Or they might say something like, "Tell me more," "What then," "Can you say more," or "That's really interesting." This kind of response encourages the other person to go on expressing ideas and feelings, knowing full well he or she is being heard and accepted. Just like communicating, "I love you," with a loving touch, or by not interfering with a child's activities, this kind of communication shows acceptance and builds better relationships. Think about someone you consider a good listener—someone who doesn't interrupt you and who knows how to communicate the message, "I am still here and still interested in you." That person probably says things like, "Uh huh, and what then?" As a parent, you

can be that kind of listener to your child. This will help to build a better parent-child relationship, establishing the foundation for the child to share personal feelings and problems with you as he or she grows up.

5. There is a fifth way to help you to communicate love and acceptance and to build a better relationship with your child—by joining in some of your child's activities. It may sound like I'm contradicting what I said before about staying out of your child's activities, but there is an important difference here. I am suggesting that you join in, but that you follow two basic ground rules: First, it is necessary for you to ask to join if you haven't been invited. Second, and most importantly, you must take the role of a follower and let your child keep the role of leader or boss during the activity. Notice the important differences. You join some of your child's activities, but you don't direct those activities once you become involved. This is another way that you can demonstrate acceptance of your child—by accepting what he or she is doing. If *you* start an activity and your child joins in, then you are the leader. If *your child* starts to build a house with blocks and you join in, then you are the worker and your child is the boss.

Let's look at some examples of these ways of communicating love and acceptance.

Five-year-old Tommy is outside playing on the slide with his friends. His mom is walking by; as Tommy reaches the top of the steps to slide down, his mom yells out, "Be careful Tommy!"

Q Is Tommy's mother showing acceptance of his activities? *(Pause for parents' response.)*

Q How could this mother have shown Tommy love and acceptance in this situation? *(Pause for parents to discuss their ideas.)*

Yes. She could have just stood there and watched Tommy with a smile on her face. Or she might have said, "Boy, that looks like a lot of fun!"

Now think about this next example. Are the parents showing acceptance here?

Six-year-old Jeff was really excited. His grandmother had mailed him a model dinosaur kit and it had just arrived that afternoon. Taking the kit to the basement workshop, Jeff labored over it for hours. When his mom went down to the basement for something, she noticed Jeff was gluing the head onto the tail. Another time, Jeff's dad went down to get a screwdriver and saw that the directions for the kit were still in the sealed plastic cover. Neither parent said a thing.

Q Were Mom and Dad showing acceptance of Jeff's model building? How did they do it? *(Pause for parents to discuss their ideas.)*

Yes. Jeff didn't ask for help, and his mom and dad let him do things his way. Now, let's talk about the same two situations, but we'll change them a bit.

This time, Tommy's mother lets Tommy slide and play with his friends without commenting on his every move. Tommy, having played all he wanted, walks over to his mother, who is talking with her neighbor. Her neighbor happens to be Jeff's dad. Without stopping her conversation, Tommy's mother reaches down, tousles Tommy's hair, and cups his head in her hand. Then Jeff's dad says, "I have to go." He goes to his basement workshop, where Jeff is still hunched over the dinosaur model. Dad begins to pick up and organize the pieces of the model. Dad doesn't notice Jeff's frown. He says, "I bet these directions could really help! I know they'd help me if I were doing this model. You can't do a job right if you don't follow the directions."

Q Now, what did our two parents communicate this time? How did they do it? *(Pause for parents' response.)*

Yes. Tommy's mother accepted his behavior. She also reached out and touched him, showing him her affection. On the other hand, Jeff's father took control and communicated with both actions and words that Jeff wasn't doing things right. Jeff was told and shown that he was unacceptable.

6. There is a sixth way to help build a good parent-child relationship. Using the helpful praise and helpful criticism techniques we talked about in the second session, you can also deposit more positive feelings into your relationship savings account. Helpful praise and helpful criticism will help your child develop positive feelings about himself or herself, and your child will, in turn, feel closer to you. *(Pause for parents to discuss their ideas.)*

For a moment, let's review these six ways of building a better parent-child relationship. *(Write the categories from Figure 10 on the board.)*

First, you can say, "I love you." Second, you can use touch and gestures to communicate love and acceptance for your child. Third, you can let your child work on his or her own activities in your presence without trying to take over. Fourth, you can learn to be a good listener for your child. Fifth, you can join in some of your child's activities when invited, accepting the role of worker or follower in those activities. Finally, you can use helpful praise and helpful criticism to help your child feel good about himself or herself.

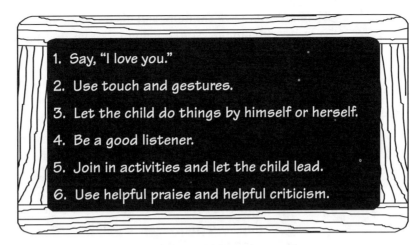

Figure 10. Six ways to build a better parent-child relationship.

Keep these six techniques in mind as you consider the following situation:

Jeannette joyfully and excitedly tells her mom and dad that she won a prize in her preschool class. With a big smile, she tells how neat it was to win the game she played with her classmates.

Now, how would you show acceptance of Jeannette regarding this experience? Take a moment to think about our six ways. *(Point to the board.)* In a minute we'll list on the board some of the possible ways to show acceptance in this situation. *(Pause for the group to think, and then ask parents for suggestions. Write each suggestion on the board beside the correct category. Some possible correct responses are: Stand there with a proud smile, reach out and hug her, say, "Tell me how it went" or "That's neat!")*

Now I'm going to add to this story about Jeannette.

It's now bedtime. Jeannette is being tucked into bed by her mom and dad. She fidgets under the covers for a few minutes and finally says, "Mom and Dad, I want to tell you something. You know the prize I said I won? Well, I really found it on the floor in the hall. I knew it was Billy's prize, but I really wanted it!" Jeannette starts to cry. "I put it in my pocket. I just had to tell you I won the prize so I could keep it."

Q Now, how could you show your love and acceptance for Jeannette? Talk about this for 3 minutes with the person sitting next to you, and then we'll make another list on the board. *(Some possible constructive responses are: Mother reaches out and looks at Jeannette with a concerned expression. Mother says, "You are upset by what you did," or "Have you decided what to do next?" Let the group discuss the situation for 3 minutes. Then write their suggestions on the board and discuss them.)*

The board (Figure 10) reads:

1. Say, "I love you."
2. Use touch and gestures.
3. Let the child do things by himself or herself.
4. Be a good listener.
5. Join in activities and let the child lead.
6. Use helpful praise and helpful criticism.

Here are two more examples. In each example, think about how we could change the situation to build a better relationship by showing acceptance and love for the child.

After supper, 5 year-old Andrew throws himself on the floor in front of the television. He lies there and listens to his dog, Ralph, whining. Dad can hear Ralph whining, too. He knows that Ralph hasn't been fed yet and that this is one of Andrew's daily chores. Dad walks by, gives Andrew a light kick on the leg and says, "Get your lazy self out there and fix Ralph some dinner!"

Q How would you rewrite that story so Dad's response builds a better relationship with Andrew? I'm going to pass out some cards, and I want you to write down what your response would be. Also write down which category on the board your response would best fit. *(Pause to allow parents to write down their responses.)*

Now I'd like you to listen to one more situation.

Four-year-old Melissa is busy playing house with all her dolls. It's a lazy Sunday for the family, and Dad has been taking a nap. He wakes up and goes to look in on Melissa. Melissa looks up as her Dad enters the room and says, "Daddy, come play with me and my children. You can be the big brother, but I'm the mommy."

On the back of your card, write down what this dad could do to foster a good relationship with Melissa. Again, write the category your response fits best. *(Pause for this to be completed.)*

Now, I would like you to form small groups of three or four people. Talk about what you wrote on your cards. Share with each other the responses you thought would help to build better parent-child relationships. I'll move from group to group, and in about 15 minutes we'll talk about the suggestions each group came up with. *(Allow about 15 minutes for discussion. Then ask someone from each group to briefly describe the suggestions the group came up with.)*

Now I want to share some final thoughts with you. We talked about some really important ways to build better relationships with your children. These ways help our children know, experience, and feel our love for them. These ways are all like depositing positive feelings in the parent-child relationship account, an account of love and good will. You might not always be able to make a deposit. You might be angry, or irritable, or busy. Or you might need to discipline your child. At these times, you will have to make a withdrawal from the account.

But keep in mind that if you keep a healthy balance of positive feelings between you and your child, withdrawing from that account when it's necessary will not bankrupt your relationship with your child. Remember to keep the emphasis on making deposits, not withdrawals.

Depositing and withdrawing are not the whole story. We are trying to help our children develop into competent, worthwhile individuals. The best way for you to help is to maintain a positive, strong, and respectful relationship with your child.

General Discussion

Let's talk for a few minutes about your reactions to today's session.

(Encourage parents to share their feelings and reactions. Ask parents to talk about how they can apply these ideas with his or her own children. After one parent talks about his or her own family situation, you might say, "Mr. Smith sees one way that these ideas can help his family. Does anyone else see how they might use these ideas at home?")

Discussion of the Home Practice Assignment

The home practice assignment for this week will help to encourage you to use the six different ways to show your child love and acceptance. It is important that you try to use all six ways. Some will be easy and natural for you, whereas others may seem awkward or unnatural. Please try to record or remember your reactions so that we can share them with the group. The assignment will help you discover more ways to build a positive relationship with your child and to help your child build a positive self-concept.

Learning to Recognize Your Child's Feelings Through Reflective Listening

Introduction

The previous sessions have revolved around the need for parents to communicate love and acceptance to their children. This session talks about one important method of communicating—reflective (or active) listening (listening for feelings).

The style of parent-child communication described here is built on the work of a number of parent educators, child development specialists, psychotherapists, and other mental health professionals. The fundamental premise behind this approach is the belief that children's social skills develop and their ability to solve problems is enhanced when their parents communicate in ways that model and encourage reflection of feelings and motives (Applegate, Burleson, Burke, Delin, & Kline, 1985).

Both clinical experience and the available research base suggest that the development of self-regulatory behavior is enhanced in the context of a parent-child relationship that acknowledges and explores the interpretation and meaning of each other's behavior, feelings, and goals. This process or way of behaving has the additional benefit of enhancing the relationship itself. Individuals who experience being understood and who feel free to express their feelings and thoughts within a relationship come to value that relationship and will try to protect it from any disruption. Moreover, the participants come to trust each other, and opposition to each other's requests or expectations is reduced. Interactions become less stressful and confrontive as understanding and trust grow.

Haim Ginott (1965) described a way of communicating that will help parents avoid "fruitless dialogues" with their children (p. 20). When parents try to reason with their children, frustrating conversations often result, because children resist verbal interchanges when they feel that they are being preached to or criticized. Ginott's recommended communication method requires that statements of understanding precede statements of advice or instruction. Essentially, Ginott emphasized the importance of recognizing the feelings behind a child's remarks and of indicating to the child that those feelings have been understood. Once a child knows that he or she has been heard and understood, that child is more likely to listen positively to what his or her parent has to say.

Ginott's method integrates within the parent-child relationship the same qualities that Rogers (1957) emphasized as pivotal within the therapist-client relationship. Rogers suggested that the qualities of empathy, unconditional positive regard, and congruence are essential to the therapist for success in the therapeutic relationship. In 1989, Teybur echoed the importance of empathy and nonjudgment within the therapeutic relationship. The psychotherapy literature, as well as later research on empathy, has important implications for improving communication between parents and children.

Rogers (1959) defined *the state of being empathetic* as the accurate perception of another's frame of reference and emotional experience, as well as the meaning that the other perceives in life events. Rogers suggested that empathy involves sensing "the hurt or the pleasure of another as he (the client) senses it and to perceive the causes thereof as he perceives them." (pp. 210-211). More recently, Rogers (1975) reconceptualized empathy as a process rather than a state of being. He describes several facets of this process:

> [Empathy] involves being sensitive, moment to moment, to the changing felt meanings which flow in (the) other person, to the fear or rage or tenderness or confusion or whatever, that he/she is experiencing. It means temporarily living in his/her life, moving about in it delicately without making judgments....It includes communicating your sensings of his/her world...To be with another in this way means that for the time being you lay aside the views and values you hold for yourself in order to enter another's world without prejudice. In some sense it means that you lay aside yourself and this can only be done by a person who is secure enough in himself that he knows he will not get lost in what may turn out to be the strange or bizarre world of the other, and [who] can comfortably return to his own world when he wishes. (p. 4)

Experienced therapists suggest that empathy from a therapist makes it possible for clients to self-explore and to move forward in therapy (Karasu, 1992; Teybur, 1989). Rogers (1975) describes the positive consequences of a therapy relationship rich in empathy that may contribute to a client's willingness to self-explore and to implement change.

Empathy dissolves alienation. When a client receives empathy from his therapist, he or she feels understood by someone else and perceives the relationship with that person as positive. Empathic understanding allows the recipient to feel valued, cared for, and accepted for who he or she really is. The client receives this message, "...this other individual trusts me, thinks I'm worthwhile. Perhaps I am worth something. Perhaps I could value myself. Perhaps I could care for myself" (Rogers, 1975, p. 7).

An important aspect of empathy is its accepting, nonjudgmental quality. Rogers (1975) felt that acceptance is the highest expression of empathy because a therapist has to form a nonevaluative opinion in order to accurately and sensitively understand the client. As the client becomes aware that the therapist is not judging him or her, the client's capacity for self-acceptance is increased.

Rogers concluded his 1975 article with the following statement:

> There are...situations in which the empathetic way of being has the highest priority. When the other person is hurting, confused, troubled, anxious, alienated, terrified; or when he or she is doubtful of self-worth, uncertain as to identity, then understanding is called for. The gentle and sensitive companionship of an empathetic stance—accompanied of course by the other two attitudes (genuineness and caring)—provides illumination and healing. In such situations deep understanding is, I believe, the most gracious gift one can give to another. (p. 9)

Although Rogers was referring to the therapy relationship, his words appropriately describe the understanding and concern a parent might communicate when his or her child is expressing emotion. The skill of reflective listening—listening empathically and mirroring the child's emotions—is an important one for parents to incorporate into their communications with their children. Reflective listening is an effective method for expressing acceptance and understanding, as well as for opening pathways to communication.

In his *Parent Effectiveness Program*, Gordon (1970) listed several reasons why active listening (another term for reflective listening) is a helpful parenting skill. He also described the basic parental attitudes necessary to use active listening effectively. These attitudes are similar to those described by Rogers, particularly with regard to the effectiveness of understanding and acceptance when they are communicated. Gordon describes 6 basic parental attitudes:

1. The parent must want to hear what the child has to say, and be willing to take the time to listen.

2. The parent must genuinely want to be helpful to the child when the child presents a particular problem.

3. The parent must be able to truly accept the child's feelings, whatever they are and no matter how much they differ from the parent's.

4. The parent must have a deep feeling of trust in the child's capacity to handle his [or her] feelings and to work toward constructive solutions to his [or her] own problems.

5. The parent must appreciate that feelings are transitory and changeable. He or she must not fear the child's expression of feelings.

6. The parent must be able to see the child as someone separate from himself [or herself], with particular attitudes, feelings and perceptions. The parent should not feel threatened by a child who does not conform to parental attitudes, values, and beliefs. (Gordon, 1970, pp. 59-60)

In Summary. The concept of reflective listening has its foundations in the practice of client-centered psychotherapy and is a useful method of communication within the parent-child relationship. Ginott (1965) and Gordon (1970) incorporated the idea of reflective listening in their writings on parent education. Reflective (or active) listening is introduced as a helpful skill for developing open and trusting parent-child communication.

Special Notes for the Mental Health Professional

It is critical that the skill of reflective listening be presented and learned in the context of the positive relationship-building skills presented in earlier sessions. Although reflective listening can be a very useful tool, its use can only be effective in changing a child's behavior if the parent-child relationship already contains warmth, love, mutual concern and sharing, positive regard, and so forth, to draw from. If these qualities are absent from the relationship and the reflective listening occurs without a positive emotional base, parent-child communication is unlikely to improve. In such instances, the child is likely to perceive that the parent is insincere or pretending to show concern. When the parent's actions do not indicate that the parent is truly concerned, reflective listening can actually harm the parent-child relationship.

The last part of the lecture/discussion in this session emphasizes necessary precautions with reflective listening: (a) the basic attitudes described by Gordon (1970) must be present in the parent for reflective listening to be effective, and (b) parents must understand that when these attitudes are absent, children will detect the emptiness of their parents' remarks, and communication will break down.

The skills presented in this session and the next are difficult for parents to learn. It is critical that parents practice these skills until they feel comfortable using them. An additional review/practice session may be necessary before you move on to introduce any new material. You will find notes for an optional review and practice session on reflective listening immediately following this session. Keep in mind that the skills presented here will be useful to parents in future sessions, and they should be reinforced heavily before new material is presented.

Parents also need to practice active role-playing to internalize these skills. You may find that parents try to intellectualize and talk about reflective listening instead of practicing the skill. Examples and role-playing activities are included in this session to give parents ample opportunity for practice. To learn these essential skills, parents must take part in the role-playing activities and complete their home practice assignments. You can also help parents become familiar with these skills by modeling them during your interactions with group members.

When presenting the concept of reflective listening, point out that parents can reflect their child's feelings and express their own understanding without either being permissive or lowering their standards. If cursing is unacceptable, for example, it remains unacceptable. Still, a parent may choose to ignore a child's cursing *initially* and to respond, instead, to the child's feelings of anger and frustration. The unacceptability of cursing can be discussed at a later time, when the child's feelings have been vented and he or she is in a better frame of mind to listen and work toward solving the problem.

Session Objectives

1 To sensitize parents to the need for responding to everything their child communicates, including words and feelings.

2 To show parents how to communicate to their children that they understand their children's feelings.

3 To help parents develop the skill of recognizing feelings implicit in their children's communications; to help parents learn to relate an understanding of those feelings to their children.

4 To help parents understand some of the precautions they should use along with reflective listening.

Sequence

- Review and sharing of home practice (10 - 15 minutes)
- Lecture/Discussion (25 minutes)
- Small group triads (20 - 25 minutes)
- General discussion (30 - 40 minutes)
- Discussion of the home practice assignment (5 - 10 minutes)

 Materials

Sets of 12 note cards, each containing a situation for the practice exercise

Review and Sharing of Home Practice Experiences

Last session we discussed four ways of communicating love and acceptance to your child. You had a home assignment to practice using these different ways.

 Who would like to describe a situation in which they used one of the four ways? *(Be very reinforcing to the volunteers. Encourage all parents to consider other methods of communicating love and acceptance in each situation presented.)*

Lecture/Discussion

Reflective Listening

Today I will suggest ways that you can improve your communication with a child. These techniques are sure to work for everyone, but they take practice. All parents want a good relationship with their child. We want them to love us, and they want to love us and feel close to us.

Remember that we talked about building relationships with our children by communicating love and acceptance. A positive parent-child relationship teaches your child that he or she is lovable, worthwhile, competent, and responsible. Now we'll talk about two new ways to build a better relationship and communicate love to your child.

The first way is to recognize how your child is feeling, and the second way is to let your child know you understand those feelings by communicating them back to the child.

If you think about it, you'll realize that your children communicate their feelings in many ways. Sometimes they use simple words like, "Mommy, I love you," or "You're mean, I hate you." No communication problem—these words are easy to understand. Sometimes, though, children communicate their feelings in words that are not so simple—words that take some figuring out. Here are two examples of communication that needs some figuring out:

It is Saturday afternoon. Billy, age 4, says to his father (in a mildly pleading tone of voice), "Are you going to work all day, Daddy?"

Sally, age 6, has a new baby sister. One day, she asks her mother (in a mildly angry tone of voice), "Why do you let that noisy old baby sleep in your room?"

The words that Billy and Sally use don't communicate their feelings as clearly as a simple "I love you" or "I hate you." To understand these children, you have to listen to more than the actual words. You need to listen to the tone of voice and think about what the child's feelings are and what his or her intent might be. *(Read the first example again.)* You can see that Billy wanted his father to play with him. *(Read the second example again.)* Sally was expressing her feeling of being left out.

There is another way that children express their feelings. Think about these two examples.

Belinda is sent to her room for misbehaving. She doesn't have to say she is angry. Her mother sees her frown and hears her storm up the stairs. Mom also hears Belinda's bedroom door slam.

Something is wrong. Frank came home from school and went straight to his room. He didn't say, "Hi" like he usually does.

You can see that understanding your child's feelings is like listening to a song. You have to pay attention to the music as well as the words. When you look at your child's facial expression and gestures and listen to his or her tone of voice, you will recognize the feelings behind the words.

If you learn to recognize your child's feelings but do nothing with that recognition, you are wasting a real opportunity to build a closer relationship. When you recognize your child's feelings and express your understanding of those feelings, it pulls the two of you closer together. When a friend recognizes that you are upset and says, "You seem a little upset today," he shows you that he notices and cares about how you feel. If he shows good sense and doesn't say anything else, he gives you a chance to share your problem if you want to. That sharing of feelings brings the two of you closer together.

When you don't listen to your child's feelings, two negative things can happen. First, you miss the chance to build your relationship and to communicate love and acceptance to your child. Second, you are not likely to understand your child's communication fully, and you may actually close yourself off as a source of help and understanding for your child. Here are three examples of parent-child communication. As you listen to them, think about why these children (particularly if they are teenagers) don't talk to their parents or come to them for help.

1. **Child** (*dejected tone of voice*): "I don't think I want to go to chorus any more."

   Parent (*firmly, with annoyance*): "Let's not hear any more of that. You're going to chorus."

2. **Child** (*angrily*): "That Sarah is a rotten bitch."

   Parent (*annoyed and angry*): "Listen, young lady, don't ever let me hear you talk like that again!"

3. **Child** (*pleading*): "Mom, do I have to do it now?"

   Parent (*annoyed and angry*): "Patrick, do your chores now. Do you hear me?"

You can see that the parents' replies in these situations are not going to improve these parent-child relationships. Each response contains a threat— the threat to use parental power or force. In its own way, each parent tells the child that he or she is not worthwhile and that the way he or she thinks is wrong. In each example, the parent is telling the child, "You shouldn't talk like that; I can't accept you."

Here are the same examples with different parental responses —ones that are helpful:

1. **Child** (*dejected tone of voice*): "I don't think I want to go to chorus any more."

   Parent (*concerned*): "Jim, you sure sound unhappy."

2. **Child** (*angrily*): "That Sarah is a rotten bitch."

   Parent (*concerned*): "Sometimes she really gets you angry."

3. **Child** (*pleading*): "Mom, do I have to do it now?"

   Parent (*firmly*): "You would like to do something else?"

Now let's try to recognize the ways you can help and hinder your relationship when you talk to your own child. Remember that using power is destructive to positive relationships, and so is giving away power by being too permissive. Your goal is to understand your child's feelings and to share that understanding with your child. This way, your child will know that you accept and respect him or her.

Now I'm going to read some conversations between parents and children. Each situation will have three possible parental replies: one based on power, one based on permissiveness, and one based on recognizing the child's feelings.

Child:	"Mom, we aren't having asparagus again, are we?"
Parent 1:	"You don't have to eat it."
Parent 2:	"It sounds like you don't like the vegetable."
Parent 3:	"Stop your griping."

Exactly. Parent number 2 was listening for the child's feelings. Let's try another one.

Child *(longingly)*:	**"Will Daddy be home soon?"**
Parent 1:	**"You miss him."**
Parent 2:	**"Stop pestering. He'll get here when he gets here."**
Parent 3:	**"Why don't you call him and ask him to come home soon?"** *(Again, ask parents to identify the use of power, permissiveness, and reflective listening. If you feel that the parents need more practice, use one or more of the following examples.)*
Child *(angrily)*:	**"I hate school and I'm not going tomorrow."**
Parent 1:	**"Don't say things like that. It can't be that bad."**
Parent 2:	**"It sounds like you had a bad day at school."**
Parent 3:	**"If it's that important to you, you can stay home tomorrow."**
Child *(crying)*:	**"Mom, Jane's being mean to me. She took my crayons away."**
Parent 1:	**"Jane, give Lucy her crayons. You should know better than to take things from your little sister."**
Parent 2:	**"Jane took your crayons and you're unhappy and angry with her."**
Parent 3:	**"Lucy, if you'll stop crying, maybe I can understand what you're saying."**
Child *(excitedly)*:	**"I've been wishing our scout troop would go camping, and now we're going. I can't wait!"**
Parent 1:	**"I'm so glad. You sound really excited about the trip!"**
Parent 2:	**"We'll have to ask your Dad if you can go."**
Parent 3:	**"That's nice. I'll help you start packing."**
Child *(frustrated)*:	**"Dad, this homework is dumb. It's too hard. Can you help me?"**
Parent 1:	**"Sorry, but I'm watching the news right now. Keep trying and I'll help in a while."**

Parent 2:	"Sure I can help. Let's see what the problem is."
Parent 3:	"You sound pretty frustrated. That must be a tough homework assignment. I'll be with you right after the news."
Child (proudly):	"Mom, we got report cards today and I didn't get any Cs. Aren't you proud of me?"
Parent 1:	"Yes! And you seem pretty happy about it too."
Parent 2:	"See, I told you that hard work would pay off."
Parent 3:	"Of course I'm proud of you. Let's have an ice cream cone to celebrate."
Child:	"But I want to go over to John's house. I hate you. You never let me do anything."
Parent 1:	"Well, if you're going to act like that, I'd rather you did go to John's. Go ahead."
Parent 2:	"You are angry at me. But I can't let you go to John's when his parents are not home."
Parent 3:	"Don't you talk back to me. I said no, and that's final."

You're all beginning to understand the differences between these three types of responses. You're on your way to knowing how to communicate with your child by listening for his feelings.

You could have responded to the above examples by answering what the children said rather than how they said it. For example, a parent could have responded "yes" to the asparagus question, or "no" to the question of whether Daddy would be home soon. But then, only part of what the children said would have been heard. Listening to the feelings *behind* the words is also important.

Let me clarify this difference a bit more. Your child does not always need to have his or her feelings communicated back—especially when the child is only asking for information. The time when reflecting the child's feelings is most helpful is when the child wants more than just information. If a child says, "I'm leaving for school now," it would seem silly to say, "You feel like leaving now." But, if your child whines, "I just hate school. Why do I have to go," the child is asking for and needs more than information. This is a time to listen to your child's feelings and to communicate that you understand those feelings.

Okay, let's practice some situations where listening for feelings will help build a better parent-child relationship. I'll read you a conversation where the parent is using either power or permissiveness. I want you to change the parental response to a reply that shows that you, the parent, are listening for feelings.

Child:	**"Will I always wake up when I go to sleep?"**
Parent:	**"Don't be a baby! Of course you always wake up after sleeping."**

Q Now this parent has used power, and missed the feelings being expressed along with what the child is saying. What could the parent have said that would have reflected an understanding of the child's feelings? *(Pause for parents' responses. Try to get several different reflective responses that show an understanding of the child's fear.)*

Good job. Those examples showed an understanding of not only the words, but the child's feelings as well. Here is another one.

Child *(anxiously)***:**	**"I don't want to go in the pool. It's too cold and I don't like the water."**
Parent:	**"You don't have to go in if you don't want to."**

Here the permissive parent has also missed the whole message the child is sending.

Q What are some responses you could make to the child that would express your listening and understanding of his feelings? *(Pause for parents' responses. Get several possible responses, and summarize what they have said: The parent in the example should reflect the child's concerns and fears.)*

Great. Now you're ready to try more exercises in listening for feelings. This time, I'll give you an open message, as if I were the child. After I'm finished, let me know what you think I'm feeling. If that's not quite what I'm feeling, I'll give you another version of the same message. But if you are understanding exactly what I'm feeling, I will tell you right away. Everyone will get a chance to try this exercise. Who would like to try first? *(Read each example and pause for parent response. In the first few examples, you can prompt parents by giving them the initial part of their responses: "I bet you are feeling _____, or "You seem to be very _____." For the purposes of this exercise, it is more important for the parent to communicate the child's feelings than for the parent to converse with the child.)*

1. *(Angry and indignant.)* **"Boy, do I hate my new teacher. She is so crabby and she's too strict."**

   (Response: You're angry at your new teacher.)

2. *(Pleading.)* **"I don't want to eat these baked potatoes. I hate them."**

   (Response: You don't like potatoes, and you feel I will make you eat them anyway.)

3. *(Pleading and forlorn.)* **"I don't have anything to do today. What can I do? I wish there was something to do!"**

   (Response: You're bored and lonely.)

4. *(Angry and confused.)* **"I hate Julie. She always cries and gets her way. If I don't do what she wants, she goes home."**

   (Response: You're angry and confused.)

5. *(Stubborn and indignant.)* **"I don't want to take a bath. I'm not even dirty. I hate baths anyway. Why do I have to take a bath every day?"**

   (Response: You don't want to take a bath. Note that it is not yet clear what is behind this. Parents are better off using a short reflection and then listening for what comes next.)

6. *(Tearfully.)* **"Fran won't let me play with her dolls. She's mean. Make her give me some dolls to play with."**

   (Response: You're angry with Fran.)

7. *(Child hurts finger with hammer.)* **"Ouch! Ow! It hurts! (Sob) Ow!"**

   (Response: It sure does hurt!)

8. *(Pleading.)* **"I want to sleep in your room. I don't like to sleep in my room. Can I sleep with you and Daddy?"**

   (Response: You're lonely in your room.)

9. *(Pleading and annoyed.)* **"Times have changed since you were a kid. You're old-fashioned. All the other girls my age wear lipstick now."**

   (Response: You want to wear lipstick like the other girls so you won't feel left out.)

10. *(Tearfully.)* **"John always asks Billy to go to the park. He never asks me."**

    (Response: You feel left out and lonely.)

11. *(Confused.)* **"I don't know what to do. Sometimes I want to go."**

    (Response: You're confused.)

12. *(Angrily.)* **"I'm not going to clean up my room. I hate to clean it up. It's my room, and I like it messy."**

    (Response: You don't want to be told what to do.)

13. *(Initially matter-of-fact, but becoming more dramatic.)* **"I don't want to eat my dinner tonight. I'm not hungry. Just don't make me anything. I couldn't eat anything tonight, not the way I'm feeling."**

    (Response: Something has upset you.)

14. *(Angrily.)* **"I wish I weren't a kid. I'll be glad when I grow up. It's no fun being a kid."**

(Response: You sure sound unhappy. Can you talk about what upset you?)

Now, some of you may have found identifying the feelings in these children's messages difficult. Sometimes it *can* be hard, but remember that practicing listening for feelings will make you more comfortable with the skill. Reflective listening does seem strange at first, but parents learn very quickly after they see how their children respond to having their feelings understood. You will see your child's eyes brighten when he or she realizes that you understand the feelings behind the words. This will be so rewarding that you'll find yourself practicing this skill more and more and getting better and better at using it. That's what's great about reflective listening—it builds better relations with your child quickly and positively, and it keeps building.

So, listening for feelings is a skill worth practicing and working for. It brings you and your child closer together. This closeness helps teach your child that he or she is worthwhile, lovable, competent, and responsible. Remember that using power or force withdraws positive feelings from the relationship savings account. Well, the closer your parent-child relationship gets, the less you will need to use power in discipline, and the less you will have to withdraw from your relationship account.

Practice Exercise in Reflective Listening

(Divide the group into triads. Parents in these small groups will take turns playing child, parent, and observer. Give one set of 12 situation cards to each triad—these situations are described below. Have the "child" read a card and allow the "parent" to respond. The two should continue talking for 2 to 3 minutes. The observer should provide the "parent" with feedback regarding the appropriateness of his or her responses. You should move among the triads, providing encouragement and feedback.)

Let's divide up into groups of three so we can do some role playing. Each of you will take a turn being parent, child, and observer. This is how the exercise will work. First, the person playing the child will read from a card to set the scene and begin the conversation. The parent will respond to the child by listening and reflecting the feelings behind what the child said. Parent and child should continue talking for 2 or 3 minutes, with the parent using a listening for feelings statement at least one more time during the conversation. The observer should pay close attention and then point out any other moments when a listening for feelings statement would have been appropriate. The child should pay close attention to the parent's responses and share his or her reactions with the parent after they finish talking. When you play the role of the child, remember to think about how you are feeling, what you are thinking, and how you want to respond.

Each person should get four cards. You will play the child in the four situations on those cards. Each person will also get turns as parent and observer. Once you finish four cards, another person becomes the child, and you take a turn playing parent or observer. Keep working until all the cards have been used. Any questions?

(To prepare for this exercise, print these situations, one to a card, on as many note cards as you will need for your parent groups):

1. **Five-year-old Mary has just come in from playing outside. She is crying and says to her mom, "Mommy, I don't like Sue anymore. She won't play with me in my store, she wants to play kickball with Nancy."**

2. **Terry is working on his model car as his dad walks into the room. Terry says (excitedly), "Dad, look how I fixed my car! Doesn't it look great with the decals?"**

3. **Martha, age 3, begins to cry when her parents are leaving for the evening. The babysitter tries hard to console her, but Martha just cries louder. She reaches for her mom and says, "Martha go, too."**

4. **John, age 7, has just come home with a test that he failed. He says, "I hate school."**

5. **Mark, age 7, calls excitedly to his mother, "Mom, Dad said we can go skating on Saturday. I wish it was Saturday already!"**

6. **Christy, age 6, just started school. Her mother is having a hard time getting Christy ready on her fourth school day. Christy says to her mother (pleading and stubborn), "I don't want to go to school today. I want to stay here with you and play with my puppy."**

7. **Beth, age 6, has been invited to two different parties on the same day. She comes to her mother and asks, "Mom, what do I do now? Should I go to Jane's party or Tom's party?"**

8. **Jeff, age 8, wants to go on a weekend camping trip with his friends. His father had to tell him that he couldn't go because Jeff would miss his mother's birthday party. Jeff says (angrily), "Why do I have to be at her party? I never get to do what I want to do."**

9. **Susie's mother is in the hospital with her new baby. Susie says to her father one night at bedtime, "When is mommy coming home? I want her to read my book."**

10. Mike, age 7, has been trying hard to finish cleaning his room so he can go outside. His mother comes to see how he is doing, but he is only half finished. Mike says (pleading), "Can't I go out and play now? I really have been working hard. See how neat my bed is?"

11. Angela, age 5, wants to play ball with her older brother Jim, who is 8. Angela comes to her father and says, "I want to play, but Jim won't let me. He laughs when I ask him and says I'm not big enough. Make him let me play, Dad."

12. Steve, age 4, watches as his mother is rocking his new baby sister. He walks over to the chair, smiles at the baby and leans over to kiss her. Steve says to his mom, "I want to rock my baby too. Can I please hold her?"

Precautions To Use With Reflective Listening

Before we stop today, I want to cover one more point. There are some rules of caution to follow when you use reflective listening. Remember, whenever you listen for your child's feelings and reflect them back, you are signaling your child to talk more and to continue to express himself or herself.

There are times and conditions when you won't want to encourage your child to continue expressing feelings. And there are some conditions where listening for your child's feelings may lead to more conflict or get in the way of building a positive relationship. So there are actually times when listening for feelings won't be helpful. You can't predict every situation where listening for feelings will have a negative affect on your relationship, but I can give you five situations where you definitely should not use listening for feelings.

Your child is expressing feelings you cannot accept. Here's an example: Mrs. Jones is a very sensitive person, and her 7-year-old son says to her, "I hate you. You're very mean." Now, this is very likely to upset Mrs. Jones, so she needs to examine her own feelings and reactions first. Once she understands her own feelings, she will be better able to help her son explore his.

You don't have the time to let your child express himself or herself fully. For example, you are about to leave the house and have to be on time for an appointment. Your daughter stops you and says, "Mom, I don't want to stay with the babysitter again today." By responding, "You're unhappy because I need to leave you again," you are opening the door for more conversation. You don't have time to talk, however, and you may have to cut your daughter off abruptly. If you cut her off after you encouraged her to express her feelings, she will feel even more upset than she did before.

You cannot help your child at that particular time. If you are occupied or too busy to stop and help when your child asks for it, don't signal your openness to more communication by giving a listening for feelings response. Rather than cut your child off in the middle of expressing feelings, it would be better to wait until the next time he or she asks, or to go back to the child's concerns at a later time.

If you are not willing to build your own trust in your child's problem-solving ability, don't encourage the child to talk about his or her problems by listening for feelings. If you are not comfortable with your child's decision-making, don't encourage the child to talk about his or her problem and some possible solutions. And remember, you will put your child down if, in the end, you impose your own solution to the child's problem. From such an experience, your child will start feeling that you're not really interested in what he or she has to say—because at the end of the communication you tell your child what to do anyway. This feeling will damage your child's sense of being worthwhile and competent and, thus, it will damage your relationship.

You don't see your child as a separate person with a right to his or her feelings. As a separate person, your child is entitled to disagree with you, to think you are wrong, and even to think you are foolish sometimes. You may believe that a child should not disagree with the parents. For example, your daughter may feel strongly that you are unfair because you won't let her stay overnight at a friend's house when the parents are not at home. If you are not prepared to hear her objections to your decision, or if you do not think she should disagree with you, don't say that you understand that she is angry and encourage her to express that anger. You should never encourage your child to talk about something when you are not willing to listen. This will only frustrate you and your child.

When you are trying to decide whether it is appropriate to use reflective listening, ask yourself the following questions: *Am I willing to allow my child to express these feelings and talk them out? Will I put my child down or cut my child short because I can't accept what he or she will say?* If the answer to the second question is yes, it is not an appropriate time to use listening for feelings.

General Discussion

Can anyone see how you might apply reflective listening in your own family situation? *(Encourage parents to explore how they can use this skill to improve relationships at home, especially with their children.)*

(Note: If you plan to hold the optional training session, you should add the following request at this point.) For next session, I'd like each of you to write down one situation in which you have discussed a problem with your child. Don't write your name on the situation, just describe it. During our next session, we will use all your problem situations to practice the reflective listening skills you learned today.

Discussion of the Home Practice Assignment

The home practice assignment for the coming week is one of the most difficult assignments you will face. You will be trying to encourage your children to share their feelings and trying to show them you can accept their feelings. Unfortunately, it is possible they will express feelings or share feelings that are honest, but not what you want to hear. Most importantly, it is precisely at those times that your child may feel the greatest love and acceptance from you, and your relationship will grow. Your child probably will know that you don't *agree* with what he or she is saying, but also that you *understood* his or her feelings! Once children feel understood, they are in a better position to consider alternative reactions or alternative behavior.

You should be alert to the possibility that your child will notice a change in your own behavior. If your child does notice, acknowledge the change and tell your child you are working on learning new ways of showing how much you love him or her.

References

Applegate, J. L., Burleson, B. R., Burke, J. A., Delin, J. G., & Kline, S. L. (1992). Reflection-enhancing parenting as an antecedent to children's social-cognitive and communicative development. In I. E. Sigel (Ed.), *Parental belief systems: The psychological consequences for children* (pp. 3-39). Hillsdale, NJ: Erlbaum.

Ginott, H. (1965). *Between parent and child*. New York: MacMillan Company.

Gordon, T. (1970). *Parent effectiveness training*. New York: Peter H. Wyden.

Karasu, T. B. (1992). *Wisdom in the practice of psychotherapy*. New York: Basic Books.

Rogers, C. R. (1957). The necessary and sufficient conditions of therapeutic personality change. *Journal of Consulting Psychology, 21,* 95-103.

Rogers, C. R. (1959). A theory of therapy, personality, and interpersonal relationships as developed in the client-centered framework. In S. Koch (Ed.), *Psychology: A study of a science* (Vol. III, pp. 184-256). New York: McGraw-Hill.

Rogers, C. R. (1975). Empathetic: An unappreciated way of being. *The Counseling Psychologist, 5*(2), 2-10.

Teybur, E. (1989). *Interpersonal process in psychotherapy: A guide for clinical training*. Pacific Grove, CA: Brooks/Cole.

Session 6A

Reflective Listening—Review and Practice (optional)

Special Notes for the Mental Health Professional

This follow-up session for reflective listening is difficult to script, because you can anticipate neither what situations the parents will bring from home nor their reactions in the role-playing activities. It is important, however, to provide parents with opportunities to practice this new and sometimes difficult skill. As you move from group to group during the role-playing activity, remind parents of the basic steps behind reflective listening. When necessary, you might want to step in and play the "parent" in order to demonstrate appropriate reflective listening. The following ideas should be reviewed during this session or modeled during the role-playing:

1. *Joining with the child.* Parents should reflect their child's feelings as many times as is needed until both they and the child have a clear picture of the child's feelings, motivations, or goals.

2. *Fostering problem ownership.* Once the child's feelings have been expressed and understood, the parent might want to ask the child what the child would like to make happen or what the child would like to do to solve the problem. The parent could assist the child with this problem solving by asking about the effect the child's solution might have on the child and on others, by asking about alternative solutions and their effects, or by asking if the child might think about the problem and come back to the solution later.

3. *Reflective listening continues throughout the above process.* Parents should continue to reflect the child's feelings during the child's problem-solving. Examples might include, "It is frustrating to think about different solutions—you're getting angry with me."

4. *Reflective listening is not only for use in negative or problem situations.* Parents must be encouraged to use reflective listening in positive situations as well. The skill is particularly useful for sharing a child's good feelings and achievements.

Session Objectives

1 To review the idea of reflective listening.

2 To provide parents with additional practice and discussion of reflective listening.

Sequence

- Review and sharing of home practice (10 minutes)

- Role plays of parents' problem situations (40 - 50 minutes)

- General discussion (15 minutes)

- Discussion of the home practice assignment (5 - 10 minutes)

 ## Materials

Box at the room door labeled, "Place Problem Situations From Home Here"

Additional problem situations printed on index cards as a back-up for discussion

Review and Sharing of Home Practice Experiences

(As parents arrive, ask them to place their problem situations in the box at the door.)

Last session, we talked about recognizing your child's feelings through reflective listening. This skill can help in problem situations, and it will help you build a better parent-child relationship. Sometimes it is difficult to find the feelings behind the words your child is saying. This session will give you an opportunity to practice finding those feelings and reflecting them back to your child.

 How were your experiences at home using reflective listening with your children? Any questions or problems? *(Pause for parents' response. Encourage parents to respond to each other's questions and problems.)*

Role-Playing Problem Situations

Now I would like you to divide up into groups of three so we can do some role playing. We're going to do the same thing we did last session, but this time we will use the problem situations you brought from home. *(As parents break into groups, remove the problem situations from the box and divide them into sets of three or four. Give a set of situations to each group. Each group should have at least three situations to work with. If you run out of situations, use the list of eight additional problem situations provided below.)*

Remember that each of you will take a turn being parent, child, and observer. The person playing the child will read the problem situation and begin the conversation. The parent will respond by listening and reflecting the feelings behind what the child said. Parent and child should talk for 2 or 3 minutes, with the parent using reflective listening as many times as possible. When the conversation is finished, the observer should point out other moments when reflective listening would have been appropriate. The child should also pay attention to the parent's responses and to his or her own reactions so the reactions can be shared with the parent after they finish talking. I'll be moving from group to group, helping out if you need me. (*Move from group to group, facilitating the role-playing and stepping in to provide help or suggestions where necessary.*)

Additional Problem Situations for Role-Playing Activity

1. Eight-year-old Kathy rushes home after school. She bursts through the door, runs up to her mom with a big smile on her face and says, "Look Mommy! I got straight A's on my report card! I even got an A in math!"

2. Sarah, age 8, has been playing Monopoly with her older sisters. After about an hour she comes into the living room and says to her father, "Dad, I'm a terrible Monopoly player. Every time I play with them I lose all my money and have to go to jail. I'm never going to play Monopoly again!"

3. Gary's mother has been busy all day, getting ready for a dinner party. She is in the kitchen arranging crackers on a plate. Gary, age 7, walks in and says, "Boy, Mom, do those crackers look stupid! Why are you spending all day working on this stupid party, anyway?"

4. Dylan is 3 years old. His mom has just had a new baby and is coming home from the hospital today. When his mother walks in the front door holding the baby sister, Dylan stands in the hallway and says, "Mommy, go away! You and baby go out! Get out!"

5. Jennifer, age 5, has been trying hard to build an airplane with her tinker toys. She finally gets the airplane to stand up on its own. She turns to her mother and says, "My airplane can stand, and it's ready to fly!"

6. Eric, age 7, and his father are at the zoo watching the gorilla. At 4:30, Eric's father says, "Time to go, Eric. It's almost time for dinner." Eric says, "Oh Dad, I'm not hungry. Let's just stay and watch for a little while longer."

General Discussion

Great! You are all learning to use reflective listening effectively.

Q Does anyone have any questions about or problems with this skill? (*Pause for parents' response.*)

Remember the rules of caution to use with reflective listening: When you hear and reflect your child's feelings, you are sending the child a signal to talk more and express himself or herself fully.

There are times when you might not want your child to continue expressing feelings; these are the times when you shouldn't use reflective listening. If you cannot accept your child's feelings, don't encourage the child to continue. Never use reflective listening when you don't have the time to listen and help your child with problem solving. Finally, if you cannot put your trust in the child's problem-solving ability, or if you do not feel that your child has a right to his or her feelings, do not use reflective listening.

An easy way to remember these rules of caution is to ask yourself two important questions: *Am I willing to allow my child to express these feelings and talk them out? Will I put my child down or cut my child short because I can't accept what he or she will say?* If the answer to the second question is yes, it's not an appropriate time to be listening for feelings.

Sharing Yourself

Introduction

A great deal has been said in previous lessons about listening to and responding to children. Several skills have been introduced as techniques for facilitating open communication between parent and child. Whereas it is important that children feel comfortable expressing themselves to their parents, it is just as important that parents feel comfortable expressing their feelings and ideas to their children. Parents must openly communicate in such a way that children learn to listen to and accept their parents. This is a second, important skill that helps to build open, loving, and respectful relationships between parents and children.

The counseling and psychotherapy literature provides a basis for the self-sharing skill introduced in this session. Rogers (1957) mentions *congruence*, or *genuineness*, as one of three qualities in a therapist that he feels are essential to the establishment of an effective client-therapist relationship. He defines congruence as the act of being transparent, that is, hiding nothing of one's own experience in a relationship. Rogers feels that the therapist, by being genuinely free and open, is offering the possibility of an existential encounter between two real persons, thus creating a therapeutic atmosphere within the relationship. In later works, Rogers (1961, 1975) states that, in ordinary interactions among colleagues, it is probable that congruence is the most important element. This genuineness involves the straightforward expression of the therapist's own negative and positive feelings. According to Rogers, congruence becomes the basis for living together in an atmosphere of intimacy and realness (1975, p. 3).

Jourard (1971a, 1971b) studied *self-disclosure* and defined it as the act of fully, spontaneously and honestly revealing oneself to another person. Jourard found that self-disclosure from one person increased self-disclosure in the other and feelings of closeness between both individuals in a relationship. Recent research on self-disclosure in the therapeutic relationship (Stricker, 1990) supports Jourard's findings. In his book on self-disclosure in psychotherapy, Stricker states that self-disclosure, or the mutual revealing of self, is at the very heart of a successful, growth-promoting relationship.

Thus, it seems clear that the act of making one's feelings, attitudes, beliefs, and thoughts known in an honest, straightforward manner is important to developing an intimate, trusting relationship with another person. It is also clear that self-disclosure, or genuineness, can be fostered in others through modeling. Therefore, self-disclosing parents are likely to facilitate patterns of communication with their children in which both negative and positive feelings and opinions can be freely expressed by parents and children in a climate of mutual love and respect.

Gordon (1970) discussed self-disclosure as a way of ensuring that the parent's needs and rights are accounted for without disparaging the child's feelings and wishes. Gordon introduces the I-message for use in situations where a parent feels that his or her own needs are being violated. I-messages will help the parent gain the child's attention in order to achieve a mutually satisfying resolution. Gordon indicates three reasons why he believes I-messages can be effective:

1. Communicating openly to a child the effect of that child's behavior on a parent is less threatening than judging, name-calling or focusing on the child's assumed motive; therefore, open communication is less likely to provoke resistance and rebellion.

2. The child is given responsibility for his or her own behavior and allowed an opportunity to do something about it.

3. The parent, by honestly communicating his or her feelings, encourages the child to express feelings as well. This flow of honest communication fosters an intimate interpersonal relationship between parent and child, one where there is mutual trust and acceptance.

Gordon (1970) suggests the I-message technique as an intervention strategy when parent-child conflicts arise. Gordon also introduces the idea of self-sharing statements as a skill to be learned by parents so they can facilitate intimate interactions with their children. Self-sharing is presented as an ongoing method of building a positive parent-child relationship in both positive and negative situations, rather than as an intervention technique. In this way, self-sharing differs from Gordon's concept of the I-message, which focuses on clarifying problem ownership as a means of conflict resolution. A child may ignore the parent's I-message and, as a result, the parent's expectation that the I-message will make the child more reasonable will be disappointed. Thus, an I-message may actually lead to greater frustration or to a feeling of being rejected or devalued for the parent. When a parent sees self-sharing as a relationship-building skill instead of a behavior management technique, it's not a traumatic event for the parent if a child ignores an I-message.

Special Notes for the Mental Health Professional

As in previous sessions, practicing the new skills presented in this session is of paramount importance. Parents are probably not accustomed to the idea that it is all right to express *their* positive and negative feelings to their children. For this reason, parents need to practice self-disclosure until they feel comfortable communicating in this manner. Participation in the practice exercises and completion of home practice assignments are essential to learning this skill. Again, you may want to plan an extra group session devoted to practice and role-playing before moving on to new material. You can also encourage self-sharing statements and ease parental anxiety by sharing your own thoughts and feelings constructively as you interact with the group members. For example, you might say something like, "I don't think I am doing a good job of explaining this idea," or "I don't think I am understanding your situation," or "I am encouraged to hear of your success with this skill."

It is important not to mislead parents about when to use self-disclosure. It is not an intervention strategy for times when communication has broken down or times of conflict. This skill is a relationship-building strategy, not a panacea for avoiding or resolving parent-child conflicts. If used consistently and appropriately in the context of fostering honest interpersonal interaction between parent and child, self-disclosure can be very effective. However, the use of such an approach in a relationship that is not particularly positive may result in frustration and hurt feelings for parent, child, or both. For this reason, you should encourage parents to share only *positive* feelings as they begin to practice this skill with their children. Parents must be made aware that their children may not respond to (or may even ignore) their statements of negative feelings. If negative feelings such as unhappiness, hurt, or anger have been shared with no response from the child, parents may become resistant to using these self-sharing communications. Encouraging parents to use positive self-sharing communications at first will help to avoid this problem.

The general discussion period in this session should focus on parents' reactions to expressing their feelings openly to their children. It is particularly helpful to point out that it is natural for a parent to feel vulnerable about self-sharing in situations where he or she may be ignored, rejected, or put down. This may be a good time to introduce the idea of negative self-talks (please refer to Sessions 16 through 19 for a review of this idea). Addressing the danger of such negative self-talks as, "If my child doesn't react favorably to my self-sharing, then my child doesn't care about my feelings," would be quite appropriate at this point. This is also an excellent time to reemphasize the importance of reflective listening (see Session 6) in helping a child to feel both heard and understood. During this session, parents experience the sharing of feelings in the same way their children did in the home practice exercises for Session 6. Parents can now discuss, from their new vantage point, the positive effects of using reflective listening in their communications with their children.

Session Objectives

1. To help parents build their relationships with their children by sharing positive and negative feelings and ideas in constructive ways.

2. To help parents recognize the types of communication with their children that can be destructive to the parent-child relationship.

3. To help parents set reasonable expectations for themselves in terms of sharing their own feelings.

Sequence

- Review and sharing of home practice (5 - 10 minutes)
- Lecture/Discussion (20 - 30 minutes)
- Practice exercise (20 - 30 minutes)
- General discussion (20 - 40 minutes)
- Discussion of the home practice assignment (5 - 10 minutes)

Materials

Blackboard (or large marking board)

Chalk (or markers)

Eraser

Movable chairs, arranged in a circle

Extra parent-child situation examples printed on 4 x 5 cards

Review and Sharing of Home Practice Experiences

Last session we talked about the importance of recognizing and reflecting your child's feelings as a way of building a closer and stronger parent-child relationship. Who would like to share the results of the home practice assignment with the rest of us? *(Encourage parents to respond, asking follow-up questions and prompting as needed.)*

Lecture/Discussion

Sharing Your Thoughts and Feelings

First, I want to review what we've talked about in our previous sessions as they lead up to what we'll be talking about today. Remember that the parenting skills you've been learning are designed to help you build closer and more positive relationships with your children. Your goal is to help your children to believe in themselves and to experience themselves as worthwhile and competent. When you communicate love and acceptance, you demonstrate respect for and belief in your children. These communications teach your children to respect and believe in themselves. When you use reflective listening to recognize your child's feelings, you teach your child that his or her feelings are both important and acceptable.

There is another way to build a closer relationship with your child, and that's what we'll be talking about today. Simply put, this new way to build your positive relationship involves sharing yourself with your child. What does that mean? It means that you let your child know and experience your own thoughts and feelings. Remember when we talked about evaluating your parent-child relationship? One of the signs of difficulty in the relationship is when a parent uses *destructive communication*. Destructive communication means communicating thoughts and feelings in a way that will not improve the parent-child relationship.

Let's consider some common examples of destructive communications between parents and children. One type of destructive communication occurs when a child has a problem and the parent solves that problem by telling the child the solution. Children cannot solve all problems without help, and parents sometimes need to give the child some information. But when you communicate solutions to your child, you send a hidden, destructive message

111

that says, "You are not competent enough to deal with this problem without my help." If a parent is almost always giving solutions to the child, then that parent's communication will be damaging to both the parent-child relationship and the child's developing sense of competence. Here are three examples of such destructive communication.

1. **Jimmy, age 4, is slowly picking up his toys and blocks and putting them away. The job is going slowly, because Jimmy tries to carry as much as possible on each trip, dropping many of the toys and blocks on the way to the toy box. His father says, "Jimmy, if you carry less you can get the job done faster. You would make more trips, but you wouldn't have to keep stopping to pick up the toys you drop."**

2. **"Susie, if you want your sand castle to stand, you need to build it farther from the water."**

3. **"Jeffrey, if you call each of our neighbors, maybe one of them will have a sleeping bag you could borrow."**

Each of these examples represents a situation in which either the child can be expected to eventually find the solution or the situation will teach the child the solution. The child will learn from the consequences of his or her behavior. The child doesn't need the parent to provide a solution.

A second type of destructive communication involves using the word you. When you want to share yourself with your child and build a closer relationship, you must understand the destructiveness of communications that use the word you. Here are four examples: *(Write the sentences in Figure 11a on the board, leaving enough room to write a new sentence beneath each.)*

In each of these examples, the child is being blamed and judged, yet he or she may not know exactly why. In each case, the parent is also giving the child a solution.

Now, sometimes this kind of communication is useful to parents, because it solves the immediate problem. But our focus today is on building better ongoing relationships with your children, and communications involving either a statement using the word you or giving the child the solution to a problem will not help you do that. In fact, these statements are a drain on the relationship. When you tell your child something using the word you, you are drawing a kind of line between the child (you) and the parent (I). Closeness involves sharing and being on the same side; creating an I-you division does not help you build a closer and more positive parent-child relationship.

There is a more constructive way to communicate with your child. First, you must recognize that parents often have strong feelings and emotions that need to be expressed. Your feelings, ideas, values, expectations, and standards are important, and they should be communicated to your child. The question is, how can you do this so that it helps you build a closer parent-child relationship?

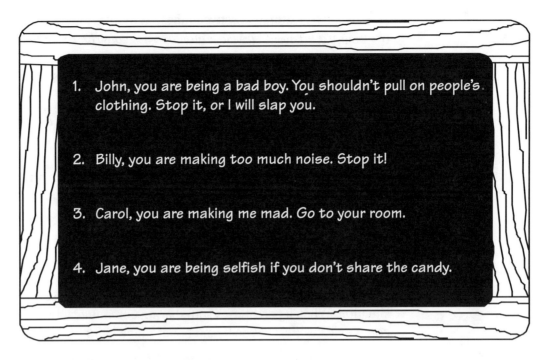

Figure 11a. Examples of destructive *you* statements.

Now, let's return to the four examples of destructive communication using the word *you* and restate them in a more constructive way, a way that is designed to build the parent-child relationship by using self-sharing statements: *(Write the four constructive statements beneath the four destructive ones.)*

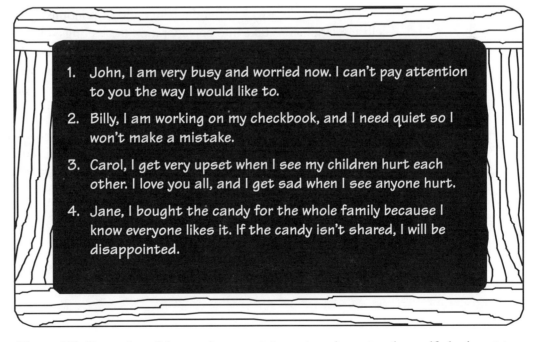

Figure 11b. Examples of destructive *you* statements and constructive, self-sharing statements.

What is the difference between these examples and the original ones? *(Pause for parents' response. You may wish to write the responses on the board.)* You can see that these new examples are more personal. The parents are sharing their own feelings, ideas, expectations, and standards. They are helping to build a closer parent-child relationship.

Note that this new set of sentences contains the word *I* instead of *you*. *(Write I and you on the board.)* Sentences that start with the word *I* and don't include the word *you* communicate the speaker's feelings, ideas, values, and expectations. This speaker is opening up his or her private world and saying, "I want you to know me and be close to me." Such self-sharing communications tell the listener, "You are somebody special."

Also notice that self-sharing communications don't involve providing solutions; they contain no advice, no warnings, and no counseling, and they don't put responsibility or blame on the other person. The child hears directly what the parent thinks and feels, and still is free to choose what to do in the situation. When a parent uses self-sharing communication, he or she communicates trust, respect, and belief in the child.

If a parent doesn't have a strong relationship with the child, then the child may ignore the parent's shared feelings, ideas, values, and expectations. This is one of the risks involved in using self-sharing communication. You could find out that your relationship with your child isn't as positive as you would like it to be. Your child may ignore your feelings and needs and continue with the problem behavior you were communicating about. So, make sure you're not trying to use self-sharing communication as a way to control your child's behavior.

Self-sharing is a way to build a better, closer relationship. People with close relationships take into consideration the feelings, ideas, values, and expectations of the people they love and feel close to. Self-sharing is a way in which close families influence each other's behavior, but the goal of the method is closeness, understanding, and love. The goal is not to gain power over one another.

Sometimes, parents use a *false I* when they try to use self-sharing communications. This occurs when a message starts with the word *I* and then actually includes solutions or some blame or judgment of the child. It is important to learn the difference between disguised destructive messages and real self-sharing messages.

Here are some examples: *(Write the sentences from Figure 12 on the board.)*

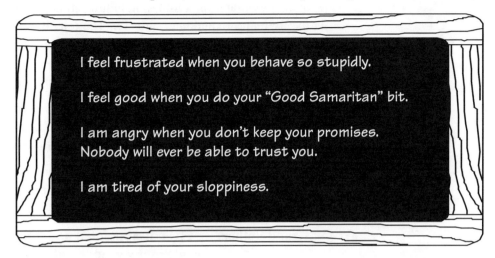

Figure 12. Disguised destructive messages.

In each of these statements, there is a sense of "I feel" from the speaker, but name-calling, sarcasm, and solution-sending are also present. The form of self-sharing is there, but not the spirit.

So far, we've identified three kinds of communication that affect the closeness of your relationship with your child: destructive, false self-sharing, and genuine self-sharing. *(Write the three headings from Figure 13 on the board, and then describe the points under each as you write them on the board.)*

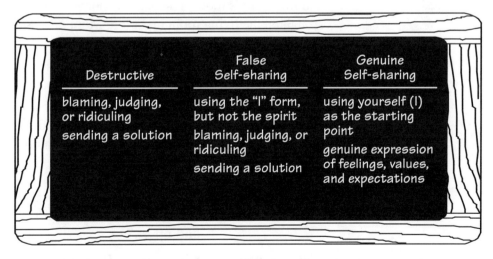

Figure 13. Three kinds of communication that affect the closeness of a parent-child relationship.

I am going to read you two stories. Use the chart on the board to decide what kind of message each character in the story is sending.

It's been a long week and a very hard day for Mr. and Mrs. Brown. Dinner is over and the family, including Timmy's grandmother, is relaxing in the living room and watching TV. The telephone rings. Timmy's kindergarten teacher tells Mr. Brown that Timmy was cursing that day in school. After the call, Mr. Brown tells the whole family, including Timmy, what the teacher said. Each person has something to say to Timmy:

Dad:	**"When I hear these stories from your teacher I get angry and disappointed, because you behaved like a lousy, rotten kid. I could break your neck."**
Mom:	**"Timmy dear, you really ought to know better. You can see how you've upset your father and the whole family."**
Grandmother:	**"I feel disappointed and kind of sad. I have a lot of pride in my grandchildren. I wonder what might have happened in school."**

Given what was said, to which adult will Timmy probably feel closest? Can you identify which adult is using each communication style on the board? *(Take a few minutes for parents to answer and discuss their impressions.)* Exactly. Timmy's mom used destructive communication. His dad used the word *I*, but the spirit of Dad's message was still destructive. Timmy will probably feel closest to his grandmother, because she is genuinely sharing herself, using "I" statements, and she is not blaming, judging, or giving Timmy a solution. Let's try another one.

Rosemary, a 6-year-old, is playing with her toys in the living room. Before long, they are scattered all over. It is getting close to dinner time, and Rosemary's mom is on her way home from work. Dad wants to straighten the living room up before Mom gets home. He asks Rosemary to clean up her toys. Rosemary says, "Okay," but 15 minutes pass and the room is still a mess. Rosemary's father gives her three different messages in the following conversation:

Father:	**"Now Rosemary, I don't like to scold you, but you should expect me to scold you when you don't do what you're supposed to do. Now get going."**
Rosemary:	**"But Dad, I was busy."**
Father:	**"Rosemary, when you promise to do something, I count on it. Then if it isn't done, I get disappointed and upset."**
Rosemary:	**"Okay, okay, I'll put them away. You don't have to get mad."**
Father:	**"Not get mad! Ha! I get really angry when you play dumb with me. Of course I get angry when you don't do what you're supposed to do!"**

Which one of the three responses will help Rosemary feel closer to her father? Can you identify the destructive comment, the phony sharing comment, and the genuine self-sharing communication in Dad's replies? *(Allow time for parents' discussion and analysis. Reinforce and then summarize the discussion.)*

You have the basic idea. Next we'll practice giving self-sharing replies to some common things children do and say. I will give you some examples of bad parent communication. Each time, I want you to change the response to one that involves genuine self-sharing.

Child: **"I really love you, Mommy."**

Mother: **"That's nice, John."**

What might be a self-sharing response to this child? *(Pause for parents' response. If necessary, prompt parents by providing the initial part of their response, i.e., "I feel _____" or "When you say that, I feel _____." Continue to prompt, as necessary, as you discuss the following examples.)*

A child is jumping up and down on the sofa while Dad is resting. The father says, "Stop being a pest or you'll get a smack, young man."

What would be a self-sharing response? *(Pause for parents' response. It might be, "I am trying to rest. I am very tired, and I don't want to play right now.")*

Mother watches her 5-year-old daughter helping her 3-year-old daughter. Mother says, "You are a good girl when you help your sister."

What would a self-sharing communication be? *(Pause for parents' response. It might be, "When I see you help your sister, it makes me feel good inside. It's like seeing love in action.")*

Billy keeps interrupting while his father is trying to repair the lawn mower. Dad says, "Billy, stop bothering me. I am busy. Do you hear me? Get going!"

What would be a self-sharing reaction? *(Pause for parents' response. It might be, "Billy, I am very busy and it's important to me that I finish this job soon. Each time you interrupt me, I forget what I was doing and I could make a mistake and ruin the machine.")*

You all seem to understand how to give a self-sharing response to your child. Can anyone think of a situation or a typical child's remark that we could use to practice some more self-sharing responses?

(Pause for parents' response. List the situations and comments the parents describe on the board. Collect 9-12 responses. If necessary, use one or more of the extra examples in the following list to bring your total to 12. Once the list of examples is complete, divide the group into triads. Explain that the small groups will now role-play, just as they did during Session 6. Each group

member will take a turn being child, parent, and observer. In this exercise, however, parents will practice both self-sharing communication and reflective listening when they play the parent.)

(Use the following extra examples for use in the role-playing exercise if needed:)

1. **Sally, age 8, has just come home from school. She runs into the living room where her mother is resting. Sally says, "Mama, please fix me some cookies and milk so I can have a picnic with Jerry. I need them right away!"**

2. **June, age 5, continues to run through the house after repeated attempts by her mother to stop her. Finally, June knocks against a table, and her mother's favorite plant falls to the floor and is ruined. June, looking scared, says to her mother, "I didn't mean to break your flower, Mommy."**

3. **Seven-year-old Dylan makes a pretty card for his father's birthday. He proudly gives it to his father at breakfast, saying, "Happy birthday, Daddy. I made you a card!"**

4. **John, age $3^1/2$, gets very frustrated while trying to ride his tricycle backwards in a straight line. After several attempts, he begins to cry and scream loudly. This becomes very annoying to his mother, who is trying to read nearby. John yells, "I can't make it go right! This is a stupid tricycle!"**

5. **Stephen, age 7, asks to help his father wash the family car. "Dad, can I help you wash the car today? Then it'll look just like new!"**

6. **Mary, age 4, has once again lost her doll. Her mother is talking on the phone when Mary comes to her in tears saying, "Mommy, my baby got lost again. Please find her."**

7. **Peggy, age 8, is responsible for taking the trash out after dinner every night. For the past two nights, however, she has gone out to play soccer right after dinner, forgetting to empty the trash. This is the third night; the garbage is piling up, and Peggy says, "I'm getting really good at making goals 'cause I've practiced so much."**

8. **Tommy, age 10, is involved in many different activities. He is constantly asking his parents to drive him places. After making several requests during the week, Tommy comes to his father on Saturday and says, "Dad, can you take me over to Kenny's? I'll call you when I'm ready to come home, okay?"**

9. **Scott, age $2^1/2$, gets very mad at his mother as she tries to dress him. He hits her and says, "No! Scott do it!"**

10. **Laurie, age 7, has been chosen by her teacher to play the lead part in the class play. Laurie excitedly tells her parents, "Mrs. Smith wants me to be Goldilocks in our play. She said that's a real important part."**

Practice Exercise in Role-Playing

(Use the following directions for the small group role-playing activity:)

Now you'll use the situations and comments on the board to practice self-sharing statements and reflective listening. I want you to move into groups of three the way you did for our last role-playing activity. Again, you'll each have a chance to be the child, the parent, and the observer.

1. The child will begin by explaining the situation, and will then initiate the conversation by saying his or her line. During the role-playing activities, the child should pay attention to his or her feelings and reactions to the parent's responses.

2. Each parent should respond with a self-sharing statement. Continue the conversation for 2 or 3 minutes, and make sure to use a self-sharing statement at least once more. Use reflective listening when it seems appropriate. Pay attention to your feelings during the role-playing activity.

3. The observer must pay close attention to the parent's statements as well as how the child is responding to those statements. Afterward, the observer should be prepared to tell the parent how appropriate the self-sharing and reflective listening statements were and to give suggestions as to other times such statements could have been used.

There are 12 examples. After you finish each of the situations, take a few minutes to discuss what happened and get feedback from the observer. *(During the role-playing activity, move from group to group, making sure everyone is understanding and performing the assigned role successfully. Give cues where needed. If appropriate, share some of the small group responses with the whole group at the end of the exercise.)*

Before we finish this session, I want to remind you that self-sharing responses do help parents to build a closer relationship with their children. You will not always be able to give self-sharing responses, however, and you should not expect that of yourself. Although self-sharing responses must occur regularly if you are to become close to your child, they will not always be possible. *(Pause.)* Remember, self-sharing responses are not given to manipulate a child, to make the child feel guilty, or to control the child's behavior. People with close relationships consider the feelings of others. People in a close relationship will often decide not to do something because of how it will affect the other person. This will happen in your relationship with your child only as that relationship grows stronger. If you use self-sharing to manipulate or control your child, the child will learn to share his or her own feelings as a way of manipulating and controlling others. This will damage both your own parent-child relationship and your child's future relationships as well.

General Discussion

What are some of your reactions to the idea of sharing yourself with your child? How can you start using self-sharing and reflective listening in your own families? *(Pause for parents' response. Encourage parents to apply the new self-sharing and reflective listening skills to their own situations. Remember to address parents' reactions to sharing feelings with their children.)*

In our next session, you'll get some additional practice with these three techniques for building better, stronger relationships with your children:

1. Communicating love and acceptance

2. Using reflective listening

3. Sharing yourself by communicating your own thoughts and feelings.

Discussion of the Home Practice Assignment

Please be sure to bring your home practice exercises for this week to our next session, because we'll be using them to practice these three techniques.

References

Gordon, T. (1970). *Parent effectiveness training.* New York: Peter W. Wyden.

Jourard, S. M. (1971a). *Self-disclosure: An experimental analysis of the transparent self.* New York: Wiley.

Jourard, S. M. (1971b). *The transparent self.* New York: D. Van Nostrand.

Rogers, C. R. (1957). The necessary and sufficient conditions of therapeutic personality change. *Journal of Consulting Psychology, 21,* 95-103.

Rogers, C. R. (1961). *On becoming a person.* Boston: Houghton Mifflin.

Rogers, C. R. (1975). Empathetic: An unappreciated way of being. *The Counseling Psychologist, 5,* 2-10.

Stricker, G., & Fisher, M. (Eds.). (1990). *Self-disclosure in the therapeutic relationship* (pp. 61-71, 75-88, 103-115, 157-172, 277-289). New York: Plenum.

Building a Relationship—Review and Practice of Three Techniques

Special Notes for the Mental Health Professional

Encourage sharing, but take care when you point out any parental errors, as parents are particularly vulnerable during this sharing exercise. It is a good idea to use praise and to incorporate the ideas presented in Session 2 along with the tutoring techniques suggested in Session 22.

Sequence

- Review and sharing of home practice (5 - 10 minutes)
- Review of the three techniques for building better relationships (5 - 10 minutes)
- Practicing the three techniques (50 - 65 minutes)
- Discussion of the home practice assignment (5 - 10 minutes)

Review and Sharing of Home Practice Experiences

Q What were some of your reactions to the home practice assignment from Session 7? *(Pause for parents' response. All parents should get a chance to speak and share their home practice experiences.)*

Lecture/Discussion

Building Better Parent-Child Relationships

Today we are going to use the situations you brought with you to practice building better relationships with your children. First, let's take a moment to review the three ways you can do that.

One way is to communicate love and acceptance. *(Write this on the board.)* This type of communication can range from simply saying that you love or appreciate your child to demonstrating that love through actions such as touching or sharing in your child's activities—but without taking over. Two other specific ways to communicate love and acceptance are letting your child enjoy his or her activity without your interference or direction and allowing your child to experience that you, the parent, are a good listener.

Another technique for building better relationships is to listen for feelings. *(Write this on the board.)* When you listen for feelings, your child experiences you, the parent, as understanding and accepting of his or her feelings along with the words. This lets your child know that you recognize his or her feelings as important and the experience increases and strengthens the parent-child bonds.

A third technique is sharing yourself by communicating your own thoughts and feelings. *(Write this on the board.)* The identifying characteristics of genuine self-sharing communications are that they include the word *I* and that they do not state solutions or use any judgmental words.

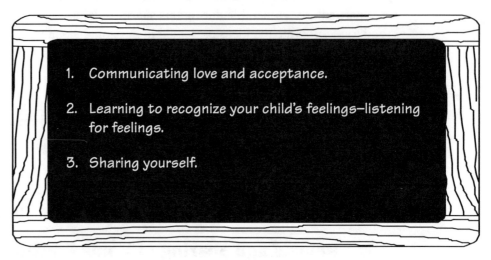

1. Communicating love and acceptance.

2. Learning to recognize your child's feelings—listening for feelings.

3. Sharing yourself.

Figure 12. Three techniques for building better parent-child relationships.

Practicing the Three Techniques

I think we can give some of the examples you brought with you a try. *(The remainder of this session should be spent on practice. If your parents don't provide enough good situations for the role-playing activity, suggest one or more of the unused examples from Session 7. Have the parents consider and point out how each of the three major techniques can be used in every example they present. The use of role playing, first in the large group and, eventually, in small groups of four, is helpful for practicing these techniques. You should start out as a major actor in the large group's role playing. Later, when small groups are formed, you should act as consultant and coach.)*

8 Providing Discipline

Discipline in the Parent-Child Relationship

Introduction

When we hear the words *discipline a child*, the idea often seems to be to *punish* a child. Discipline is a word derived from Latin that means "to teach," and it is in this sense that we will approach the topic.

The purpose of this session is to help parents explore their belief systems about discipline. The basic approach is to consider discipline in the context of the overall parent-child relationship (Belsky, Lerner, & Spanier, 1984). The central goal is not abstract consideration of which are good or poor discipline techniques, but rather to develop an understanding of the need to match any disciplinary action to the specific situation. What will be the immediate and long-term effects of a specific approach be on the parent-child relationship? What impact will a disciplinary action have on the child's self esteem, on the child's working model of self? What approach in a specific situation will increase the likelihood that the child will internalize the values and expectations of the parent?

Discipline and limit setting need to be presented as essential parental teaching functions that are designed to help ensure that their child will be able to function effectively in a social world (Fry, 1993; Miller, 1984). The issue is not to impose parental will, but to help children recognize that they are making choices and that different choices result in different consequences. Thus, discipline can be understood both from the perspective of what the parents do in relation to their child, and also from the standpoint of self-discipline. Self-discipline is the quality of self-regulation that a child develops as a result of appropriate parental guidance. The lessons of discipline are learned gradually and need to be adjusted as the child grows and develops. A 3-year-old may be taught not to hit someone who takes his or her toys, but, by age 6, children need to learn the more complex task of when to seek help and when to physically defend themselves against others' aggression. Parents should be encouraged to reflect on the attitudes and beliefs that their children may be developing as a result of the discipline approaches they currently use (Shaw & Scott, 1991). In short, parents need to understand the role of discipline from both their own and the child's perspectives. What is the immediate problem? What message is the parent's action sending the child about himself or herself and about how the child should handle similar problems in the future (Ginsburg & Bronstein, 1993)?

The research literature (e.g., Dishion, Patterson, & Kavanagh, 1992; Gottman & Katz, 1989; Patterson, 1982) suggests that the extremes of parenting styles—unresponsive or permissive versus overcontrolling or authoritarian; involved or warm versus distant or rejecting—are associated with children's behavior (i.e., unresponsive or permissive parental interactions have been found to be linked to children's angry and noncompliant behaviors). Chamberlain and Patterson (1995) describe the impact of different disciplinary approaches on the parent-child relationship and the question of child compliance.

Session Objectives

1 To show why extremely permissive or extremely restrictive discipline should be avoided; to demonstrate that moderate discipline, whether permissive or authoritarian, is the most effective.

2 To help parents recognize the extreme ranges of discipline that are possible.

3 To help parents recognize that discipline must be constructive, not revengeful. Discipline should provide a learning situation in which the child can internalize standards set by his or her parents.

4 To demonstrate how parental warmth moderates the effects of discipline.

5 To point out the importance of consistency in discipline. Consistency leads to emotional security and smoother functioning in families.

Sequence

● Review and sharing of home practice (5-10 minutes)

● Lecture/Discussion (30 minutes)

● General discussion (30 - 40 minutes)

● Discussion of the home practice assignment (5 - 10 minutes)

Review and Sharing of Home Practice Experiences

Q What were some of your reactions to the home practice assignment from Session 8? *(Pause for parents' response. All parents should get a chance to speak and share their home practice experiences.)*

Lecture/Discussion

Discipline as a Positive and Constructive Process

Today we are going to discuss discipline. *(Write the word Discipline on the board.)* For many people, the word discipline sounds harsh and old-fashioned, and it is often associated with punishment, fear, and pain. But this is a negative way to look at discipline. Today we will be discussing discipline as a positive and constructive process. Discipline is a process of guiding your child in his or her development by providing appropriate learning situations. Discipline is not a way to *make* your child do the right thing; rather, it is the process of helping your child learn and want to do the right thing.

Optional Exercise

Before we begin our discussion of discipline, I thought it might be helpful if we all tried to get in touch with our memories of how our own parents disciplined us. *(Take a long pause.)*

Q Who would like to share some of the ways your parents disciplined you? It is probably best if we talk about methods our parents used frequently. *(Pause for parents' response. If no parent is willing to begin, this would be a good time for you to share a disciplinary method from your own childhood, in order to get the exercise going.)*

Q Do these examples remind you of some of the methods that your own parents used? *(Pause for parents' response.)*

As parents, we often wonder if the way we discipline our child is the best way. You might ask yourself, "Am I too permissive?" *(Write the words Too Permissive on the board.)* You may wonder if you give your children full rein to do what they want to do whenever they want to do it.

At the opposite extreme you might ask, "Am I too restrictive?" *(Write the words Too Restrictive on the board.)* Do you demand strict obedience to your commands, without letting your child question, or even discuss, the rules?

It is unreasonable to think that giving a child complete freedom will help the child develop into a normal, well adjusted adult. Overly permissive parents go too far in one direction. They place few restrictions on their child, letting the child interrupt their conversations, eat his or her meals whenever he or she chooses, and leave possessions and playthings all over the house. In short, permissive parents allow their child's undesirable behavior to be practiced, learned, and developed. When these undesirable behaviors occur outside the home, they can lead to terrible consequences for the child. Here's an example of what an overly permissive mother might say about her 4-year-old daughter:

It's beginning to be really difficult to get Jane to bed at night. At 8:00, I tell her it's time for bed, but she stays up and plays anyway. Sometimes I think she's gone to bed, and then I hear her playing in her room. She often comes out and watches television with us. I let her, but I would really like her to go to bed when I tell her to. Oh well. She'll go to bed when she gets tired. I don't want her to think I'm a dictator.

This 4-year-old stays up until 10:00 or 11:00 every night, leaving her parents almost no time to be alone together. This mom is too lenient. Jane is getting her way at the expense of her parents' needs. Jane's mom is not using any control or placing any limits on her behavior. Jane is being taught to be selfish.

Children who have few—if any—controls and limits placed on them experience a variety of problems as they grow up. Bedtime and mealtime limits, such as starting meals on time, going to bed after Dad reads a story, or having your day end at a regular time, are all very important. Being in a predictable world helps children to develop a sense of time and a feeling of security. Limits also help children learn that living in a social world requires being concerned about the feelings and rights of others.

Research shows that a child whose parents have been overly permissive often grows up lacking in self-control. That child as an adult might very well be selfish, unmanageable, uncooperative, and inconsiderate of others.

Overly restrictive parents err in the opposite direction. They may think that they are being strict for the sake of their child, but this strictness tends to hide their love from the child. Overly restrictive parents often give constant directions and frequent punishment, and they tend to insist on perfection from their children. Here is an example of a conversation between an overly strict mother and her son:

Mother:	**It's 8:00, Johnny. Time for bed.**
Johnny:	**Oh mom, do I have to? Why can't I stay up just a few more minutes?**
Mother:	**8:00 is bedtime. Don't ask questions. Just go to the bathroom and then to bed.**
Johnny:	**But…**
Mother:	**No buts. Do what I say, or you'll wind up with a spanking.**

Johnny gets up slowly, and his mother smacks him for taking too much time. This mother is overly controlling. She gives a command and then expects it to be obeyed immediately. Johnny is given no explanation as to why he can't stay up a little later; he is only threatened with a spanking.

Research shows that when parents are overly strict, one of two patterns is likely to develop in their children. In the first pattern, the children of strict parents learn to be timid, shy, and withdrawn from others. They tend to be unhappy and to play by themselves, afraid to make friends and play with others. In the second pattern, these children often develop into self-centered, aggressive individuals, who can become uncooperative and argumentative. In fact, individuals who are frequently spanked as children often exhibit aggressive and destructive behaviors as adolescents and adults.

You can see that using either extremely permissive or extremely severe discipline methods can be harmful to your child. Children who are disciplined with either of these methods are more likely to develop emotional problems and aggressive or destructive behaviors later on in life. Finding a moderate, middle ground in discipline is the key to helping your child grow into a mature, responsible, and well adjusted adult.

(Write the words Moderate Discipline on the board.)

Assume that you want to be moderate in your methods of discipline. Now the question becomes, "How do you know when you are being too severe or too permissive?"

Q What guidelines can you think of that might indicate discipline that is too severe? *(Pause for parents' response. Make sure you discuss or summarize the following four situations that might lead a parent to choose severe discipline.)*

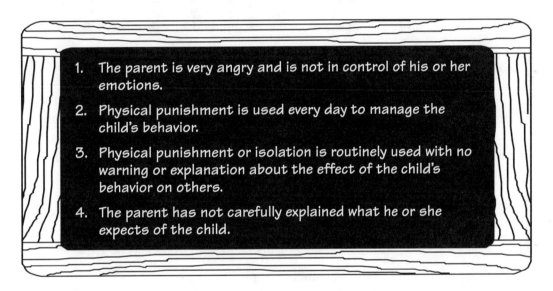

1. The parent is very angry and is not in control of his or her emotions.

2. Physical punishment is used every day to manage the child's behavior.

3. Physical punishment or isolation is routinely used with no warning or explanation about the effect of the child's behavior on others.

4. The parent has not carefully explained what he or she expects of the child.

Figure 14. Four situations that exemplify severe discipline.

Q What signs would indicate parenting that is too permissive? *(Pause for parents' response. Make sure you discuss or summarize the following four situations that might lead to overly permissive parenting.)*

Here are some examples of overly permissive and overly strict discipline:

Jimmy's parents are having company at 7:00. Jimmy, age 4, has been put to bed; as usual, he refuses to stay there. His parents say nothing and allow him to stay up, hoping he will soon get tired. As the company arrives, Jimmy runs to the door and begins charming the guests. By 10:00, Jimmy is sipping people's drinks, interrupting conversations with his tumbling act, and getting piggy-back rides from the guests. By 10:30, he is cranky and crying, and he insists that his mother stay in his room until he falls asleep—usually around 11:00.

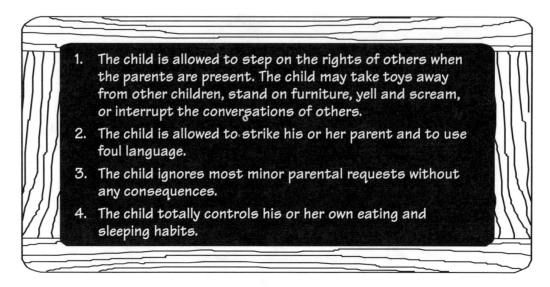

Figure 15. Four situations that exemplify overly permissive discipline.

Jimmy's parents are overly permissive. They have allowed Jimmy to stay up past his bedtime, disrupt conversations, and disturb their guests. If Jimmy had experienced and learned to accept limits in the past, this situation might have been very different. If Jimmy's mom or dad had explained (in the past) why he had to go to bed and had insisted that he remain in his room, he would have become accustomed to bedtime limits. This disruption and annoyance might have been avoided altogether. Remember, children are always learning. The night of his parents' party, Jimmy learned to be self-centered, to ignore the rights of others, and to believe he is the center of the world. With permissive parenting, Jimmy will continue to learn these lessons; and what he learns will undoubtedly cause him trouble as he grows up.

Here's another example:

Mrs. Johnson takes her 4-year-old daughter, Sharon, to the playground. When they get to the park, Mrs. Johnson says, "Sharon, you must play in the sandbox first. I'll tell you when it's okay to go on the swing and the slide. Remember, don't get your clothes all dirty like a nasty girl." Later on, Mrs. Johnson feeds Sharon some candy, placing each piece in Sharon's mouth so Sharon won't get all messy. When Sharon wanders about 100 feet away, her mother gets very upset. Mrs. Johnson yanks Sharon by the hand, gives her a smack on the bottom, and says, "How many times have I told you not to leave my sight?"

Q How would you rate this parent? Is she permissive or overly strict? *(Pause for parents to respond that this mother is overly strict.)*

Exactly. Mrs. Johnson was dominating and controlling Sharon by giving her too many commands and restrictions. Although she was trying to be a good and concerned mother, Mrs. Johnson went too far. She has now become a dictator or a prison guard. She wants to prevent all possible accidents and mistakes, so she demands a degree of self-control and memory that no 4-year-old child is likely to have.

Here's another example:

Mrs. Archer says to her son: "No Tom, you can't play with your blocks today. I know you are disappointed, but I've told you that you have to pick the blocks up before bedtime. Last night I had to pick them up. I'm tired at night, and I don't want to do your work. I know you are sad, Tom, but you can play with your blocks tomorrow." Tom starts crying loudly. His mother says, "Tom, if you keep crying, I will put you to bed. I know you are disappointed, but you can't play with the blocks today." Mrs. Archer walks away.

Q How would you describe this interaction? Is Mrs. Archer overly permissive, overly restrictive, or something else? *(Pause for parents' response.)*

Yes. Mrs. Archer handled Tom with firmness, but her discipline is reasonable in terms of her expectations, the consequences she imposes, and her sensitivity to Tom's feelings.

Now let's consider a situation that calls for discipline and see if you can decide on an appropriate moderate discipline for this child:

Four-year-old Jimmy just scribbled all over the dining room wall with red crayon. This is the first time this has ever happened.

Q What might an overly permissive parent do? *(Write the words Too Permissive on the board. Pause for parents' response. Write their responses under the heading.)* What might an overly strict parent do? *(Write the words Too Restrictive on the board. Pause for parents' response. Write their responses under the heading.)*

Q What might moderate discipline be like in this situation? *(Write the words Moderate Discipline on the board. Pause for parents' response. The discussion should include suggestions like: "Jimmy, you wrote on the dining room walls and now they are messy. I'm very proud of our house, and I want it to look neat. If you want to draw, I will help you get a big piece of paper. First, you have to clean up the mess you made. After you clean up those marks, you can play some more.")*

Let me summarize what we've talked about so far.

1. Children need discipline.

2. Discipline should provide the child with an experience from which he or she can learn. This means presenting the child with a clear picture of what you expect, and why you expect it.

3. Being too permissive or too strict causes problems as the child grows up.

4. All parents are too permissive and too severe sometimes. That's okay as long as most of the discipline that a child experiences is moderate.

There is one very important idea to remember about discipline and its effects on children: The destructive effects of either permissive or strict discipline can be moderated by the amount of love and warmth in your parent-child relationship. For example, a permissive parent who has a disconnected or negative parent-child relationship may actually increase the destructive effects of his or her discipline on the child. Likewise, an overly strict parent who is distant, cold, and insensitive to the child's feelings will increase the destructive effects of his or her discipline.

Think again about that relationship "savings account." When there are plenty of warm, positive feelings in the account, the destructive effects of either strict or permissive discipline methods are decreased. The more warm, gentle, and affectionate you are as a parent, the healthier your child's development will be—regardless of your discipline style. Parents who tend toward permissiveness, but who are also warm and affectionate, often produce children who are friendly, independent, and self-confident. These children can be really good problem-solvers. Warm and loving parents who tend toward the restrictive end of the continuum tend to raise children who are polite, neat, less aggressive, and more considerate of others. These children are less likely to get into trouble at home and at school than children of cold, distant, and restrictive parents. Both types of children are happy and well adjusted. *(Pause.)* It doesn't matter whether a parent uses moderate permissiveness or moderate restrictiveness, as long as that parent avoids the extremes and demonstrates plenty of love and warmth.

Here are some parent-child interactions which contain signs of love, warmth, and affection:

Child: **Dad, look at the picture I drew at school today.**

Father: **That's really pretty. It looks like you worked very hard on it. You should be pleased with your work.**

Child: **Yeah. It was a lot of fun, too. Now I'm drawing another picture in the kitchen.**

Father: **Well, it's getting close to your bedtime.**

Child: **Dad, can't I stay up a little longer so I can finish it?**

Father: **All right. But when you're finished, you have to go to bed.**

Child: **Okay, Dad. Thanks.**

This is an example of a warm, permissive father. He demonstrates his warmth by showing appreciation for his son's drawing and by praising him. We consider him permissive because he let his child stay up past bedtime to finish something the child considered important.

Here's another example:

Four-year-old Mary comes into the kitchen while her mother is fixing dinner.

Mary: **Mommy, I'm hungry. Can I have a snack?**

Mother: *(In a firm tone of voice.)* **No, Mary. If you have a snack now, you won't want to eat your dinner.**

Mary: **Please Mommy. Do you want me to starve to death?**

Mother: **Of course not. But you can't have a snack now. We'll eat dinner in 15 minutes, and I'll save you two cookies for a special dessert.**

Q We might call this mom warm and restrictive. Why? *(Pause for parents' response, which should include the following ideas: Mother is warm because of the friendly interchange and because she gave a reasonable explanation for her decision. She is restrictive, because she was firm with Mary and did not give in to Mary's request.)*

Now, listen to another example. Try to figure out what kind of discipline this parent is using.

Five-year-old Rachel is watching her mother mow the lawn.

Rachel: **Mom, I want to help mow the lawn. Can I?**

Mother: *(In an annoyed tone of voice.)* **You asked that last week. What did I tell you then?**

Rachel: **You said no. But can I do it today?**

Mother: **No.**

Rachel: **Why not, Mom?**

Mother: *(No response.)*

Rachel: **Why, Mom?**

Mother: **Stop asking me stupid questions and stay out of the way of the lawnmower.**

Q How would you describe this method of limit-setting, and why? *(Pause for parents' response.)*

Q What might a warm, restrictive parent say? *(Pause for parents' response, which should include the following idea: "Rachel, I would like your help when you get older. A lawn mower is dangerous, and I don't want you to get hurt. Would you like to hold the handle with me for a while?")*

Yes, this mother shows warmth. She gives Rachel a reason why she cannot mow the lawn, explains her reason, and tells Rachel that she will be allowed to use the lawn mower when she gets older.

So far, we've learned three things about discipline:

1. Discipline does not have to be the harsh, old-fashioned, punishing method. It can be constructive. Discipline can provide your child with a learning situation in which he or she can develop the standards of behavior you expect.

2. Extreme permissiveness and extreme restrictiveness both have damaging effects on a child's development. When a parent uses either method in the extreme, the child is more likely to develop emotional and behavior problems.

3. Moderate discipline, whether permissive or restrictive, is the better practice. When combined with warmth and affection for your child, moderate discipline of either type provides optimal results.

Now there's one last important point about discipline, and that is that discipline should be applied *consistently*. (*Write the word Consistency on the board.*) Sometimes, your discipline will be inconsistent. After all, we are not machines. Consistent discipline, however, makes your child's world more predictable. If your child knows what you will do in certain circumstances, he or she will know what your expectations are and how to behave in those circumstances. Children who are exposed to very inconsistent discipline have no way of knowing what will happen as a result of what they do. The rules are always changing, or they have never been clearly stated. These children cannot develop standards of behavior, because their parents' standards are always changing.

It is not important that we do the same thing every time—that would be impossible. What we can do, however, is teach our children to predict changing rules by explaining how certain situations might change the existing rules. Here are two examples of how a parent might do this:

Dad usually puts the children to bed and talks with them or reads to them before they go to sleep. On nights when he isn't feeling well or doesn't have the time, he can change the bedtime limits by explaining, "Tonight I am tired and don't feel like talking. I would like you to go to bed quickly."

A mother who normally tolerates a noisy home might explain, "I am upset about something today, so I need your help. Please play as quietly as you can."

It also helps if the look on your face matches the words you are using. In the first example, the father might naturally have a tired look on his face. In the second, the mother will probably look sad. These facial expressions are reinforcing the signal that the *specific situation* is changing the rules.

Many parents find it helpful to develop a specific signal that tells their child the parent "has had it." When the child sees this signal, he or she knows it's time to walk softly. This signal could be a look, a word, or both. The signal should not be frightening or threatening, and it should not be overused. When you do use a signal like this, you must follow through with your child. This means imposing consequences when your signal is ignored. Let me give you an example:

When Dad sees his son, who is normally called Mike, approach a limit, he will say something like this *(in a soft and deliberate manner)*: **"Michael, (pause) do you hear me? I want you to either sit down and watch TV or go to bed."**

The first part of Dad's statement is the signal, and it's always the same. When Mike hears the words, "Michael, do you hear me?" he knows he has reached a limit. Whenever his father says, "Michael, do you hear me?" Mike knows that what his father says next is a firm rule that must be obeyed.

General Discussion

Q Does anyone already have a signal like the one I just described? Did any of your own parents use a signal like that with you? (Let parents *discuss these questions.*)

Q Are there any questions or reactions to what we've discussed?

Discussion of the Home Practice Assignment

This week's home practice assignment will help you to become more aware of your own parenting style—how permissive or restrictive you are with your child and how much warmth you show in your interactions. As you are completing the assignment, you may realize that there are some specific areas or issues where you tend to become more or less restrictive or where you tend to show more or less warmth. By reviewing these situations, you will be in a better position to decide whether your actions and responses are helping or hurting your relationship with your child.

References

Belsky, J., Lerner, R. M., & Spanier, G. B. (1984). *The child in the family* (pp. 66-70). Reading, MA: Addison Wesley.

Chamberlain, P., & Patterson, G. R. (1995). Discipline and child compliance in parenting. In M. H. Bornstein (Ed.). *Handbook of parenting*. Mahwah, NJ: Erlbaum.

Dishion, T. J., Patterson, G. R., & Kavanagh, K. A. (1992). An experimental test of the coercion model: Linking theory, measurement, and intervention. In J. McCord & R. E. Tremblay (Eds.), *Preventing antisocial behavior: Interventions from birth throughout adolescence* (pp. 253-282). New York: Guilford.

Fry, D. P. (1993). The intergenerational transmission of disciplinary practices and approaches to conflict. *Human Organizations*, *52*, 176-185.

Gottman, J. M., & Katz, L. F. (1989). Effects of marital discord on young children's peer interactions and health. *Developmental Psychology*, *25*, 373-381.

Ginsburg G. S., & Bronstein, (1993). Family factors related to children's intrinsic/extrinsic motivational orientation and academic performance. *Child Development. 64*, 1461-1474.

Patterson, G. R. (1982). *Coercive family process*. Eugene, OR: Castalia.

Miller, A. (1984). *For your own good*. New York: Farrar, Straus & Giroux.

Shaw, J. M., & Scott, W. A. (1991). Influence of parent discipline style on delinquent behavior: The mediating influence of control orientation. *Australian Journal of Psychology*, *43*, 61-67.

9 Managing Children's Behavior

Introduction to Sessions 10-15

The six sessions on managing children's behavior form a sequence designed to teach the basic concepts of behavioral psychology. You must approach this material with the highest degree of warmth and interpersonal sensitivity, avoiding any appearance of a mechanical delivery style. There should be no difference between your presentation of this new material and your presentation of the more humanistic approaches presented in earlier sessions. Each of the skills learned by parents early in the program is essential to, and compatible with, the behavioral principles you will present in the following sessions. Encourage (and continue to remind) parents to use reflective listening and self-sharing in combination with these new behavioral principles. In the context of a good parent-child relationship, these behavior management techniques will help clarify communication, provide structure for conflict resolution, and allow parents to attain their positive goals. The idea of using behavioral principles to impose one's will on another person—or to train children as one would train a dog—is a complete contradiction of the goals and objectives of this Early Childhood Parenting Skills Training Program.

In the first of these six sessions, Who Owns the Problem?—Resolving Conflicts, parents will become aware that not *all* of their children's problems are the parents' problems and that children have the *right* to work through their own problems.

In the second of these sessions, Using Behavior Modification Principles, parents will learn and practice a variety of basic skills and ideas essential to the successful use of behavioral modification principles with children.

In the third session, parents will focus on the way consequences can encourage and discourage specific behaviors. They will learn how to recognize the specific things that are important and reinforcing to their own children as a way of building a stronger parent-child relationship.

The fourth, fifth, and sixth sessions deal with recording behavior and setting consequences, using appropriate reinforcers, and using the ABC behavior modification method on oneself.

Session
10

Who Owns the Problem? — Resolving Conflicts

Special Notes for the Mental Health Professional

This first session is divided into three parts: (a) Parent Problems, (b) Child Problems, and (c) Shared Problems. This three-part design will help parents learn how to analyze problems and will also free parents from the burden of being constantly responsible for solving all the problems that involve their children.

Parents may express guilt about not helping their children when they have problems, and this issue must be addressed. To offset this guilt, emphasize the fact that when children work out problems for themselves they build strength for handling future problems with an enhanced sense of their own competence. As parents begin to understand how important it is for children to solve their own problems, the parents' discomfort and guilt are usually lessened. As you discuss the idea of shared problems, be sure to help parents understand how reflective listening and self-sharing can help them to resolve conflicts or, at least, help them to clarify a conflict or the issues underlying that conflict.

The exercises at the end of this session will demonstrate the limits of reflective listening and self-sharing. Emphasize that reflective listening and self-sharing won't work when a parent is unwilling to compromise or when the ongoing parent-child relationship is not a healthy one. You may find that some parents will report (almost triumphantly), "We tried, but we are still in conflict." This discussion of irreconcilable differences will actually become the springboard for the concept of negotiating compromise agreements. Parents should be advised that, when they must *enforce* a decision or a solution on a younger child, they can't always expect good-natured compliance; they must learn to recognize the child's true feelings through reflective listening. With older children, parents should be encouraged to persevere in the technique of negotiation, because imposed solutions rarely work with teenagers.

Session Objectives

1 To help parents become aware that not all of a child's problems are the parent's problems, and that children have the right to work through their own problems.

2 To help parents see how listening for feelings, self-sharing, and showing acceptance can help children solve their own problems.

Sequence

- Review and sharing of home practice (20 - 30 minutes)
- Lecture/Discussion (30 - 40 minutes)
- General discussion (30 - 40 minutes)
- Discussion of the home practice assignment (5 - 10 minutes)

Materials

Blackboard (or large marking board)

Chalk (or markers)

Eraser

A note card for each member of the group containing the two role-playing exercises

Handout: Three Types of Problem Ownership

Review and Sharing of Home Practice Experiences

Encourage parents to share their experiences. But this is an area where parents often have very fixed ideas. Discussions on this subject may get very intense. As the professional, you must provide balanced support for both permissive and authoritarian points of view. Remember that successful and happy people have been raised in homes with both points of view.

Lecture/Discussion

Managing Problem Behaviors

You have already learned several skills for building good relationships with our children. Our main purpose in the recent sessions was learning to communicate to our children that they are worthwhile, competent individuals.

There is a very close relationship between how competent and worthwhile a child feels and how that child behaves. You can test this idea with yourself. When you feel good about yourself, how do you behave? Usually, it is hard to behave in any way except one that expresses that good feeling. Just like you, your child will behave in more positive ways when he or she feels worthwhile and competent as a person. This is a major benefit of building a positive parent-child relationship that is based on feelings of competency and being worthwhile.

In this session, we'll focus on how some of the relationship-building skills you have already learned can be used to help manage a behavior that is a problem for you or your child. In your parent-child relationship—as in all relationships—things don't always go smoothly. It is not always possible to be building our relationships. There are times when problems or upsets arise in every family. These are expected and normal events that all families deal with.

Your first task as a responsible parent when there is a problem or crisis is deciding who owns that problem or crisis. Sometimes problems belong only to the parent; sometimes they belong only to the child; and, sometimes, the problem can be shared by two or more family members, because the problem involves something family members need from each other. *(Write the diagram shown in Figure 16 on the board.)*

137

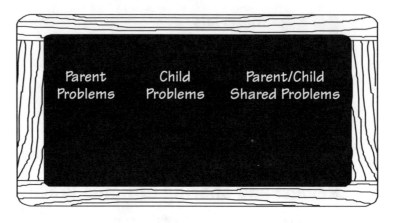

Figure 16. Three types of problems.

There are many times when a problem really belongs to your child. Often, as parents, we make the mistake of thinking that all of our child's problems are *our* problems. That's not always true. In fact, if we behave as if this were true, we will be undercutting—and sometimes even damaging—our child's sense of self-worth and competence. *Remember—children have a right to their own problems, and they have a right to work through those problems for themselves.*

How can you tell if a problem belongs only to your child? The simplest way is to ask yourself, "If this problem isn't solved or if it doesn't work out, will it affect me in any substantial way?" Will you lose your job, your wife, your friends? Will you be ridiculed and shamed by your neighbors? This idea—that a child can own a problem without the parent being any part of it—may seem strange at first. Parents naturally want to help and protect their children. But to solve any problem, we must learn to identify who owns that problem.

First, let's consider some problems owned only by the parent:

The Green family has moved to a new neighborhood. Mrs. Green has no friends and misses all her old neighbors. Her husband and children love her, and they know she feels lonely and sad. They care about her, but they also know that she owns this problem and that she must solve it for herself.

Mr. Green is working a new sales territory with a new product. He has always been a great salesman, but this past month things haven't been going well. The people in the new area have different ways of doing things, and Mr. Green feels he is just not accepted. His family knows that he has a problem. They love and care about him, but they know that he must solve this problem for himself.

Now let's consider some problems that belong to children, some that belong to parents, and some that belong to both because of some conflict of interests and needs. Here are three problems that belong to the child:

1. **Rose is feeling rejected by her friend, Mary, who is playing with a new girl on the street.**

2. **Bill is upset because he can't play soccer well.**

3. **Kathy is unhappy when she cannot find her toys.**

And here are three problems that belong to the parent:

1. **Your child keeps walking on the furniture.**

2. **Your child keeps interrupting your conversation with a friend.**

3. **Your child leaves his or her toys around the house.**

Now here are three problems that are shared by the parent and the child:

1. **Your child wants to go swimming, and you want to stay home and work in the garden.**

2. **You are having company for dinner, and your child wants to invite two children over for a slumber party.**

3. **When the family plays a game, your youngest child cannot stand to lose, so he disrupts the game for everyone.**

First, let's consider the situation in which your child owns the problem or crisis. The best parenting skill to use here is reflective listening. You certainly don't have to solve a problem that isn't yours. Further, you know that your child can—if you allow it—solve many of his or her own problems. For example, if you communicate to your child that you understand that he or she is upset, you can also communicate that it is acceptable for the child to have these feelings and that you believe your child is capable of handling the problem. Compare this to your own experience. When you complain about *your* work, do you really want someone to step in, take over, and solve your problems?

Q If another person solved your problems and took over all the time, how would it affect your personal sense of worth and competence? Would you feel competent and worthwhile if this kept happening? (*Pause for parents' response.*)

This same sort of thing happens with children. A child who is upset likes and wants to be understood, but the child also wants to work on his or her own problems. How often have you heard your child say, "Mom, I'd rather do it myself." The child whose problems are solved by a protecting parent quickly becomes either resentful or passive and dependent.

Now let's talk about family situations when the child's problem is also a problem for a parent or for the whole family. The most effective parenting skill in this situation is strong and direct communication of how you feel or think. This self-sharing communication offers many benefits. First, you let your child know how you are affected by a problem you share. Second, you allow your child the freedom to do something (or nothing) about the problem. Third, you eliminate blame or shame, because these negative feelings will only cause your child to resist solving the problem. Fourth, by openly and honestly expressing your feelings, you include your child in resolving the problem. Self-sharing communicates a shared responsibility with your child, rather than blaming, threatening, or making the child feel guilty. This sense of shared responsibility can only enhance your child's sense of his or her own competence.

Common sense tells us that reflective listening and self-sharing communications will not solve all the problems that might occur in a family. But they will often help—especially when you already have a particularly good parent-child relationship. In later sessions, we'll talk about other ways to manage your child when reflective listening and self-sharing don't work. For now, let's concentrate on using these two important skills to help solve problems. Remember, these methods are only useful when a good relationship already exists. That's why it's important to keep using the relationship-building skills you have already learned and practiced.

When you use reflective listening and self-sharing communication, you must first know where the ownership of the problem lies. Let's identify who owns the problem in the following examples. *(Encourage all parents to participate.)*

1. You discover your daughter, Ellen, in her room crying softly. You ask if she is hurt, and she tells you that her feelings are hurt because the girls next door won't let her play in their treehouse. Who owns this problem? *(Ellen owns this problem—her feelings are hurt and she must decide what to do and what to think about the girls next door.)*

2. You are entertaining some friends one evening, and your 10-year-old daughter strides in, exclaiming that she's never seen so many nerds gathered together in one room before. Who owns the problem? *(This may be a shared problem. The daughter may be feeling bored or left out. The parent has to decide if he or she is embarrassed or shrug off the event while protecting the guests from such comments.)*

3. Your 6-year-old son, Thomas, is wandering around the playground equipment during a family picnic at the park. You notice that he wanders here and there but never plays with anyone or uses any of the outdoor equipment. Who owns this problem? *(Thomas owns the problem if he is distressed by the circumstances. The parent owns the problem if he or she wants Thomas to behave differently.)*

4. Eleven-year-old Anthony wants a model airplane. You give him permission to go across town to buy it, with the understanding that he will be back in time for dinner. Dinner time comes and goes with no sign of Anthony. It is just starting to get dark when he walks in. Who owns the problem? *(The parent owns this problem—the parent*

is upset and worried at the moment, and his trust in Anthony is diminished. In the future, when the parent does not trust Anthony or sets firmer limits on his behavior, Anthony may have a problem. Anthony might also have a problem if the parent decides to punish him or if the parent communicates through a self-sharing message such as, "I was very worried and scared when you didn't come back for supper. I love you, and I was afraid something might have happened to you." In the case of both the punishment and the self-sharing message, Anthony must make some decisions about the situation for himself.)

You have all carefully sifted out what's really important in each of these situations. We can see that some parts of a situation are problems for the child, some for the adult, and some are shared problems.

You probably noticed that each of us defined the problem a bit differently. That's normal. In so many situations, there is no one solution (or no one interpretation) of what is important or what is happening. How you interpret a situation also determines what you might do. In general, as part of their desire to be responsible, parents define more of their children's problems as belonging to themselves than is reasonable.

Q Can anyone think of a situation that includes a problem belonging to a child? *(Reinforce the efforts of all parents who speak up. Review a few situations to be sure the concept of child ownership is clear.)*

Q Would anyone like to share a situation in which it is not so clear who owns the problem. Just describe the situation without giving an opinion about who might own the problem. The rest of us will try to figure out who owns the problem—or who owns which part of it. *(Pause. Allow a parent to describe the situation, then ask other parents to try and figure it out. Reinforce all parents who speak up. Repeat this activity with as many examples as are necessary to clearly communicate the ideas.)*

Now we'll do a role-playing activity where all of you together will play the part of my parent. I will be the child in some of the examples we just talked about. During this exercise, I want you to get a feel for the power that reflective listening and self-sharing can have in managing a child's behavior. Remember this very important point: When the ownership of the problem is yours, and you let me know that clearly, I may return an equally clear, self-sharing message to you. If and when I do that, your best option is to use reflective listening until you can try to reach me again with your self-sharing messages. In other words, keep weighing my responses to determine whether the problem is yours or mine. *(At this point, use two of the situations suggested by parents in the group. As the child in each situation, demonstrate as dramatically as possible—without being unrealistic—the impact your parents' reflective listening and self-sharing behavior has on you. After each role-playing situation, encourage group members to share their impressions.*

Summarize what you hear them saying as well as what they seem to be ignoring.)

If you are going to use reflective listening and self-sharing as problem-solving methods, you will need some practice. I would like you to organize yourselves into groups of two. Husband and wife should not work together. In this exercise, you'll have an opportunity to play the role of the parent and of the child. Remember, as the parent, you must decide who owns the problem and what response would be most helpful. You may need to repeat a scene two or three times until you are satisfied with your response. *(Allow a few minutes for groups to organize themselves and spread out as much as possible.)*

Now I'm going to give each of you a card containing two situations. In the first situation, one of you should be the parent and the other the child; for the second situation, you'll switch roles. Start each situation with the child speaking to the parent.

SITUATION 1:

You are trying to have your 7-year-old son take care of his room. It's Saturday morning, and you have asked him to make his bed and clean his room. He says, "Why do I have to make my bed and clean my room? My friends don't have to. You're mean."

SITUATION 2:

You walk into the living room and find your child crying. He says, "I must be dumb; nobody likes me. I never have anyone to play with."

Figure 17. Two role-playing situations to illustrate problem ownership.

As a reminder, this handout contains some suggested responses to the three types of problem ownership: parent, child, and shared. *(Distribute the handout page shown in Figure 18 to each member of the group.)*

Child Owns Problem

1. Allow your child time and space to solve the problem.

2. Try reflective listening as your first approach.

3. Assist in problem resolution if your assistance is requested by the child and if the request doesn't create a problem for you.

Parent and Child Share Problem

1. Describe the problem using self-sharing communication.

2. Use reflective listening in response to your child's comments By doing this, you are asking, "How can we solve this problem together?"

3. You may need to repeat Steps 1 and 2 several times before a solution to the problem emerges from the discussion.

4. Comments such as, "We really need to find a solution," "There must be a way to solve this," or "Let's try harder to figure this out" tend to help you and your child resolve the problem.

5. Step 4 should not be used if you are unwilling to compromise or change your position. Instead, you should restate your position and then use reflective listening. Such an assertion of parental authority to solve shared parent-child problems should be rare.

Parent Owns Problem

1. You may use self-sharing communications if your child can reasonably be expected to help you solve the problem.

2. You can request assistance from your child with the understanding that your child can ignore your request if he or she believes it creates a problem for him or her.

Figure 18. Recommended parental reactions to problem ownership situations.

General Discussion

Now I would like you all to share your reactions to this exercise in terms of both the parent's and the child's role.

Q Can you see how reflective listening and self-sharing might help you in situations with your own child? *(Pause for parents' response.)*

Q Can anyone see some problems with these ways of responding? *(Pause for parents' response and attempt to help parents understand that these methods have limits—they won't work when a parent is unwilling to compromise or when the parent-child relationship is not a positive one.)*

Q Does anyone have any reactions which they would like to share about this week's session? *(Pause for parents' response.)*

Discussion of Home Practice Assignment

This week's home practice assignment will help you sort out what are *your* responsibilities and problems as a parent and what problems are *your child's*. It often happens that children will try to make their problems a problem for their parents, and some parents assume all of their children's problems as their own. This assignment will help you to see what is happening in your own situation. Remember—by allowing your child to own and work on his or her problems, you are building the child's feelings of self-competence and responsibility. Finding a toy for a crying child may be easier than having the child solve the problem, but what does your action teach the child about his or her competence and responsibility?

Three Types of Problem Ownership

Child Owns Problem

1.   Allow your child time and space to solve the problem.

2.   Try reflective listening as your first approach.

3.   Assist in problem resolution if your assistance is requested by the child and if the request doesn't create a problem for you.

Parent and Child Share Problem

1.   Describe the problem using self-sharing communication.

2.   Use reflective listening in response to your child's comments. By doing this, you are asking, "How can we solve this problem together?"

3.   You may need to repeat Steps 1 and 2 several times before a solution to the problem emerges from the discussion.

4.   Comments such as, "We really need to find a solution," "There must be a way to solve this," or "Let's try harder to figure this out" tend to help you and your child resolve the problem.

5.   Step 4 should not be used if you are unwilling to compromise or change your position. Instead, you should restate your position and then use reflective listening. Such an assertion of parental authority to solve shared parent-child problems should be rare.

Parent Owns Problem

1.   You may use self-sharing communications if your child can reasonably be expected to help you solve the problem.

2.   You can request assistance from your child with the understanding that your child can ignore your request if he or she believes it creates a problem for him or her.

PAR Psychological Assessment Resources, Inc./P.O. Box 998/Odessa, FL 33556/Toll-Free 1-800-331-TEST

Using Behavior Modification Principles

Introduction

This second session in the sequence begins the process of presenting and practicing a variety of basic skills and ideas essential to the successful use of behavior modification principles with children. The focus of this session is on teaching and strengthening desirable behavior and discouraging undesirable behavior. This is an ideal opportunity for you to present one of three excellent videotapes on the subject. But the session can also be presented in the regular lecture/discussion format, without a vidotaped presentation. This chapter presents an outline for each of these formats. Before you decide which method you prefer, review the list of tapes presented at the end of this chapter. This will help you to determine the most appropriate way to present the material to your particular group of parents.

Special Notes for the Mental Health Professional

During this phase of the training, you will find the parents in your group will often want to tackle *entire problems*. Trying to teach a set of skills step-by-step while some of the parents are concerned with a whole problem can be difficult. There are ways you can deal with this situation. As you present the specific skills, maintain the group focus on the specific ideas you are discussing. After you have presented all the material, the group discussion can focus on whole problems and whole solutions. Remember to incorporate the principles and skills of behavior management into these discussions. Don't worry about "stealing the thunder" from an upcoming session. Parents will tolerate redundancy much better having their immediate concerns ignored.

Session Objectives

1. To help parents understand that they are their children's teachers and that parental behavior influences what children learn.

2. To help parents understand that knowing the consequences of an act can determine an individual's future behavior.

3. To help parents understand that behavior change is best accomplished in small steps.

4. To demonstrate the effectiveness of behavior modification and to discuss the basic ideas of reinforcement.

Sequence for a Session That Includes a Videotape Presentation

- Review and sharing of home practice (5 - 10 minutes)
- Lecture/discussion (30 - 52 minutes)
- Videotape (24 - 30 minutes)
- Discussion of the home practice assignment (5 - 10 minutes)

 ## Materials

Blackboard (or large marking board)

Chalk (or markers)

One of the three videotapes listed at the end of this chapter

Videotape playback unit with large monitor for group viewing

Review and Sharing of Home Practice Experiences

Q Who would like to share the results of their home practice assignment? *(Pause for parents' response.)*

Q Did anyone have any specific reactions to, or any problems with, the assignment? *(Encourage all parents to share their experiences, being careful not to pressure them.)*

Lecture/Discussion

Behavior Modification

In the next few sessions we will discuss and then practice a very powerful method of managing children's behavior called *behavior modification*. Some of you may have heard this term before. Later in this session we'll watch a videotape about behavior modification techniques. But before we watch the tape, I'd like to go over a few ideas that form the basis of the behavior modification method. There are three ideas that are basic to effective behavior modification. *(Write the three ideas shown in Figure 19 on the board.)*

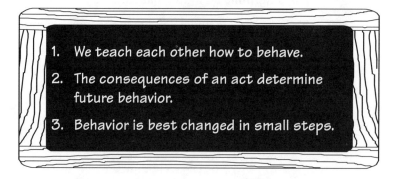

1. We teach each other how to behave.
2. The consequences of an act determine future behavior.
3. Behavior is best changed in small steps.

Figure 19. Three basic concepts of behavior modification.

Let's talk about each of these basic concepts.

The first idea is, "We teach each other how to behave." Here is an example of what this means.

You've just put your 15-month-old daughter to bed, but she has decided that she does not want to stay there. She does not like being alone in the room, so she cries and you go in to see what is wrong. You check the diaper pins, the room temperature, and the blanket. The crying stops, and you leave. In a minute, she begins to cry again and you go back to the room to check on her again.

Can you see that your child is teaching you how to behave at the same time you are teaching her how to behave? She teaches you that you shouldn't leave her in her room alone. Her behavior, particularly the crying, teaches you to stay with her. At the same time, you are teaching your child that when she cries you will come to her room. Here's another example:

Your baby is beginning to enjoy a variety of foods, so you decide to buy a jar of pureed peas. At dinner, you open the jar of peas and try to give your baby a spoonful. The baby takes the peas in his mouth, spits them out, and begins to fuss. You slowly put the lid back on the pureed peas and put them away. *(Pause.)*

You can see again how people teach each other how to behave. In this example, the baby has taught you not to buy pureed peas. You have taught the baby that, if he spits out food and fusses, he will not have to try that food again.

All people teach each other how to behave, but the closeness of the parent-child relationship makes parents and children very important teachers for each other.

Let's look at the second idea, "The consequences, or results, of an act determine future behavior." Listen to this example:

Your child asks you, "Why does a boat float?" You feel embarrassed about not knowing exactly what to say, so you just look the other way or pretend to be very involved in what you are doing. Later on, your child asks you, "Where does Uncle Charlie live?" Again, you are busy, and the child's question is ignored.

What will happen to your child's question-asking if this is your common reaction? The chances are good that he or she will stop asking questions. The consequence of asking questions is that the child gets ignored. The child doesn't like to be ignored, so he or she will probably stop asking questions. Let's look at another example:

It's Saturday morning, and you are doing your grocery shopping. At the check-out counter, your daughter asks for a piece of candy, but you tell her she can't have sweets until after lunch. When she hears this, she screams, throws herself on the floor, and has a temper tantrum.

You feel embarrassed, and you know the only way to make her stop is to buy her some candy. You pay the cashier for a candy bar, give it to your daughter, and tell her to be quiet.

Okay, the child's behavior in this example is screaming and throwing herself on the floor. *(Write "Screams, throws self on floor, has a temper tantrum" on the board.)*

Q What was the consequence of this behavior? What happened after the behavior? *(When parents respond correctly, write "Parent gave child candy" on the board.)*

Exactly. Remember that knowing the consequences of an act can determine future behavior.

Q What do you think will happen to this child's tantrum behavior as a result of this consequence? Is there likely to be more or less tantrum behavior in the future? *(Pause for parents to respond that the tantrum behavior is likely to be repeated.)*

Consequences determine behavior. When the consequences of a behavior are pleasurable, there will be more of that behavior in the future. When the consequences of a behavior are unpleasant, there will be less of that behavior. In the first example, the consequence of the child's question-asking behavior was being ignored. Being ignored is unpleasant, so the child will probably ask fewer questions in the future. In the second example, the consequence of throwing a tantrum was to get some candy. Candy is a pleasant consequence, so the child will probably throw more tantrums in the future.

The last basic idea about using behavior modification principles is that behavior is best changed in small steps. These small steps should work toward a goal established by the parent. Think about teaching your 5-year-old to make his bed. If you have your child watch you make the bed a few times and then tell him to do it by himself, what do you think might happen? He would probably have a hard time making the bed, and he would quickly get discouraged. He just wouldn't be able to make the bed all alone.

Q Can anyone think of a better way to teach a child to make his bed? *(Pause for parents' response. Summarize responses as follows.)*

We see that there are many effective ways of teaching a child to make his bed. No matter which method you use, the key to success is to break the job into parts or steps and slowly add each new step as the child learns. Just putting the pillow on the bed or tucking in the sheet might be a first step. Slowly, over a couple of weeks, all the steps in making the bed can be added.

Behavior Modification and the Learning Process

Tonight, we're going to watch a tape that shows how behavior modification can help children learn. As you watch the tape, keep the three basic concepts of behavior modification in mind. *(Point to the ideas on the board.)* The ideas we talked about are: 1. We teach each other how to behave; 2. The consequences of an act determine future behavior; and 3. Behavior is best changed in small steps. This tape will show you just how powerful this technique of behavior modification can be. The changes in behavior you will see are quite dramatic. *(Show the videotape. After the tape is finished, encourage parents to share their responses or to ask any questions they may have.)*

In the next few sessions, you'll all get a chance to become more successful at managing your children's behavior. We'll talk about using the ideas we discussed today, and you'll learn how to set appropriate consequences for your child's behavior and how to break tasks down into smaller, learnable steps or parts.

Sequence for a Session Without a Videotape Presentation

● Review and sharing of home practice (5 - 10 minutes)

● Lecture/Discussion (30 - 40 minutes)

● Discussion of the home practice assignment (5 - 10 minutes)

 ### Materials

Blackboard (or large marking board)

Chalk (or markers)

Review and Sharing of Home Practice Experiences

Q Who would like to share the results of their home practice assignment? *(Pause for parents' response.)*

Q Did anyone have any specific reactions to, or any problems with, the assignment? *(Encourage all parents to share their experiences, being careful not to pressure them.)*

Behavior Modification and the Learning Process

Your reactions to your children will determine, in part, what behaviors they develop, what behaviors will continue to occur, and what behaviors will disappear. Just as people are always reacting to each other, so our children are always reacting to us and learning from our reactions to their behavior.

Still, parents can't be expected to constantly monitor how their behaviors and reactions will affect their children. With a child's minor or unimportant behaviors, your reactions are probably of little importance—that's because you don't really need to affect those behaviors. When you are concerned about developing, maintaining, or stopping a behavior, you do have to pay attention to your reactions,especially in any situations where that important behavior might occur. Your reactions in these situations become the consequences of your child's behavior. This brings us to two important ideas: First, consequences determine behavior; and second, children learn best in small steps.

In the next few sessions we will discuss and then practice a very powerful method of managing children's behavior called *behavior modification*. Some of you may have heard this term before. I'd like to go over a few ideas that form the basis of the behavior modification method. There are three ideas that are basic to effective behavior modification. *(Write the three ideas shown in Figure 19 on the board.)*

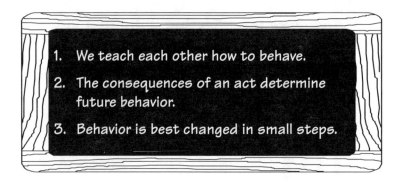

Figure 19. Three basic concepts of behavior modification.

Let's talk about each of these basic concepts. The first idea is, "We teach each other how to behave." Here is an example of what this means.

You've just put your 15-month-old daughter to bed, but she has decided that she does not want to stay there. She does not like being alone in the room, so she cries and you go in to see what is wrong. You check the diaper pins, the room temperature, and the blanket. The crying stops, and you leave. In a minute, she begins to cry again and you go back to the room to check on her again.

Can you see that your child is teaching you how to behave at the same time you are teaching her how to behave? She teaches you that you shouldn't leave her in her room alone. Her behavior, particularly the crying, teaches you to stay with her. At the same time, you are teaching your child that when she cries you will come to her room. Here's another example:

Your baby is beginning to enjoy a variety of foods, so you decide to buy a jar of pureed peas. At dinner, you open the jar of peas and try to give your baby a spoonful. The baby takes the peas in his mouth, spits them out, and begins to fuss. You slowly put the lid back on the pureed peas and put them away. *(Pause.)*

You can see once again how people teach each other how to behave. In this example, the baby has taught you not to buy pureed peas. You have taught the baby that, if he spits out food and fusses, he will not have to try that food again.

All people teach each other how to behave, but the closeness of the parent-child relationship makes parents and children very important teachers for each other.

Let's look at the second idea, "The consequences, or results, of an act determine future behavior." Listen to this example:

Your child asks you, "Why does a boat float?" You feel embarrassed about not knowing exactly what to say, so you just look the other way or pretend to be very involved in what you are doing. Later on, your child asks you, "Where does Uncle Charlie live?" Again, because you are busy, the child's question is ignored.

What will happen to your child's question-asking if this is your common reaction? The chances are good that he or she will stop asking questions. The consequence of asking questions is that the child gets ignored. The child doesn't like to be ignored, so he or she will probably stop asking questions. Let's look at another example:

It's Saturday morning and you are doing your grocery shopping. At the check-out counter, your daughter asks for a piece of candy, but you tell her she can't have sweets until after lunch. When she hears this, she screams, throws herself on the floor, and has a temper tantrum. You feel embarrassed, and you know the only way to make her stop is to buy her some candy. You pay the cashier for a candy bar, give it to your daughter, and tell her to be quiet.

Okay, the child's behavior in this example is screaming and throwing herself on the floor. *(Write "Screams, throws self on floor, has a temper tantrum" on the board.)*

Q What was the consequence of this behavior? What happened after the behavior? *(When parents respond correctly, write "Parent gave child candy" on the board.)*

Exactly. Remember that knowing the consequences of an act can determine future behavior.

Q What do you think will happen to this child's tantrum behavior as a result of this consequence? Is there likely to be more or less tantrum behavior in the future? (Pause for parents to respond that the tantrum behavior is likely to be repeated.)

Consequences determine behavior. When the consequences of a behavior are pleasurable, there will be more of that behavior in the future. When the consequences of a behavior are unpleasant, there will be less of that behavior.

In the first example, the consequence of the child's question-asking behavior was being ignored. Being ignored is unpleasant, so the child will probably ask fewer questions in the future. In the second example, the consequence of throwing a tantrum was to get some candy. Candy is a pleasant consequence, so the child will probably throw more tantrums in the future.

Let's look at another example.

Jimmy, a 6-year-old, is always a slowpoke. He keeps Mom, Dad, and sometimes the whole family waiting for him whenever they plan to go somewhere—a fishing trip, running errands, or visiting friends. Jimmy always has good, original reasons: he can't find his shoes, he isn't dressed, he's busy with a project, or he can't be found. And every time, either Jimmy's family waits for him or a family member helps him get ready. One day, Jimmy's father decides that the next time they are going somewhere and it's time to leave, Jimmy will be told once— just like everyone else—and if he isn't ready there will be one of two consequences: If someone is available to take care of him, Jimmy will have to stay home. If not, he will have to sit in the car by himself for 15 minutes after the family arrives at their destination.

Think about this example carefully. Jimmy's behavior is being a slowpoke and making the whole family wait for him. *(Write on the board, "Slowpoke, holds up family.")*

Q What was the consequence of Jimmy's behavior—for Jimmy— before his father decided to change the pattern? *(Pause for parents' response and then summarize: The consequence was positive—Jimmy's family made it easier for him.)*

Q What would you expect to happen to Jimmy's behavior, given these positive consequences? *(Pause for parents to respond that the behavior will continue to occur or will occur more often.)*

Q Once Jimmy's father tried a different reaction to Jimmy's behavior, what were the possible consequences of that behavior for Jimmy? *(Pause for parents to respond that the consequences were missing family outings or having to stay in the car by himself.)*

Q What would you expect to happen to Jimmy's behavior, given these new consequences? *(Pause for parents to respond that he would probably try to avoid these unpleasant, punishing consequences.)*

154

From these examples, you can see that there are three kinds of consequences for behavior. First, behavior can be ignored. Ignoring a behavior causes it to occur less often. Second, behavior can lead to positive, or enjoyable consequences. These positive consequences will cause behavior to continue or to increase. Third, behavior can lead to negative, unpleasant consequences. These negative consequences will cause the behavior to be decreased or changed. *(Write the consequences shown in Figure 20 on the board:)*

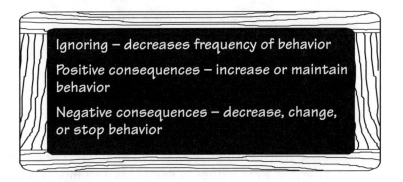

Ignoring – decreases frequency of behavior

Positive consequences – increase or maintain behavior

Negative consequences – decrease, change, or stop behavior

Figure 20. Three kinds of consequences that determine future behavior.

Now I'll give you some examples of situations where these ideas might apply. In each situation, see if you can determine what the consequences are for the child in terms of the parent's behavior and what effects we should expect in terms of the child's behavior.

Mary, age 7, is the oldest three sisters. The youngest sister is 12 months old. The middle sister, who is 4 years old, has a serious heart condition. Mary's parents are very busy, because they have a sick child and a baby to care for. Mary is a big help to her parents, and her mother and father praise her for helping and even brag about Mary to their friends. Recently, however, Mary's mother has been annoyed by Mary's frequent complaints that she feels sick. Mary's mother explains to her husband that the children's health is important to her. It takes a great deal of time to put Mary to bed, take her temperature, feel her sore spots, and listen carefully to her complaints. Mom doesn't want to ignore Mary if she is really sick, but she suspects that Mary isn't really feeling ill.

This is a short story, and many details had to be left out. Still, with what I told you, can you identify the consequences of just two of Mary's behaviors?

Q First, what happens as a result of Mary's helping her parents? *(Pause for parents to respond that Mary's parents praise and brag, which is a positive consequence.)*

Q Exactly. Because the consequences are positive, what will happen to Mary's helping behavior? *(Pause for parents to respond that it should increase or be maintained.)*

Q What happens as a result of Mary's complaints about feeling sick? *(Pause for parents to respond that Mary's mother pays more attention to Mary, nurtures her, and helps her feel loved.)*

Q What will probably happen to Mary's complaints about being sick? *(Pause for parents to respond that the complaints should continue or increase.)*

Because we have identified the consequence of Mary's complaining behavior, we now know the reason for her complaints. We know that she is complaining because she wants and needs some special nurturing and attention. If you were Mary's parents, you could make that special nurturing and attention a consequence of some constructive behavior instead. That way, Mary can readily give up her complaining because she will have a more constructive way of getting what she needs. Now, here's another example:

Mr. Arthur loves to make model airplanes, and he was delighted when his 8-year-old son Fred showed an interest in model airplane building. One day, Fred brings in one of his own models to show his father:

Fred: **"Look, Daddy. I finished the model."**

Father: **"Well, let's see. It looks pretty good."**

Fred: **"I made the wings just like you said."**

Father: **"No you didn't Fred. See, they don't fit together properly. You rushed through in your usual, sloppy way. *(Pause.)* Didn't I tell you to glue it one part at a time and to wait until the first part dried before gluing the second part? That's why the body is so crooked. If you aren't patient, it will turn out to be a mess every time. This plane looks as messy as your room does!"**

Q What was the consequence of Fred's building the model and showing it to his father? *(Pause for parents to respond that the consequence was being criticized. Fred probably won't do it as often, and he might even stop building models with his Dad altogether.)*

Q What other consequences might have decreased Fred's model-building behavior? *(Pause for parents to respond that punishing consequences would decrease the behavior. Point out that ignoring Fred's efforts would also tend to decrease the behavior.)*

Ignoring can be total, such as looking at Fred's work and then just walking away, or it could involve giving a brief response such as, "That's nice" and then going on to talk about something else. The effect of either kind of ignoring would be that Fred is less likely to come to his father, or less likely to build model airplanes, or both.

The last basic idea about using behavior modification principles is that behavior is best changed in small steps. These small steps should work toward a goal established by the parent.

One of the most common errors made by adults who try to change the behavior of their children is that the adult sets a goal for the child and then tries to get the child to reach that goal in steps that are just too big for the child. The child achieves positive consequences only for a perfect or total performance. If the goal is too big, or if the steps to reach that goal are too big, there will be no positive consequences for the child. The helpful adult must break down the behavior to be learned (or unlearned) into a series of small steps with positive, rewarding consequences following each step.

Think about trying to teach your 5-year-old to make her own bed.

Q If you have her watch you make the bed a few times, and then tell her to do it by herself, what do you think might happen? *(Pause for parents' response.)*

Yes. She would probably have a hard time making the bed and she would quickly get discouraged. She just wouldn't be able to make the bed by herself.

Q Can anyone think of a better way to teach a child to make her bed? *(Pause for parents' response. Reinforce parents and summarize responses as follows.)*

We see that there are many effective ways of teaching a child to make her bed. No matter which method you use, it is important to break the job into small, achievable steps and then slowly add each new step as the child learns the previous one. Just putting the pillow on the bed or tucking in the sheet might be a first step. Slowly, over a couple of weeks, all the steps in making the bed would be learned.

In the next few sessions, you'll all have an opportunity to practice successful skills for managing your children's behavior. We'll talk about using the ideas we discussed today, and you'll learn how to set appropriate consequences for your child's behavior and how to break tasks down into smaller, learnable steps or parts.

General Discussion

Q Does anyone have any reactions which they would like to share about this week's session? *(Pause for parents' response.)*

Discussion of the Home Practice Assignment

In the next few weeks, you will be learning about a method for managing your child's behavior called behavior modification. Behavior modification is a very powerful set of techniques for helping your child. But, like all powerful "medicines," there are some real dangers involved in using behavior modification techniques. The biggest danger is that it works so well that you can get all tangled up with the method and forget to keep working on the quality of your ongoing relationship with your child. And remember that your reflective listening and self-sharing skills must always play a large part in managing your child's behavior.

Recommended Readings

Barclay, D. R., & Houts, A. C. (1995). Parenting Skills: A review and developmental analysis of training content. In W. O'Donohue & L. Krasner (Eds.), *Handbook of psychological skills training: Clinical technique and applications* (pp. 195-228). Boston: Allyn & Bacon.

Barkley, R. A. (1987). *Defiant children: A clinician's manual for parent training*. New York, NY: Guilford.

Clark, L. (1985). *S.O.S! Help for parents*. Bowling Green, KY: Parents Press.

Dangel, R. F., & Polster, R. A. (1988). *Teaching child management skills*. New York: Pergamon.

Forehand, R., & McMahon, R. J. (1981). *Helping the noncompliant child: A clinician's guide to effective parent training*. New York, NY: Guilford.

Graziano, A. M., & Diament, D. M. (1992). Parent behavioral training: An examination of the paradigm. *Behavior Modification, 16*, 3-38.

Hersen, M., & Ammerman, R. T. (1989). Overview of new developments in child behavior therapy. In M. Hersen (Ed.), *Innovations in child behavior therapy*. New York: Springer.

Painter, G., & Corsini, R. J. (1990). *Effective discipline in the home and school*. Muncie, IN: Accelerated Development.

Patterson, G. R. (1986). *Living with children: New methods for parents and teachers* (Rev. ed.). Champaign, IL: Research Press.

Videotaped Introductions to Behavior Modification

1. *Parents and Children: A Positive Approach to Child Management*

   VHS, 24 minutes
   Research Press, Department J
   P. O. Box 9177
   Champaign, IL 61826
   Phone: (217) 352-3273/Fax: (217) 352-1221

   This videotape uses realistic examples of common parent-child interactions combined with running commentary by a child management consultant. The program covers such concepts as strengthening and maintaining desirable behavior, eliminating undesirable behavior, teaching new behavior, using various types of rewards, and using time out.

2. *Child Management*

   VHS, 30 minutes
   Research Press, Department J
   P.O. Box 9177
   Champaign, IL 61826
   Phone: (217) 352-3273/Fax: (217) 352-1221

   This videotape illustrates some practical techniques for parents to encourage appropriate behavior, discourage inappropriate behavior, and handle behavior problems both at home and at school. This program comes with a discussion guide and is recommended for use with parents of elementary school-aged children.

3. *Parent-Child Interaction Series*

   VHS, Two 26-minute programs
   Health Sciences Consortium
   201 Silver Cedar Court
   Chapel Hill, NC 27514
   Phone: (919) 942-8731

   These two programs describe and illustrate behavior modification skills that encourage desirable behavior, discourage undesirable behavior, and use mild punishment. This series of two programs is recommended for use with parents of children ages 2-8 years.

Consequences That Increase and Decrease Behavior – Selecting Behaviors to Change

Introduction

In this session, parents are to focus on the consequences that help to encourage (increase) and discourage (decrease) specific behaviors. Under your guidance, parents begin to realize how the use of reinforcers will help them to understand the uniqueness of their own children. They learn to view the process of identifying and recognizing the specific things that are important and reinforcing to their own children as a way to build a stronger parent-child relationship. In fact, through good reflective listening, the parent can easily learn what is reinforcing to his or her child. Parents must also realize that self-sharing communications, particularly those involving positive feelings, are very powerful social reinforcers for children.

Special Notes for the Mental Health Professional

It is important that you present the skill of pinpointing and describing specific behaviors as an essential ingredient in parent-child communication as well as in developing a program of behavior management. If parents are having difficulty with descriptive language, discuss a number of examples that use the specific concerns of the parents in your group. It is important to point out the way misconceptions and misunderstandings can easily occur when the language used is nondescriptive.

Session Objectives

1 To help parents understand and utilize the concept that behaviors that are reinforced will increase and behaviors that are punished will decrease.

2 To help parents gain skill in identifying possible reinforcers for their own children.

3 To help parents understand that withholding reinforcers is one form of punishment.

4 To help parents identify behaviors that can be changed through behavior modification.

5 To help parents understand the importance of accurately recording the frequency of specific behaviors as the second step in any behavior modification program.

Sequence

● Review and sharing of home practice (5 - 10 minutes)

● Lecture/Discussion (40 minutes)
    – The concept of reinforcement
    – Identifying possible reinforcers
    – Using punishment
    – The importance of identifying specific behaviors
    – Using descriptive language
    – Recording the frequency of specific behaviors

● General discussion (20 - 30 minutes)

● Discussion of the home practice assignment (5 - 10 minutes)

Materials

Blackboard (or large marking board)

Chalk (or markers)

Eraser

Review and Sharing of Home Practice Experiences

(Review and discuss home practice as usual.)

Lecture/Discussion

Positive and Negative Consequences

Last session, we focused on how parents and children teach each other to behave, how consequences determine future behavior, and how it is helpful for parents to teach their children new behaviors in small, achievable steps. These three ideas form the basis for behavior modification. You also saw that behavior modification is a very powerful tool for teaching children. Knowing how to use this technique will make you more effective teachers of your children. *(Pause.)*

In this session, we'll talk specifically about how positive and negative consequences—reinforcements and punishments—determine behavior. First, let's consider how people learn. One important way that people, especially children, learn is through reinforcement and punishment. Behavior that is reinforced will be repeated; behavior that is punished will not be repeated. In other words, reinforcement will increase a behavior, whereas punishment will decrease it.

As I said, reinforcement and punishment are two kinds of consequences. They are two things that can happen after your child behaves in a certain way; they are the possible results of your child's behavior.

From the recipient's point of view, reinforcement is something pleasant or enjoyable, and punishment is something unpleasant—something to be avoided. Suppose you are working on an assembly line in a factory and you come up with a great idea. You know that your idea will make the work more enjoyable for everyone at the plant and will, at the same time, increase production. You take your idea to the boss and she says, "Great idea. I'd like to think about it a little longer, but I think we'll use it. You know, I think your idea might win the bonus award for " 'suggestion of the month.' " Would the boss's reaction to your idea be a reinforcement or a punishment? *(Pause for parents' response.)*

Exactly. It would be a reinforcement, because her response to your idea was pleasurable for you. Now, we know that behavior will occur more often when it is reinforced, so you will probably tell your boss about your ideas more often.

Now, let's assume that you get another idea a few months later, and you take that idea to your boss. This time, she says, "Look, just worry about your own job. Leave the thinking to somebody who gets paid for that." You would probably experience this response as unpleasant. The boss's discouraging statements could be called a punishment, because they were unpleasant and you would certainly want to avoid any repetition of the experience. In the future, you will probably think long and hard before sharing another idea with your boss.

Let's consider a situation in which a child has behaved in a certain way:

One Saturday morning, your 11-year-old son mows the lawn without being asked. You say, "It makes me happy to see you do such a good job on the yard without being asked."

Would your statement to your son be a punishment or a reinforcer? *(Pause for parents to respond that it is a reinforcer.)* Right. Chances are that it is very pleasant for him to hear your praise. And, because behaviors that are reinforced occur more often in the future, you have increased the chance that he will be helpful on other occasions without being asked.

When teaching your children, you will want to make reinforcement the consequence for behaviors you would like to see more often. And for behaviors you'd rather not see any more, you will either avoid giving any reinforcer, or you will make punishment the consequence.

This is not always so easy. To help you master this technique, let's look more closely at the concepts of reinforcement and punishment. A reinforcer, as I said, is something pleasant or enjoyable. What are some pleasant, enjoyable reinforcers for children? *(Write the three categories of reinforcers shown in Figure 21 on the board. As parents offer examples, write each under the appropriate category. Don't talk about the three categories at this point, but make sure you get several examples for all three. You should be prepared to stimulate examples by providing some ideas based on the last session.)*

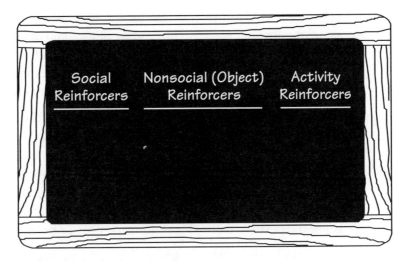

Figure 21. Three categories of reinforcers.

As you see, I've divided your examples into three types or categories of reinforcers. We can call all these reinforcers "social reinforcers," and these "activity reinforcers." This column contains "nonsocial or object reinforcers." *(Point to each category as you name it.)*

All three kinds of reinforcers can be used as consequences for child behaviors you want to see more of. I divided them into categories just to make it easier for us to talk about the different types and to help you realize that there are three different types of reinforcers.

Remember that consequences determine behavior, and that behavior that is followed by reinforcement is likely to occur again in the future. Part of your job as a parent is to teach your child by providing or arranging reinforcing consequences for valued behaviors. When you do this, your child learns the behaviors you want him or her to learn.

Q From this list, which reinforcer would you choose when your child puts a shirt on by himself or herself for the first time? Let's assume you want your child to repeat this behavior in the future. *(Pause for parents' response. Emphasize the idea that many different reinforcers are possible; each parent chooses the type he or she feels is best for the child and the specific situation.)*

Here's another example:

Suppose you would like your 6-year-old son to help his brother more often. One day, the younger boy holds up his empty glass. Your older son says, "Would you like more milk? I'll get it for you."

Q How might you reinforce your older son's helping behavior? *(Pause for parents' response. Many responses will be acceptable.)*

Great. Now you see there are many different reinforcers that would probably increase the frequency of his helping behavior. Children don't need to be given candy or toys as reinforcers. In families with close relationships, social reinforcers, such as kind words, praise, and appreciation, are most often used. Activity reinforcers—allowing the child to do something he or she wants to do—can also be very effective. And sometimes, even the closest of families will use nonsocial reinforcers like candy or gifts.

The flip side of reinforcement is punishment. We've talked about punishment before. You know that, if you use punishment wisely as a consequence for a particular behavior, that behavior will occur less often in the future. Remember that punishment can also have an unwanted effect. Punishment that involves the threat or use of power can cause a break-down in the parent-child relationship. Frequent use of any kind of punishment can strain the positive feelings a child has for his or her parent.

Generally, the most effective and least damaging type of punishment is the withholding of reinforcers. We'll talk about this type of punishment in more detail during a later session.

There is one last, but very important, point to consider. You must remember that the effectiveness of a reinforcer depends on the child's point of view, not the parent's. If a child feels that something is enjoyable or pleasant, then it will be an effective reinforcer. If a child feels that something is unpleasant, then that something will be an effective punishment. Here's a good example of what I mean.

In elementary school, many of us had the experience of being sent out into the hall as a punishment. But for many children, standing in the hall was more interesting and more fun than staying in the classroom. Consequently, making us stand in the hall when we misbehaved was ineffective as a punishment—it didn't decrease our misbehavior. As a matter of fact, standing in the hall was probably a pleasant experience, so it reinforced our misbehavior. What the teacher thought was a punishment was actually a reinforcer that made us misbehave more often.

The same thing can happen with what parents think are rewards. Taking a child fishing, to a baseball game, or to some other activity that doesn't interest the child is a punishment, regardless of how reinforcing that activity might have been to that parent when he or she was a child. Giving a child candy or money when the child already has all he or she wants is not an effective reinforcer. So your task as the parent is to determine which reinforcements your child will want and then to use those reinforcements to influence (or modify) your child's behavior.

By reinforcing the behaviors you like in your children and by not reinforcing or punishing behaviors you do not like, you can be an extremely important influence on your child. In many ways, you are influencing the type of person he or she is and will become. You can think of using reinforcement as informal behavior modification. Simply catching your child in a positive behavior and reinforcing that behavior is a very powerful teaching technique.

Sometimes, parents are concerned about a particular behavior they see in their child. This might be a behavior you would like to see more frequently, but don't see very often. For example, you might want your child to help around the house or make more of an effort to get along with a brother or sister. Or you might be concerned about a frequently-occurring behavior that you're not too crazy about. For example, your child might be fighting with other children or wetting his or her pants. Behavior modification can effectively increase or decrease the frequency of a particular behavior in your child.

There are four essential steps in successfully developing and implementing a formal behavior modification program. The first step is to pinpoint a specific behavior. *(Write on the board: "1. Pinpoint a specific behavior.")*

Let's look at the example I just mentioned.

Suppose your two sons, ages 6 and 4, just can't seem to play together without fighting, fussing, or crying. You want them to be able to play well together.

To use behavior modification with this problem, you must be very specific about the behavior you want to increase. You might think that playing well together is specific enough, but it's not. Playing well together can mean many different things. It can mean not hitting, not crying, sharing toys, playing together, or just playing in the same room without arguing. It could even mean that the little brother always lets the big brother decide what they are both going to do. In order to be successful in changing your child's behavior, you have to be very specific about the behavior you want changed.

Q How can we describe "playing well together" in a way that would pinpoint a specific behavior? *(Pause for parents' response. Ask the group to validate, or approve, the suggestions offered by the group members. Ask if the response that one group member has given means the same thing to the other parents. Also, introduce the idea that specifying behavior includes specifying the situation. For example, "not hitting little brother when playing in your room" is specific and manageable.)*

Now that you understand that successful behavior modification depends on pinpointing a specific behavior, let's look at another example.

Suppose you are a psychologist and a parent comes to see you. The parent says, "My daughter is aggressive. She doesn't get along with anyone, and she is always misbehaving."

Q What specific behaviors did the parent describe? *(Pause for parents to respond that there were none.)*

Right—none. Now, suppose another parent comes to you and says, "My son is shy and withdrawn. When someone new says hello to him, he looks down at the ground and doesn't reply."

Q What specific behaviors have been described here? *(Pause for parents to respond that the son puts his head down and doesn't respond to greetings from strangers.)*

Q What about shy and withdrawn? Are they specific behaviors? *(Pause for parents to respond, "No.")*

I think you've got the idea. A specific behavior is something you can see and something that you can describe so that another person will have no doubt about exactly what you are describing. Here are some more examples. Tell me whether or not they are specific behaviors:

1. **Saying, "Thank you" when given a piece of candy.** *(Specific.)*

2. **Getting along with little brother.** *(Not specific.)*

3. **Straightening up her room.** *(Not specific.)*

Q How could you make the last example (straightening up her room) a specific behavior? *(Pause for parents to suggest hanging up clothes, making bed, putting toys away, etc.)*

Q If you wanted your child to be more independent, what specific behaviors might you try to reinforce? *(Pause for parents to suggest behaviors such as playing alone for 15 minutes, putting on a coat without help, getting a cup of water without help, etc.)*

The second step in behavior modification is to pick a specific behavior and then count the number of times it occurs. How often a behavior occurs is called that behavior's frequency. You must record both how often and in what setting that specific behavior occurs. *(Write on the board: "2. Record frequency.")*

Here's an example:

Amanda's parents were concerned because she was often not stopping at home after school before going to a friend's house to play. The parents became worried, because they couldn't be sure that Amanda had gotten home safely. They were concerned about a specific behavior: Amanda's not coming home immediately after school. They could count how often this happened. If Amanda did this every day without fail, her parents could say it happened once per day on every school day. Sometimes, Amanda would come straight home and sometimes she wouldn't. The frequency of Amanda's behavior might be counted as the number of times per week that she failed to come home. One week she might fail to come home twice, and another week it might happen four times.

The frequency of a behavior tells how often that behavior occurs in a given period of time. Frequency is a useful measure for a number of reasons. First, it helps you see how serious a problem really is. It may seem like your children are always fighting when they actually fight only two or three times a day. It might seem like your daughter never feeds the dog without being asked when she actually remembers to do it twice a week without coaxing. Recording the frequency of a behavior helps you get a clear idea of how serious that problem really is. It also helps you see if there is any change in a behavior as a result of your managing its consequences.

When you record the frequency of a behavior, it is important to be consistent about when the record is made and how often the behavior is corrected. For example, you may want to count every occurrence every day. But if the behavior has been singled out as a problem only at meal time, you would want to record its frequency only at meal time.

If you are not consistent about recording at the same time every day, the normal day-to-day fluctuations in the behavior might not tell you how effective your behavior modification program is. Let's use the example of reinforcing your child's independence. On Monday, you decide to record how often your child plays alone for 15 minutes. You record the behavior during the 3 hours between breakfast and lunch. On Tuesday, you record the same behavior during the 3 hours before bedtime. Now, let's say that the behavior record indicates that your child played alone more often on Monday than she did on Tuesday. Does this record show that her independent behavior is decreasing? Not necessarily. The record might actually show that the specific behavior, in this case playing alone, occurs more often during one part of the day than during another part of the day. You want your record to accurately reflect a behavior's frequency before you try to change that behavior.

How you actually go about counting a behavior's frequency depends partly on the behavior you have chosen to count. Sometimes, the simplest method is to carry a piece of paper and pencil with you, making a mark on the paper each time the behavior occurs. At the end of the day (or some other designated time period), you just count up your marks, and you have a record for that day.

It is usually best to choose one or two specific time periods during the day for observing and recording how often the behavior occurs. This is easier to handle than trying to keep a record all day long. One mother who was interested in getting her boys to share their toys chose to record behavior during one, 40-minute time period each evening, just before bedtime.

There are a number of other methods for recording behavior. One Little League coach felt that his players played better and enjoyed the game more when they were praised and encouraged by their teammates. He wanted to increase praise and encouragement, so he decided to record the frequency of those behaviors. To get an accurate record of how often these reinforcing statements were made by his players, he kept his left pocket full of small pebbles. Whenever he heard one team member praise or encourage another, he moved a pebble from the left pocket to the right pocket. At the end of every game, he could count the pebbles in his right pocket and have a fairly accurate record. This recording method didn't interfere with his coaching at all, and his players weren't even aware of what he was doing.

General discussion

We'll talk about some other methods of recording behavior in our next session. For now, does anyone have any questions or comments about this session?

Discussion of the Home Practice Assignment

Everyone needs to get some practice with basic behavior recording. For home practice, I want each of you to pinpoint one specific behavior that you would like to see more often from your child. Keep a record of that behavior's frequency during the week. You'll find all the necessary forms and instructions in your Workbook.

There's a completed sample behavior record there also. The sample shows a behavior the parent wishes to see less of: leaving toys and clothes around the house. Remember that your assignment is to specify a behavior that you want to see your child do more often. Later on, you'll be using behavior modification to change your child's behavior. But for now, it is important that you master the first step in behavior modification—accurately recording behavior frequency. You can see that we are also approaching learning one step at a time—because that's the best way to learn. So use this week to practice only recording the frequency of your child's behavior. Don't try to change the behavior. Bring your behavior frequency record with you next week. It will give you a good idea of how often that specific behavior occurs before you begin the behavior modification program.

Recording Behavior and Setting Consequences

Introduction

The next three sessions focus on using the principles of behavior modification to record behavior and establish appropriate positive and negative consequences to change that behavior. Parents often object to the idea of recording behavior as a part of formal behavior contracting. This is also the aspect of behavior management programs that parents most often fail to do. You should emphasize that the specific behavior must be recorded accurately and consistently. Children have a right to expect an accurate and fair accounting of their behavior. Inaccurate and inconsistent behavior recording can become a source of considerable anger and frustration for the child.

Special Notes for the Mental Health Professional

The difficulties associated with accurate and consistent behavior recording are the best reason why parents shouldn't use a formal behavior modification program unless there is a special problem behavior that is very important to them or to their child. Having this special need provides the necessary motivation to sustain a formal program with consistent recording. If such a need isn't present, the parents will probably not have enough motivation to sustain the requirements of the program. During the discussion of how to set up a successful behavioral modification program, parents should realize that each program needs to have a specific goal that determines when the program will end. And this goal must be discussed with the child. Failure to discuss the goal with the child when the program is first set up can lead to negative feelings, because the child loses control of when the program will end.

Be prepared to handle parent objections to, biases about, and criticisms of behavioral principles. Maintain a nondefensive, open, and accepting demeanor at all times, and respond to any challenges from the parents in a calm and matter-of-fact manner. This is a good time for you to model reflective listening skills. The most helpful approach is to use reflective listening while helping the parents in your group identify the basis for their beliefs about the behavioral principles you are teaching. This will help the parents to become more objective and more open to the ideas you are presenting.

Parents may bring up the issue of "bribing" their child into good behavior. This issue is best handled by pointing out how their child might view this situation and what effect it might have on the child. Parents should be prepared to present the behavioral program to their child as a structure that will help the child reach goals that the child values. When a child sees the program in this way, he or she will be more willing to commit to working toward a behavioral goal. Parents need to recognize that behavioral programs work best when the child is committed to the goals and activities, or procedures, involved in the program. Imposing a program on an unprepared or unwilling child is likely to result in failure, whereas discussing the program thoroughly and openly with the child increases its chances for success.

Session Objectives

1 To help parents set up behavior modification projects, specify exact behaviors, and record exact behaviors.

2 To provide parents with a variety of behavior recording procedures, including self-monitoring, that can be successful in different situations.

3 To help parents set consequences of behavior.

4 To show parents that to increase a behavior they must set a positive consequence.

5 To reinforce the idea that behavior change is best accomplished in small steps.

6 To help parents practice setting up a behavior modification program for use with their own children.

7 To help parents evaluate the results of their programs.

8 To help parents practice setting consequences in a behavior modification contract.

Sequence

- Review and sharing of home practice (5 - 10 minutes)
- Lecture/Discussion (40 - 50 minutes)
    - Description of alternate recording methods
    - Discussion of setting consequences
    - Practice in setting up a program
    - Discussion of evaluating the results of a program
    - Discussion and practice in negotiating behavior modification contracts
- General discussion (30 - 35 minutes)
- Discussion of the home practice assignment (5 - 10 minutes)

 ## Materials

Blackboard (or large marking board)

Chalk (or markers)

Eraser

Handout: Sample Behavior Modification Program

Handout: Blank recording charts for each parent

Review and Sharing of Home Practice

(Encourage and reinforce sharing of home practice experience.)

170

Accurately Recording Behavior

During this past week, you've all been keeping a record of a specific behavior in your child that you want to see more of. I hope you all brought those records with you tonight. Last week, I said that the first two steps in setting up a successful behavior modification program are pinpointing a specific behavior to be changed and finding out exactly how often the behavior is occurring by keeping a record of its frequency.

Q What behaviors have you chosen to work on? *(Pause for parents' response. If no one volunteers, call on someone. Direct group reaction to the behaviors chosen. Help the group decide whether each chosen behavior is specific enough to be reliably recorded. Ask if this is a description of an observable behavior or an evaluation of the child's personality/character. One example of this might be, "the child takes other children's toys" versus "the child is mean." Have individual group members present the behavior they have chosen to modify; then ask if anyone has a question about the behavior he or she has chosen. Have the group react, but make suggestions if necessary.)*

As a group you're studying a wide range of behaviors. How did the recording go? I'm sure most of you found out that accurately recording behavior frequency is not always as easy as it sounds.

Q Did anyone come up with methods for counting behavior frequencies that they especially liked? Did anyone have problems with recording? *(Pause for parents to respond to each question. If no one volunteers, call on someone who has already described the behavior they are counting. Lead the group response to the different recording methods being employed. Be sure the discussion includes the following points: Is the recording method reliable? Is it easy to administer? Where is the recording taking place? Could any improvements be suggested? Will this method work with any of the behaviors that other group members have chosen to modify?)*

I would like to tell you about one additional recording system you might find useful. Sometimes it is possible to have your child keep a record of his or her own behavior. An example of a behavior your child could easily record is tooth-brushing. For example, a simple chart containing the days of the month might be placed in the bathroom, and your child could just mark the chart each time the child brushes his or her teeth. This method would be very easy for you, and children often enjoy keeping records of their own behavior.

As another example, suppose you wanted your child to help with certain household chores. You could provide an empty can or other container for the child's room and you could keep a bag of marbles or some other token on hand. Then, every time your child completed one of the chores, you could give him or her a marble to put in the can. At the end of the recording period, the number of marbles in the can would provide a record of the number of times your child helped around the house. (Pause.)

Q How might your child record his own behavior of taking out the garbage after dinner or feeding the dog? *(Pause for parents' response.)*

Q What if the behavior is getting up in the morning without being called several times? How could your child record that behavior? (Pause for *parents' response.)*

You see that there are many behaviors your child can easily keep a record of. This may actually be the best recording method for the specific behavior you have chosen to modify. (Pause.)

Let's review the steps involved in a behavior modification program. Last session, I mentioned that there are four steps and we talked about the first two: pinpointing behavior and recording its frequency. *(Write on the board, "1. Pinpoint behavior" and "2. Record behavior frequency.")* The third step is setting the consequences of the behavior. *(Write on the board, "3. Set the consequences.")*

Remember that a consequence is something that happens after or as a result of a certain behavior. You already know that behavior is determined by its consequences. According to the first law of learning, behavior that is followed by a pleasant or reinforcing consequence tends to be repeated, and behavior that is not followed by pleasant consequences or that is punished tends not to be repeated.

Because you are all working toward increasing a desirable behavior in your child, we'll talk about how to set the consequences that will increase the frequency of a behavior. You want the behavior to be followed by a reinforcer. In other words, you will want to set a pleasant consequence. When we talked about reinforcers last week, I mentioned three general types: social, nonsocial or object, and activity.

Q Can someone give me an example of a social reinforcer? *(Pause for parents' response.)*

Q What about some examples of object reinforcers? *(Pause for parents' response.)*

Q What are some good activity reinforcers for children? *(Pause for parents' response.)*

Now I'll tell you about a formal behavior modification program developed by two parents.

172

Mr. and Mrs. Kotch were very upset by the fact that their 5-year-old son, Paul, was bullying his 2-year-old brother Mark. Paul would hit Mark for no apparent reason, yell at him and call him names, or pull toys away from him and knock him down. The Kotches tried to share their feelings with Paul. They talked with him about their concern for Mark's safety and their desire to have a happy home. Despite their increased attention and their open and frank discussion with Paul, his behavior toward his little brother didn't change.

Mr. and Mrs. Kotch decided to try a formal behavior modification program. They each decided to pinpoint one specific behavior they wanted to change. Mrs. Kotch chose to record the number of times Paul hit or pushed Mark; Mr. Kotch chose to record the number of times Paul said something kind or friendly to Mark. The Kotches decided to record these two behaviors every night at the same time: after supper and before bedtime, from 7:00 to 8:00 p.m.

(Put the basic graphs shown in Figures 22 and 23 on the board, but don't include the treatment data yet. Explain how to read the graphs.)

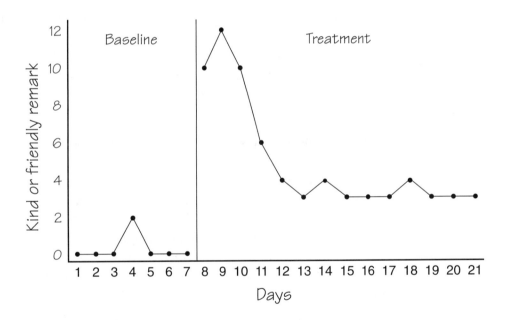

Figure 22. Mr. Kotch's behavior recording chart.

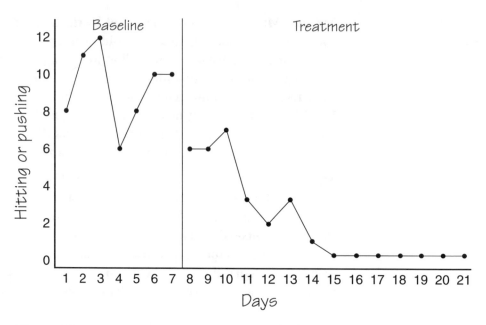

Figure 23. Mrs. Kotch's behavior recording chart.

Let's consider what might have happened if Mr. and Mrs. Kotch had set up the behavior modification program differently at first. What if they had said, "Paul, we can't stand the way you behave. You are mean and cruel. If you keep being mean, you'll grow up to be just another rotten kid. Because we love you, we are going to give you a chance to change and be nice. After supper, if you are nice to Mark, you can stay up an extra 15 minutes and we will give you a snack."

Q With the approach I just described, it is not likely that Paul's behavior will change. Can you spot some of the problems with this approach? *(Pause for parents' response. The answers should include the following ideas: judging and scolding attacks the child's self-worth; name-calling will upset the child, and he will be less likely to hear the rest of the message; the parents did not use small steps or frequent reinforcements; instead, they required a total cure; the parents did not describe the specific behavior they were talking about; the parents did not explain what specific behaviors they were calling "mean.")*

At the beginning of the second week of their program, the Kotches had a conference with Paul. They repeated their concerns and proposed an agreement. Each time Paul said something kind to Mark or helped him, Paul would get a roasted peanut—one of his favorite foods. To keep track of how many peanuts he earned, a marble was placed in a jar every time Paul said something kind to his brother. It was also agreed that if he didn't hit or push Mark between supper and bedtime, Paul could stay up an extra 15 minutes and have a glass of milk with Dad while Mom put Mark to bed. When Paul earned this special time, his father used it to praise Paul's accomplishments.

Now let me show you what happened as a result of Mr. and Mrs. Kotch's behavior modification program. *(Plot the treatment data shown in Figures 22 and 23 in graphs on board.)* The effect of the program on Paul's hitting and pushing behavior can be seen clearly. The effect we see in Mr. Kotch's graph of the incidence of kind words needs a little more explanation. At first, Paul earned a lot of peanuts by saying about one kind sentence to his brother each minute. After a while, the novelty wore off, and it was hard for Paul to constantly be thinking of kind things to say. So Paul's kind words occurred less often. Still, as we can see on the graph, the change in Paul's behavior has remained. He now rewards his brother—not every minute—but more often than he did before.

Notice that this behavior modification program used all three kinds of reinforcers.

Q What were the specific reinforcers used by the Kotches? What kind of reinforcer was each? *(Pause for parents to respond: Social – Daddy's praise. Nonsocial – roasted peanuts. Activity – staying up 15 minutes extra/special time with daddy.)*

We've talked about formal behavior modification, and you've seen some examples. Now I'd like you to practice setting up a program. You'll divide into groups of three or four and work in teams. *(Groups should be approximately equal.)* Each group will outline their program on this sheet of paper. *(Distribute the handout from the end of this chapter to one person in each group.)* You'll notice that the first step in the program—pinpointing a specific behavior—has already been filled in. You'll be completing the other two steps: recording frequencies and setting consequences. You'll have 5 minutes to decide how to go about changing the specific behavior. Fill in the frequencies you think you might see if you were recording this child's behavior. *(Assist groups as needed. Make sure parents are very specific about recording procedures and delivering consequences.)*

Q Time is up. How did this group *(point to one group)* go about getting Cindy to brush her teeth? *(Have each group discuss their proposed program. Get reactions from other groups as to the reliability and feasibility of the suggested recording procedures, appropriateness of the consequences, ease of administration of consequences, etc. Discuss each group's proposal in this manner.)*

You might be thinking that behavior modification is not really all that new or different. Setting consequences is something many of you have already used to manage your child's behavior. For example, you might have a rule that your child can only have dessert if he eats his dinner, or that he can only watch television after he finishes his homework. These are definite examples of behavior modification programs, and they are not new. But there are two things that may be new to you: the large variety of behaviors that can be taught using these procedures and how to use these procedures in a systematic way to ensure successful results. This systematic method is particularly important with behaviors that must be learned and that will only change slowly. This brings us to the fourth, and final, step in behavior modification—evaluating the results. *(Write on the board: "4. Evaluate the results.")*

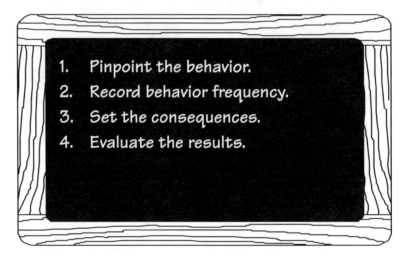

Figure 24. The four steps in behavior modification.

Let's take one of the examples I just mentioned. Suppose you are trying to get your child to eat his dinner. You notice that he hasn't eaten any vegetables the last 4 nights, and you decide to set a consequence. He can have dessert only if he has eaten all of his vegetables. The first night, he doesn't eat any dinner and asks for dessert. You tell him you would like to give him dessert, but the rule is he can only have dessert if he eats his vegetables. He still doesn't eat any vegetables. The next night, the same thing happens. After 5 days of this, he still is not eating any vegetables. You evaluate your results, and you realize that you have not been at all successful. You decide to take another look at your program.

Q Can anyone suggest why this program isn't working? *(Pause for parents' response.)*

Exactly. After you set the consequence for a behavior, you must continue to record the frequency of that behavior and use your record to evaluate the results. You have to remember that there is usually not an immediate change in behavior. Children will often try to test you to see if you really meant what you said. When your child is sure you did mean what you said, his or her behavior will begin to change. If the behavior doesn't begin to change, there is something wrong with one of the four steps in your program.

One final point about setting consequences: Setting consequences is a lot like negotiating a contract. The object is not to force something on your child, but to develop an arrangement that will benefit both of you. The process of setting up this contract provides an excellent opportunity for using the relationship-building skills we talked about in our earlier sessions. It gives you a great opportunity to listen to your child's feelings and accept them. As you saw in our example of the Kotch family, parents can best communicate by sharing themselves, not by passing judgment. In all contract negotiations, the strongest agreement comes about when both sides use reflective listening and self-sharing. This give and take is necessary. When a positive parent-child relationship exists, agreements can be reached in which all the parties reach their goals.

You've practiced recording behaviors, and now you'll practice setting consequences. We'll do a little role-playing using relationship-building communications to determine the appropriate consequences to use with a child. If someone will volunteer to practice setting consequences, I'll play the child. Your task in the role-play will be to determine some reinforcers that will work with the child I'm pretending to be. *(If no one volunteers, call on a group member to negotiate a behavioral contract with you as the child. Reinforce the parent and suggest appropriate techniques. Encourage all the group members to take a turn at role playing with you as the child.)*

Remember, The more you practice these techniques, the more natural they will become.

General Discussion

 Does anyone have any concerns or questions about what we are doing and how it may work in your particular family situation? *(Pause for parents' response. Encourage and reinforce honest discussion and parents' attempts to relate these ideas to their own home situations.)*

Discussion of the Home Practice Assignment

In the home practice assignment for this week you will be designing a behavior modification program for use with your child. You may select as the target behavior any behavior that you would like to see your child do more or less frequently. One important decision that you will need to make in selecting a target behavior is whether you want to focus on reducing a negative behavior or want to help your child to develop a positive behavior that is incompatible with the negative one. Often when we focus on negative behavior, we think of punishing our child for every occurrence of the behavior. In most cases, if we reinforce or reward a positive behavior that is incompatible with the negative behavior, the negative behavior will begin to disappear. For example, if your child is getting ready to leave for the nursery school or day care and has his or her shoes on "before the big hand on the clock is pointing straight up," the child would get a special treat. This positive behavior would be incompatible with dawdling and not getting dressed in time. The review section in this week's home practice describes how you might select a positive behavior to reinforce (that is incompatible with the negative behavior) and how to record your observations. The assignment will give you the opportunity to use not only the behavior modification skills we have been discussing, but also your reflective listening skills.

Remember, a behavior modification program works best when the child has been involved in its design. It is important to talk about the target behavior with your child, discussing why a change would be good for your child. If your child would like to work on a different but equally important behavior, consider going with the child's choice. Your child's input on the design of all phases of the program is very important to its success. What your child actually finds reinforcing is more important than your guesses about reinforcers. Therefore, you need to discuss the reinforcers you plan to use with your child.

Next week we will review how your behavior modification programs are going.

Behavior Modification Recording Chart

Name ___Cindy, age 5_____ Date ___March 10_____

1. Specific behavior to be changed: ___I want Cindy to brush her teeth sometime___
   ___between the time she finishes dinner and when she goes to bed._____

   _____

   Incompatible positive behavior (optional) _____

   _____

   _____

2. Time and place of observation: _____

   _____ observations per _____ every _____
      (number)   (minute/hour/day)   (day or week)

   What will be counted?_____

3. Results of observation before setting consequences:

	Day 1	Day 2	Day 3	Day 4	Day 5	Day 6	Day 7
Specific (negative)							
Incompatible (positive)							

4. Consequence will be _____

   _____

   _____

5. Results of observation after consequences were set:

	Day 1	Day 2	Day 3	Day 4	Day 5	Day 6	Day 7
Specific (negative)							
Incompatible (positive)							
	Day 8	Day 8	Day 10	Day 11	Day 12	Day 13	Day 14
Specific (negative)							
Incompatible (positive)							

PAR **Psychological Assessment Resources, Inc.**/P.O. Box 998/Odessa, FL 33556/Toll-Free 1-800-331-TEST

Using Behavior Modification Principles With Appropriate Reinforcers

Session Objectives

1 To provide feedback and elicit reactions concerning the parents' ongoing behavior modification projects.

2 To make parents aware of Grandma's Law (Premack Principle) and help parents understand that any activity a child enjoys can be a reinforcer.

3 To demonstrate withholding reinforcement and time-out as methods of decreasing undesirable behavior.

4 To help parents generate answers to issues or solutions to problems that arise in their use of behavior modification.

Sequence

● Review and sharing of home practice (10 - 20 minutes).

● Lecture/Discussion (40 - 45 minutes)
  – Discussion of activity reinforcers
  – Discussion of methods of decreasing an undesirable behavior
  – Discussion of common objections to behavior modification principles

● General discussion (20 - 30 minutes)

● Discussion of the home practice assignment (5 - 10 minutes)

Materials

Handout: Blank Recording Chart

Review and sharing of home practice

(Encourage and reinforce sharing of home practice experience.)

Lecture/Discussion

Recording Procedures

Let's start today's session by talking about the behavior modification programs you've been working on. Some of you may still be recording your child's behavior, and others may already be using consequences and reinforcements. First, let's talk about the recording procedures you selected and your experiences recording your child's behavior. *(Pause for parents' response. If no one starts, ask who is still recording, and ask that person to describe the recording procedures he or she is using. Be as reinforcing as possible.)*

It sounds as if everyone has a good understanding of recording procedures and the different ways they can be used. Now, how are things going for those of you who are already using reinforcers and consequences in your programs? *(Pause for parents to bring up their projects. If no one volunteers, ask parents directly. During this discussion, be sure to emphasize the importance of including a gradual fade-out of extrinsic reinforcers in the original agreement. Reinforce parents' contributions. Reinforce parents who mention using reflective listening and self-sharing during the initial phase of setting up the program and identifying appropriate reinforcers. Explain again that if a program is not working, it probably has design problems. You might mention that even professional psychologists sometimes have to adjust their behavior modification programs. Offer to help parents whose programs are not working to carefully review the specific behavior they want changed, the recording procedure they chose, and how they set the reinforcers.)*

Lecture/Discussion

Activity Reinforcers

I want to briefly review last week's discussion about reinforcers that will increase a desirable behavior in your child. I mentioned three basic groups of consequences that can be reinforcing. There are social reinforcers, such as praise and affection, activity reinforcers, like watching television or talking with Mom and Dad, and nonsocial or object reinforcers, such as candy or peanuts. We'll take a closer look at activity reinforcers during this session.

Activity reinforcers are just as powerful as any other type of reinforcer, but they have two extra values. First, they usually fit easily into the regular family routine. And second, using activity reinforcers as consequences means you have to pay closer attention to what your child does and likes, and you must also use reflective listening and self-sharing to discover what reinforcer will work best. Here's an example of what I mean:

Mrs. Green was having a hard time getting her daughter, Jane, to brush her teeth before she went to Kindergarten every morning. Jane would brush her teeth without argument if her mother was standing there, but she wouldn't take any responsibility for it. Yelling and threats didn't seem to change the situation. Mrs. Green decided to use her reflective listening skills.

Mrs. Green:	**"You sure don't like to brush your teeth in the morning, Jane."**
Jane:	**"It's dumb."** *(Mrs. Green remains silent.)*
Jane:	**"It's no fun!"**

Mrs. Green:	"You would do it if it was fun?"
Jane:	"Yeah. Like when you brush your teeth, Mom. *(Mrs. Green has an electric toothbrush.)* That's fun."

Mrs. Green used her reflective listening skills, and she learned more about Jane. Because of what she learned, she was able to come up with the following formal behavior modification program using an activity reinforcer:

Mrs. Green:	"Jane, I worry about you. If you don't take good care of your teeth, you could get cavities. I'll tell you what. If you brush your teeth in the morning before school without me reminding you, you can use the electric toothbrush to brush your teeth before you go to bed."

For Jane, the reward for brushing her teeth was the chance to brush her teeth. At first it doesn't seem to make sense. But, when you think about it, you see that a reinforcer is something rewarding, something that's fun, something that's important to the individual receiving it. By maintaining a close relationship with your child and by using reflective listening and self-sharing, you will have a better understanding and appreciation of your child and what he or she finds reinforcing.

Here's another example of how a mother solved a problem by using her communication skills along with a behavior modification program involving an activity reinforcer.

Mrs. Hand belonged to a family that socialized a good deal. Every other Sunday afternoon, relatives would visit. Mrs. Hand found that getting ready for company was too much for her. It involved lots of rushing around and yelling at the kids. One Sunday, she told her 10-year-old son, James, to vacuum and dust the living and dining rooms. James started to do the vacuuming, but reluctantly, grumbling to himself. Usually, Mrs. Hand would yell even more when James did this, but this Sunday she decided to try something different. She used reflective listening and then spoke:

Mrs. Hand:	"James, you sure are mad about having to vacuum and dust the living room and dining room."
James:	"Yeah." *(Mrs. Hand waits in silence.)*
James:	"Mom, why do I have to do this job? It's not an important job like polishing the silverware. I like to help, but I don't like to vacuum and dust."
Mrs. Hand:	"James, it is important to me to be ready for company when they get here. If polishing the silverware would be important to you, then you can polish the silverware as soon as you finish cleaning the living and dining rooms."

This agreement solved the problem of getting willing help from James for the Sunday clean-up. Again, we see that what some people would call harder work—polishing silver—was used to reinforce a desirable behavior. Let's look at another example.

Joanie and her mother had a running battle over Joanie's homework. It wasn't that she didn't do it, but that she waited until late at night to start working on it. That meant that Joanie had to stay up very late to get her work finished. Mom felt that Joanie needed more sleep than she was getting. When Mom looked closely at the problem, she realized that it was happening because Joanie was watching television after dinner instead of getting right to work. Joanie and her mother discussed the situation and decided on a new rule. Joanie had to finish her homework each evening before she was allowed to watch television. The behavior change was dramatic. Joanie began her homework promptly after dinner and still had time to watch some TV and get to bed at a reasonable time.

This is an example of a very effective way to use an activity reinforcer to increase behavior. In this case, the behavior Joanie's mom wanted to increase was doing homework early in the evening, and the activity reinforcer was watching television.

Last week I mentioned that behavior modification is not really a new technique. In fact, the example of Joanie and her Mom demonstrates a technique so old that it is sometimes called *Grandma's Law*. Grandma's Law involves arranging the order of activities to achieve a desired result. This is the technique that Grandma first used when she said you could have a piece of pie after you took your bath. When there are two behaviors that can occur in a particular situation, one that your child enjoys and one that the child dislikes but you think is important, you can arrange it so your child can do the one he or she likes *after* the one you feel is important. That's Grandma's Law.

Now, listen to this statement:

"I'll take you ice skating, but I want you to pick up your toys first."

Q Is this an example of Grandma's Law? *(Pause for parents' response.)*

Yes, it is. The important behavior which is less likely to occur on its own is done first. The behavior desired by the child is used as a consequence. What about this remark:

"Okay, you can go to the movies. As soon as you get back, I want you to rake the lawn. You promised me yesterday that it would be finished by now."

Q Is this an example of Grandma's Law? *(Pause for parents' response.)*

Right. This is not an example of Grandma's Law. The highly desired behavior—going to the movies—comes first. The behavior the parent thinks is important—keeping a promise to help—is not being taught very well.

Q Can you think of other examples of Grandma's Law? *(Pause for parents' response.)*

I want to emphasize one more thing about selecting activity reinforcers for children. There are some activities that most children enjoy. Watching television is a good example. Almost all children enjoy television a great deal, and this activity is a strong reinforcing consequence. Some activities, however, should not be used as reinforcers unless you know that they will work with your child. For example, some young children love to set the table or dry the dishes. Some like to wash the car or rake the lawn. For some children, a very desirable activity is answering the phone. These are simple, normal, everyday activities, so many parents miss the potential they have as reinforcers.

If you tune in to the activities your child particularly enjoys, you will find a list of very powerful reinforcers. And think about the special meaning this will have for your child. When you suggest a consequence activity that is a really special treat for your child, it shows your child that you care enough to know what he or she likes to do and that you understand his or her world, at least a little bit.

For example, suppose your 10-year-old daughter really likes to make Jello® or brownies. One day, you are in a hurry and you are trying to get the house cleaned up before company arrives. You say to her:

> **"Honey, I really have a lot to do, and I don't think I can finish it all before the guests come. I'll tell you what. If you make the beds and clean the hall, you can make Jello or brownies for the company."**

Because this is an activity your daughter particularly likes, she will probably help you with the housework. At the same time, you have communicated to her that you understand what she likes and doesn't like. Watching what your child enjoys doing is one way to identify activities that will be good reinforcers.

Lecture/Discussion

Unpleasant Consequences

So far, we've talked mainly about increasing desirable behaviors. It is usually more effective to concentrate on rewarding rather than punishing. Rewarding produces a change in the specific behavior and, at the same time, it can also increase the strength of your parent-child relationship. Sometimes, though, it is necessary to withhold rewards or to punish a child in order to decrease some undesirable behavior. Let's look at some examples of how parents have decreased problem behaviors by using behavior modification.

Mrs. Ward's 6-year-old son, Billy, frequently soiled his pants. She kept a record for 5 days and found that the soiling occurred one to three times daily. She also discovered that one consequence of Billy's soiling was that she washed and changed him, giving him a good deal of attention. She decided to set a different consequence. From now on, when Billy soiled himself, she would give him clean clothes only after he washed his pants out. On the first day with the new consequence, Billy soiled himself once. Then he didn't soil himself again until the 21st day of the program, and that was the last time it happened. Mrs. Ward was very satisfied with the results of the new consequence.

This example shows how you can effectively withhold reinforcers to decrease an undesirable behavior. It also shows how we sometimes teach our children bad habits without even realizing what we are doing. All the attention Mrs. Ward had been giving her son was very pleasant and enjoyable for him, and it actually reinforced his soiling behavior.

Here is another example of using an unpleasant consequence effectively to decrease an undesirable behavior.

Scott, age 4, and Philip, age 6, were brothers who frequently fought with each other over toys. When they argued and hit each other, it upset their mother. So she told the boys that she was upset and that she realized they were both angry with each other. She then told both boys that, each time an argument began and they started hitting each other, they would have to sit on the steps going upstairs. One brother would have to sit on the bottom step and the other on the top step. And they would have to sit there for 5 minutes. In a few days, the number of arguments and fights had dropped from about 10 per day to only once or twice a day.

This mother used a time-out procedure as an unpleasant consequence. When the problem behavior occurred, the boys had to take a time-out from playing.

Time-out is one of the most effective mild punishments for decreasing undesirable behavior in children ages 2 to 12 years. Time-out is a consequence that involves isolating the child from the flow of family activities and from eye contact with the parent for a specified period of time. The child must stay in the designated time-out location until the time is up. Choose a place that is boring and one that will not present any danger to the child. For younger children, ages 2 to 4 years, this might be a straight-backed chair facing a wall in a room near you. For 5- to 12-year olds, choose a hallway, the middle of a set of stairs, or some other location away from you. The time-out location should never be your child's own room or any other room in the house where he or she would have access to some form of entertainment.

The process of handling time-outs will depend on your child's level of development. Time-outs need to be explained well in advance of their first use with any child. Younger children will probably need to rehearse the procedure, putting a doll or some other object in time-out so the child can understand exactly what is expected. Be sure to match appropriate feelings with your words. You might say something like, "It's sad that Dolly (or Teddy) has to go into time-out, but Dolly decided not to do what we asked. Dolly will get out of time-out soon, and we'll be happy together."

But with older children, you can first explain the procedure and then walk the child through it. Let your child know that time-out is a consequence that will be applied when he or she doesn't comply with a request to do or stop doing something. Emphasize that you will repeat your request once and then, if the child still doesn't comply, he or she will be placed in the time-out location for the specified amount of time, usually 1 minute for each year of the child's age. You can use a kitchen timer or other timing device that will signal you and your child when the time-out is over. When the timer sounds, the child is automatically released.

After you explain the time-out procedure to your child, select one or two behaviors to which time-out can be applied in a reasonable manner. Remember that the procedure needs to be consistently followed whenever your child refuses to comply with your request regarding the target behavior. When the undesirable behavior occurs, the first step is to ask your child to stop the behavior. If the child refuses to comply, you repeat your request once and let the child know that he or she is now "making a decision." At this point, it is essential for your child to understand that time-out is really his or her decision. For example, you might say, "You are making a decision now. Either pick up the toy or go to time-out." or "You hit your brother again. Go to time-out now." You can use any phrase that lets your child know that the time-out penalty is invoked for failure to comply with your request. Time-out must *always* be enforced when you threaten to use it.

Not being able to play, even for short periods of time, is a very negative experience for children. Longer periods of time, such as 30 minutes or more, tend to be less effective. This is particularly true with younger children, because they lose the link between their behavior and the consequence after 5 or 10 minutes. More frequent time-outs of shorter duration provide more learning trials for young children. The general rule should be 1 minute of time-out for each year of the child's age. Of course, the time-out clock starts only after the child is quiet and continues only as long as the child stays in the time-out location. Younger children may cry or talk when they are in time-out, but you should ignore this minor noise. With older children, you might require silence during time-out. If the child makes noise when time-out silence is required, or if the child leaves the specified time-out location, the time-out clock starts over.

At the end of the time-out, when the timer rings, ask your child, "Why were you sent to time-out?" You shouldn't scold or explain, and your child should not be expected to apologize. If you don't get a clear answer, then repeat your original request or describe the child's undesirable behavior in as few words as possible. This is the last step in the time-out. When the child is released, everything should be forgiven and not mentioned again. You should always praise your child for good time-out behavior. For some 5- to 10-year-olds, occasionally releasing them early from time-out as a reward for good behavior helps to ease any tension in your relationship.

Obviously, children don't want to be in time-out. They find it unpleasant. But, when time-out is consistently applied, children do learn to accept it. Normally, only a few time-out sessions are all that is required. However, resistance to the time-out procedure is not uncommon.

For children ages 2 to 4 years, this resistance will typically follow one of five patterns:

1. *Delaying or refusing to go to time-out.* If this happens, quickly carry the preschooler or toddler to the time-out location.

2. *Making noise during time-out.* If this happens, you have two options: ignoring the child or letting the child know that time will be added to the time-out if the noise continues.

3. *Escaping from the time-out chair.* You have five options for dealing with this behavior. I will present them in decreasing order of preference:
   – Place the child back in the chair, stand beside the chair, and harshly command the child to say put.
   – Firmly place your hand on the child's leg or shoulder, look away, and command the child to stay in the chair. Say nothing else.
   – Stand behind the chair and firmly hold the child in place.
   – Sit in the chair yourself, holding the child firmly in your lap. Tell the child you will start the timer after he or she stops trying to get away. Then, ignore the child completely; avoid responding to any remarks.
   – Spank the child. Remember, this is not a recommended option!

4. *Not leaving the time-out chair after the timer rings.* You should ignore this. It's the child's choice.

5. *Continuing to cry or scream after leaving the chair.* If this happens, try ignoring the child for a couple of minutes. If the child continues, firmly tell the child to stop, saying something like this: "You are making a decision. If you continue to cry, you will go back to time-out." Then, if the child continues, repeat the time-out procedure.

In children ages 5 to 10 years, resistance to time-out will typically follow one of four patterns:

1. *Delaying or refusing to go to time-out.* If your child doesn't respond, tell the child that additional minutes will be added if he or she doesn't go to the time-out location immediately. If the child still

resists, count 10 seconds silently to yourself, and then tell the child you are adding 1 minute to the total time-out. This should be repeated up to an additional 5 minutes. If the child is still resisting, explain that, in addition to the extra time-out minutes, he or she will also lose certain privileges. In some situations, if the behavior penalty is sufficiently punishing, you may choose to substitute the behavior penalty for the time-out. For example, the child might lose the privilege of watching television for the entire evening as a behavior penalty for resisting time-out. The child will soon learn that the consequences of not going to time-out are worse than accepting the time-out. Remember, you are working toward compliance with the time-out procedure, and reasonable behavior may take a while to emerge in your young child.

2. *Making noise during time-out.* If this occurs, you have two options: ignoring the child or adding extra minutes to the time-out if the noise continues.

3. *Escaping from time-out.* Tell your child that, for each 10 seconds he or she is absent from the specified time-out location, an additional 1 minute will be added to the time-out clock. Again, the maximum would be 5 minutes additional time-out. If that doesn't work, an additional behavior penalty or loss of privilege should be imposed. Your child will quickly learn that accepting the time-out is better than the behavior penalty or loss of privilege.

4. *Making a mess in the time-out location.* You need to realize that this is another attempt on your child's part to punish you or coerce you into not using time-out. Maintain a calm, matter-of-fact tone. Tell your child that he or she must clean up the mess before leaving the time-out location. Don't act shocked or scold the child.

If your child continues to resist time-out, even after you successfully apply these principles, it may be time for you and your family to seek professional assistance in managing your child's behavior.

Q Can you think of any of your own children's behaviors that might be handled with a time-out? *(Pause for parents' response. Reinforce suggestions.)*

Usually, when parents begin to learn behavior modification procedures, they develop some reservations about the techniques. There are some questions that parents often ask, and I'd like to spend the rest of this session helping you decide how you would answer these questions. Let's do it this way: I will be the person who has the questions. You will all play the role of someone who uses and supports these behavior modification procedures and who refutes the questions that I present. I'll ask the questions the way someone who doesn't accept behavior modification might ask them, and you will answer my questions the way someone who supports behavior modification would respond. Ready? *(Pause for parents' questions.)*

Question 1: *(Questioning tone of voice.)* **It sounds to me like you are bribing children.**

(Summarize parent responses. The responses should include the following ideas: Bribery involves getting someone to do something wrong or bad. Pay for honest work is entirely legitimate.)

Question 2: *(Irate tone of voice.)* **What gives you the right to decide for your child what he or she will do? It sounds like manipulation to me.**

(Summarize parent responses. The responses should include the following ideas: Parents make many decisions for their children. This is part of a parent's job—guiding and teaching. Parents control many behaviors without even realizing it—as we saw in the example where the boy was soiling his pants. The question isn't whether or not you, the parent, will control your child's behavior, because in many ways you already do. The question is whether you will control wisely and with forethought.)

Question 3: **It seems to me that you are asking us to become an "if-then" sort of family. If you do this for me, then I'll do that for you.**

(Summarize parent responses. The responses should include the following ideas: Formal contracting is not a technique that you will use all the time—only some of the time, when it seems to fit the situation best. There are other child management techniques that parents can use. As good teachers, parents should always try to positively reinforce desirable behaviors.)

Question 4: **This whole behavior modification thing is artificial. Kids should learn how to behave without getting paid for it.**

(Summarize parent responses. The responses should include the following ideas: "Should" is a moralistic, irrational concept. Kids learn what they do learn because of the reinforcements that follow certain behaviors. What is important is making sure that children do learn what they need to learn, not whether they "should" or "ought" to have learned something in a different way. Regarding artificiality, many behaviors and natural reinforcers already exist in the home. It is simply a matter of better organizing them. Whenever artificial reinforcers are used, they are used to get the behavior under control. Then the artificial reinforcers are slowly replaced with social reinforcers such as praise or affection, and finally with self-pride in accomplishment.)

Question 5: **Do you expect me to record and develop a behavior modification program to teach my child everything and to handle every problem behavior?**

(Summarize parent responses. The responses should include the following ideas: Formal behavior modification programs, including accurate behavior

recording, are special techniques that parents can use for special problems, particularly those that haven't been solved using less systematic procedures.)

General Discussion

Q I hope this discussion has helped you to formulate some of your own answers to these questions. Are there any other questions you may have? (*Pause for parents' response. If possible, have the group respond to individual parents' questions at this point. This is also a good time to remind parents of the less formal behavior management techniques they learned in earlier sessions.*)

Discussion of the Home Practice Assignment

That's all for this session. You'll be continuing with your behavior modification projects during the coming week. Pay particular attention to identifying activities that your child really enjoys. Next session, we'll be reviewing your projects, so don't forget to bring your recording charts. I have additional blank recording charts in the box at the door for anyone who needs them.

Behavior Modification Recording Chart

Name _____ Date _____

1. Specific behavior to be changed: _____

   _____

   _____

   Incompatible positive behavior (optional) _____

   _____

   _____

2. Time and place of observation: _____

   _____ observations per _____ every _____

      (number)   (minute/hour/day)   (day or week)

   What will be counted? _____

3. Results of observation before setting consequences:

	Day 1	Day 2	Day 3	Day 4	Day 5	Day 6	Day 7
Specific (negative)							
Incompatible (positive)							

4. Consequence will be _____

   _____

   _____

5. Results of observation after consequences were set:

	Day 1	Day 2	Day 3	Day 4	Day 5	Day 6	Day 7
Specific (negative)							
Incompatible (positive)							
	Day 8	Day 8	Day 10	Day 11	Day 12	Day 13	Day 14
Specific (negative)							
Incompatible (positive)							

PAR Psychological Assessment Resources, Inc./P.O. Box 998/Odessa, FL 33556/Toll-Free 1-800-331-TEST

Session 15

Using the Behavioral Modification Method on Yourself

Session Objectives

1 To help parents successfully complete the behavior modification projects they have set up with their children.

2 To point out that behavior modification procedures can also be applied to oneself.

3 To evaluate parents' objections and problems with behavior modification.

Sequence

● Review and sharing of home practice (5 - 10 minutes)

● Lecture/Discussion (40 - 50 minutes)
 – Review examples of behavior modification projects
 – Discuss the use of behavior modification with the parent's own behaviors

● General discussion (20 - 30 minutes)

● Discussion of the home practice assignment (5 - 10 minutes)

Materials

Blackboard (or large marking board)

Chalk (or markers)

Eraser

Review and Sharing of Home Practice

(Encourage and reinforce sharing of home practice experience.)

Lecture/Discussion

Sample Behavior Modification Programs

Let's start off by reviewing the projects you are working on with your own children. How are they going? *(Wait for parents' comments. Reinforce the first person to speak and try to get the group to respond to any questions or comments before you react.)*

Q Have any of you found the use of different reinforcements, Grandma's Law, or other behavior modification methods useful in ways that don't involve a formal program? *(Pause for parents' response.)*

Next I would like to describe a few behavior modification programs that have been developed by parents to change their children's behaviors.

Susie, an 8-year-old girl who had often been sick as a young child, developed the habit of climbing into her parents' bed in the middle of the night. Her parents wanted this behavior stopped, so they developed the following formal behavior modification program. First, they recorded Susie's natural behavior and found that Susie came to their room 8 out of 10 nights. Susie was told she would receive a nickel every night she stayed in her own bed. During the next 10 nights, she came to her parents' bed only twice. During the following month, she came only once and was returned to her bed promptly. After 2 months on the program, Susie's parents told her that she didn't need the program any longer, and it was stopped. It is important to note that all during the program, Susie's parents combined large doses of praise and affection with each nickel they gave Susie. They spoke with pride about Susie's accomplishments. In short, they made a big deal about her growing up and not doing the things she used to do when she was little.

Q Does anyone have a reaction to this story? *(Pause for parents' response. Highlight the pairing of social and nonsocial reinforcers in this example. Discuss the problem of how to phase out extrinsic reinforcers.)*

Here's another example: *(Draw the graph shown in Figure 25 on the board. Add the data as you explain each step in the program.)*

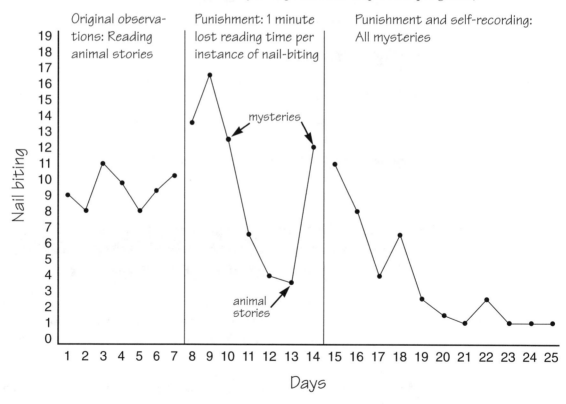

Figure 25. Graph of Carol's nail-biting modification program.

Mrs. Chen wanted her 10-year-old daughter, Carol, to stop biting her fingernails. She had tried a number of methods through the years and

none of them worked. She noticed that Carol chewed her nails most often when she was reading. If Carol didn't read very much for a week or so, her nails would start to grow. The idea of having Carol stop reading seemed just as bad as having bitten fingernails. Mrs. Chen observed Carol for a week. She recorded Carol's nail-biting behavior for the first 30 minutes of Carol's 1-hour reading period before bedtime. *(Plot data on first portion of graph.)* She then told Carol she would subtract 1 minute of reading time for each time Carol put her fingers in her mouth while she was reading. During the next week, Carol was punished frequently for the first 3 days and the last 2. *(Plot data on second portion of graph.)* In fact, her behavior was worse than when the program began. When Mrs. Chen investigated further, she found that Carol's nail-biting was worse when she was reading mysteries. During the third week, the same punishment was used. But there was one important difference. This week, Carol was to read with a golf counter in her hand. Each time she bit her nails, she recorded it herself. *(Plot data on third portion of graph.)* And you can see the effect on the nail-biting.

Q Do you have any questions about this behavior modification program? *(Discuss the problem of baseline recording under dissimilar conditions. Highlight different possible methods of self-recording for children: stars on charts, graphs by the bed or in the bathroom, etc.)*

Here's another example:

(Draw the graph shown in Figure 26 on the board. Add the data as you explain each step in the program.)

Mrs. Patterson was unhappy with the dependent behavior of her youngest son. Mark, age 4, was frequently whining and playing under Mrs. Patterson's feet. He seemed to have frequent, minor "boo-boos," and he would not get out his own toys to play by himself. Mrs. Patterson found herself helping too often, holding Mark, and "making it better." She realized she was reinforcing the very behavior she didn't like by giving Mark so much of her attention. She decided to ignore, as much as possible, all of Mark's dependent behaviors and to reinforce any independent behaviors, such as playing alone for 10 minutes or more, fixing his own scrapes, and getting out his own toys.

The graph shows that before the program started, Mrs. Patterson rarely reinforced the behaviors she wanted to see. Because Mrs. Patterson *was* responding to Mark's dependent behavior, she was reinforcing the very behaviors she disliked. The combination of ignoring dependent behavior and rewarding independent behavior worked, but not right away.

So you can't always expect immediate results from your behavior modification program. With some behaviors, such as temper tantrums, things often get worse for 3 or 4 days before they begin to get better.

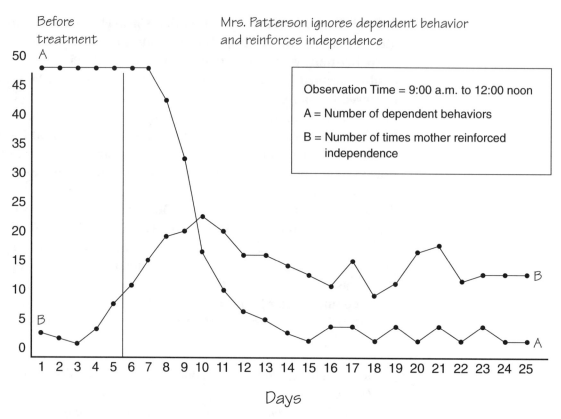

Figure 25. Graph of Mark's dependent behavior.

The other important thing to notice about this graph is that Mrs. Patterson's behavior also changed. Mark was occasionally dependent, as all 4-year-olds are. At first, Mrs. Patterson was not training her child to be independent, because she responded to and reinforced his dependent behavior with her attention.

Lecture/Discussion

Modifying Your Own Behavior

Behavior modification programs may be seen as ways of changing a child's behavior. It is also interesting to note that these programs do as much to change a parent's behavior as they do the child's. After parents set up and run a behavior modification program, they often find their own behavior has changed in the following ways:

1. Parents pay closer attention to the child's specific behavior and needs.
2. Parents behave more consistently.
3. Parents reward and reinforce their children's behaviors more often.
4. Parents feel more confident in managing their children's behavior.

198

5. Parents "catch" their children being good more often. They reinforce this behavior, which gives them a new outlook on managing children's behavior.

So far, we have talked about a number of ways that behavior modification procedures can be used to change children's behavior. Before we leave this topic, I'd like to point out one other important approach to changing children's behavior.

Sometimes, an effective way to make changes in a child's behavior is to focus on and make changes in the behavior of the person who is teaching that child. For example, in an earlier session, we talked about the importance of reflecting your child's feelings by responding to the feelings behind what the child says rather than to the actual words the child uses to express his or her feelings. Reflecting feelings is a behavior many parents are not accustomed to and they frequently feel a little uncomfortable doing it at first. You may be feeling this way when you use reflective listening with your child.

A simple behavior modification procedure can help you get beyond this initial period of discomfort and help you to make reflective listening a welcome habit. You can keep a record of how often you reflect your child's feelings by keeping a tally, by moving some sort of counter from one pocket to another, or by using one of the other recording methods we've talked about. At the end of each day, write down your score and keep a daily chart to see how well you are progressing. Often, just seeing your own progress is enough of a reinforcer to keep you at it. The important benefit of improving your relationship with your child is a powerful reinforcer as well. After a short time, reflecting feelings will come naturally to you.

Parents can also help one another to change behaviors. For example, in one family, the husband wanted to stop yelling at the children. His wife offered to wash the car on Sunday afternoon if her husband could go 7 days without yelling at the children more than 20 times all together. Each night the couple recorded the number of times Dad yelled. In each succeeding week, a new agreement was negotiated. The couple reduced the allowed yelling to 15 times, then 10 times, then 7, and so on.

You can also help yourself with Grandma's Law. For example, you may want to take the kids to the park on Saturday, but you also want to watch a baseball game on television. Simply tell yourself that you can't watch the game until after you take the kids to the park. *(Pause.)* Or you may need to finish the ironing on a day when there's a television show you want to watch. Instead of having your dessert before the vegetables, finish the ironing before the show comes on.

Q Can you think of other behaviors you can effectively manage with the procedures we have talked about? *(Pause for parents' response.)*

Q Last week, we discussed some objections people often raise about behavior modification. Now that you have had more experience with these techniques, can you think of any other problems or objections? *(Pause for parents' response. Write the parents' responses on the board. Do not respond to or refute any of the parents' comments. When all of the objections have been raised, encourage the group to respond.)*

Q What do you think about the first problem listed? Can things be handled in a way that would keep this from happening? *(Summarize parents' reactions and then fill out their responses if you believe some important point was missed.)*

General Discussion

The behavior modification procedures you've been learning are very effective ways to manage behavior. They are often used by psychologists and psychiatrists to treat serious behavior problems. You can use these procedures by either designing a specific program or by just remembering the idea that reinforcers increase behaviors and that ignoring decreases behaviors.

I would strongly recommend that, in the future, you only use a specific formal program to deal with the few behaviors that are either very disturbing or very important to you or to your child. Behavior modification is a powerful tool, but formal programs take time and energy. A formal program can even create more of a problem for you than the specific behavior if that behavior is of minor importance to you.

Q Any questions or reactions? *(Pause for parents' response. Respond to questions or reactions. Praise parents, using constructive praise.)*

Discussion of the Home Practice Assignment

The home practice assignment for this week involves three parts:

● First, you are being asked to continue using the behavior modification program you designed for your child.

● Second, you are asked to write down any concerns you have or problems you see developing as a result of your using any of the behavioral methods suggested.

● Third, you are invited to design a behavior modification program for changing one of *your own* behaviors. If you choose to design a formal program, you should follow the same steps you used with your child. If you decide to apply some other method to change your own behavior, such as Time-Out or Grandma's Rule, then simply specify the target behavior and your goal for change.

Special Notes for the Mental Health Professional

If your group will not be continuing to the sessions on "Managing Your Feelings," you will need to provide at least one follow-up review session after this one. During this session, you should review the home practice assignment on behavior modification and also allow the group to participate in an open forum, discussing the entire program and the parenting skills it provided.

10 Managing Your Feelings

Introduction to Sessions 16-19

The four-session sequence entitled Managing Your Feelings presents concepts based on the principles and techniques of Rational Emotive Therapy (RET). Although you may not be familiar with these concepts, a number of well written books on the subject are available from the Institute of Rational Living, 45 East 65th Street, New York, NY 10021.

The recommended readings listed at the end of this chapter cover the general principles of RET and how to use these RET principles successfully with parents and children; the supplemental readings provide additional information about RET techniques and the teaching of these principles.

This first session in the sequence, The ABCs of Understanding Emotions, is designed to teach three major ideas that will help parents use RET to manage their own emotions: (a) negative emotions limit the effectiveness of parent-child interactions, (b) the conclusions parents draw about their interactions with their children are based on their own belief systems, and (c) the emotional reactions we have to situations are based on our conclusions about those situations.

The second session in the sequence, Applying the ABC Model to Your Interactions With Your Child, is, in many ways, the most critical. At this point, parents often make statements that reject (or are critical of) the RET approach to managing feelings. Parents need to be aware that the A-B-C analysis is most appropriate for situations that occur *repeatedly*, causing repeated upsets and negative emotions.

The focus of the third session is parent-parent interaction. You should keep in mind that this session can create conflict between spouses in the group, particularly if they do not have a strong interpersonal relationship. If you anticipate such a problem, you might want to restrict the focus of the discussion to parent-parent interactions in relation to their child.

In the final session of the sequence, parents learn how to analyze the situations in their lives that can lead to negative emotions and to explore more rational ways of looking at situations that can lead to better interpersonal relationships.

This four-part sequence on managing your feelings is the one that new parenting skills trainers often single out as one of the most stressful portions of the program to present. On the other hand, it is one portion that parents often judge to be the most helpful to them. In many ways, this sequence is the most challenging to parents' self-images and identities. If you are new to parenting group training, it is *not recommended* that you use Short Course 1, which often addresses emotionally charged materials.

The ABCs of Understanding Emotions

Special Notes for the Mental Health Professional

This session will explore three major concepts that will help parents learn to use Rational Emotive Therapy (RET) to manage emotions:

1. Strong negative emotions limit effective parent-child interactions.

2. Parents draw conclusions, called self-statements, about specific interactions with their children based on the parents' personal beliefs about parent-child interactions in general.

3. The emotional reactions that we have to interactions are caused by these self-statements.

First, parents must recognize that when they are experiencing strong negative emotions, their ability to effectively interact with their children is usually reduced. Second, parents should understand that the conclusions they draw about specific interactions they have with their own children are based on their personal beliefs about interactions between people in general. In RET, these instantaneous conclusions are called self-statements. Third, parents learn that strong emotional reactions to an interaction with their own children are the direct and automatic result of their self-statements. You should devote as much time as is necessary for your group to understand these three basic ideas *before* you introduce the ABC Model.

Some parents will resist the ideas presented regarding the ABC Model. You must accept these objections as natural and reasonable reactions to a new way of thinking. Parents are to be reassured that the A-B-C analysis is not applicable to all situations, but is most useful when a given situation occurs again and again, with the same negative emotions and upset occurring again and again. The A-B-C analysis will permit parents to see if their reactions are irrational and/or not helpful in such situations.

After you present the ABC Model, it will be helpful to ask parents in your group for examples of specific interactions they have had with their own children (activating events—Step A), their conclusions, or self-statements, following these interactions (belief statements—Step B), and their feelings or reactions to these situations (consequent emotions and behaviors—Step C). When parents provide examples from their personal experience, it helps everyone in the group recognize that they do experience self-statements at Step B, regardless of how brief or fleeting these statements may be.

The concepts in the second half of this session are best presented by developing a chart on the board that is similar to the Practice Sheet for ABC Analysis in the Parents' Workbook. Emphasize the fact that the feelings and behavior that occur at Step C are the logical and inevitable consequences of the self-statements at Step B. Therefore, although the emotions and reactions are related to the situations, they are *caused* by the self-statements at Step B. As parents work through the ABC Analysis in reverse, they can often predict the self-statement that is likely to occur at Step B.

Another helpful technique is to describe two parent-child interactions and ask the group members to write their emotional reactions to each situation on the front of a 3 x 5 card and their self-statements on the back. The cards are then shuffled and redistributed to the group. Each parent reads the emotional reaction on the card and the group tries to guess what self-statement produced that emotional reaction. Using this method, parents receive valuable feedback anonymously, and they can also see what a variety of self-statements are possible in any situation. This is a very effective way to reduce the parents' natural tendency to believe that their own self-statement about a situation is the right way (or the only reasonable way) to view that situation. Use this discussion as an opportunity to point out that the way different individuals *think* about a situation determines the different emotional reactions they will have to the situation.

Session Objectives

1. To help parents gain a basic understanding of the rational- emotive theory of behavior.

2. To demonstrate how rational-emotive theory can be used to analyze parent-child interactions.

3. To help parents learn a technique for increasing their rational control over the overt and covert responses they have in parent-child interactions.

4. To help parents begin to investigate their self-statements in problem situations with their own children.

5. To provide parents with practice situations that demonstrate and encourage the use of rational-emotive theory in interactions with their children.

Sequence

● Review and sharing of home practice (5 - 10 minutes)

● Lecture/Discussion (50 minutes)

● General discussion (30 - 40 minutes)

● Discussion of home practice assignment (5 minutes)

 ## Materials

Blackboard (or large marking board)

Chalk (or markers)

Eraser

Review and Sharing of Home Practice Experiences

Q How are your projects going? Is anyone having problems with your project? Is anyone disappointed in the results? Does anyone have specific questions about your project? *(Pause for parents' response. Help parents answer questions, adjust their programs, etc.)*

Lecture/Discussion

The ABC Method

During this session, you'll be learning a method that will help you to manage your feelings and your behavior. You will find this method particularly helpful in situations where you need to manage your emotional reactions to your child in order to effectively manage that child's behavior. Hopefully, in the next few sessions, you will all begin to understand that you can control your feelings and reactions and that they are, for the most part, determined by what happens in a given situation. Our goal is for each of you to learn that you own your emotions.

When people get angry, they often do things they later wish they hadn't done. For example, a parent may spank a child because the parent is angry or upset. Or a wife may not speak to her husband for an hour or more because he came home late from work, forgetting that it was his turn to make dinner. If you asked the parent in the first example about his or her behavior, the response might be, "I couldn't help it. I just got mad." The wife in the second example might reply, "He made me so damn mad, he's lucky I didn't throw something at him."

Strong negative emotions, such as anger, can lead to behavior that doesn't work well for anyone involved. When you are angry at your child, for example, it is hard to step back and decide what might be the most effective way to handle the situation. The parent who spanked the child might have chosen a better method of handling the child's behavior if that parent had been able to manage his or her own angry and upset feelings. Of course, other negative emotions, like guilt, fear, depression, and anxiousness, can also get in the way of effective behavior. Let's consider some common situations that lead to strong emotions and, possibly, to ineffective, and often counterproductive, behavior.

> **Mrs. Smith told her two boys, ages 4 and 5, that she was going to wax the kitchen floor that afternoon, and she wanted the boys to be sure not to step on it until it dried. Two minutes after she finished the floor, the boys burst through the door and ran through the kitchen. At that moment, Mrs. Smith said to herself angrily, "How inconsiderate! (Pause.) They don't care about how much work I do, and they obviously don't care about how I feel."**

Q What do you think happens next? (*Pause for parents' response. Write the responses on the board.*)

Q How do you think this mother feels toward her children at this moment? (*Pause for parents' response.*)

Right. Her boys will probably get a good scolding, and they may even get spanked because Mrs. Smith is angry. Given what she told herself about the situation—her self-statement—it is obvious why the boys will be scolded or spanked. It was possible, however, for this incident to turn out differently. (*Pause.*)

Imagine that when the boys run through the kitchen Mrs. Smith says to herself, "I knew it! I should have locked that door. When those two are playing tag, it's a miracle that they don't run into a tree."

Q Given this second example of a self-statement, what do you think would happen? (*Pause for parents' response. Discuss the possibility of Mrs. Smith getting angry and scolding or spanking the boys after the second example. Suggest that Mrs. Smith would probably remember to lock the door in the future. She might also ask the boys to take a time-out watching her redo the floor before resuming their play.*)

This example shows that there are often a number of different things we might say to ourselves about situations, and that each of these different self-statements could lead to different reactions. Here's another example:

The Jones family is getting ready for lunch. While no one is noticing, 3-year-old Mary Beth tries to pour a glass of milk from a full half-gallon. Milk splashes all over the place. Mary Beth's mother looks at the mess and thinks (*expressed dramatically*), "How many times have I told her not to touch the milk carton. She is a stubborn little girl and she's going to have to find out who's boss."

Q What do you think this mother is likely to do next? (*Pause for parents' response.*)

Q How will she be feeling toward Mary Beth? (*Pause for parents' response. Discuss possible reactions.*)

Basically, I think we all agree that after Mary Beth spilled the milk, her mother became angry and probably scolded or punished Mary Beth. Let's replay this example a bit differently:

The milk has just splashed all over the table. Mother turns and says to herself (*with exasperation*), "Oh no! Now the floor needs to be cleaned and Mary Beth's clothes are a mess! I'm going to have to teach that child what she can lift and how to pour."

Q What do you think is likely to happen next? (*Pause for parents' response. Discuss probable events.*)

Again, both types of self-statements are possible, and each would probably lead to a different reaction. *(Discuss some likely consequences of the second example: Mother is not angry, remembers to teach Mary Beth to pour, asks Mary Beth to clean up the mess, etc.)*

These examples demonstrate something that most people tend to forget: events and other people don't determine what we do and feel. What we tell ourselves about situations determines the way we will react and what we will do; and what we say to ourselves in a given situation is a direct result of what we believe about that situation. Mary Beth's mother might believe that children disobey parents just for spite, and this might lead her to react with overly-angry, ineffective behavior. On the other hand, she might believe that children make mistakes because they have not learned how to do something. In this case, her response to Mary Beth's mistake would be to teach her how to pour milk. Mother's second, more rational, reaction would result in Mary Beth learning to pour milk, and this would prevent further spills from occurring. You can see how rational beliefs can lead to rational reactions and more effective results.

Now I would like to try an exercise that should make this even clearer. Close your eyes, and imagine a situation with your child in which you experienced a strong negative emotion that led to your engaging in an ineffective behavior. Try very hard to remember exactly what happened that day. Where were you? What were you doing? What was your child doing? What happened before you felt angry, or sad, or anxious? Now, for a few minutes, I want you to let yourself feel the feelings you had on that day. *(Pause for 1 or 2 minutes.)* Good. Now, I want you to step back, and look at how you are feeling. How can you manage that emotion? Don't try to make it go away; just try to change it a little. How can you change your strong negative reaction to a reaction that would allow you to effectively manage your child's behavior? *(Pause for several minutes.)*

Q How did you change your reactions? What did you tell yourself about the situation to help you react in a more rational manner? *(Pause for parents' response. Ideally, some parents will report that they changed their emotional reactions to these situations by changing the way they were thinking about the situations.)*

Good. You can begin to understand a little more about what happens in these situations. What you believe about a situation influences both how you feel about it and how you react to it. But you can change your feelings and reactions to problem situations by helping yourself to think differently about those situations. *(Draw the ABC diagram shown in Figure 27 on the board.)* We'll be using this ABC diagram a number of times today and in the next few sessions. The diagram will help you understand and remember what determines how you react to the situations in which you find yourself.

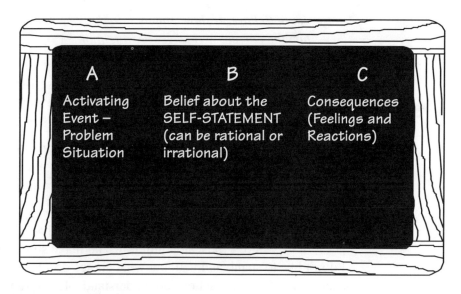

Figure 27. The basic ABC model.

One very important point to consider about the things we tell ourselves is whether or not they are rational. Are the things we say to ourselves sensible—do they agree with the facts? Would other people agree with what you are saying to yourself about the situation?

Let's consider some situations—Step A—and the idea of rational versus irrational self-statements—Step B.

Situation 1. Mrs. Smith is having a party at her house for grown-ups. Her only child, Jim, is 3 years old. Jim has been playing alone in his room for some time. He comes out of his room and says to his mother, in front of her company, "I hate you. These people are just a bunch of stinkbugs."

Following this incident, Jim's mother gets angry, feels hurt, and punishes Jim. This is her reaction, Step C.

Q What did she probably say to herself in her self-statement, B, which led to her reaction? *(Pause for parents' response. Draw out the idea of rejection—"He doesn't love me; I am embarrassed; my guests think I'm a bad mother." Mother's reaction might be, "I'll show you. If you hurt me, I'll hurt you." Ask the group to decide if it is rational for this mother to believe her child really doesn't love her or was trying to hurt her.)*

Now let's assume that Jim's mother doesn't get upset at Step C, and that she talks to Jim briefly, but gently. *(Pause.)*

Q To have a different reaction at Step C, what might this mother say to herself at point B? *(Pause for parents' response. Answers might be, "Poor kid, we've been ignoring him. I guess he was desperate for attention. Now my friends know I have a spirited boy. Nevertheless, I'm*

207

going to have to show Jimmy I don't like what he did, and then show him the correct way to get my attention.")

In her first reaction, this mother's self-statement was irrational, and it led to her punishing Jimmy. In the second reaction, her self-statement was rational, and it helped her find a way to teach Jim what she expected of him. Let's consider another situation.

Situation 2. Mr. Jones spots his 3-year-old son, John, sticking bobby pins into an electric outlet. Mr. Jones rushes over to John, pulls John's hands away from the outlet, and begins to scold the child and slap his hands.

In this case, Step B probably went like this: "That's dangerous! He could get seriously hurt. I must stop him now and make sure he doesn't do it again. I don't like to spank and yell, but what choice do I have?" Given this self-statement, Mr. Jones' actions are understandable. More importantly, they seem sensible and rational. In this case, the emotional upset and punitive behavior at Step C make sense. What if Mr. Jones had said to himself, "What John is doing is dangerous, but if he gets a shock he will learn his lesson?" The likely consequences of this self-statement would be for Mr. Jones to do nothing. His self-statement would not be rational at all!

This way of looking at behavior is not a way of avoiding negative feelings. I am not suggesting that you should never have a negative emotion. There are times when fear, anger, sadness, and guilt are reasonable and rational reactions. But these feelings aren't reasonable or rational if they occur frequently, last for a long period of time, or interfere with your effective management of your child's behavior.

You can see that it is not only situations and interactions with your children that lead to your getting upset. What you say to yourselves about those situations and about the people with whom you interact actually influences your reaction. This idea is important, because it places the responsibility for your emotions and feelings squarely where it belongs: with you. Using rational self-statements can help you to learn not to say, "He made me mad," or "She made me so angry that I spanked her." *(Pause. Speak slowly and deliberately as you explain the next point.)*

Clearly, the ABC model shows that you have a choice. Your reactions and feelings at Step C are not completely determined by what happens at Step A. What you say to yourself at Step B and how rational these self-statements are will determine how you will react at Step C.

Now let's consider some of the common objections people make to the ABC model. Some people say, "If I tell myself something different from my natural reaction, I will be a phony." That's a pretty negative thing to say about yourself. I can see why a person who says this might not want to use the ABC model. Who would want to do something that would make you feel like a phony?

But let's see if that statement is sensible. To begin with, we all have beliefs and ideas that guide how we act. Does anyone believe we were born with our beliefs and ideas? No! We learned them. Sometimes we were aware of beliefs as we were learning them, and other times we weren't. You may have admired an older cousin, so you copied his or her way of looking or talking—and maybe even the way that cousin thought about things. You also learned your moral beliefs, although you may not recall when or how. This behavior you copied and your unconsciously learned moral beliefs are both equally real, not phony, parts of who you are.

If you begin to think about things in a different way, for example, by using the ABC model, it will feel strange at first. It will be like learning a new language. Would learning a new language make you a phony? No. Obviously, the only problem that's left is that you feel uncomfortable. It is probably worth feeling a little uncomfortable if it will make you a more effective and more sensible parent. *(Pause.)*

Another reaction people sometimes make to the ABC model is, "Well, this point of view seems to excuse everything children do, placing all the blame on the poor upset parent." This reaction is made up of two parts, both of which are false. First, there is nothing in the ABC model about excusing ineffective and unacceptable behaviors in children. Parents have standards and limits for children's behavior, and both are needed—for the child's sake as well as the parent's.

Actually, this model can help you teach limits and standards to your child more effectively, because the model helps you make rational decisions about how to feel and behave in a particular situation. The ABC model may help the parent, who is upset at step C, to determine what it was at Steps A and B that led to the upset. For example, a father might be upset when his son leaves toys all over the playroom floor and doesn't put them away after he has finished playing.

It is reasonable to expect a 5-year-old to pick up and put away his toys. If the father gets upset and spanks the child, that father probably said to himself, "I have told him a thousand times and he just won't listen. He is asking for a spanking. If I don't teach him to be neat now, he will never learn. He'll probably be an irresponsible slob when he grows up."

If the father examined the situation using the ABC model, he might say to himself, "What am I saying at Step B that is causing me to be so upset?" *(Pause.)*

What part of what the father said is rational, and what part is irrational? Let's examine some of the self-statements this father might use to help guide his own reactions. *(Write the statements shown in Figure 28 on the board.)*

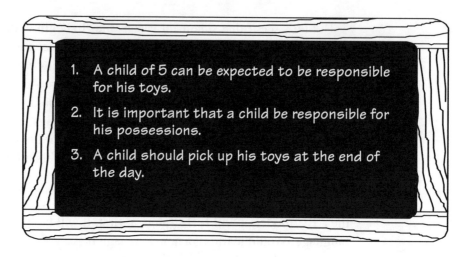

Figure 28. Rational beliefs or self-statements.

Now, here are some irrational self-statements that this father might use. As you listen to these statements, think about why they might be irrational. *(Pause after reading each statement aloud to discuss the irrational nature of the belief involved.)*

1. **A 5-year-old should put his toys away each time he finishes playing with them during the day. (*Ask how a child of 5 knows he is finished playing with the toys.*)**

2. **This child was "asking for it." (*Point out that it is not likely that a child wants to be hurt or punished.*)**

3. **If this child does not pick up his toys, he will become an irresponsible slob as an adult. (*This is a very extreme reaction. How likely is it to occur?*)**

4. **The child should want to share his father's concern with neatness. (*It would be nice if a child shared that concern, but is it reasonable to expect such a young child to be concerned with neatness?*)**

Let's consider another situation:

Imagine a father watching his 7-year-old son and a friend playing football on a large field near their house. The field is used as a ball field by all the neighborhood children. Suddenly, a large group of older boys come along and tell the two youngsters to get lost, because they have a big football game. The father watches as his son and the friend walk off the field; they are disappointed, but not arguing. The father experiences a strange mixture of emotions. He is furious, hurt, and disappointed. When his wife asks why he is upset, he relates the story, saying, "Margaret, our son just let himself get pushed around. He never stands up for himself. I don't know what to do. He gets it from me. That's just the way I was as a boy, and you know how people at work treat me."

Q Now what is the activating event at Step A? *(Write "A" on the board, and then pause for parents to respond. Write the responses on the board. Remember, Step A is the situation—watching the son get forced off the field by the older boys.)*

Q What is the emotional reaction at Step C? *(Write "C" on the board, and then pause for parents to respond. Write the responses on the board. Step C is the father's feelings of hurt, anger, and disappointment.)*

Q What is Step B— the father's belief about this situation—that leads to his reaction? *(Write "B" on the board, and then pause for parents to respond. Write the responses on the board. Make sure the responses include the following irrational statements this father was probably telling himself: This one incident is typical of the child's behavior in general; I feel worthless, and now I will have a worthless son; a child ought to stand up for his rights at all times; it is terrible to retreat.)*

Excellent. I think you are all developing a skill for handling these examples. Now I would like to experiment with the ideas we have been discussing.

Q How many of you can remember being alone in a dark room when you were young? *(Pause for parents' response.)*

Good. This should be easy for you, then. I am going to turn off the lights in this room. I'd like you all to close your eyes and try to recall being put to bed and lying in the dark. *(Shut off the lights and speak softly.)* I want you to try to remember how you felt. *(Pause.)* Concentrate on remembering just what it was like to lie there in the dark. *(Pause. Wait 30-45 seconds, and then turn on the lights.)* Now let's see how many different feelings you had. I'd like each of you to describe how you felt in that circumstance when you were young? *(Erase the board, leaving only the A, B, and C. Write all the parents' feelings under the C.)*

Now, what did you believe about being in the dark that led to your feelings? *(Pause. Write these beliefs under the B on the board.)*

What could you have said to yourself about the dark that would have helped you to react differently—more rationally— at C? *(Write the responses on the board.)*

To summarize, we've learned that it isn't a situation or a person that causes us to get upset and angry. Whether or not we get upset depends on what we believe about the situation and what we say to ourselves. Now, if you are concerned and annoyed in a particular situation, it may be because your self-statement (based on what you believe about that situation) is rational. But if you are frequently angry or upset, these negative reactions may well be caused by some irrational self-statement. By learning to become aware of what you believe about situations that involve your child, and discovering whether your self-statements are rational or irrational, you can begin to manage your own reactions to your children more effectively. That's how using the ABC model can help you improve your interactions with your children.

General discussion

Any questions or reactions? Who would like to share their reaction to tonight's session? *(If no one responds, you might ask someone whose expression indicates some concern: "Mr./Mrs._____ you seem to be a little uncertain or concerned about this.")*

Discussion of the Home Practice Assignment

This week for homework you have some situations to analyze in your Workbook. After you complete the assignments, I would like each of you to write down a description of a situation at home with your own child that often leads to your being upset. Describe the situation and your emotional reactions. Be sure you include the things you usually do or say. Please don't put your name on the paper. We'll use your descriptions next week for some practice with the ABC model, but we'll keep the identity of the writers secret.

Applying the ABC Model to Your Interactions With Your Child

Special Notes for the Mental Health Professional

This second session in the sequence on Managing Your Feelings is, in many ways, the most critical one. You need to be prepared for feedback that rejects, or is highly critical of, the RET approach to managing feelings. These parental objections tend to cluster around three main ideas:

1. RET is just a way to rationalize problems and deny them.

2. Using this idea would make me a phony, because emotions should just happen naturally.

3. Parents feel unable to give up responses such as "she made me mad" or "he made me feel guilty" as the correct way to view their world.

As a professional, you must accept these objections as natural and reasonable reactions to a new way of thinking. Reassure the parents that the A-B-C analysis is not appropriate to all situations, and tell them that they will find it most useful when a given situation occurs again and again, and they respond with the same negative emotions and upset again and again. The A-B-C analysis will help parents to determine whether their reactions are irrational and, therefore, not helpful to them or to their child.

Session Objectives

1 To review the rational-emotive theory (RET) of behavior and its relationship to managing feelings.

2 To help parents apply RET in sample parent-child interactions.

Sequence

- Introduction and review (5 - 10 minutes)

- Questions and reactions (10 - 15 minutes)

- Small group discussion of homework assignment (20 - 30 minutes)

- Discussion of common irrational beliefs (20 - 30 minutes)

- General discussion (20 - 30 minutes)

- Discussion of home practice assignment (5 - 10 minutes)

Materials

Blackboard (or large marking board)

Chalk (or markers)

Eraser

Box labeled, "Place Your Problem Situations Here" placed at the door of the room

Lecture/Discussion

Review of the ABC Model

(As parents arrive, have them place their written problem situations in a box at the door. Supply blank cards to any parents who forgot to bring theirs.)

Last week, we discussed the ABC model of managing your feelings. We'll be referring to the model several times this evening, so I'll draw the diagram on the board again. *(Draw the A-B-C diagram on the board.)*

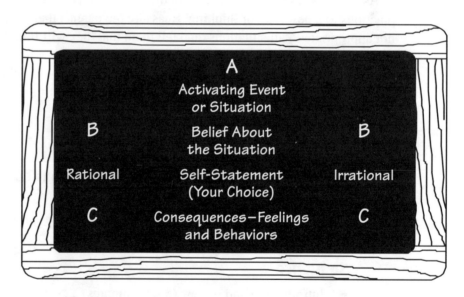

Figure 29. The ABC model for analysis.

Do you remember one important thing we learned about behavior in our last session? *(Point to C.)* Your reactions are not caused by the event or situation at Step A. *(Point to A.)* Instead, they are caused by what you tell yourself about the event or situation. *(Point to B.)* When your self-statements are rational, they lead to effective problem-solving. When your reactions to a situation that occurs over and over again are repeatedly strong, negative emotions like anger, there's a good chance that your self-statement has been an irrational one. *(Pause.)*

214

Q Are there any questions about the ABC model or any of the material we covered last week? *(Pause. Wait until some interaction begins, and then encourage responses.)*

Discussion of the Home Practice Experiences

The first topic today will be your home practice assignment from last session. I'd like you to break up into groups of four. Married couples or other partners should not be in the same group. Each group should discuss the answers to all four problem situations in the home practice. In about 20 minutes, I'll ask each group to share the answers they have come up with. *(Go from group to group, making sure each group is on task and providing assistance with their discussion where appropriate. While groups are discussing the homework, you should also look over the anonymous problem situations in the box at the door. After about 20 minutes, call on one group for their answers to problem 1, a second group for answers to the problem 2, and so on. For problem 4, write the entire analysis on the board in the A-B-C diagram.)*

Lecture/Discussion

Common Irrational Beliefs

Great. You've all come up with ideas that show you are thinking about how to use the model. Now that you have had some practice with the general technique, it's time to focus on what is probably the most important part of the ABC method—the idea of examining irrational beliefs.

You have already learned that your belief about a situation will determine your reaction or behavior in that situation. When your beliefs are rational, they are easily supported by facts. Irrational beliefs, on the other hand, are simply not based in reality and cannot be supported by facts. To help you understand what I mean, here are two common beliefs that people have about children. I'll read the statements, and then we'll try to examine the evidence for each. *(Read the following statement:)*

1. **"Children should always obey their parents."**

Q What is the evidence for this belief? *(Encourage parents to provide both supporting and contradicting evidence for this statement. As they suggest evidence, examine its validity by asking the following questions: "Is this evidence really true? How do we know it's true? Why must it be true? Is there any other way to think about this?" Help parents reach the conclusion, through this close examination and questioning, that this belief is irrational because it is "absolute." Ask parents how someone who holds this belief might behave toward his or her child. Would that behavior be effective? How might changing this belief change the parent's behavior?)*

Great. Let's try another one:

2. "It is important for children to learn right from wrong."

Q What is the evidence for this belief? *(Again, use the questions listed above to examine the validity of this rational belief about children. It is important that parents reach an understanding that this belief is rational because it is based in reality, because it is not absolute or insupportable in nature, and because it is likely to lead to effective parenting behavior.)*

Good. One thing you might notice about this irrational belief *(point to the first belief statement)* is that it contains the word "should." Many irrational beliefs contain the words *should, must, always,* or *never*. When you tell yourself something about your child that contains one of these words, chances are you are telling yourself something irrational.

Now I'm not suggesting that you beat yourself up if you find that you have an irrational belief. It just suggests that you are a good person who sometimes acts in ineffective ways with your child because of beliefs that don't make sense. That's probably true of every parent at one time or another. By determining which of your beliefs are irrational, you can quickly increase your effectiveness with your child. And remember, some beliefs may be rational in some situations and irrational in others. For example, you might hold the belief that children should obey their parents, but you will be a more effective parent if you are flexible and open to times when your child might have a solid, rational reason for disobeying you. People are often surprised by how strongly they hold a belief and how difficult it is to think about alternative ways of looking at a situation.

Let's look at some of the common irrational beliefs that parents have about raising their children. As I read each belief, think about the evidence that supports it, and ask yourself how realistic that evidence is.

(Read each of the nine irrational beliefs presented in Figure 30. After you read each one, ask parents to briefly discuss why the belief is irrational. Also ask parents to identify at least one alternative way of thinking about the belief.)

1. Parents are always right.

2. Children disobey their parents because they don't love and respect their parents.

3. If my child doesn't pick up his or her toys every day, my child will become a lazy, good-for-nothing person when he or she grows up.

4. Children must never show anger or sadness.

5. When I tell my child to do something, he or she should do it exactly the way I say it should be done.

6. Children should always get along with their brothers and sisters.

7. A good parent must do everything possible to minimize pain, difficulty, and frustration in his or her child's life.

8. If I get angry or don't want to be around my child, then I am a bad parent.

9. A parent should always know how to handle his or her child.

Figure 30. Common irrational beliefs about parenting.

General Discussion

Now that we've practiced identifying irrational beliefs and examining them, let's look at some of the real-life situations you put into our box this evening. *(Return to the board. Leaving the frame of the A-B-C diagram intact, erase the content of the last problem situation. Read each of the parents' anonymous problem situations aloud, and then explore it using the diagram.)*

Q   What is Step A in this problem?

(Pause for parents' response. Although it may be a struggle for parents to answer, remain patient and relaxed. Lead the group through the analysis of each situation, filling in each space of the diagram as parents supply appropriate answers. It is important to emphasize that situations can be evaluated in a number of ways and how some of these evaluative thoughts make more sense than others in the particular situation you are examining. Encourage parents to use the techniques they've been learning to examine their irrational beliefs and determine if they are supportable with facts. Remind parents that examining the reasons or rationale behind evaluative thoughts may prevent negative emotions and promote effective problem-solving.

Note the tone of the discussion. By communicating acceptance in your words and the tone of your voice, you can prevent this exercise from deteriorating into a judgment session. Continue to point out that there are many different possible self-statements. The ones that are based in reality are the most help; the ones that are not based in reality do not help and they may even make a situation unnecessarily worse.

Involving the parents in the group in working out answers to the problems in this section is vital to the success of this whole sequence on managing feelings. Don't supply your own answers. Be prepared for a long pause before the first volunteer speaks up, but wait it out. Let your facial expression and words reinforce the parents who do volunteer, particularly at the beginning of the discussion. Continue analyzing as many of the anonymous situations as time allows.)

Discussion of the Home Practice Assignment

For home practice during the next week, I want you to continue examining your interactions with your children. Pay particular attention to your self-statements in situations where you experience strong negative emotion and have difficulty making a rational decision about how to react. As soon as the problem situation is over, sit down and write a quick note to yourself about your reactions. Write down as much as you can remember about your self-statements during the interaction with your child. Ask yourself how you evaluated what was happening. What did you believe about your child's behavior? Use the blank forms in the Workbook to help you analyze your situation. The home practice assignment also contains a discussion of eight common, self-defeating ideas that frequently lead to irrational self-statements. If you examine these ideas carefully, you will see that they are often part of the self-statements that accompany strong, repeated emotional upsets.

As the week goes on, begin to work on making your self-statements more rational when you interact with your child. If you start to get angry in a situation, ask yourself, "What do I believe about this situation that is making me angry?" "Is this belief rational? Does it match the facts about my child and about children in general?" Look at your belief carefully, and ask yourself if you can find facts to support it. Begin to look for alternative self-statements when you can't find any supporting facts. Ask yourself the following questions:

1. What can I tell myself about my child's behavior that will lead to a rational reaction on my part?

2. What do I want to happen in the situation? What is my goal?

3. What is the best way to reach this goal with my child?

In our next session we will begin by discussing this process. Remember, the goal is not to change your behavior overnight. The goal is to become more aware of your rational and irrational self-statements and how they affect your effectiveness as a parent. As you learn to use rational self-statements in interactions with your child, you will find your behavior changing as well.

Parent to Parent Interactions: Controlling Your Emotions

Introduction

This third session in the sequence often produces some of the liveliest group discussion. Parents have now had an opportunity to practice the ABC method of analysis at home, and they will try to enlist the support of other group members for the reactions and self-statements they normally use when interacting with their children. Parents may also try to challenge you. For example, if you encourage them to examine alternative self-statements, they may suggest that you just don't understand *their* unique situation.

At this point, it is best to allow parents to answer each other's questions whenever possible. Input from a variety of sources and the group process tend to facilitate change and acceptance of that change in individual parents. The Workbook home practice assignment that asks parents to examine eight common self-defeating ideas provides an excellent stimulus for discussion. Parents often recognize one or more of these ideas as the basis for some of their own self-statements. This can be both reassuring and upsetting to these parents. If the group dynamics surrounding this assignment engage parents in lively and productive discussion, you may want to postpone the next session to allow parents to devote an extra session to sharing their parent-child situations and reactions.

The focus of the new material in this third session is on parent-parent interaction. You should keep in mind that this material can create conflict between the spouses in your group, particularly if they do not have a strong interpersonal relationship. If you anticipate such a problem, you might want to restrict the focus of the discussion to parent-parent interactions in relation to their child.

Special Notes for the Mental Health Professional

One effective technique for use with parent couples who are having difficulty in this session is to have the couple role-play situation A from the homework assignment. The group members then write down what they think the couple's reaction will be at Step C and what the self-statement will be at Step B. The group can then discuss the couple's actual reaction and probable self-statement of each parent in the couple. The role-playing couple must watch and listen to the group, but they may not participate in the discussion until the group has reached some form of consensus.

Session Objectives

1. To review the rational-emotive theory of behavior.

2. To demonstrate how to apply RET theory as a way of analyzing parent-parent conflicts and personal problems.

3 To discuss some possible objections to the rational-emotive approach.

4 To provide parents with practice in analyzing problem situations.

Sequence

● Lecture/Discussion (30 minutes)

● Small group discussion of problem situations (20 - 30 minutes)

● Review and sharing of previous home practice (20 - 30 minutes)

● Discussion of home practice assignment (5 - 10 minutes)

Materials

Blackboard (or large marking board)

Chalk (or markers)

Eraser

6 sheets of paper, each containing two of the six problem situations (one sheet for each group of 4 parents)

Lecture/Discussion

Review of the ABC Model

For the past two sessions, we've been discussing the ABC model for managing feelings. You remember that emotions such as anger, fear, and depression are not caused just by the situation itself, but by the situation plus what we tell ourselves about the situation. Here's the diagram we used before. *(Draw the diagram shown in Figure 31 on the board.)*

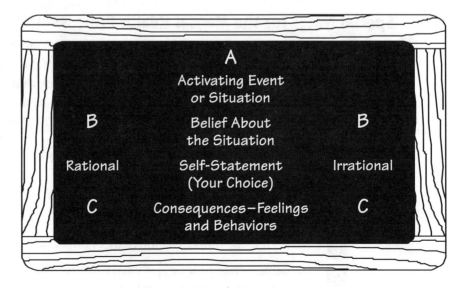

Figure 31. The ABC model for analysis.

220

A is the situation or event. B is the belief or self-statement about that situation. Remember that these self-statements can be rational or irrational. C is the reaction, which can be behavior, or feelings, or both. And what happens at C depends on A and B.

In the past two sessions, we talked about situations and problems involving parents and children. You now understand that when your self-statement (what you tell yourself about a situation) is rational, the reactions and feelings that follow are also rational; and these reactions and feelings are often effective in helping you meet your goals for the situation. Good problem solving results from rational self-statements. Of course, parent-child problems are not the only ones that can benefit from rational self-statements. Consider the following situation. *(As you read the example, fill in the blanks in the diagram for points A and B only, as shown in Figure 32.)*

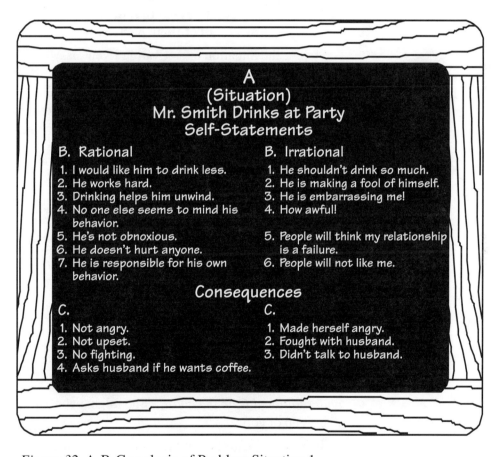

Figure 32. A-B-C analysis of Problem Situation 1.

1. **Mr. and Mrs. Smith have just returned home from a party. It used to be that every time they went to a party, they would argue all the way home and for most of the next day. Tonight there is no argument. Mrs. Smith thinks she knows what has made the difference. She has learned to manage her feelings. At parties, Mr. Smith drinks more than Mrs. Smith would like him to. In**

221

the past, Mrs. Smith would get quite upset about this. She recalls having self-statements that went something like this:

> "He shouldn't drink so much. He is making a fool of himself and embarrassing me. *(Pause.)* How awful. What kind of a relationship will my friends think I have if John gets drunk all the time and doesn't respect me. Nobody will like us!"

Tonight, however, Mrs. Smith is not angry nor upset. When she examines her self-statements this evening, they go something like this:

> "I wish John wouldn't drink so much at parties. But he is responsible for his behavior. I guess he drinks to unwind, and he's not really obnoxious when he drinks. Our friends certainly seem to like him, or they wouldn't keep inviting us to all of their parties."

Step A, the Situation or Activating Event, is Mr. Smith drinking at a party. Step B, the self-statement, has changed from "He shouldn't drink so much. He is making a fool of himself. My friends probably think my relationship is a failure. People will not like me." to "I would like him to drink less. He works hard and drinking helps him to unwind. No one else seems to mind his behavior. He's not obnoxious, and he doesn't hurt anyone. He is responsible for his own behavior."

Q In the past, when Mrs. Smith's self-statements were about being embarrassed and her husband being a fool, how do you think she behaved and felt? *(Pause for parents' response.)*

Yes, her reaction at Step C used to be anger and arguing with her husband, *(Write "Anger" and "Arguing" under Irrational C on the board.)* and this wasn't effective in managing her feelings, and it certainly wasn't changing her husband's behavior.

Given Mrs. Smith's new, rational self-statements, we see that she isn't upset or ashamed of her husband for drinking more than she thinks he should. This time, the reaction doesn't include fighting or anger. *(Write "No fighting" under Rational C on the board.)* She might even ask if her husband would like a cup of coffee.

You can see how Mrs. Smith learned to manage her feelings. She examined her self-statements, changed them to more sensible or rational statements, and now she can behave in a more reasonable way when her husband drinks at parties.

This shows you how the A-B-C analysis can work toward improving parent-parent relationships. In this session and the next, we'll focus on using the A-B-C analysis in a variety of situations, not only for those involving children. But before we do that, let's examine some objections to the A-B-C analysis that generally arise after a few weeks of practice with this method.

Common Objections to the ABC Model

The example that was just described may have raised at least one objection. Some of you may be thinking that the A-B-C analysis forces you to accept a lot of things that you would rather not accept. It forces you to give in or "surrender." For example, when Mrs. Smith's self-statements were rational rather than irrational, she probably decided that it would be best if she did not nag her husband about his drinking at parties. In other words, she accepted the fact that he would drink at parties and that he might drink more than she wanted him to. She did accept something she didn't like. She lost the "drinking at parties," battle because she finally refused to make it a battle.

One of the very important lessons for adults to learn is knowing when it makes sense to fight. That is, learning to recognize which issues or situations have a chance of being improved by fighting and which probably don't. The A-B-C analysis helps you decide which issues or situations deserve your fighting spirit and which do not.

Let's look again at Mrs. Smith's self-statements. *(Point to the diagram on the board.)* Her irrational self-statements were based on her beliefs that Mr. Smith was making a fool of himself, that Mrs. Smith's friends would consider her relationship a failure, and that her friends would not like her anymore. When she examined these three beliefs, she realized that they were irrational in light of the facts. It seemed that Mr. Smith was not such a fool—at least the rest of the people at the party didn't seem to think so. The idea that his drinking made her relationship a failure in her friends' eyes was not sensible, because the couple continued to be invited to their friends' houses. You may recognize that the final self-statement, the belief that her friends would not like her anymore, fits into one of the eight common self-defeating beliefs discussed in the Workbook assignment from last week—the need for constant love and approval.

Certainly, Mrs. Smith needs friends and it is important to her to be liked. But how much is she willing to pay for this? Is she willing to battle her husband every week over the number of drinks he is allowed? It seems that, in the past, Mrs. Smith held the self-defeating belief that it was necessary to be constantly loved and approved of by everyone else. And this self-defeating belief is probably what led her into battle with her husband after every party. She was afraid that someone would disapprove of her, and she would do whatever she felt she had to do to avoid that disapproval. The A-B-C analysis allowed her to see that the real issue, the issue that should be dealt with, was her unlimited need for constant love and approval. In the past, she had been regularly upsetting herself, not examining her self-statements, and attacking her husband for drinking too much. The battle went on every week because the real issue, the self-defeating belief that constant love and approval is necessary, could not be resolved. In fact, it wasn't even being addressed.

When conflict or bad feelings exist between parents, and these negative reactions occur again and again about the same issues, the real basis for such feelings is probably some irrational, self-defeating beliefs held by one or both parents. These problem situations cannot be solved until both parents examine the beliefs behind their self-statements.

When you recognize an irrational self-statement, examine the belief behind that statement. What is the evidence for that belief? Is the belief true, or is there another way to think about this situation? For Mrs. Smith, the belief that constant approval is necessary was the basis for her statements about being a failure, having a foolish husband, and so forth. When Mrs. Smith could find no evidence for this belief, she began to realize that she had to change her beliefs and self-statements to better match reality. By finding an alternative way of looking at her problem, Mrs. Smith began to understand that her real battle was handling her need for constant approval and love.

So, the A-B-C analysis does not encourage surrender. It encourages you to be more selective about where you choose to fight. By examining your beliefs and self-statements, you can learn to recognize the real issues and then deal with them in more constructive ways. *(Pause for parents' reaction.)*

When you apply the A-B-C analysis to those interactions with your partner that frequently lead to anger or hurt feelings, you can strengthen your ongoing relationship. Evidence shows us that the better parents get along, the more competently and reasonably they raise their children, and the happier their children will be.

Also, one of the most powerful ways children learn to behave is by watching the behavior of the people around them, especially the people they love. If you want your child to develop the ability to analyze his or her self-statements, you might share your own self-statements with your child, at least once in a while. You can show your child examples of rational and irrational self-statements—from your own experience. This is the way your child will learn that he or she has a choice about how to react, and you are teaching your child two very important things: how to evaluate self-statements and choose the more rational, more effective ones and how to control his or her feelings. *(Pause for parents' reactions.)*

Now you understand how the ABC model can be applied to improve both parent-child and parent-parent interactions. It has a third use as well: helping you get along better with yourself and helping you solve problems that are strictly personal. The second problem situation example illustrates how the ABC model can be applied to a personal problem. It also illustrates another of those eight common self-defeating ideas from your last Workbook assignment.

2. **Several years ago, a television show ran a spot about a hospital that was developing a new program for people who have cancer. There is a great deal of fear and dread associated with cancer. It is truly a frightening disease. It is also true, however, that people**

can live for many years after having contracted certain forms of cancer. The aim of that new hospital was to help control the spread of cancer in a patient and to help the patient handle the natural fears about having cancer and dying. The approach seemed successful overall, but one patient was not buying it. The doctors could not convince her that the remainder of her life was worth facing. She was deeply depressed and refused treatment.

Of course, it doesn't make sense to refuse treatment when you're sick, and the emotions this woman was experiencing were decidedly negative. Let's analyze this situation using the ABC model. *(Erase the previous diagram, and begin a new one as you present the situation shown in Figure 33.)*

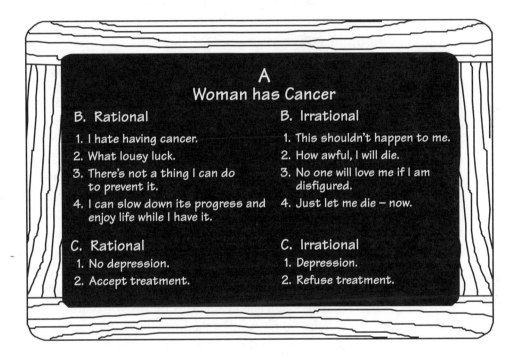

Figure 33. A-B-C analysis of Problem Situation 2.

The A, of course, is that the woman has cancer. *(Write "Cancer" under A.)* The Irrational C is that she is deeply depressed and is refusing treatment. *(Write "Depression" and "Refuse treatment" under Irrational C.)*

Q What self-statements might have led to the Irrational C? *(Pause for parents' response. Write answers under Irrational B: "It shouldn't happen to me. How awful, I will die. No one will love me if I am disfigured. Just let me die—now!" Bring out the idea that the woman is not accepting reality. She is saying, "It shouldn't happen to me; if I am disfigured, no one will love me.")*

Q What self-statements would have been more rational in this situation? *(Pause for parents' response. Write the appropriate suggestions under*

Rational B: "I hate having cancer. What lousy luck. There's not a thing I can do to prevent it. I can slow down its progress and enjoy life while I have it.")

Exactly. And then for the reaction here at Step C, we would probably have "No depression" and the woman would "Accept treatment." In this example, the woman's insistence that reality should not be what it was led to depression and very poor problem solving. Self-statements caused by the belief that an event or person ought to be different are always irrational. At times, we all wish that reality were different, but to say that it *should* be different suggests that there are no reasons for reality being the way it is. The idea that reality should be different is not only illogical, it is self-defeating. Reality is the way it is, and saying it should be different does not lead to mature acceptance of reality or to good problem solving. It generally leads to negative emotions like depression, self-pity, and anger.

It may sound like I am saying that, as a result of attending these sessions, you should never experience another negative emotion. I don't mean that at all. What I do mean is that, by examining your self-statements in a problem situation, you can make a judgment about whether or not your reactions or feelings are reasonable. At first, you will probably react to problem interaction and feel much the same way about them as you did before you began this course. The only difference, at first, may be that, after you experience an emotionally charged situation, after A, B, and C have already occurred, you might sit down and take a closer look at what really happened. You might recognize that one or more of your self-statements at Step B were not totally sensible and that your reactions and feelings at Step C were not as reasonable and effective as you would have liked them to be. But, as I mentioned before, the kinds of situations husbands and wives get really upset about are usually repeated again and again. This means you will soon have another chance to challenge and get rid of the irrational part of your self-statements. This is a difficult task, and it will only be accomplished through repeated practice. The kinds of negative situations we've been talking about will give you the opportunity for that repeated practice as you work toward managing your feelings and the behavior of yourself and others.

Q Are there any questions about the A-B-C analysis or anything else we've covered so far? *(Encourage questions.)*

Small Group Discussion

Now I want you to divide up into groups of four. This time, I would like spouses or partners to be in the same groups. Each group will receive two problem situations involving adults. The problem situation will be Step A in the A-B-C analysis. Each group should complete the A-B-C analysis for both situations, including the possible rational and irrational beliefs or self-statements and reactions. Then we'll discuss some of these analyses as a group. *(When parents break into groups, give a slip of paper to each group with two of the six problem situations shown in Figures 34-39. Move from group to group to assist them in the exercise as needed. Allow the groups to discuss their situations for 5-8 minutes, then ask each group, in turn, to share their analyses of the two problem situations. Each of the situations provides an example of at least one of the eight common self-defeating ideas mentioned in last week's Workbook assignment. Encourage each group to examine the self-statements and reactions. Continue to point out the self-defeating beliefs behind irrational self-statements. As you discuss each group's analyses, complete the A-B-C diagram for each situation on the board. Be sure to include the major points shown in Figures 34-39.)*

3. **Mr. Brill was a very successful accountant. He was not a very successful mechanic, however. On weekends, he frequently worked on the family car, but he created more problems than he solved. What self-statements could Mr. Brill choose, and what might his reactions and feelings be?**

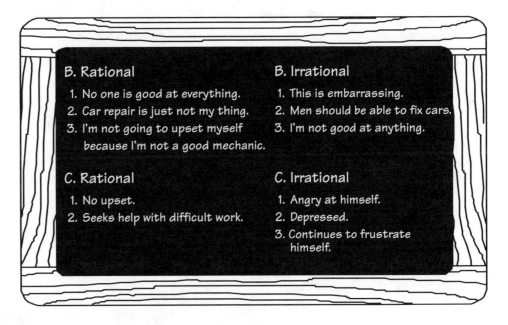

Figure 34. A-B-C analysis of Problem Situation 3.

4. **Mrs. Buck was a homemaker, and she wasn't very happy. Her life seemed meaningless, and her daily routine really seemed like a rut. What self-statements could Mrs. Buck choose, and what might be her reactions and feelings?**

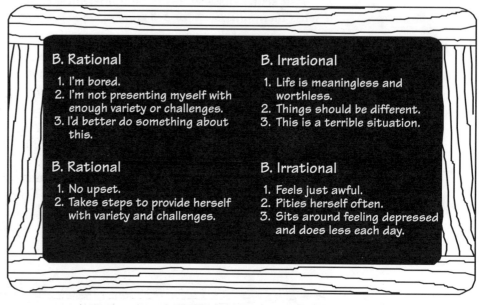

B. Rational

1. I'm bored.
2. I'm not presenting myself with enough variety or challenges.
3. I'd better do something about this.

B. Irrational

1. Life is meaningless and worthless.
2. Things should be different.
3. This is a terrible situation.

B. Rational

1. No upset.
2. Takes steps to provide herself with variety and challenges.

B. Irrational

1. Feels just awful.
2. Pities herself often.
3. Sits around feeling depressed and does less each day.

Figure 35. A-B-C analysis of Problem Situation 4.

5. **Mr. Rush got off work at 4:00 p.m. After a very hectic day, he was anxious to get home and relax. He waited for the bus, but when it came he realized that he only had a $10 bill. The bus driver said, "Sorry, Mac. No way I can make change for that. You'll have to get change somewhere and catch the next bus." Mr. Rush said, "Don't give me that! Look, just let me ride home tonight, and I'll give you the fare tomorrow." The bus driver replied, "Hey, I can't let anybody on the bus without paying the fare. I've got a schedule to keep. So long." What self-statements could Mr. Rush choose, and what might be his reactions and feelings?**

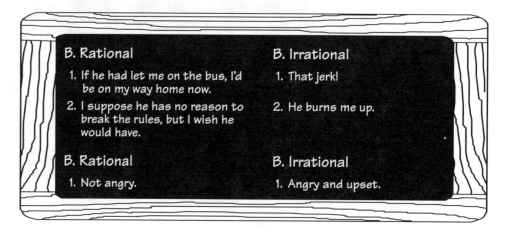

B. Rational

1. If he had let me on the bus, I'd be on my way home now.
2. I suppose he has no reason to break the rules, but I wish he would have.

B. Irrational

1. That jerk!

2. He burns me up.

B. Rational

1. Not angry.

B. Irrational

1. Angry and upset.

Figure 36. A-B-C analysis of Problem Situation 5.

6. Ralph enjoyed his job very much. He was doing something he had wanted to do for a long time. The only part of the job he didn't like was his boss. Ralph knew that if he performed well on the job he could get a promotion and make more money. But he really disliked his boss. Sometimes, Ralph worked hard to get his promotion, but at other times he did the very least amount of work he could get away with. What self-statements could be influencing the amount of work that Ralph does, and what are his feelings and reactions likely to be?

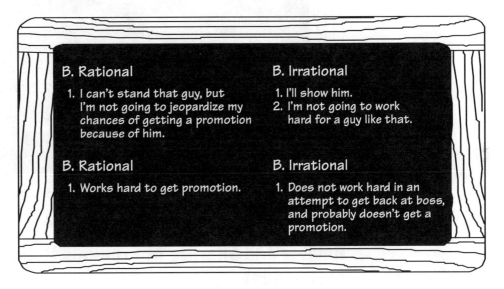

Figure 37. A-B-C analysis of Problem Situation 6.

7. They had had such a beautiful relationship. At least that's what Nancy thought until Ned suddenly left her. What self-statements could Nancy choose, and what might be her reactions and feelings?

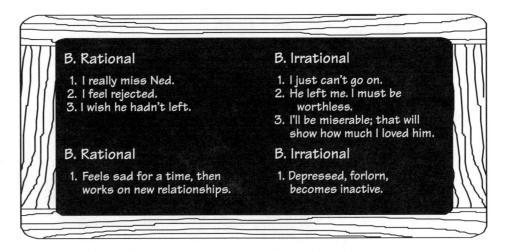

Figure 38. A-B-C analysis of Problem Situation 7.

8. In the past, Gladys used to get upset because George would come home from work obviously troubled about something that he refused to discuss with her. She used to get upset and then feel very depressed. She is beginning to be successful at refusing to upset herself. She is trying to change her self-statements. What might have been her self-statements and reactions in the past? What are they now?

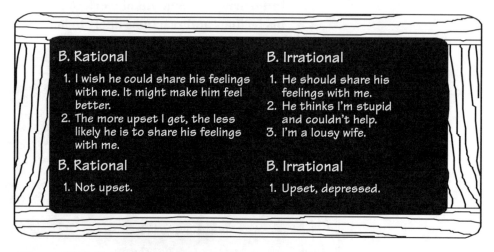

Figure 39. A-B-C analysis of Problem Situation 8.

Review and Sharing of Previous Home Practice Assignment

Q Who would like to share the A-B-C analysis from their home practice exercise with the group? *(Encourage volunteers to describe the situation and then share their A-B-C analyses. Continue to point out the successful identification of irrational and rational self-statements and reactions.)*

Discussion of the Home Practice Assignment

In this week's home practice, you'll be analyzing two situations according to the ABC model. One of the situations or events can be in relation to anything or anyone you choose, but one must be a situation between you and your partner. The more openly and honestly you complete this assignment, the greater its benefit to you. Your task will be difficult, because you will be challenging some of your lifelong beliefs.

Use the same technique you used for last session's home practice. As soon as your problem situation is over, sit down and write out as much as you can remember about it. Include your beliefs about what happened, what you told yourself about the situation, and how those self-statements determined your reaction or feelings. This time, write down at least one alternative way of thinking about each problem situation you encounter.

Next session, we'll go over any of the situations you are willing to share. There will be a box at the door of the room to deposit your home practice situations when you arrive next week. We will go over each set of situations, self-statements, and reactions you put in the box. Please don't put any real names on the sheets. That way, we can work on each situation anonymously.

Handouts for Small Group Discussion

The handouts on the following six pages are designed to facilitate small group discussion of the ABC model for managing emotions successfully. These handouts provide the framework for practical experience in the A-B-C analysis.

A
Situation

Mr. Brill was a very successful accountant. He was not a very successful mechanic, however. On weekends, he frequently worked on the family car, but he created more problems than he solved. What self-statements could Mr. Brill choose, and what might his reactions and feelings be?

B
Self-Talk Possibilities

Rational	Irrational
_____	_____
_____	_____
_____	_____
_____	_____
_____	_____
_____	_____

C
Likely Actions & Feelings

Rational	Irrational
_____	_____
_____	_____
_____	_____
_____	_____
_____	_____
_____	_____

PAR Psychological Assessment Resources, Inc./P.O. Box 998/Odessa, FL 33556/Toll-Free 1-800-331-TEST

A
Situation

Mrs. Buck was a homemaker, and she wasn't very happy. Her life seemed meaningless, and her daily routine really seemed like a rut. What self-statements could Mrs. Buck choose, and what might be her reactions and feelings?

B
Self-Talk Possibilities

Rational

_____
_____
_____
_____
_____
_____
_____

Irrational

_____
_____
_____
_____
_____
_____
_____

C
Likely Actions & Feelings

Rational

_____
_____
_____
_____
_____
_____
_____

Irrational

_____
_____
_____
_____
_____
_____
_____

A
Situation

Mr. Rush got off work at 4:00 p.m. After a very hectic day, he was anxious to get home and relax. He waited for the bus, but when it came he realized that he only had a $10 bill. The bus driver said, "Sorry, Mac. No way I can make change for that. You'll have to get change somewhere and catch the next bus." Mr. Rush said, "Don't give me that! Look, just let me ride home tonight, and I'll give you the fare tomorrow." The bus driver replied, "Hey, I can't let anybody on the bus without paying the fare. I've got a schedule to keep. So long." What self-statements could Mr. Rush choose, and what might be his reactions and feelings?

B
Self-Talk Possibilities

Rational

_____
_____
_____
_____
_____

Irrational

_____
_____
_____
_____
_____

C
Likely Actions & Feelings

Rational

_____
_____
_____
_____
_____

Irrational

_____
_____
_____
_____
_____

PAR Psychological Assessment Resources, Inc./P.O. Box 998/Odessa, FL 33556/Toll-Free 1-800-331-TEST

A
Situation

Ralph enjoyed his job very much. He was doing something he had wanted to do for a long time. The only part of the job he didn't like was his boss. Ralph knew that if he performed well on the job he could get a promotion and make more money. But he really disliked his boss. Sometimes, Ralph worked hard to get his promotion, but at other times he did the very least amount of work he could get away with. What self-statements could be influencing the amount of work that Ralph does, and what are his feelings and reactions likely to be?

B
Self-Talk Possibilities

Rational	Irrational
_____	_____
_____	_____
_____	_____
_____	_____
_____	_____

C
Likely Actions & Feelings

Rational	Irrational
_____	_____
_____	_____
_____	_____
_____	_____
_____	_____

PAR Psychological Assessment Resources, Inc./P.O. Box 998/Odessa, FL 33556/Toll-Free 1-800-331-TEST

A
Situation

They had had such a beautiful relationship. At least that's what Nancy thought until Ned suddenly left her. What self-statements could Nancy choose, and what might be her reactions and feelings?

B
Self-Talk Possibilities

Rational	Irrational
_____	_____
_____	_____
_____	_____
_____	_____
_____	_____
_____	_____

C
Likely Actions & Feelings

Rational	Irrational
_____	_____
_____	_____
_____	_____
_____	_____
_____	_____
_____	_____

PAR Psychological Assessment Resources, Inc./P.O. Box 998/Odessa, FL 33556/Toll-Free 1-800-331-TEST

A
Situation

In the past, Gladys used to get upset because George would come home from work obviously troubled about something that he refused to discuss with her. She used to get upset and then feel very depressed. She is beginning to be successful at refusing to upset herself. She is trying to change her self-statements. What might have been her self-statements and reactions in the past? What are they now?

B
Self-Talk Possibilities

Rational	Irrational
_____	_____
_____	_____
_____	_____
_____	_____
_____	_____
_____	_____

C
Likely Actions & Feelings

Rational	Irrational
_____	_____
_____	_____
_____	_____
_____	_____
_____	_____

PAR Psychological Assessment Resources, Inc./P.O. Box 998/Odessa, FL 33556/Toll-Free 1-800-331-TEST

Session 19

Managing Emotions in Your Parenting Partnership

Introduction

This session is the last in a four-part sequence of training in "managing your feelings." Its purpose is to practice and reinforce the information and concepts presented in the earlier sessions. Session 16 presented the basic principles of Rational Emotive Therapy. The ABC model for analyzing our reactions to situations helps parents to recognize that the Events that occur at Step A do not automatically cause the emotions and reactions that occur at Step C. Rather, it is the thoughts, interpretations, and beliefs that occur at Step B (no matter how automatically or instantaneously they occur), leading an individual to assign a particular meaning to the Event, that cause the reactions at Step C. As the Mental Health Professional, your focus is helping parents learn to slow down the process so they can examine the rationality of their self-statements at Step B. This is the key to gaining control over and effectively managing their feelings. Parents should be encouraged to consider alternative self-statements and to explore ways to refute their current self-statements.

In Session 17, parents moved from a purely intellectual understanding of the ABC model into the difficult work of challenging their comfortable, and often automatic, self-statements. The list of common irrational beliefs about parenting helped parents to realize that they are not "stupid" or "alone" in this struggle. Returning to this list and asking parents to suggest additional examples is a good technique for helping parents learn to refute their own irrational beliefs.

The focus of Session 18 was applying the ABC model to parent-to-parent and parent-to-other interactions. The clear message in this session was that the skills for managing one's emotions and feelings are applicable to all interactions. Thus, the skills can be developed and integrated into our interactions as parents, spouses, friends, employees, and so forth.

Five key ideas will be presented in this session:

1. Our emotions, feelings, and behaviors following an event are caused by what we think about the event, that is, the meaning we assign to the event.

2. Rational thinking leads to control over our emotions and to better problem solving.

3. All people have pockets of irrational beliefs that cause them pain and difficulty in certain situations.

4. To build a successful parenting partnership, each partner must communicate and understand the other partner's beliefs about the child.

5. Parents must receive emotional support, and they must feel safe when they share their personal feelings and beliefs with their partners.

239

Special Notes for the Mental Health Professional

Depending on the progress of the group, it may be useful, or even necessary, to repeat this session using the same preparatory home practice assignment—the one at the end of Session 18. At this stage of the training program, groups in which parents feel safe and encouraged will naturally evolve into less structured and more problem-focused support groups. This is an option you may wish to offer to your parents. From this point on, the support group could focus on applying the parenting skills they have learned to individual problem situations faced by members of the group. Other group members become consultants, providing emotional support and concrete ideas about how to cope with the specific situation. If you have done your job well, your role will change from group leader to resource professional. In some instances, the group may even choose to continue to meet without you after the formal schedule of sessions has been completed!

Session Objectives

1 To provide parents with guided practice in analyzing situations in their own lives that lead to negative emotions.

Sequence

● Discussion of home practice (5 - 10 minutes)

● Introduction (10 - 15 minutes)

● Group discussion of problem situations supplied by parents (40 - 50 minutes)

● Lecture/Discussion of common irrational beliefs about the parenting partnership (30 - 40 minutes)

● Discussion of the home practice assignment (5 - 10 minutes)

 ## Materials

Blackboard (or large marking board)

Chalk (or markers)

Eraser

Box placed at door labeled, "Place Problem Situations Here"

Extra paper or note cards

Pencils

(As parents arrive, have them place their problem situations from the home practice assignment in the box at the door.)

I hope everyone remembered to bring in an anonymous problem situation from the home practice assignment. I have some paper and pencils here. We have a few minutes before we begin, so anyone who forgot to bring in a problem situation or would like to offer another one can feel free to do so now. *(Pause 2-3 minutes to allow parents to fill out cards and put them in the box.)*

During the past three sessions, we've been talking about how you can manage your feelings by using the ABC model. You have learned this method can be used in a lot of different situations. Tonight, we are going to talk about the problem situations you brought in to share with the group. Before we start, I want to be sure you know that these situations will be talked about without using your names. It's natural to feel a little uncomfortable about writing down a real-life situation about yourself or one that involves you and your spouse or partner, but remember we won't be using any names.

This is our final session on managing your feelings. It will be an important experience to listen to other people in the group using the ABC model with your own situations. The usefulness of this new technique for managing your feelings will depend on how well you can figure out problem situations by yourself or with the aid of your spouse or partner. This session should be quite helpful in providing an example for you to follow when you are on your own. First, I'll draw our A-B-C diagram on the board again. *(Draw the diagram shown in Figure 40 on board.)*

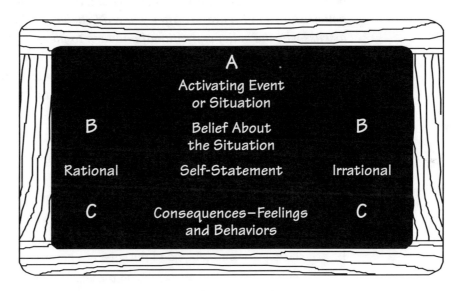

Figure 40. The ABC model for analysis.

Group Discussion of Problem Situations

And now we'll discuss the problem situations you brought to share with the group. Each situation will be the A in the A-B-C analysis. We'll be completing the A-B-C analysis as a group, filling in the possible rational and irrational self-statements, reactions, and feelings. After we complete the diagram for each situation, we'll discuss that situation. *(Read each problem situation aloud to the group, and then facilitate the A-B-C analysis and discussion. Fill in the diagram on the board for each situation. Allow parents to discuss the completed diagram, then erase the information, leaving the diagram for use during the next discussion.)*

(During the discussion of each situation, your focus should be on helping parents identify and examine the irrational beliefs behind the self-statements they identify. Ask them to identify the evidence behind each irrational belief and to determine whether that belief is really true. Guide the group to discover alternative beliefs or other ways of looking at the situation.)

Great. I think you've all caught on to the way you can use the A-B-C analysis in a variety of situations.

Lecture/Discussion

Discussion of Common Irrational Beliefs About the Parenting Partnership

Now let's review some common irrational beliefs that many people hold about their parenting partnership. We will examine the evidence behind these beliefs just as we did two weeks ago. *(Read aloud each of the irrational beliefs shown in Figure 41. After you read each one, ask parents to briefly discuss why the belief is irrational and then to identify at least one alternative way of thinking about the situation or the belief. Ask the same questions used in Session 17 to examine irrational beliefs about parenting. Remember to have parents describe how parenting partners who hold these beliefs might behave toward each other and toward their children.)*

1. If my partner respects and loves me he must back up my decisions about the children.
2. Parents should never disagree in front of their children.
3. A single parent can never do as good a job as two parents.
4. Good parents should always agree with each other about how to discipline their child; good parents are never inconsistent.
5. I must agree with my parenting partner's methods, or it will create problems in our relationship.
6. Mothers instinctively know how to care for children, and fathers should always listen to their partner's advice.
7. My relatives should take care of my child exactly the way I do. I am the parent, and I know best.

Figure 41. Common irrational beliefs about the parenting partnership.

Good. Now you can really see how examining your own irrational beliefs can improve your relationship with your child, your relationship with your partner, and your effectiveness as a parent. Remember, irrational beliefs usually lead to self-defeating behavior. By finding alternative ways of looking at a situation, you will often behave more successfully and more effectively in that situation.

Discussion of the Home Practice Assignment

For next session, continue your home practice assignments. Remember to keep asking yourself about the evidence behind your beliefs or your self-statements. During our next session, we'll talk about how your practice using the ABC model to analyze your own situations is going.

Recommended Readings (for sessions 16 through 19)

Basic Readings

Bernard, M. E. (Ed.). (1991). *Using Rational-Emotive Therapy effectively: A practitioner's guide*. New York: Plenum.

Dryden, W., & DiGiuseppe, R. (1990). *A primer on rational-emotive therapy*. Champaign, IL: Research Press.

Ellis, A., & Grieger, R. (Eds.). (1986). *Handbook of rational-emotive therapy*. New York: Springer.

Supplemental Readings

Dryden, W. (1990). *Rational-emotive counseling in action*. London: Sage.

Ellis, A., & Dryden, W. (1987). *The practice of rational-emotive therapy*. New York: Springer.

Yankura, J., & Dryden, W. (1990). *Doing RET: Albert Ellis in action*. New York: Springer.

Section III

Single Session Lectures or Workshops

Optimizing Your Child's Development—
Ages 0-48 Months

by Suzanne Button

Introduction

Parents often hear about how important it is to help their children learn. Parents want their children to do well in school and grow up to be "successful" adults. What parents do not usually realize, however, is the importance of children's emotional development. Young children need to learn the emotional basics so that they can begin to form happy, healthy relationships at home and school. Successful relationships are as important as learning information in helping children approach tasks like reading and problem-solving with confidence.

During the first 4 years of life, children develop the foundation for their ability to form relationships and control their emotions. Between birth and age 4, children gradually develop a basic sense of who they are. For this development to occur in a positive way, children need to have experiences that teach them they can handle their own emotions, enjoy their environment, and communicate successfully with the people they love.

Now, you may be saying to yourself, "I want my child to feel loved and confident, but I have no idea what you mean by 'emotional development.' It all sounds pretty vague." When I speak of emotional development, I am talking about the development of two sets of skills: the ability to form positive interpersonal relationships and the ability to control one's emotions. Many parents know that they want to help their children develop the ability to form strong, healthy relationships and to control their emotions, but parents are not sure what they can do to foster this development.

That's what we'll be talking about today. I will describe the basic stages of emotional development that your baby goes through and then give you some simple, concrete strategies for helping your baby learn what we call *emotional intelligence*. *(Distribute pens or pencils and the handout from the last page of this session.)*

Session Objectives

1. To introduce parents to the concept of emotional development.

2. To teach parents the early stages of emotional development.

3. To teach parents simple, concrete methods for helping their young children develop emotionally.

Sequence

- Introduction (10 minutes)
- Lecture/Discussion of the normal stages of emotional development and appropriate methods for facilitating each stage (60 - 90 minutes)

Materials

Blackboard (or large marking board)

Chalk (or markers)

Eraser

Handout for parents: Stages of Emotional Development

Pens or pencils

Lecture/Discussion

Normal Stages of Emotional Development and the Parent's Role as Facilitator

First, we'll take a brief look at the six stages of emotional development that every young child goes through in the first 48 months. These stages are listed on your handout, and you'll find plenty of space for you to record your own ideas as we discuss these stages. After I describe each stage, we'll talk about the specific steps you can take to strengthen your child emotionally. Think about how you might work these steps into your family's lifestyle.

Remember, it will be important for you to adjust these ideas to fit your child, your family schedule, and your general lifestyle. You are the expert on your child. Every child is unique, and every child goes through the stages of emotional development at a slightly different pace. Every family is unique, too. As I suggest ways you can help your child develop emotionally, think about how you can adapt these suggestions to fit your own family's style and schedule. During this session, I encourage you to record the ideas that occur to you about your own child's development and how you can help with it. *(Write the following heading on the board.)*

0-3 Months: Self-regulation/Self-interest/Interest in the World

Many people think that infants feel very little pleasure or pain, but research shows this is not the case. Soon after birth, infants can respond to different sounds, feelings, and faces, and they also react to their experiences. During their first months of life, infants must learn how to calm themselves and how to keep from being overwhelmed by the almost constant stimulation from their environment. They also learn to be curious about the world around them. How do they accomplish this? They use their senses and their attention to regulate their own emotions.

When a baby is first born, he or she has little ability to screen out sights, sounds, or smells, so the baby attends to every sensory experience coming from inside or outside his or her body. When a very young baby is wet, for example, he or she is likely to feel extremely uncomfortable and to cry very loudly. The experience of discomfort is so strong that the baby is distracted from all other activity. But during the first few weeks of life, that baby begins to control the amount of discomfort he or she feels when the diaper is wet. The baby gradually develops an ability to feel a moderate amount of discomfort with the diaper while, at the same time, maintaining an active interest in the surrounding world. You may have noticed that your baby's reaction to a wet diaper seemed to diminish as he or she grew a little older.

As you might guess, your baby's ability to regulate feelings and your baby's interest in the surrounding world develop hand in hand. As your baby learns to tolerate and then to regulate emotional reactions, he or she remains interested in learning about other people and other things. And this early interest in the surrounding world forms the basis for the child's interest in learning later on.

As a parent, you can take some simple steps to foster your infant's emotional development during this first stage, which usually occurs from birth to about 3 months of age. Your goal at this stage should be to help your child feel calm and soothed when he or she experiences strong sensations such as hunger, gas, or loud noise. Your infant is almost programmed to accomplish this goal if he or she receives a little necessary help from her caregivers. Your job is to help provide a consistent, responsive environment for your child. Even though your infant doesn't seem to be responding to you yet, the emotional environment that you provide will allow your child to regulate his or her feelings and begin to respond to you.

Take lots of special time with your infant. Look into your child's eyes, smile, and talk in a loving, soothing, pleasure-filled voice. Watch your child carefully, and respond to the way your child feels and expresses emotions. What do I mean by this? Well, some babies like to be stroked and held, others prefer to be talked to, and some love to hear their parents singing. Try out all the different ways you can think of to show your love to your baby, and see which method gets the best response. By communicating in your baby's preferred style, you help the baby feel secure about communicating with you. In other words, you will support your baby's emotional development more and more as you learn to accurately read his or her emotional states and signals.

Listen carefully to the quality of your baby's cries. Parents can learn to recognize a hungry cry, a gassy cry, and a "come-and-play-with-me" cry. By learning this language of cries, you will know when your baby wants to play or stop playing, when your baby needs physical attention, and when your baby needs some quiet, nonstimulating time. When you respond to these cries appropriately, you help your baby return more quickly to the calm, alert state that frees the baby to explore and learn about the environment. In addition, as you help your baby experience relationships in ways that are comfortable and responsive without being intrusive, you are providing an opportunity for your child to learn to control his or her own feelings, little by little.

Many people don't realize that babies have individual preferences for communication. A baby who doesn't like noise, for example, may become overwhelmed and fussy when people talk in loud voices. On the other hand, a baby who prefers being talked to may get irritated when he or she is held quietly for a long period of time. It is important to remember that each baby has different preferences for communicating. *(Write the following heading on the board.)*

3-7 Months: Falling in love—forming the first relationship

When your baby begins to interact with other people, he or she has entered into the next stage of emotional development. From 3 to 7 months of age, babies form their first relationship—with their primary caregiver. You will be able to tell when this stage begins, because your baby will start to show a preference for you. Your baby will smile and gaze at you, brighten at the sound of your voice, and relax in your arms.

At this stage, your baby is ready to learn about how a loving relationship can be supportive, positive, and pleasurable. In fact, the quality of your relationship with your baby at this stage will teach him or her what to expect from other relationships in the future. It can also teach the baby that relationships are supports for his or her development. Your baby's future interpersonal relationships are strongly influenced by what he or she learns in this first relationship with you. Your goal at this stage is to establish regular communication between you and your baby and to demonstrate that relationships can be safe and pleasurable.

Your baby will reach out to you by smiling, by gazing, and by laughing. Your job at this stage is to respond. Just as you did in the first stage, you must observe and respect your baby's pace and style of interaction. Your baby will often smile and vocalize to you. This is a signal that he or she is ready for interaction. Whenever you can, smile back, talk back, and make some sort of contact. Spend special time with your baby, sharing the joy of these loving interactions and encouraging them to continue and to lengthen.

But remember to respect your baby's pace. Watch for signs that your child needs to take a break from interaction for a while. When you pick up that signal, give your child a chance to be calm, to suck his or her hand and stare off into space, or even just to look away from you for a few moments. These are ways your child has of practicing that emotional regulation I talked about earlier. Let your child take a break, but be ready to respond enthusiastically when he or she signals for more interaction.

Try to "woo" your baby. Encourage interaction for longer periods of time, but remember to be gentle about adding time or intensity to your interactions. The more time and space you give your baby as he or she is building up to longer and more loving interactions with you, the more your child will be able to enjoy them. And it will also help your child to build a stronger sense of self. *(Write the following heading on the board.)*

4-10 Months: Communicating with a purpose

As your baby forms a unique relationship with you, he or she will begin to practice communicating with a purpose. Your child will tell you, through movements, facial expressions, and vocalizations, what he or she needs from you emotionally. At this stage, your baby must learn that he or she can communicate emotional needs to another human being, who will, in turn, respond to those needs.

Your job as parent is to respond to your baby's emotional states by maintaining control over your own emotions and paying attention to what your baby does and feels. Observe your baby, and respond in kind when he or she communicates with you. If your baby smiles and laughs in a silly way, show your own silliness and joy in response. If he or she looks very sad, speak in a comforting voice or hold your baby for a while. If your baby makes a fussy face or kicks his or her legs and feet, be soothing in the way that you know will really work. Even if you only have time to smile or speak in response, make sure you react to all your baby's communications.

The more you respond to your baby's emotional needs, the more he or she will come to feel self-confident about getting those needs met. This feeling of success about interactions with you will spill over into relationships with other people. Most importantly, this emotional communication is the beginning of all communication that your child will eventually learn. The more your child learns that he or she can communicate effectively with you, the more motivated your child will be to work toward more grown-up methods of communication—like speaking and writing—in the future. *(Write the following heading on the board.)*

9-18 Months: Developing a complex sense of self

You will notice when your child begins to develop a more complex sense of self. Your child will begin to express his or her own unique personality in very noticeable ways. Your child is beginning to put together everything learned so far, and this is expressed as a forming personality style. Your baby will begin to do things that you haven't taught, to show preferences for food or toys, to play simple jokes, or to act shy or aggressive.

Your job is to encourage this developing personality by respecting your child's preferences and encouraging his or her originality and creativity. Show an interest in the games your child makes up. If your child does something new and exciting, give lots of praise.

At this stage, you can help provide a foundation for your child's positive self-esteem by showing lots of interest and excitement about this developing personality. You can also help your child improve the new skills that seem to appear on their own. For example, if your daughter is building a sand dune in the yard while you are working in the garden nearby, look at her occasionally and smile, giving her praise for her independent accomplishment. Ask her if she can make a tunnel all by herself. Always praise independent efforts, but encourage your child to take these new abilities even further.

It's important to remember that teaching is *not* the goal of this stage. At this time of life, children are programmed to explore, develop, and learn on their own when they are provided with a stimulating and supportive environment. The goal here is to follow your child's interests and actions by showing interest, giving encouragement, and having enthusiasm for what your child does. You might occasionally show your child something new or provide some new toys or materials to play with, but formal teaching isn't necessary to foster positive development at this stage. *(Write the following heading on the board.)*

18-30 Months: Emotional ideas

Emotional ideas are the beginnings of your child's imagination. Your child can have an emotional picture of a person or an event and can remember that picture after the person is gone or the event is over. This is an important skill, because it helps your child become more independent from you. If you leave your child at a day-care facility or with a babysitter during this stage, your child can begin to use imaginative ideas to remember how good you make him or her feel—and this will provide comfort while you are gone. Children who have experienced comfort and support in their relationships will begin to do and say things to calm themselves that they remember their parents doing or saying in order to calm them at some time in the past. These children are learning to regulate their own emotions.

Emotional ideas are important because they form the basis for your child's developing imagination. Children learn through pretend play, and their emotional ideas form the basis of this play. When your child begins to pretend play, you will know that he or she is beginning to form emotional ideas. Your job at this stage is to show interest in the pretend play and to participate as much as possible. But remember that your role in your child's play is that of a follower—your child is the leader.

Like many parents, you may get tired of pretending for long periods of time, especially when your child wants to play the same game over and over. Still, your participation will encourage your child to use imagination and to explore feelings through play. Try to be patient and enthusiastic, but participate *only* when you can do so without being irritated or bored. It is important that you communicate encouragement and excitement when your child uses emotional imagination. *(Write the following heading on the board.)*

30-48 Months: Emotional thinking

This stage in early emotional development is very important. *Emotional thinking* develops when your child is able to remember your positive feelings in situations outside of your relationship. Your child will take the sense of encouragement and interest that you have communicated up to this point and carry that encouragement and interest into other relationships and situations.

If your child feels understood and valued by you, he or she will have a more confident sense of self-worth. As a result, your child will approach other people and new situations with optimism and self-confidence.

Emotional thinking also allows your child to work through any emotional problems that he or she may encounter. When your child gets upset, for example, he or she will use your example of speaking calmly to regain self-control. Your child will learn to expect that others will help—as you have always helped in the past—and will turn to others readily for help to feel calmer and to regain emotional control. Toddlers who do not feel valued and understood by the adults around them often exhibit poor emotional development. For example, they may withdraw or become aggressive when they are upset.

Your child's ability to imagine what it would be like to be independent of you or what it is like to be close to you is also an important part of this learning process. You may have noticed your child pretending to be angry or sad. This is your child's way of practice handling emotions in the ways that have become familiar through interactions with you. By playing along with these pretend games and giving your child hints about how to cope with difficult emotions, you can help your child learn to handle feelings independently as he or she grows older.

Your child will need some help developing the ability to think emotionally. He or she will begin to act out make-believe dramas that have emotional themes and will need your help and support when acting them out with you. For example, if you are playing with your daughter and she pretends to be the "mean" mother, what should you do? It is best to respect her need to act mean, while commenting that she sometimes feels like her own mommy is mean. If your son pretends to get on a train and say goodbye, you can say goodbye, but reassure him that you will be there when he gets back.

Again, it is important to observe your child carefully during this stage. By paying attention to the themes in your child's pretend play, you can find out what emotional struggles he or she is acting out and trying to master. By commenting on those struggles in a supportive, understanding way, you can help your child to work through them with support and encouragement.

For the rest of this session, I would like you to share some specific situations where you have observed your child's emotional development during one of the stages I presented. As we discuss your example, feel free to refer to the handout or to your notes. Before we begin, are there any questions about the six stages of emotional development?

(For the remainder of the session, encourage parents to discuss their own experiences with a child's emotional development. Ask parents what they noticed during each stage of their children's development, and connect their observations to the above stages with your comments. Ask parents to consider how they would respond in each situation. What else could they do? What part of emotional development is hard for them to understand? Be prepared

for the fact that most parents will not immediately be able to fit their child's behaviors into the appropriate stage. Ask the parents to describe their child's behavior, and then let the rest of the group try to figure out what is going on and what stage of emotional development the child is working on. Remind parents that, as their children progress to new stages, they may continue to exhibit behaviors related to earlier stages of development. Explain that children need support and encouragement when this occurs, regardless of their apparent mastery of past developmental stages.)

Recommended Readings

Greenspan, S. I. (1989). *The development of the ego*. Madison, CT: International Universities Press.

Greenspan, S. I., & Thorndike-Greenspan, N. (1985). *First feelings: Milestones in the emotional development of your baby and child*. New York: Viking Penguin.

Greenspan, S. I., & Thorndike-Greenspan, N. (1989). *The essential partnership*. New York: Viking Penguin.

Stages of Emotional Development:
Birth to 4 Years

Age	Stage	What Parents Can Do
0 – 3 months	Self-Regulation, Self-Interest, and Interest in the world	Spend special, loving time with your child. Respond in a predictable, sensitive manner to the infant's preferred style of experiencing feelings.
3 – 7 months	"Falling in love"– forming the first relationship	Respond to your baby's overtures. Show your affection and joy during the interaction. Allow your baby to take breaks, but encourage him or her to interact with you for longer and longer periods of time.
4 – 10 months	Communicating with a purpose	Respond to your baby's emotional communication, Try your best to meet your child's emotional needs. Smile back when your baby smiles, speak soothingly when he or she fusses, and comfort your child when he or she is sad.
9 – 18 months	Developing a complex sense of self	Show interest and excitement in your child's emerging personality. Try to respect his or her preferences. Give praise for independent accomplishments while encouraging your child to go even further.
18 – 30 months	Emotional ideas	Show interest in your child's ideas. Participate in pretend play with interest and excitement.
30 – 48 months	Emotional thinking	Comment on and support the emotional themes in your child's pretend play. Help your child work through emotional struggles by giving support and encouragement. Show enthusiasm and excitement when your child uses his or her imagination.

PAR Psychological Assessment Resources, Inc./P.O. Box 998/Odessa, FL 33556/Toll-Free 1-800-331-TEST

Session 21: Special Education and Your Legal Rights

by Suzanne Button

Session Objectives

1 To familiarize parents with special education, its goals, and the children who benefit from its use.

2 To inform parents of their rights under the Individuals with Disabilities Education Act of 1990.

Sequence

● Lecture/Discussion of children with special educational needs (30 - 40 minutes)

● Lecture/Discussion of PL 94-142 and PL 99-457 (10 minutes)

● Lecture/Discussion of how to obtain special education services (30 - 40 minutes)

Materials

Blackboard (or large marking board)

Chalk (or markers)

Eraser

Handout: Assistance Guidelines

Handout: List of additional/local resources for parents
(If available)

Lecture/Discussion

Children With Special Educational Needs

Today we'll be talking about special education programs for children. Over the past 20 years, our federal government has passed a series of laws that guarantee equal opportunity in education to all children. Before we talk about those laws, let's talk about why certain children might need special educational circumstances and why it is important to meet those needs.

Children who cannot learn by ordinary teaching methods are referred to as children with special educational needs. Special-needs children may be unable to do certain types of things because of a physical or mental handicap, or they may be disadvantaged in some specific way because of a particular disability. Because of their physical, intellectual, or emotional limitations, special-needs children are challenged beyond their capacity by regular teaching methods. To succeed in school, these children require special circumstances or special services (or both) that will help them to learn.

Special education, then, is teaching that is specially designed to meet the needs of a particular child. It may be provided in the regular classroom, in a special education classroom, or in a combination of classroom education and special one-on-one tutoring. Wherever it is provided, special education is designed to identify and capitalize on the individual strengths and abilities of the special-needs child.

Some people argue that special education is just too expensive. Why should our tax dollars go toward building access ramps, hiring special teachers, or buying special buses? It is expensive for schools to provide special education, but it would be even more expensive not to provide it. If the special-needs child succeeds in school, he or she is more likely to grow into a self-supporting adult. Adults who are self-supporting don't need welfare or institutionalization. That's why it's actually less expensive in the long run to pay for special education for a limited amount of time than it is to support individuals who have handicaps or disabilities for their entire lives.

(Throughout the following discussion, use a Question and Answer format to encourage parents to suggest each of the 7 major categories shown in Figure 42. As parents mention each category, list it on the board. First, encourage parents to identify and define a handicap or disability and then to describe the special educational needs that would be involved. Be sure to cover any remaining categories and provide information to supplement what parents do not know.)

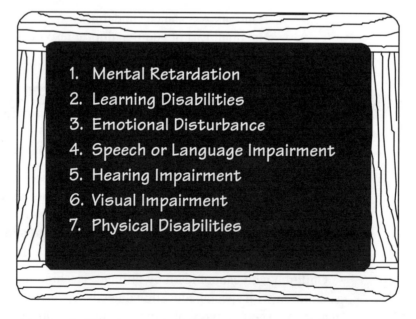

1. Mental Retardation
2. Learning Disabilities
3. Emotional Disturbance
4. Speech or Language Impairment
5. Hearing Impairment
6. Visual Impairment
7. Physical Disabilities

Figure 42. Handicaps or disabilities of children with special needs.

Q What handicaps or disabilities might cause a child to have special educational needs?

What special educational circumstances might such a child need?

1. Mental Retardation

Definition:

Children with mental retardation learn and mature more slowly than their peers. It is important to understand that children with mental retardation differ significantly from their peers in learning ability only. This means they have the same capacity for making friends, caring about other people, and relating to others that all children do.

Special educational needs:

Because mental retardation occurs in varying degrees of severity, children with this disability are usually placed in an educational setting according to the severity of their cognitive and social delay. Education of children with mental retardation often focuses on readiness skills—these are the skills that prepare a child for learning—such as sitting and paying attention to a teacher, following directions, using language, motor coordination, social skills, and self-help skills. In the upper grades, special education may focus on preparing the child for the work place and for independent living.

2. Learning Disabilities

Definition:

Children with learning disabilities are those who have average or above-average intelligence, but have specific problems with listening, thinking, speaking, or performing an academic skill. Children with learning disabilities are unable to perform at age-appropriate levels in the area of their disability. This category includes many different areas of difficulty, such as difficulty paying attention, inability to distinguish different sounds from each other, and inability to recognize the differences between certain letters of the alphabet.

Special educational needs:

Children with learning disabilities usually require specific instruction—by a tutor, a regular classroom teacher, or a special education teacher—that is designed for the specific disability. Depending on the disability, behavioral management techniques, special learning strategies, or appropriate technological assistance may also be required. Children with attentional difficulties may also benefit from appropriate medication.

3. Emotional Disturbance

Definition:

Children with emotional disturbance exhibit one or more of the following behaviors for an extended period of time and to a degree of severity that interferes with their ability to learn, to relate to adults, and to form successful relationships with their peers: aggression, disruptive or destructive behavior, fear, nervousness, depression, withdrawal, and frequent, unexplained physical complaints. Because of their emotional difficulties, these children often behave in ways that make it difficult, or even impossible, for them to succeed in a regular classroom.

Special educational needs:

Depending on the severity of their behavioral disturbance, children with emotional difficulties may be educated in the regular classroom using special behavioral management techniques or in a special classroom for emotionally disturbed children. In either case, children in this category usually receive some sort of psychological treatment as well. In addition, their parents and teachers are often taught special techniques to handle their behavior problems.

4. Speech or Language Impairment

Definition:

Children with speech or language impairment may have difficulty making the sounds required to produce their native language. Children with speech disorders may be unable to produce a particular sound, to produce adequate vocal sounds, or to control the rate and rhythm of their speech. Children with language disorders may have difficulty comprehending or using language itself. In either case, the child's speech or language impairment interferes with communication to the degree that it affects the child's ability to succeed in the regular classroom.

Special educational needs:

Children with speech or language impairments usually receive some sort of speech or language therapy in conjunction with special teaching methods in the regular classroom.

5. Hearing Impairment

Definition:

Children with hearing impairment suffer from deficits in hearing that are severe enough to interfere with educational performance.

Special educational needs:

Hearing impairments are usually addressed using a total communication approach. Children are encouraged to make maximum use of the hearing they do possess. They are taught skills such as speech-reading and sign language to augment their hearing and provided with technological assistance, such as hearing aids or computer-assisted instruction, when necessary. Depending on the severity of their impairment, children with hearing deficits may be educated in a regular classroom (along with regular tutoring sessions), in a special education classroom, or in a special school for the hearing impaired.

6. **Visual Impairment**

Definition:

Children with visual impairment suffer from visual deficits that are severe enough, even with eyeglasses or other correction, to interfere with educational performance.

Special educational needs:

Visual impairments must be addressed by modifying classroom teaching methods, because these traditional methods are primarily visual. Visually impaired children are also encouraged to make maximum use of the sight they possess; they are provided with large-type or Braille books, and they are taught mobility skills. Depending on the severity of their impairment, children with visual deficits may be educated in a regular classroom (along with regular tutoring sessions), in a special education classroom, or in a special school for the visually impaired.

7. **Physical Disabilities**

Definition:

Children with physical disabilities suffer from non-sensory impairments that interfere with successful functioning in the regular classroom. Physical impairments encompass a wide range of neurological, congenital, and other physical conditions. Examples of physical impairments include cerebral palsy, spina bifida, muscular dystrophy, juvenile diabetes, and physical complications as a result of AIDS.

Special educational needs:

In the absence of any other, nonphysical impairments, the special educational needs of the physically impaired student will generally involve modification of the physical environment of the classroom to provide access and mobility for the child. In addition, physically impaired students may need special devices or special instruction to help them perform academic tasks which require physical movement.

Good. Now you can see that special education may include special teaching methods, special learning environments, psychological services for children and their families, or special methods of disciplining children.

Special education should be designed to capitalize on the abilities and strengths of the individual child who is receiving the special services.

Lecture/Discussion

PL 94-142 and PL 99-457

In 1975, the federal government enacted Public Law (PL) 94-142, the Education for All Handicapped Children Act. In 1986, the government amended that Act, and called the amendments PL 99-457. After additional amendments in 1990, the original Act with all its amendments is now called the Individuals with Disabilities Education Act, or IDEA. IDEA guarantees free, appropriate education and related services for every child over the age of 2 years. It also provides financial incentives for states to provide early intervention and assistance for infants and toddlers who have special needs.

If you have a child with a handicap or a disability who is over the age of 2 years, you are legally entitled to an appropriate education for that child at no additional cost to you. In this case, *appropriate* means an education that meets your child's special needs. If your child is physically disabled, for example, he or she may need wheelchair access to the school and may also need to be transported in a special school bus. If your child is mentally retarded, your child may be entitled to small-group instruction with appropriate materials. If your local school system cannot provide appropriate educational services for your child, the law requires that school system to provide and pay for an alternative placement as close to your home as possible. For example, if your child is severely disabled in some way and needs to be educated in a residential setting, your local school system is required to pay the total cost of that residential setting, including room and board.

If your special-needs child is not yet old enough to attend school, you may be eligible for certain preschool services, physical and medical therapies, and in-home assistance. A child under the age of 2 years may be eligible for an early intervention program, if one is provided by your local government. *(Write the following heading on the board.)*

LRE–Least Restrictive Environment

According to IDEA, every special-needs child has the right to be educated in what is called the LRE, or least restrictive environment. This means that special-needs children should be placed with nondisabled children in regular classrooms as much as possible. Special services should be no more intensive than necessary, and a child should only be placed in a separate class or school when supplementary services, such as tutoring or learning aids, are not sufficient to allow the child to succeed within the regular classroom.

Obtaining Special Education Services

Now, what should you do if you think your child may need special educational services? The first thing to do is contact your child's teacher and the school. The law guarantees that your child's school (or your local early intervention program) must address your concerns by providing an appropriate assessment of your child's potential disability. In addition, the law requires that you be fully informed about this assessment and that you give your full consent. Let me give you an example:

Cory Taylor is 8 years old and in the third grade. He is an energetic boy who enjoys running and playing with his friends. For the past 2 years, Cory has had difficulty in reading and arithmetic. His parents and teachers have given Cory extra help at home and arranged for extra help at school, but he still can't get passing grades. When his parents help him with homework, Cory tries very hard to listen to what his parents tell him, but he cannot seem to get things right. Cory's parents call his teacher, who says that she thinks Cory might need special education services. Cory's teacher refers him to the in-school screening committee, consisting of the school principal, the school psychologist, and Cory's teacher. The committee reviews Cory's schoolwork and report cards for the last 2 years and decides that a more formal assessment of his educational needs is called for. At this point, Mr. and Mrs. Taylor are notified of the committee's decision and asked for their permission to do this formal evaluation of Cory's abilities.

Any formal school assessment should be designed to address the specific problems your child is having. For example, a child who is getting A's in math and failing reading should, in all likelihood, be assessed for a reading disability. In addition, this assessment should be administered in your child's native language and should not be discriminatory in any way. The assessment should be as focused or as extensive as necessary, given your child's specific problem(s). Most importantly, you should be informed of the results of this assessment during a legally-required eligibility meeting attended by your child's teacher, a representative of the school's special education department, and at least one of the individuals who evaluated your child. This is how the process usually goes:

Once the Taylors give their consent, Cory is given a full evaluation. He is seen by his pediatrician, the school psychologist, the special education teacher, and the school's speech and language specialist. Each professional gives Cory several tests and uses the special procedures necessary to determine Cory's abilities and his present level of functioning. Cory's parents are then invited to attend an eligibility meeting about Cory. At this meeting (which is also attended

by the director of special education, Cory's teacher, and the school nurse), the school psychologist presents the results of the assessment. Cory's parents and the team of professionals discuss these results, review his school records, and discuss experiences each has had when working with Cory. After reviewing all of this information, the professionals at this meeting agree that Cory has mild retardation and is, therefore, eligible for special education services—a special education program designed to help him succeed in school.

Once your child is identified as eligible for special education, another meeting must be held to develop a plan for your child's educational program. During this meeting, you and the professionals attending should develop an individualized education program, or IEP. Remember, this IEP is a legally required plan that must provide five things. *(Write the five requirements shown in Figure 43 on the board.)*

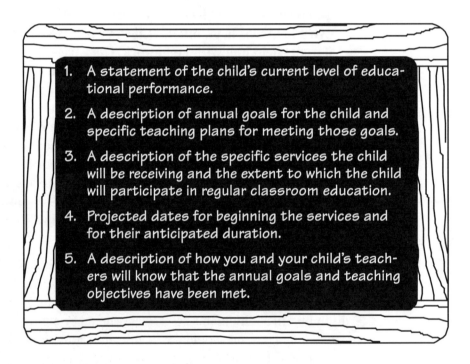

1. A statement of the child's current level of educational performance.

2. A description of annual goals for the child and specific teaching plans for meeting those goals.

3. A description of the specific services the child will be receiving and the extent to which the child will participate in regular classroom education.

4. Projected dates for beginning the services and for their anticipated duration.

5. A description of how you and your child's teachers will know that the annual goals and teaching objectives have been met.

Figure 43. The five requirements on an IEP.

Let's look at what happens in Cory's case:

Cory's parents are informed of the place, date, and time of Cory's IEP meeting. At this meeting, Cory's parents meet with his teacher, the school psychologist, a special education teacher, and the special education director to develop a specific educational plan for Cory. The group decides that Cory would do well in a special education classroom, or resource room, for two periods each day. During those two periods, Cory will work with a special teacher and with other mentally retarded students on basic readiness skills. Cory will spend the rest of the school day—lunch, recess, art, and social studies—with his regular classmates. At this meeting, the professionals write an IEP that includes descriptions of the goals for Cory, teaching objectives for meeting those goals, and criteria for knowing that the goals have been met. Cory's parents and all the professionals present sign this IEP, which is then implemented the following week. Cory begins to spend part of his day in a resource class and part of his day with his regular classmates.

Finally, the law requires that each child's IEP must be reviewed and updated every year. In addition, each child must be reevaluated every 2 years (with parental consent) to determine the most appropriate and least restrictive environment to meet his or her continuing educational needs. Cory's story ends like this:

Cory is doing well in both his regular class and his resource class. After each academic year, his parents and teachers update his IEP, including new goals and objectives for Cory. Every 2 years, Cory is reevaluated to ensure that his educational needs are being met in the least restrictive environment possible.

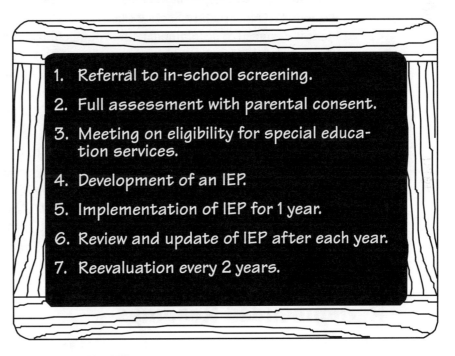

1. Referral to in-school screening.

2. Full assessment with parental consent.

3. Meeting on eligibility for special education services.

4. Development of an IEP.

5. Implementation of IEP for 1 year.

6. Review and update of IEP after each year.

7. Reevaluation every 2 years.

Figure 44. The IEP process.

Let's review this process again. *(You may wish to write the seven steps shown in Figure 44 on the board.)* A child who may be eligible for special education services should first be referred to an in-school screening committee by his teacher or parents. If a full assessment is called for, the parents must consent to this assessment before it begins. The assessment should be nondiscriminatory, administered in the child's native language, and appropriate for the child's specific disability. After the assessment is complete, parents and specialists attend an eligibility meeting to determine whether the child is eligible for special education services. If the child is eligible, a second meeting is held during which parents and professionals design an IEP. This IEP is implemented for 1 year, after which the child's progress is reviewed and the IEP updated. Any child receiving special education services should be reevaluated every 2 years to ensure that appropriate services are being provided to meet the child's needs.

As parents, you should be involved throughout this process. You should be informed about exactly what is happening with your child, and you are entitled to review your child's records if you have any questions. If you feel that your child is not getting appropriate services, you may obtain an independent evaluation for your child or request an independent hearing before an impartial third party. *(Pause.)*

If you have a child under 4 years of age who has a handicap or disability, you should call your local Head Start program or your local school system for information about obtaining appropriate services. Again, after you give your consent, your child is entitled to a timely, appropriate evaluation. If your child is identified as developmentally delayed or disabled, you are entitled to a written Individual Family Service Plan, or IFSP. This plan resembles the IEP, but it is designed to accommodate the young child at home and at school. Through the IFSP, your child might receive special preschool services, medical services, or in-home education. You may also be entitled to parent training, respite care, or other types of support. Like the IEP, each IFSP is individually designed to maximize the abilities of the disabled preschool-age child, and each IFSP will be unique. *(Pause.)*

This has been a brief overview of special education law and your rights under that law. Let's use the rest of our time to talk about any questions you might have about special education. *(Take a few minutes to answer questions briefly. Make sure to have a list of resources available to give to parents whose concerns are beyond the scope of this session. National resources and pertinent literature are listed in the Annotated Bibliography at the end of this book. Also, distribute the handout at the end of this chapter before you close the session.)*

Recommended Readings

Gallagher, J. J., Trohanis, P. L., & Clifford, R. M. (Eds.). (1989). *Policy implementation and PL 99-457.* Baltimore, MD: Paul H. Brooks.

Hallahan, D. P., & Kauffman, J. M. (1991). *Exceptional children.* Englewood Cliffs, NJ: Prentice-Hall.

La Morte, M. W. (1993). *School law: Cases and concepts.* Boston: Allyn & Bacon.

Osborne, A. G. (1988). *Complete legal guide to special education services.* West Nyack, NY: Parker.

Turnbull, H. R., III. (1990). *Free appropriate public education: The law and children with disabilities.* Denver, CO: Love.

Valente, W. D. (1994). *Law in the schools.* New York: Macmillan.

Assistance Guidelines
Consumer Concerns Regarding Children with Special Needs

Typical complaints: Inadequate assessment of a child, the absence of an Individual Education Plan or Individual Family Service Plan, inadequate or missing services, or the lack of an impartial hearing.

Process: First, parents should express their concerns to the school system's Director of Special Education. After all efforts at the local level are exhausted, the following complaint procedures may be followed:

1. Address complaints to the Office for Civil Rights of the Department of Education in the region where your school district is located. Your complaint must be filed within 180 days of the violation.

2. The complaint should be as brief as possible, but should include all of the following:
    *   name, address, and phone number of person making the complaint
    *   name, address, and phone number of person who has been the victim of discrimination or inappropriate services
    *   a description of that individual's disability
    *   name and address of the school, institution, or facility that caused the discrimination or inappropriate services (NOTE: The program must receive federal funds in order for the law to give you protection.)
    *   a description of the problem and the dates involved
    *   a description of all attempts to solve the problem, and what has happened as a result of these efforts

3. Sign and date the complaint. Attach copies (*not* the originals) of all relevant correspondence about the complaint.

You will be contacted by an investigator for further information; the school or facility will also be asked to present its side of the story. If your complaint is accurate and the school or agency is not in compliance, the Department of Education has the authority to require compliance.

WARNING: No complaint should be filed as a means of harassing a school or agency. If the school will no longer talk to the parents about their child's situation and the parents honestly feel that the law has been violated, a complaint will force the school or agency to confront the issue. The school or agency will have to either produce facts to back up its actions or change its practice.

Two major federal laws may be of help: PL 94-142 and PL 99-457. Collectively, these laws are called the Individual with Disabilities Education Act (IDEA). Copies of the laws are available from: Superintendent of Documents, U.S. Government Printing Office, Washington, DC 20402, (202) 783-3238.

Sources of assistance:

National Center for Law & the Handicapped, Inc., 211 W. Washington Street, Suite 1900, South Bend, IN 46601, (219) 288-4751

Center for Law & Education, Inc., Gutman Library, 6 Appian Way, Cambridge, MA 02138, (617) 495-4666

Children's Defense Fund, 1520 New Hampshire Avenue, NW, Washington, DC 20036, (202) 483-1470

Helping Your Child With Schoolwork

by Richard R. Abidin and Suzanne Button

Session Objectives

1 To teach parents to effectively support and encourage their children's independent completion of school work.

2 To help parents learn how to recognize when their children need special help with schoolwork and how to provide their children with that help.

3 To teach parents when their children's educational needs are beyond the parent's capacity and provide suggestions for seeking outside tutoring when such assistance is called for.

Sequence

- Introduction (5 minutes)
- Lecture/Discussion of homework plan (15 - 20 minutes)
- Lecture/Discussion of tutoring children (20 - 30 minutes)
- Lecture/Discussion of monitoring parent's tutoring (20 - 30 minutes)
- Lecture/Discussion of seeking outside tutoring (15 minutes)

Materials

Blackboard (or large marking board)

Chalk (or markers)

Eraser

Handout: Helping Your Child With Schoolwork

Introduction

Most of you have had difficulty, at one time or another, getting your child to do his or her homework. For some parents, getting homework completed becomes a tiresome chore, one that involves arguing, constant supervision, and all the frustration that comes with having to go through an unwelcome process night after night. It's also hard for some parents to recognize when their child is really struggling with a particular subject and needs extra help. Some parents are unsure about when they should step in to help their child and about what kind of help they should be giving.

Today, I'll be talking about a basic plan to help you get your child to do homework more willingly. If this plan is put into place, it can make homework an easier experience for both you and your child. We'll also talk tonight about how and when to offer tutoring or other assistance when your child is struggling with his schoolwork. *(Distribute the schoolwork handouts provided at the end of this chapter.)*

Lecture/Discussion

Homework Plan

This handout will be a good reference for our discussion. Feel free to make notes as we move along. Although the Homework Plan is fairly simple, you might want to make a few notes to yourself about how you can use the plan at home. This homework plan has 4 stages: *(Write the steps presented in Figure 45 on the board.)*

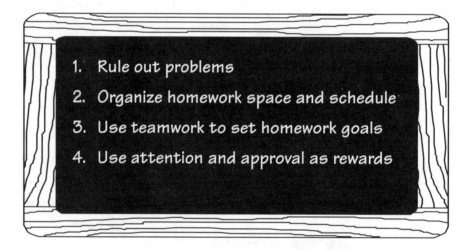

1. Rule out problems
2. Organize homework space and schedule
3. Use teamwork to set homework goals
4. Use attention and approval as rewards

Figure 45. A 4-step homework plan.

Rule out problems. It is important to rule out any real problems that your child might have with schoolwork in general before starting this plan. For example, have your child's vision and hearing been checked? Also, if you think that your child may be suffering from a learning disability or an attention deficit, you might want to talk to your child's teachers about your concerns before starting this plan. Finally, think about your child's age level and academic abilities. Is the amount of homework appropriate for your child's age level? Does the difficulty level of the homework match your child's ability level? If you are concerned about any of these questions, speak with your child's teachers before beginning. It is important that your child not be overwhelmed by schoolwork, because a child who is truly overwhelmed will be learning negative attitudes toward schoolwork. And that, in turn, will make it very difficult to motivate your child.

Even if you don't have any of these concerns, it is a good idea to let your child's teacher know that you are considering the new plan. If the teacher knows that you're starting a homework plan, he or she can reinforce your efforts by praising and supporting your child for completed homework assignments. Your child's teacher might also be able to tell you what subjects seem to present particular homework challenges and give you suggestions on ways to motivate your child to get work done.

Organize homework space and schedule. The second step is very, very important. Organizing a special study area and a consistent homework schedule with your child will set the stage for strong study habits and eliminate the need for constant reminders about homework. It will also send a message to your child that homework is important enough to set aside special space and time, and that he or she is responsible enough to handle homework independently.

Together, you and your child should choose and organize a study space. It is important to choose the space carefully, because your child will do homework *only* in this space. The space can be anything from a special seat at the kitchen table to a desk and chair in a corner of your child's room. The important thing to keep in mind is that the spot you choose must be relatively free of distractions. Obviously, a spot in the television room will not work. Try to pick a place where people won't be going in and out frequently and where noise can be kept to a minimum.

Once a room has been chosen, you should do two things. First, make sure your child has adequate light to work by and a chair and desk that are the right size and are comfortable, but not too comfortable. Remember, soft chairs and sofas are not good homework seats, because they encourage napping and daydreaming. Your child's chair should have a straight back (for sitting up straight and staying focused), and his or her feet should touch the floor when seated. Make sure that your child has pens, pencils, paper, and any other material that will regularly be needed to complete homework. The more material your child has in the study space, the less time he or she will have to spend getting organized to do homework each night. And second, you and your child must set some basic rules for the study space.

Rule 1: At homework time, the study space is off limits to siblings, friends, toys, televisions, and any non-homework materials. This rule is important because distractions can make it nearly impossible to concentrate on schoolwork!

Rule 2: Homework is always done in the study space. Remember, you are trying to help your child develop consistent study habits, and a consistent space will help accomplish that goal.

Rule 3: Although there may be certain special exceptions, homework is done at the same time each night.

When you and your child choose the time, think about your family's schedule, your child's preferences, and the amount of time the homework usually takes. For example, if your child gets very sleepy after dinner, you might want to set homework time at 4:00 p.m. That way, your child will be wide awake at study time. However, if your child is often out at soccer practice or a scouting activity after school, study time should be set for the evening. Whatever time you choose, remember that you should try to keep that time sacred for homework each night. Of course you will have to make some exceptions on special occasions or when family schedules make it impossible to stick to the set time. Remember, the more you and your child stick to a consistent study time, the more easily your child will establish consistent study habits. Are there any questions so far? *(Pause.)*

Use teamwork to set homework goals. Now we move on to Step 3 of the plan. Together, you and your child will set some basic homework goals. Once these initial goals are met, you can set more ambitious ones. Remember, as your child successfully meets each goal, your child will gain confidence in his or her overall ability to do schoolwork. Therefore, it is important to begin with small, realistic goals that you can help your child attain. It might also be helpful to write down the goals you and your child set. Post these goals where your child can see them, and go over them with your child each night.

To set homework goals, sit down with your child and talk about what problems seem to provide the most difficulty in getting homework done. If your child has trouble getting information about assignments, Goal 1 could be that your child bring home accurate information about what work must be done every day for a week. Setting up a homework notebook can really help your child achieve this goal. Have your child bring a notebook to school, write down each homework assignment, and then have the teacher check the notebook at the end of each day to make sure all the assignments have been correctly recorded. Together, you and your child can go over the notebook at study time and develop a specific plan to handle that day's list of assignments.

Perhaps your child has trouble sitting still and concentrating on homework. A helpful goal in this case might be to set a small amount of time, perhaps 15 minutes, that your child must sit and work before taking any break. The set time can be lengthened gradually each week until your child is able to sit and focus for longer periods.

Finally, make sure the goals you set with your child address the amount of work he or she will accomplish each night, the quality of that work, and the amount of supervision the child will need from you. You might start out with the goal that your child will complete two assignments each night, that you will check the work in progress three times, and that at least 50% of the work must be correct. You can increase or decrease the number of assignments, the number of times you will check the work, or the percentage that must be correct, depending on how easy or challenging these goals are for your child. Remember, it is important that the goals you set provide a challenge for your child, but this challenge must be one your child has the ability to meet successfully. If your child isn't capable of meeting the goals you set, there is only one possible result: frustration and increased problems with homework. Any questions about setting homework goals? *(Pause.)*

Use attention and approval as rewards. Once your goals are in place, it is time for Step 4: Using your attention and approval as rewards for your child. As your child begins to meet his or her homework goals, reinforce these successful efforts through words, gestures, and specific feedback. First, as your child begins, use encouraging words such as the following: "You are really working hard! You are doing a good job on your own." Use gestures— a smile, a pat on the back, ruffling the hair. At the end of the study time, give your child a kiss, a hug, or even a handshake.

But, along the way, it's essential to give your child plenty of specific, positive feedback about how he or she is doing. I'm not suggesting that you be insincere—it is important that your child know you mean what you're saying. I am only suggesting that you praise your child for *efforts* and not just for results. Pay attention to small improvements, and mention them frequently: "Wow. You got two more spelling words correct today. Good job!" or "It must feel great to know that you worked for 20 minutes without stopping just now. You're really improving." As your child's homework habits strengthen, you will be able to gradually reduce the amount of supervision and feedback you provide. But never completely abandon your child's homework efforts. Your attention, approval, and feedback will make all the difference between a child who consistently works well and a child who adopts an "I don't care" attitude about homework. Any questions? (Pause.)

Lecture/Discussion

Tutoring Your Child

Now, what if your homework plan is firmly in place, and you have given it some time to take effect, but the plan is not working? It may be time for you to provide some special tutoring for your child. Many children have difficulty with a particular subject in school, and teachers cannot always give each child the extra help needed. If you find that your child is struggling in one or two subjects, schedule a conference with your child's teacher.

Tell the teacher about your concerns, and ask if tutoring might help. Your child's teacher can suggest some specific skill areas to work with, and, after the tutoring starts, the teacher can provide ongoing feedback about your child's progress in the classroom. This kind of teamwork—parent and teacher working together—can help a child who is struggling to master difficult subjects and gain confidence.

Once you and your child's teacher agree that tutoring will help, you will be working much more closely with your child at study time. There is more to tutoring than knowing the answers to math questions, however, and it's important to always maintain a positive, supportive attitude when working with your child. Children who are struggling in a particular subject often lose confidence in their overall academic abilities, and they may have very negative feelings toward schoolwork. These feelings will often be expressed in tutoring sessions, and the way a parent handles these feelings will set the tone for the work to come. If you respond negatively or with punishment when your child expresses frustration and lack of confidence, you will make it even harder for your child to overcome his or her academic struggles. If you are interested in your child's progress, encourage your child's efforts, and remain supportive when your child fails or expresses negative feelings, then you will help your child develop a more positive attitude toward difficult schoolwork in general.

Let's look at some examples of this:

Johnny is having trouble in math. He and his father sit down after dinner to go over Johnny's subtraction problems. Johnny fidgets in his seat, drops his pencil, and looks up at the ceiling while his father is talking. Finally, he looks at his father and says, "Dad, can we go fishing on Saturday?"

Q What do you think Johnny is doing? *(Pause for parents' response.)*

Right. Johnny is avoiding math problems, because they've been frustrating in the past. It is natural for Johnny to avoid something that is difficult for him. What could his father do to help him focus? *(Pause.)* Yes. Johnny's father can praise him when he does pay attention. He can also let Johnny know that math can be hard at times and that's why Dad is there to help Johnny work through his difficulties.

Here is another example.

Maria is in the first grade, and she has fallen behind in reading. When her mother sits down to read with her, Maria says, "I can't do it. I'm dumb, and I'll never learn to read."

Q What is happening with Maria? What could her mother do about it? *(Pause for parents' response.)*

Exactly. Maria has experienced failure in reading in the past, so she believes that she will always be a failure. Her mother can acknowledge her fears and support her as they read together. Maria's mother could also praise Maria each time she tries a new word and each time she reads a new word successfully.

Here is one more example.

Sara and her father sit down for a math tutoring session. Sara's father says, "What is hard for you about math, Sara?" Sara replies, "Math is easy. It's that creep, Mr. Mark. He picks on me because he is old and nasty."

Q How is Sara handling her experience with failure? *(Pause for parents' response.)*

Yes. She is blaming her teacher for her failure. Now you can see how tutoring your child might be complicated by your child's strong feelings about schoolwork. It would be easy for you to let your child's behavior frustrate you, but if you remember that it's probably just a reaction to his or her own fear of failure and lack of confidence, it will be easier for you to remain calm. Try to communicate to your child that you are interested in the schoolwork, that you want to see him or her do well, and that you would like to help.

There are four destructive attitudes that you should avoid communicating to your child. *(Write the four destructive attitudes presented in Figure 46 on the board.)*

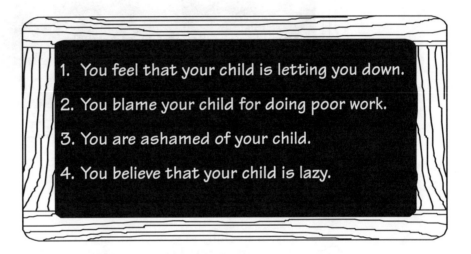

1. You feel that your child is letting you down.

2. You blame your child for doing poor work.

3. You are ashamed of your child.

4. You believe that your child is lazy.

Figure 46. Four destructive attitudes.

Here are two statements that might be made by parents. Tell me which one is destructive, and why.

"Bill, your teacher says that you are doing great in math but you're having some problems in spelling. Let's make a plan so that I can help you with your spelling for a while." *(Pause. Parents should respond that this statement is helpful because it contains praise, interest, and support. It contains none of the destructive attitudes listed above.)*

"Stephanie, I am concerned about your grade in reading. I would like to help you improve. Reading is important, and you are lazy sometimes. I know you can do better if you try." *(Pause. Although this statement contains one helpful element—the parent's interest in the child's progress, it is destructive because it suggests that the child is lazy and blames the child for not trying.)*

All the rules that apply to working on homework also apply to tutoring. Set up a special place and time for tutoring sessions, set attainable goals—starting small and working toward larger ones as your child succeeds, give plenty of praise and attention, and keep the working area free of distractions. When you are working with your child, keep the following additional tips in mind: *(Write the tips presented in Figure 47 on the board as you discuss them.)*

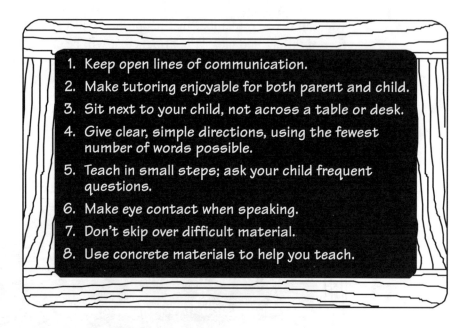

1. Keep open lines of communication.
2. Make tutoring enjoyable for both parent and child.
3. Sit next to your child, not across a table or desk.
4. Give clear, simple directions, using the fewest number of words possible.
5. Teach in small steps; ask your child frequent questions.
6. Make eye contact when speaking.
7. Don't skip over difficult material.
8. Use concrete materials to help you teach.

Figure 47. Tutoring tips for parents.

1. Keep open lines of communication.

Listen carefully to your child, and pay attention to how he or she is feeling. Remember to separate feelings of frustration with the task from feelings of annoyance with you. Be supportive and encouraging, but don't push your child too hard. By listening carefully, you will learn how to motivate your child while respecting the child's own learning pace and style.

2. Make tutoring enjoyable for both parent and child.

If you find that tutoring is a tense and frustrating experience for you and your child, try to relax and listen more carefully. Is your child trying to avoid the pain of failure because of a belief that he or she cannot succeed? Has your child's learning experience to date created a logical and reasonable belief that he or she will never learn this material? Are you getting frustrated because you think your child is "just not trying," when your child is actually afraid to fail again or when your child is embarrassed for you to see how dumb he or she is? By being supportive and making your tutoring sessions fun, you can help your child overcome these negative feelings and beliefs. More importantly, remember that learning is both an intellectual and an emotional experience. Negative feelings on the part of either parent or child can block learning.

3. **Sit next to your child, not across a table or desk.**

    When you sit next to your child, you can both see the lessons and you create a comfortable, friendly atmosphere.

4. **Give clear, simple directions, using the fewest number of words possible.**

    Young children have to learn how to follow directions as well as learn specific subject matter. Clear, simple directions that are easy to follow will help your child feel comfortable with the material and with you. When tutoring, parents commonly make the error or using too many words and talking to their child too much.

5. **Teach in small steps; ask your child frequent questions.**

    Divide the task you are teaching into small parts, and teach them to your child one at a time. For example, if you want your child to learn to read, don't expect him or her to be able to read after the first session. Set a small goal, like sounding out one or two vowels, and work toward that goal until it is reached. Check in with your child frequently. If you are teaching math problems, for example, talk about them one at a time. Asking your child questions will keep attention focused on the task at hand, and it will help you learn how to recognize what part of the material is difficult for him.

6. **Make eye contact when speaking.**

    When either of you is speaking, try to make eye contact. This will help you remain aware of your child's feelings, and it will help your child feel that you are right there as he or she masters the material.

7. **Don't skip over difficult material.**

    Encourage your child to work through difficult problems with your help. This will help to develop the habit of sticking with challenging material instead of giving up.

8. **Use concrete materials to help you teach.**

    Young children learn best when they have objects to manipulate. For example, you might use apples and oranges to illustrate addition and subtraction problems or draw pictures to represent spelling words. Let your child manipulate these materials as he or she learns.

This may seem like a long list of tips, but you will find that using these tips will make tutoring easier and more satisfying for you. Remember, use plenty of praise and don't nag, criticize, or get angry. If your child doesn't respond to a question, try restating it in a simpler way. Give clues when necessary, but never provide the entire answer for your child. When your child gets the correct answer, go over the answer again without giving any clues or praise to make sure that your child understands the material. These three additional tips might help you figure out how to praise your child's answers during the tutoring sessions. *(Write the tips presented in Figure 48 on the board.)*

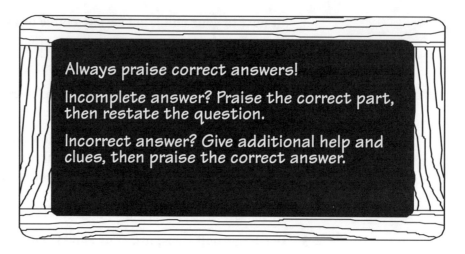

Figure 48. How to praise a child's answers.

Now, before we finish with this topic, let's look at some examples of parent-tutoring sessions. Listen carefully, and think about how you might respond to the child in each example.

Jim is solving some arithmetic problems. The first problem reads, "A boy has 5 marbles in one pocket and 5 in another. How many marbles does he have all together?" Jim says, "12."

Q What should Jim's mother say? *(Pause for parents' response. Mother should NOT say, "No, that's wrong." She should say something like, "Almost. Look at the problem and try again. How many marbles does Jim have in one pocket? How many in the other?" Mother should give clues and restate the question: "If Jim put all the marbles together in a pile, how many marbles would there be in the pile?" If Jim still gives the wrong answer, Mother could try using a concrete example: "Let's use pennies instead." Put five pennies in one pile and five in another. "Now let's add one pile to the other and see how many we have." Mother should rephrase and give clues until Jim gets the correct answer, and then she should then give plenty of praise.)*

Exactly. You can see how important it is to avoid saying "That is wrong," or "No." Those kinds of responses can be very discouraging. Let's look at one more example.

Sally and her father are working on Sally's spelling assignment. Sally's father shows her two pictures: a car and a train. He asks, "Sally, what is the first letter of each of these words?" Sally responds, "Car starts with a 'c' and train starts with a 'k.'

Q What should Sally's father do? *(Pause for parents' response. Sally's father should praise the correct part of her answer: "Very good Sally. Car does start with a 'c.' What does train start with?")*

278

Great. Sally's father should praise her for her correct answer and then continue to encourage and question her until she completes the answer correctly. Any questions?

Well, I have given you a long list of tips for tutoring. If you use these steps, I think you will find that you really can help your child improve academically. It will be helpful to you to hold on to your notes from this session. Periodically check your notes to make sure you are proceeding according to this tutoring program. After each tutoring session, ask yourself, "Was this a comfortable and satisfying interaction between myself and my child?"

Lecture/Discussion

Monitoring Your Tutoring

Once you decide to tutor your child, you must recognize that tutoring involves personal teaching skills that you may need to develop. Despite the best of intentions, we don't all have personalities suitable for tutoring. One way to develop your tutoring skills is to tape your first few tutoring sessions and review them carefully. Asking yourself the following questions will help you evaluate and improve your tutoring skills:

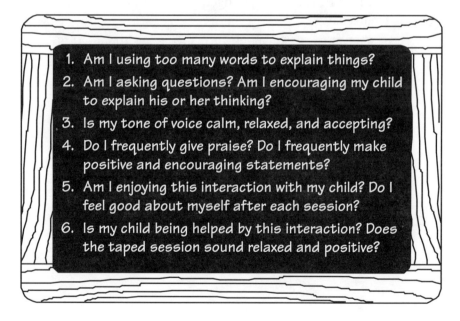

1. Am I using too many words to explain things?
2. Am I asking questions? Am I encouraging my child to explain his or her thinking?
3. Is my tone of voice calm, relaxed, and accepting?
4. Do I frequently give praise? Do I frequently make positive and encouraging statements?
5. Am I enjoying this interaction with my child? Do I feel good about myself after each session?
6. Is my child being helped by this interaction? Does the taped session sound relaxed and positive?

Figure 49. Questions for self-monitoring the tutoring.

Seeking Outside Tutoring

There may come a time when you should talk to your child's school about arranging for outside tutoring. If your child is still struggling with a particular subject after several months of tutoring, he or she may need specialized assistance in that area. Or, if you find that you cannot maintain a positive attitude because the tutoring sessions are too stressful for you or for your child, it is probably time to seek outside help. There are many ways to obtain tutoring for your child. Your child's school might be able to help; your child's teacher might be able to spend some extra time with your child after school. Local high school or college students might be willing to tutor for a small fee, or your local library may have special reading programs for children. But remember that your interest in and support of your child's education will mean more to your child's motivation and self-esteem than any specialized tutoring or outside support.

Recommended Readings

Anesko, K. M., & Levine, F. M. (1987). *Winning the homework war*. New York: Arco/Simon & Schuster.

Clark, F., Clark, C., & Vogel, M. (1989). *Hassle-free homework*. New York: Doubleday.

Kellaghan, T., Sloane, K., Alvarez, B., & Bloom, B. S. (1993). *The home environment and school learning*. San Francisco: Jossey-Bass.

Helping Your Child With Schoolwork

I. The Homework Plan

   A. Rule out problems:
- Check vision, hearing, learning problems, amount of homework, ability level.

   B. Organize homework space and schedule:
- Choose a quiet, comfortable (but not too comfortable) spot. Provide adequate light, seating, and materials.
- Set homework space rules. Homework (and nothing else) is done in the space during a specific time each night.

   C. Use teamwork to set homework goals:
- Set small, realistic goals. Write these goals down and post them; review the goals each night. Decide how much work will be done, how much supervision will be provided, and what the quality of the work should be. Set goals that challenge, without overwhelming, your child.

   D. Use attention and approval as rewards:
- Give your child plenty of positive feedback as each goal is reached. Use words, gestures, and specific praise. Give encouragement as he or she begins, and give lots of praise for each success. Pay close attention and reinforce small improvements.
- Gradually reduce supervision and feedback as your child achieves more goals, but NEVER completely abandon your child in his or her efforts to do schoolwork. Continue to give attention, approval, and feedback.

II. Tutoring Your Child

   A. Set up a tutoring plan:
- Consult with your child's teacher about what tutoring is needed. Set up a regular space and time for tutoring sessions. Decide which material you will work on and how that work will be accomplished.

   B. Avoid destructive attitudes
- Remember that your child may be feeling discouraged and isn't trying to let you down. Avoid blaming your child, communicating that you are ashamed of your child, or telling your child that he or she is lazy.

   C. Follow tutoring guidelines:
- Pay attention to your child's feelings; be supportive and encouraging.
- Make tutoring a relaxed, enjoyable experience. Avoid getting frustrated; support your child and think of ways to make the sessions fun. Sit next to your child. Make eye contact when speaking.
- Give clear, simple directions. Use as few words as possible. Don't talk too much. Break tasks into small parts. Talk about problems one at a time, and ask your child questions.
- Encourage your child to stay with difficult material. Use real objects (e.g., pennies, fruit, marbles) to teach concepts whenever possible.
- Always praise correct answers!
- Give praise for the correct portion of incomplete answers, and then restate the question.
- Give additional help and clues if the child gives an incorrect answer.

III. Monitoring Your Tutoring

- A. Am I using too many words to explain things?
- B. Am I asking questions? Am I encouraging my child to explain his or her thinking?
- C. Is my tone of voice calm, relaxed, and accepting?
- D. Do I frequently give praise? Do I frequently make positive and encouraging statements?
- E. Am I enjoying this interaction with my child? Do I feel good about myself after each session?
- F. Is my child being helped by this interaction? When I tape a session, does it sound relaxed and positive?

PAR Psychological Assessment Resources, Inc./P.O. Box 998/Odessa, FL 33556/Toll-Free 1-800-331-TEST

Communicating Effectively With Your Child's Teachers

by Richard R. Abidin and Suzanne Button

Session Objectives

1 To help parents understand the need for open communication between parents and teachers.

2 To help parents use school–home notes and parent–teacher conferences effectively.

3 To increase parents' awareness of how their feelings and the feelings of the teacher may affect their experience of parent–teacher conferences.

Sequence

● Introduction (5 minutes)

● Lecture/Discussion of school–home notes (10 minutes)

● Lecture/Discussion of parent–teacher conferences (40 - 50 minutes)

 ### Materials

Blackboard (or large marking board)

Chalk (or markers)

Pencils or pens

Paper

Handout: Useful Questions for Parent–Teacher Conferences

Introduction

It is surprising how little information most parents have about their child's experience at school. Most parents don't ask many questions of their child's teachers or make suggestions to the teachers, because the parents assume that the teachers are professional educators who will automatically know best how to handle their child's education. In addition, many parents still feel intimidated by teachers, because they remember listening to and respecting teachers when they were schoolchildren. These feelings are understandable, but it is important for parents to learn to relate to teachers on an adult-to-adult basis. Open communication between parents and teachers is a known factor in academic success: Children whose parents are actively involved in and supportive of their education usually do better in school than those whose parents are not involved. Tonight, we will talk about two ways that you can become more involved with your child's education, and both ways involve communicating openly with your child's teachers.

Lecture/Discussion

School-Home Notes

One very effective way to stay up-to-date on your child's school experiences is to ask the teacher to write school–home notes. These notes can be thought of as a sort of daily report card. Your child's teacher sends a note home every day—or on whatever schedule you and the teacher choose—updating you on your child's progress, behavior, homework, problem areas, and successes for the day, the week, and so forth. In turn, you write notes back to the teacher, letting the teacher know how the homework is going and what you have noticed about your child's behavior, and also including any other feedback, information, or questions you might have for the teacher.

If your child has more than one teacher, you might want to involve them all in the school–home note process. Establishing this process takes a little work on your part, but it is well worth the effort. A simple way to get started is to buy a spiral-bound notebook in which both you and the teacher can write every day. Your child should bring the notebook to school and then back home every day. If either you or your child's teacher does not receive the notebook on a given day, the individual who doesn't receive the notebook should assume there was a problem and make a phone call. With this method, you will be more aware of your child's progress in school, more comfortable with the teachers, and more active in your child's education because of your efforts. Any questions?

Lecture/Discussion

Parent-Teacher Conferences

The second way to remain active in your child's education is through parent–teacher conferences. Most people believe that conferences only occur when a child has misbehaved, but parent–teacher conferences can serve many purposes. A teacher may want to update you on your child's progress in school, share observations about your child's strengths and weaknesses, or let you know how your child is doing in relation to his or her ability. In addition, teachers or parents may want to compare their observations of a child at home and at school. If your child exhibits a behavior that concerns the teacher, that teacher may want to know what you think the behavior means. Your ideas are valuable, because you can help the teacher determine if the behavior is only a

284

problem at school, if it is due to a recent event in your child's life, or whether the teacher might be misunderstanding your child's behavior.

Your child's teacher also may ask for a conference because he or she needs your help. Perhaps your child is struggling in a specific academic area, and the teacher would like you to tutor your child in that area at home. The teacher can give you suggestions about how to work with your child at home, but you can give the teacher valuable information as well. After all, you have known your child longer, and you probably have some good ideas about how to motivate, support, and interact with your child.

Finally, parents may request conferences with their child's teacher. You may want to meet with a teacher to set up a school–home note program, to ask about your child's progress, or to begin the year with an understanding of what your child will be learning. If you ever have specific questions or suggestions, it is well worth your time to request a conference with your child's teacher. Any questions?

Unfortunately, many parents have difficulty when they think about meeting with their child's teacher because of all the mixed emotions that could arise during parent–teacher conferences. After all, parents usually feel that, when their child is being judged, *they* are being judged as well. Let's talk about some of the feelings you might experience during a parent–teacher conference. *(Write the three words shown in Figure 50 on the board.)*

1. Guilt

2. Fear

3. Overwhelmed

Figure 50. Parent feelings about teacher–parent conferences.

Let's discuss these feelings one at a time.

1. **Guilt.** You may feel that, if you were a better parent, your child would be a better student. Many parents blame themselves for their child's problems, becoming anxious and defensive when presented with a specific difficulty. You may also feel guilty because you have not been deeply involved in your child's education. Parents who have busy schedules often feel this way, believing that their involvement with their own work puts their child at a disadvantage.

2. **Fear.** You may be afraid of hearing that your child has serious problems. You may also fear that your child's teacher will judge you negatively. Again, these are natural fears. Try to remember that children's occasional behavior problems do not necessarily indicate serious emotional difficulties and that academic problems can usually be solved through special help and attention. Teachers want to get to know the parents of their students better so that they can work with the parents as a team to help the individual child. Keeping these things in mind will ease your fears as you go into the conference.

3. **Overwhelmed.** You may feel that you have enough pressure to handle with your job and raising a family, and that the school should take care of your child's educational problems. You may feel anger or resentment toward the teacher for not doing his or her job. Schools *are* responsible for your child's education, but teachers cannot possibly know your child better than you do. To work most effectively with your child, your child's teacher needs your ideas. That's because you have had so much more experience with your child.

It is important to keep all of these mixed emotions in perspective. Although they are natural reactions to a stressful situation, they can also keep you and the teacher from addressing your child's needs effectively. You may actually be so anxious and defensive that you can barely hear what the teacher is saying! If you listen carefully, however, you may find that the teacher needs and respects your ideas and has some interesting information for you about your child. Parent–teacher conferencing can be a rewarding experience, once you both get past your anxiety and begin to work as a team.

It is important to remember that teachers also have mixed emotions about parent–teacher conferencing. Teachers do not have all the answers, and they know it. Often the teacher is afraid of looking incompetent to you. The teacher may be afraid of looking like a bad teacher, of being blamed for a child's problems, or of being asked a question and not knowing the answer. If you remain open and supportive, it will help to alleviate the teacher's fears. Teachers may also feel guilty about not having met with you sooner or about having too many children in the classroom to give your child the individual attention that's needed. You can help by praising the teacher's efforts with your child and by remembering that he or she is really trying to help your child succeed in school.

Now, with all these emotions flying around, it's not surprising that there are times when parent–teacher conferences do not go well. Parents and teachers try to handle their negative feelings in a variety of ways. For example, parents may try to blame the school or the teacher for their child's problems; they may deny that a problem exists; they may agree with the teacher too quickly; or they may avoid the teacher completely by not responding to the teacher's request for a conference. Teachers may handle their own insecurities by talking too fast or too much during the conference, by using jargon that parents do not understand, or by talking only about the child's positive characteristics. Again, if you keep in mind that such behaviors often signal nervousness, fear, or guilt, you may be able to get past them and make the conference a productive one.

There are several concrete steps you can take to get the most out of a parent–teacher conference.

1. Try to remain aware of your own feelings. If you get anxious, angry, or fearful, take a minute to examine those feelings and to calm down. Remember that the teacher probably feels anxious too.

2. The focus of this conference is the best interests of your child, not your abilities as a parent. Keep the specific purpose of the conference in mind. For instance, you might be meeting the teacher for the first time, or discussing a behavior problem, or getting an end-of-the-year report.

3. Set your own goals for the conference. Think about questions or suggestions that you might have for the teacher. It may be helpful to write out a list of questions for the teacher before you go to the conference. This handout contains a list of 13 questions that you may find helpful when preparing for a teacher-parent conference. There's also room for you to make additional notes. *(Distribute the handout of sample parent–teacher conference questions provided at the end of this chapter.)*

4. If the teacher speaks too quickly, gently ask him or her to slow down. If the teacher speaks in jargon, be sure to ask the meaning of words you do not understand. Remember that asking about something you don't understand shows that you are interested and concerned. Making certain that you understand everything the teacher is saying will ensure that you get all the information you need from the conference.

5. Remember that you will probably have emotional reactions to the information the teacher is presenting. Try to separate your reactions from the information itself. Make sure that you are not misunderstanding something just because you are upset. Ask as many questions as you think are necessary.

6. If you feel that the teacher is holding back negative information, help by saying that you are interested in hearing both the positive and the negative things about your child. When the teacher knows that you are prepared to handle negative information, he or she may feel free to present a more accurate picture of your child's performance.

7. At the end of the conference, review what has been discussed and ask what steps should be taken to follow up. Make sure that the teacher correctly understands what you have said and that you

understand the information the teacher has presented. Take the time to clear up any miscommunication before you leave.

8. Take the time to follow up on the conference. Call the teacher in a few days with an update on events at home. Ask about progress at school, and clear up anything you might have forgotten to discuss at the meeting.

Before I open the floor for questions and further discussion, I'd like to make one final point. Remember that teachers—like everyone else—are motivated to improve situations when they feel respected for the fact that they are really trying to do what is best for your child. Your interest in your child's education alone will be a strong motivator for your child's teacher, and your offer to do what you can do to help will be much appreciated by most of the teachers you will meet.

General Discussion

For the rest of this session, I would like to discuss any questions or concerns you might have about the appropriate ways you can communicate with your child's teachers.

Recommended Readings

Carrasquillo, A. L., & London, C. B. G. (1993). *Parents and schools: A source book*. New York: Garland.

Kelley, M. L. (1990). *School–home notes: Promoting children's classroom success*. New York: Guilford.

Maeroff, G. I. (1989). *The school-smart parent*. New York: Times Books.

McLoughlin, C. S. (1987). *Parent–teacher conferencing*. Springfield, IL: Thomas.

Rich, D. (1987). *Teachers and parents: An adult-to-adult approach*. Washington, DC: National Education Association.

Useful Questions for Parent-Teacher Conferences

1.   How is my child progressing?

2.   Is my child working up to his or her ability?

3.   How well does my child work independently?

4.   Does my child participate in class discussions and activities?

5.   Is my child placed in different groups for different subjects? If so, why?

6.   How well does my child get along with others?

7.   What are my child's best and worst subjects? Why?

8.   What are my child's specific strengths and weaknesses?

9.   Does my child enjoy school?

10. What kind of testing is being done? What do these tests reveal about my child's progress? How does my child handle taking tests?

11. What specific suggestions do you have to help my child do better?

12. How can we help our child at home?

13. Do you have any observations or concerns about my child's behavior that I should know about?

PAR Psychological Assessment Resources, Inc./P.O. Box 998/Odessa, FL 33556/Toll-Free 1-800-331-TEST

Empowering Your Family to Meet Goals – Effective Use of Social Supports

by Suzanne Button

Special Notes for the Mental Health Professional

In this session, you will function as a support and facilitator while families identify their own needs, aspirations, strengths, and sources of support. Think of yourself as a resource, not as an expert. Therefore, it is important that you be thoroughly familiar with the Dunst (1988) reference (listed at the end of this chapter) and confident that you can assume a less directive, more competence-based role toward parents than may your customary approach. Because you will function as a source of information as well, you should be completely familiar with the family-oriented and help-giving services available locally. Remember, the point here is to encourage families to meet their own needs. Consequently, parents should be encouraged, through information and facilitation, to find the resources they need for themselves. If someone in the group brings up a need for which you do not have a listed resource, try helping the parent to begin a library search or putting the parent in contact with another source of information that will lead in a helpful direction.

Before you teach this session, try to contact some of the following agencies in your area: the Department of Social Services, service organizations, churches, mental health associations, police department, the Salvation Army, or the welfare department. In addition, consult your local yellow pages for other area organizations that provide support services. Gather a list of as many sources as you can, so that you can provide as much help to the parents as possible.

Session Objectives

1 To help parents identify their families' aspirations and goals and what they need to meet those goals.

2 To teach parents to empower themselves and their families by tapping into informal sources of social support.

3 To provide families with information about formal sources of social support when needed.

Sequence

- Introduction (20 - 25 minutes)
- Group Exercises
    - Identifying family needs and goals (20 minutes)
    - Identifying family strengths (10 minutes)
    - Identifying potential sources of social support (10 - 15 minutes)
    - Coming up with a plan (30 - 40 minutes)
- Questions/Discussion (10 - 15 minutes)

Materials

Blackboard (or large marking board)

Chalk (or markers)

Eraser

Large note cards, 10-12 for each group

Pens or pencils

Handout: Local Family Support Resources (if available)

Introduction

In this session, we'll be focusing on finding the right kind of support for your family's needs as a way of strengthening your family's ability to survive and grow together. Before we start, I'd like to give you a brief introduction to the way many families use social resources to grow stronger and to become more successful in meeting their goals.

All parents want the best for their families. They have wishes and dreams for themselves and for their children; they want to be effective parents and happy people. Sometimes, though, parents don't have much time to pursue wishes, dreams, or happiness because they are too busy trying to feed their families, hold down their jobs, take care of their children, and deal with other practical concerns. For many of you, taking care of basics is so tiring that you have little energy left over to pursue the special dreams and goals you may have for your family.

This is where social support comes in. Many families use their social support resources to help them meet their basic needs. You may not realize it, but you probably use sources of support in your family as well. For example, some of you may leave your children with family members when you go to work. Family members are an important source of social support. On the other hand, some of you may get together with neighbors when someone's house or yard needs fixing up. Neighbors are another source of social support for families.

The more effectively a family can tap into the many support resources available, the more effectively that family can meet its needs with energy left over for pursuing special family dreams and goals. Let me give you an example:

Henry, who works at the local grocery store as a stockman, has wanted to go to a community college and get a degree in accounting for many years. Henry has always been good with numbers, and he would like to get a better job, make more money, and someday send his kids to college, too. Henry and his wife, Dawn, have saved up enough money to pay for his college courses, but they still have a problem. Dawn works at night, and Henry works during the day. Dawn is able to work because Henry is home with their two children, who are 6 and 9 years old. They cannot afford to have Dawn quit her job, and they don't have enough money saved up to pay a babysitter.

Q What should Dawn and Henry do? *(Facilitate the discussion as parents attempt to problem-solve with this situation. If parents don't seem to be moving in the appropriate direction, ask what sources of social support Dawn and Henry might investigate for help. Possible answers include: family members who could babysit, coworkers who could trade shifts with Dawn, church members who could help out, an after-school program for the children, a day-care program at the community college. REMEMBER: You are the facilitator here. Let parents do the problem-solving themselves.)*

Some of the supports you just mentioned can be thought of as "informal" sources of support. These are the supports that are the most immediately available to everyone—you don't have to apply for them, and they are usually free. These informal sources of support include family members, friends and neighbors, church members, ministers, and coworkers. Many parents find that these informal sources of support are easier to approach for help, because an emotional connection already exists.

Sometimes, a family's important needs cannot be met entirely by these informal supports. When that happens, families often seek assistance from more formal sources of social support. What do you think these might be? *(Pause for group response.)* Exactly. Formal sources of support are those that provide services for a fee, charitable organizations, or resources that are supported by tax money. They might be individuals, like a babysitter, a doctor, or a teacher. They might also be entire agencies, like a school, a health department, or a department of social services.

Sometimes people feel that going to one of these formal sources of support is like begging or asking for a handout. It can be difficult to swallow your pride and approach an agency or a professional for assistance. Still, it is not always possible to meet your family's needs through informal sources of support. Most families—rich or poor, whatever their ethnic background—ask for outside assistance at some point in their lives. In truth, families who look for support when it is needed actually succeed more often than families who don't.

Research has found that families who tap into the social support available to them have an easier time meeting their basic needs. In addition, parents whose time and energy is not completely taken up by meeting the family's basic needs have more time to spend with their children and to enjoy family life. The more time parents have to devote to their children, the better parents they are. Finally, families who maximize their use of social support resources may have some time and energy left over to pursue some of those special dreams and goals I mentioned before.

Now I'm going to ask you to look at your own family's needs, goals, and sources of support. I'll also ask you to look at the ways you already meet your family's needs and the ways your family succeeds without any outside help at all. Our goal is to help each of you to come up with a plan for strengthening your family and reducing your stress level. Your plan will involve building your own social support system using resources both inside and outside the family.

We will do four different exercises. *(Write the four topics presented in Figure 51 on the board. Ask parents to split into groups of five or six. For the exercises in this session, married couples or partners should remain together. Give four note cards to each parent or couple.)*

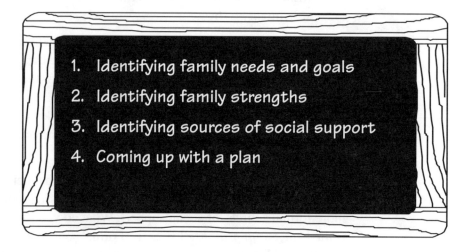

1. Identifying family needs and goals
2. Identifying family strengths
3. Identifying sources of social support
4. Coming up with a plan

Figure 51. Four steps in building a family support system.

Identifying Family Needs and Goals

The first step is to write down three of your family's most important needs. A need is anything your family has to have to survive, to be healthy, or to be relatively happy. Think about it for a few minutes first. What are the things that you feel your family needs the most? This could be new winter coats, three solid meals a day, more relaxation, or more time together. Whatever you choose to write down, make sure it is a real need for your family. It might also be helpful to write down and put a check mark beside any family needs that you have a hard time meeting without some extra help or support.

Discuss this part of the exercise *only* with your partner. Write the three needs on one of your note cards. *(Pause. Walk from group to group. Clarify the definition of "needs" if a particular group seems to be missing the point, but encourage parents to identify their <u>own</u> family's needs.)*

Good. For the second part of this exercise, I would like you to think of one important goal for your family. A goal is something you would like to see happen in your family, something you would like to get done. This goal could be a project, like painting the kitchen, or it could be a way you would like your family to be. It might also be a dream that you have for your family, like taking a vacation together, or it might be the chance to go out on a "date" with your partner on Saturday nights, without the kids. Whatever your goal is, write it down on the same card you used to write your needs. Take a minute to think this over, and talk it over with your partner as well. You will get a chance to share it with the group later. *(Pause. Walk from group to group, giving help as needed. DO NOT give parents any additional specific ideas. Instead, give them encouragement and ask facilitating questions: What are the family's interests and concerns? What do they wish would get better or easier or less stressful in their lives? What do family members do together? What would they like to do if they had the chance? If a couple seems to be particularly stuck, ask them to wait until the rest of their group has finished. Then, ask the other parents in the group to help the couple identify their goal.)*

Okay, that was good work. You can already see that you are the best experts on your own families. You know what your family needs, and you know that meeting certain goals would really make your family's life better. Now, set aside those first note cards for a few minutes, and pick up a new one.

Identifying Family Strengths

In a little while, I will ask you to think about your family's current sources of support. First, it's important to think about the ways your family meets its own needs without outside help. All families have a hard time with some areas of functioning, but all families are also especially good at handling other areas. What are the areas that your family handles well? What are your family's strengths?

Take a minute to think about this. A strength might be something practical. For example, your family might know how to get chores done quickly and well. Or a strength might be emotional. Your family members might be very appreciative of one another. Whatever they are, your family's strengths help your family to survive, to succeed, and to grow together. As you think about your family's strengths, write them down on the second note card. Try to limit yourself to five or six major strengths. *(Pause. Again, walk from group to group, facilitating as families look for their strengths. When parents are stuck, ask questions such as the following: How do your family members feel about each other? What brings your family closer together? What do family members do in a crisis? How does the family handle challenges? What does the family do together easily? How do family members communicate? What are the family rules, values, and/or beliefs? How does the family get things done? Listen carefully, and point out the strengths that emerge as parents respond to these questions. Again, be careful not to put words into parents' mouths. It is very important that parents come up with what they see as their family strengths. Take care, however, that you do not move forward until each family has identified at least two or three strengths.)*

Good work. Now I would like you to join your groups, because the next exercise will be started as couples and then finished in the groups. Please put your strength cards aside, and pick up a blank index card.

Identifying Sources of Social Support

First, each of you should write down all the sources of social support you can think of that are available to you and your family. Remember to think about informal sources, like friends and family, and about formal ones, like doctors and agencies. Talk this over with your partner, and take a few minutes to write down all the supports that come to mind. After you do this, you'll share your lists with the group. Please be as specific as you can. Name the source, and describe the specific type of support you can get from that source. *(Pause. Give parents about 10 minutes to write down sources of support.)*

Great. Now, you'll be working in your groups. For this second part of the exercise, each person should read his or her list of supports out loud to the group. *(Pause.)* As people in your group read their lists, listen carefully. Are any of the supports mentioned by other members of your group also available to your family? Are you learning about sources of support that you never thought of before? As you listen, you should add to your own list the new supports that might be helpful to your family. When all the lists have been read aloud, take a few minutes to discuss them with your group. Ask about the new supports other group members listed with which you weren't familiar. How did they discover these resources? How helpful are they? Really take the time to learn about new sources of support from each other, and add as many new sources to your own lists as possible.

While you're doing this, I'm going to write a list of possible sources of support on the board. During your group discussion, feel free to look at my list and see if it gives you any additional ideas. *(After parents complete their own lists and move into the group discussion, write the list of potential sources of support presented in Figure 52 on the board. Give parents sufficient time to complete the group activity before you begin to discuss these resources.)*

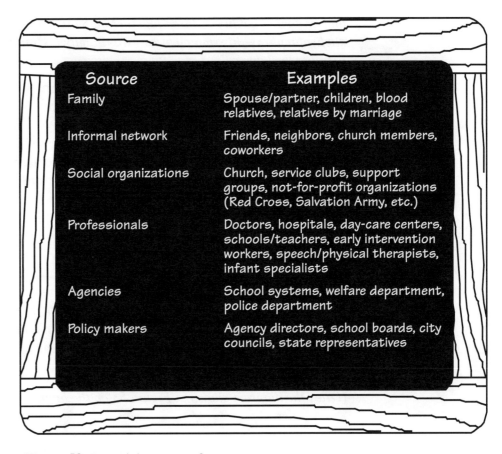

Source	Examples
Family	Spouse/partner, children, blood relatives, relatives by marriage
Informal network	Friends, neighbors, church members, coworkers
Social organizations	Church, service clubs, support groups, not-for-profit organizations (Red Cross, Salvation Army, etc.)
Professionals	Doctors, hospitals, day-care centers, schools/teachers, early intervention workers, speech/physical therapists, infant specialists
Agencies	School systems, welfare department, police department
Policy makers	Agency directors, school boards, city councils, state representatives

Figure 52. Potential sources of support.

Coming up with a plan

Now you're going to combine all the separate lists you've made up. Again, I want you to start with your partner, moving to the group for discussion after everyone is ready. What you're going to do is put your three index cards in front of you—your needs and goals, your family strengths, and your social support list—and take a look at them. *(Pause.)* Now, look at your list of needs and goals. Pick one need or goal from that list— one that you feel you could realistically make happen—and work on a definite plan to meet that need or goal. Be specific. Who would do what, and when? What alternative sources of support could you use? Who would contact the support source? How would you present your need or goal to that source?

Ask one very important question. *What gets in the way of meeting your chosen need or goal?* Does a lack of child care keep you from getting a job with more flexible hours? Are you not sure where to go to find out about certain specific services? Is there too little time or money for family activities or vacations? Now, pick up your last blank note card. Write down those things that might get in the way of meeting your need or goal. *(Pause. Give parents a few minutes to think, then move from group to group. Act as a consultant here. Ask parents why they cannot meet their need or goal, then restate their response in simple, understandable language. For example, if a father says*

297

that he cannot get his children together on Sunday afternoon to paint the kitchen, rephrase his statement as "your family does not have a schedule for painting the kitchen.")

Now look at your family strengths note card. Are there strengths on that card that will help you move through or around the obstacles you see between you and your goal? Could you take advantage of your family's closeness to get some extra child care? Can you mobilize your children to help with chores by talking about family pride? Is your family good at problem-solving? Next to your list of obstacles, write down all the family strengths that could help you overcome those obstacles. *(Pause. Again, move from group to group, helping parents connect family strengths to needs and goals. In this section of the exercise, you may be a bit more directive. Suggest ways to connect family strengths to meeting family needs and goals. Give appropriate suggestions to parents, but be careful to use their lists as your raw material and to respect their rejection of your suggestions. When you do give suggestions, it might be helpful to give them in question form. For example, "You say your family is very responsible about getting things done. What might happen if you made each person responsible for earning a small amount of family activity money each week?")*

(Draw the diagram shown in Figure 53 on the board:)

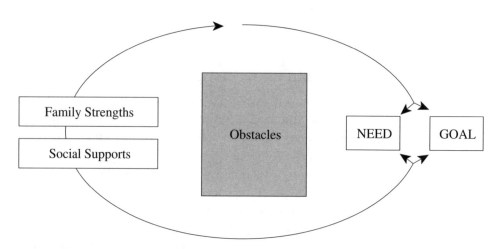

Figure 53. A plan to achieve a family goal.

Okay. The final stage of your plan will include your sources of social support. Look at your social support cards and ask yourself, "How can these sources of support help me meet my need or goal?" "How can I get around the obstacles using my family strengths and my support sources?" Be specific. Perhaps your mother can provide child care, but she cannot help with flexible work hours. You might have to go to a coworker for that. Be very thorough. Look at each source of support and ask yourself if there is any bit of assistance—no matter how small—that this support resource might provide to help you overcome the obstacles to your need or goal. Next to your list of obstacles and family strengths, write down all the supports that might help and the specific help each might provide. *(Pause.)*

Now you have come up with a rough plan for meeting your need or goal. By utilizing your family strengths and social supports, you can overcome the obstacles between you and your goal. Now I would like you to fine tune this plan in your groups. Read your plans to each other, and exchange ideas about additional family strengths and supports that might make your individual plans even more effective. *(Pause. Move from group to group, facilitating group discussion. Really allow parents to problem-solve for each other here. Let parents know about local services that might apply to their plans, giving them names, telephone numbers, etc. Make sure that each couple has come up with a basic plan for meeting their need or reaching their goal before you move on.)*

General Discussion

Terrific. Now you have some idea of how social support can help you meet your families' needs and goals. You might like to take the plans you came up with home and start using them to meet the need or goal you identified. Also, remember that you can use this method any time you need additional support to meet a need or goal. All you need to do is think about your sources of support and how they might help you work out a plan to get something done for your family. That's how you develop your plan to meet the specific need or goal. Does anyone have any questions?

Recommended Readings

Bronfenbrenner, U. (1979). *The ecology of human development: Experiments by nature and design.* Cambridge, MA: Harvard University Press.

Dunst, C., Trivette, C., & Deal, A. (1988). *Enabling and empowering families: Principles & guidelines for practice.* Cambridge, MA: Brookline.

Section IV

Annotated Bibliography of Recommended Readings

Resources for Parents

I.	Parenting	303
II.	Single Parenting	307
III.	Child Development	307
	A. Infancy Through Preschool	307
	B. School Age (6–13 years)	309
	C. Adolescence (14–18 years)	310
IV.	Divorce/Remarriage	311
V.	Children With Special Needs	313
VI.	Sexuality	315
VII.	Special Problems or Situations	316
	A. Abuse Prevention/Coping With Abuse	316
	B. Adoption	317
	C. Conflict Resolution	318
	D. Death and Dying	318
	E. Discipline	320
	F. Eating Disorders	320
	G. Environment	321
	H. Multicultural Issues	321
	I. Only Children	321
	J. Psychotherapy	322
	K. School	322
	L. Sibling Rivalry	322
	M. Sleep Problems	323
	N. Stress	323
	O. Toilet Training	323

Resources for Children

I. Materials for Children Ages 8 Years and Younger 324
    A. Abuse Prevention/Coping With Abuse 324
    B. Death/Dying/Coping With Loss 325
    C. Divorce/Remarriage 325
    D. Emotions 326
    E. Multicultural Issues 326
    F. Psychotherapy 327
    G. Sexuality 327
    H. Sibling Rivalry 327
    I. Other Situations and Problems 328

II. Materials for Children Ages 8–13 Years 331
    A. Abuse Prevention/Coping With Abuse 331
    B. Death/Dying/Coping With Loss 331
    C. Divorce/Remarriage 332
    D. Emotions 332
    E. Multicultural Issues 333
    F. Sexuality 333
    G. Other Situations and Problems 333

III. Materials for Children Ages 13 Years and Older 336
    A. Abuse Prevention/Coping With Abuse 336
    B. Adolescence 336
    C. Death/Dying/Coping With Loss 337
    D. Divorce/Remarriage 337
    E. Eating Disorders 338
    F. Emotions 338
    G. Multicultural Issues 339
    H. Psychotherapy 339
    I. Sexuality 339
    J. Other Situations and Problems 340

Resources for Parents
I. Parenting

1. Allen, J. (1984). *What do I do when?* San Luis Obispo, CA: Impact Publishers.

   This book outlines management methods for 50 common child-rearing problems, such as getting chores done, sibling arguments, and school problems. The book stresses a behavioral approach to problems and helps parents modify their children's behavior with specific management steps.

2. Baldwin, V. L., Fredericks, H. D. B., & Brodsky, G. (1973). *Isn't it time he outgrew this? or a training program for parents of retarded children.* Springfield, IL: Charles C. Thomas.

   This volume focuses on principles and techniques to develop self- and child-adaptive behavior with the retarded child. These principles focus on areas such as feeding, toilet-training, dressing, washing, and language development.

3. Bettner, B. L., & Lew, A. (1990). *Raising kids who can.* Seattle, WA: Parenting Press.

   This book presents a variety of specific strategies for fostering a sense of cooperation and responsibility in children. The authors discuss strategies in great detail and address possible obstacles to creating a more responsible, respectful environment at home.

4. Brooks, J. B. (1981). *The process of parenting.* Palo Alto, CA: Mayfield.

   This book, for the well educated parent, integrates a variety of developmental sources into a general approach to parenting. Instead of providing "pat" answers, it gives parents an informational base from which to make their own parenting decisions.

5. Butten, A. D. (1969). *The authentic child.* New York: Random House.

   The Authentic Child describes how the parent, through acceptance of self as an imperfect but striving individual, can assist his or her child to become an authentic individual. The acceptance of others and the honesty of the relationship are seen as key issues.

6. Clemes, H., & Bean, R. (1980). *How to raise children's self-esteem.* Los Angeles: Price/Stern/Sloan.

   This book provides helpful information on raising children's self-esteem. It discusses the characteristics and importance of self-esteem and outlines the conditions necessary for developing strong self-esteem. It also teaches parents how to recognize self-esteem problems in their children and how to help children with those problems.

7. Comer, J. P., & Poussaint, A. F. (1975). Black child care. New York: Simon & Schuster.

   This book focuses on the development of the black child through adolescence. Although the content is similar to that of other books on child care, the authors provide through examples and special sensitivity, a black perspective on child care.

8. DeFrancis, B. (1994). *Parents' resource almanac.* Holbrook, MA: Bob Adams.

   This book provides descriptions of a broad range of resources, as well as addresses and telephone numbers for parents to contact the organizations providing these resources. Parents can contact providers of many services, including educational options for their children, summer recreation programs, special play and learning materials, informational resources of many kinds, and emotional support for themselves or their children during difficult times or for special problems.

9. Dela-Piana, G. (1973). *How to talk with children (and other people)*. New York: John Wiley.

    This book focuses on the issue of developing good communication between parents and children. Issues such as the appropriate use of supportive, accepting, questioning, explanatory, directing, and distracting statements are covered. A variety of exercises involving sample parent-child exchanges are provided with immediate feedback to assist the reader in improving his or her own communication skills. This volume is particularly effective for parents who have a basically sound relationship with their child and who are concerned about the quality of the parent-child communication process.

10. Dreikurs, R. (1972). *The challenge of child training: A parent guide*. New York: Pantheon.

    This abridged version of Dr. Dreikurs' widely read work, *The Challenge of Parenthood*, presents a philosophy that is sensitive to the needs of children, but places the question of power and setting limits squarely in the hands of the parent. The author discusses a number of the most common mistakes parents make in child training and provides some insight to common causes for misbehavior.

11. Ellis, A. (1971). *A guide to rational living*. Englewood Cliffs, NJ: Prentice-Hall.

    This book presents the basic concepts and ideas of rational living, upon which the workshop sessions in Managing Your Feelings are based.

12. Eyre, L., & Eyre, R. (1993). *Teaching your children values*. Seattle, WA: Parenting Press.

    This book provides concrete strategies for effectively instilling parental values in children. The book divides values into two categories: (a) character traits, and (b) ways of interacting with others. Strategies are presented with examples and true stories about the authors' nine children.

13. Faber, A., & Mazlish, E. (1974). *Liberated parents and liberated children*. New York: Grosset & Dunlap.

    This is a sensitively written book by two parents who attended 2 years of workshops with Haim G. Ginott. It describes their experiences in applying his ideas.

14. Faber, A., & Mazlish, E. (1992). *How to be the parent you always wanted to be*. Seattle, WA: Parenting Press.

    This guide provides a quick and easy method for improving parenting skills. It includes two audio tapes and a workbook and helps parents deal with their children's emotions, set limits, teach cooperation, and resolve conflicts.

15. Fishel, E. (1994). *I swore I'd never do that: Recognizing family patterns and making wise parenting choices*. Berkeley, CA: Conari Press.

    This book explores the ways in which unresolved issues from a parent's childhood can prevent him or her from being the parent he or she wants to be. Topics covered include discipline, intimacy, and self-esteem.

16. Franck, I. (1993). *What's new for parents: The essential resource to products & services, programs & information, new for the '90s*. New York: Prentice Hall Books.

    This book provides a comprehensive list of national resources available to parents. Topics covered include information on education for parents and children; support for special problems or stressful times; recreation programs for children and families; professional assistance for childhood problems; and childcare, play, and learning products. The sources of information, with their contact addresses and telephone numbers, are provided.

17. Geddes, J. B. (1974). *How to parent alone: A guide for single parents.* New York: Seabury.

   The author attempts to give the single parent encouragement and advice about the process of taking care of his/her own emotional needs as the sole primary caretaker of the child. The focus is on the divorced young woman raising children of preschool and elementary school age in an urban/suburban environment.

18. Ginott, H. G. (1965). *Between parent and child.* New York: Macmillan.

   This best-selling entertaining book encourages constructive conversation between parents and their children. The nature of these talks is designed to bring a closer understanding to both parent and child about the other as a person with his own feelings and desires.

19. Glenn, H. S., & Nelson, J. (1989). *Raising self-reliant children in a self-indulgent world.* Seattle, WA: Parenting Press.

   This book outlines a plan for teaching children responsibility in the face of an environment that teaches them to "just get by." The authors stress firmness, dignity, and respect as the tools with which parents can guide their children toward self-reliance and autonomy.

20. Gordon, T. (1970). *Parent effectiveness training.* New York: Peter W. Wyden.

   This book may be read independently or used in conjunction with workshops conducted by licensed Parent Effectiveness Trainers. The principles presented are based on humanistic and client-centered psychology. This point of view places both parent and child on equal planes and suggests that harmonious adjustment and living can best be achieved by a sharing of feelings and negotiated settlement of conflicts. Although the specific skills taught are of immense value with older children, the vitality, validity, and practicality of the overall approach for children under the age of 7 is not established.

21. Krumboltz, J., & Krumboltz, H. (1972). *Changing children's behavior.* Englewood Cliffs, NJ: Prentice-Hall.

   This book is based on behavioral principles, but it is somewhat more entertaining to read than the typical work in this area.

22. Lipson, E. R. (Ed.). (1991). *The New York Times parent's guide to the best books for children.* New York: Times Books.

   This guide helps parents choose appropriate and well written books for their children. It provides short reviews of each book and is divided into age-appropriate categories.

23. Martin, A. (1993). *The lesbian and gay parenting handbook.* New York: Harper Perennial.

   This book provides information and resource lists for lesbian and gay couples who are planning on having children. Topics covered include revealing sexual preference, handling the child's concerns, dealing with the extended family, and coping with the attitudes of individuals outside the family.

24. McIntire, R. W. (1970). *For love of children.* Del Mar, CA: CRM Books.

   This book presents a sensitively written common-sense approach to child management, based on principles of behavioral psychology. This point of view, although sensitive to the concerns and development of children, is definitely a parent-centered approach. One major goal of the approach is for the child to develop a sense of responsibility for his actions.

25. Neville, H., & Halaby, M. (1984). *No-fault parenting*. New York: Facts on File.

This book, written for the well educated parent, covers childcare from birth to 6 years of age. It presents general behavioral principles, argues pros and cons of various childrearing techniques, and presents specific strategies for childcare.

26. Patterson, G. R. (1971). *Families*. Champaign, IL: Research Press.

This is a semi-program text designed to teach basic behavioral principles and is quite effective in meeting its goal. The textbook quality of the writing, however, makes it dry reading. This book is definitely parent-centered and encourages rather firm, authoritative limit-setting on the part of parents. Its greatest utility is probably with parents of children under 10 years of age.

27. Sears, W. (1983). *Creative parenting*. New York: Dodd, Mead.

This comprehensive guide to physical growth and development is useful for parents of children and adolescents. The book focuses on outlining development, but it also includes some behavior modification strategies.

28. Simon, S. B., & Wendkosolds, S. (1976). *Helping your child learn right from wrong: A guide to values clarification*. New York: Simon & Schuster.

This book focuses on a variety of activities, games, and exercises that can be used within a family to assist children in discovering their own identities and values. The structured activities provide a format which will enable both the parent and the child to explore their beliefs and values. This book provides excellent material for facilitating family discussions of important moral and relationship issues.

29. Turecki, S., & Wernick, S. (1994). *The emotional problems of normal children: How parents can understand and help*. New York: Bantam Books.

This book discusses normal emotional problems of childhood and adolescence, and provides parents with strategies for supporting their children through emotionally difficult times. Topics covered include separation from parents, peer rejection, and lying.

30. Wagonseller, B. R. (1993). *The practical parenting series*. Champaign, IL: Research Press. (Available from Research Press, Department J, P.O. Box 9177, Champaign, IL 61826).

Through example, this series of 30-minute videos helps parents cope with various special family situations. Topics covered include preparing for parenthood, coping with school systems, behavior management, adolescence, single parenting, blended families, teenage pregnancy, and parenting children with disabilities. The videos are available for rental or purchase.

31. Weisberg, A., & Buckler, C. (1993). *Everything a working mother needs to know*. New York: Doubleday.

This guide addresses a broad range of concerns that working mothers experience and provides concrete strategies for handling them. Topics covered include legal rights to maternity leave and alternative work arrangements, reducing stress on children, childcare options, and alternatives to working outside of the home.

II. Single Parenting

1. Geddes, J. B. (1974). *How to parent alone: A guide for single parents*. New York: Seabury.

   The author attempts to give the single parent encouragement and advice about the process of taking care of his/her own emotional needs as the sole primary caretaker of the child. The focus is on the divorced young woman raising children of preschool and elementary school age in an urban/suburban environment.

2. Gilbert, S. (1981). *Trouble at home*. New York: Lothrop, Lee & Shepard.

   This book addresses a variety of adolescent concerns about family relations. It describes normal family functioning and provides a list of fictional and nonfictional reading for adolescents. Topics covered include divorce, domestic violence, substance abuse, and death.

3. Marston, S. (1995). *The Divorced parent: Success strategies for raising happy children after separation*. New York: Pocket Books.

   This book dispels the myth that a single-parent home must be an unhappy one. It provides strategies for handling the stress of separation on a family and for raising well adjusted children while working on a new sense of self after divorce.

4. Weisberg, A., & Buckler, C. (1993). *Everything a working mother needs to know*. New York: Doubleday.

   This guide addresses a broad range of concerns that working mothers experience and provides concrete strategies for handling them. Topics covered include legal rights to maternity leave and alternative work arrangements, reducing stress on children, childcare options, and alternatives to working outside of the home.

III. Child Development

A. Infancy Through Preschool

1. Brazelton, T. B. (1983). *Infants and mothers: Differences in development*. New York: Dell Publishing Group.

   This book prepares parents for the first year of life by discussing developmental milestones from birth through 12 months. Information is presented through stories about real infants and parents. The author describes what the milestones at each stage of development might look like in infants with average, quiet, and active temperaments, and gives suggestions and helpful information on caring for infants with varying temperaments and rates of development.

2. Brazelton, T. B. (1989). *Toddlers and parents: A declaration of independence*. New York: Delacorte Press.

   This book provides information about and suggestions for raising a toddler (12–30 months of age) through stories about real toddlers and their parents. The author describes developmental milestones at each stage of development, discusses how to handle each stage, and presents issues with which many parents must cope. Topics covered include coping with daycare, sibling rivalry, and single parenting.

3. Brazelton, T. B. (1990). *The earliest relationship: Parents, infants, and the drama of early attachment*. Reading, MA: Addison-Wesley.

This book provides information about the importance of the first few months of life to children's healthy emotional development and offers suggestions for parents who would like to strengthen their relationship to their infants.

4. Brazelton, T. B. (1992). *Touchpoints: Your child's emotional and behavioral development*. Reading, MA: Addison-Wesley.

This easily read book outlines physical, cognitive, emotional, and behavioral development from birth to 3 years of age. The book contains sections on developmental milestones, special problems in development, and the role of various family members, friends, and professionals in facilitating healthy development in young children.

5. Christophersen, E. R. (1988). *Baby owners manual: What to expect and how to survive the first year*. Kansas City, MO: Westport Books.

This book covers the basics necessary for coping with a new baby. Each chapter covers one aspect of infant care. Chapter topics include bathing, feeding, bonding with, and soothing an infant.

6. Fraiberg, S. (1984). *The magic years: Understanding and handling the problems of early childhood*. New York: Charles Scribner's Sons.

This classic book presents the world through the eyes of small children, allowing parents to understand why youngsters behave the way they do. Developmental milestones and difficulties are described from the child's point of view, and the book provides coping strategies that are firmly based in developmental theory.

7. Greenspan, S., & Greenspan, N. (1985). *First feelings: Milestones in the emotional development of your baby and child*. New York: Viking.

This book is a resource for parents who would like to facilitate healthy emotional development in infants or young children. It describes important milestones in emotional development from infancy through the preschool years and helps parents understand and lend support during each milestone.

8. Griffith, L. L. (1986). *Rattle fatigue: And you thought you were busy before you had children*. San Luis Obispo, CA: Impact Books.

This book covering the first 3 years as a parent is divided into two sections. In Section 1, developmental milestones and typical problems are described and practical suggestions for facilitating development and handling problems are provided. In Section 2, general strategies for coping with parenting stress are discussed.

9. Ilg, F. L., & Ames, L. B. (1981). *Child behavior from birth to ten* (Rev. ed.). New York: Harper & Row.

This classic book vividly describes development during the first 10 years of life, including milestones and individual differences. Topics covered include eating, sleeping, sexuality, siblings, and discipline.

10. Sears, W. (1983). *Creative parenting*. New York: Dodd, Mead.

This comprehensive guide to physical growth and development is useful for parents of children and adolescents. The book focuses on outlining development, but it also includes some behavior modification strategies.

11. Sears, W., & Sears, M. (1994). *The baby book*. Boston: Little, Brown.

    This comprehensive and current guide for new parents covers a broad range of topics, including development, medical care, feeding, bathing, and getting on a schedule. In addition to basic information, the authors provide simple strategies for appropriate infant care.

12. Segal, M., & Adcock, D. (1985, 1986). *Your child at play series: Birth to one year, one to two years, two to three years, three to five years*. New York: Newmarket Press.

    This empirically based series is designed to enhance communication between parents and children and to increase their enjoyment of each other. The books also describe early developmental stages and provide techniques for child management during the first 5 years of life.

B. School Age (6–13 years)

1. Ames, L. B. (1979, 1981, 1985, 1989, 1990). *Your five-year-old: Sunny and serene; Your six-year-old: Defiant but loving; Your seven-year-old: Life in a minor key; Your eight-year-old: Lively and outgoing; Your nine-year-old: Thoughtful and mysterious; Your ten- to fourteen-year-old*. New York: Delacorte Press.

    This series of books about school-aged children discusses behaviors typically seen in children at each age. The author teaches parents about emotional and social development at each age and gives suggestions for coping with each age group and for facilitating healthy development.

2. Ginott, H. G. (1959). *Between parent & child*. New York: Avon.

    This classic book contains information that is still relevant today. It teaches parents how to communicate with their children in a manner that will enhance self-esteem and increase appropriate behavior; the book focuses on how to communicate during discipline, rather than on specific discipline techniques.

3. Greenspan, S., & Salmon, J. (1993). *Playground politics: Understanding the emotional life of your school-aged child*. Reading, MA: Addison-Wesley.

    This sequel to *First Feelings* provides parents with information regarding emotional development during the grade-school years. Like its forerunner, this book discusses various milestones in emotional development and includes information on how parents can support their children as each milestone occurs.

4. Meyer, R. (1984). *The parent connection: How to communicate with your child about alcohol and other drugs*. New York: Franklin Watts.

    This guide teaches parents to educate their preteens and teens about drugs and alcohol. It also presents a thorough, factual discussion of substance use and abuse and contains a section on family dynamics and alcohol.

5. Sears, W. (1983). *Creative parenting*. New York: Dodd, Mead.

    This comprehensive guide to physical growth and development is useful for parents of children and adolescents. The book focuses on outlining development, but it also includes some behavior modification strategies.

C. Adolescence (14 –18 years)

1. Bayard, T., & Bayard, J. (1983). *How to deal with your acting-up teenager: Practical help for desperate parents*. New York: Evans.

   This book is designed for parents who are truly struggling to handle their adolescents. It provides reassurance and information about strategies for handling extreme behavior problems during adolescence.

2. Bell, R., & Aeiger, L. (1983). *Talking with your teenager: A book for parents*. New York: Random House.

   This basic guide for parents of adolescents focuses on improving communication between parents and teens, but provides information and support as well. Topics covered include emotional health, sexuality, substance use and abuse, and eating disorders.

3. Bluestein, J. (1993). *Parents, teens, & boundaries: How to draw the line*. Deerfield Beach, FL: Health Communications.

   This book provides parents with strategies for handling power struggles during adolescence. It includes techniques for avoiding conflict, resolving problems, and establishing a foundation for mutual respect between teens and parents.

4. Dinkmeyer, D., & McKay, G. (1983). *The parent's guide: STEP/Teen: Systematic training for effective parenting of teens*. Circle Pines, MN: American Guidance Service.

   This illustrated book presents principles of parenting which stress the use of logical consequences, communication, and open expression of emotions when raising adolescents. It can help parents manage their children's behavior and cope with the feelings they arouse.

5. Elkind, D. (1994). *Parenting your teenager*. New York: Ballantine.

   This book provides parents with advice on raising teenagers. Topics covered include boosting self-esteem, teenage sexuality, mood swings, and curbing rudeness and power struggles.

6. Ginott, H. G. (1959). *Between parent & teenager*. New York: Avon.

   This classic book contains information that is still relevant today. It teaches parents how to communicate with their adolescents in a manner that will enhance self-esteem and increase appropriate behavior, focusing on how to relate to teenagers.

7. Meyer, R. (1984). *The parent connection: How to communicate with your child about alcohol and other drugs*. New York: Franklin Watts.

   This guide teaches parents to educate their preteens and teens about drugs and alcohol. It also presents a thorough, factual discussion of substance use and abuse and contains a section on family dynamics and alcohol.

8. Patterson, G., & Forgatch, M. (1987). *Parents and adolescents living together*. Eugene, OR: Castalia.

   This book presents basic behavioral approaches to raising adolescents. The author focuses on teaching parents to manage their children's behavior in order to increase desirable behaviors, reduce family fighting, and improve the quality of family life during adolescence.

9. Sears, W. (1983). *Creative parenting*. New York: Dodd, Mead.

   This comprehensive guide to physical growth and development is useful for parents of children and adolescents. The book focuses on outlining development, but it also includes some behavior modification strategies.

10. Steinberg, L., & Levine, A. (1992). *You and your adolescent: A Parent's guide for ages 10–12*. New York: Harper Collins.

   This book focuses on keeping family communication open throughout the teenage years. Topics covered include puberty, peer pressure, sexuality, and substance abuse.

11. Wienhaus, E., & Friedman, K. (1984). *Stop struggling with your teen*. St. Louis, MO: Speck Press.

   This book provides sound advice for parents on problem-solving and behavioral modification for adolescents. It includes specific strategies for defusing parent-child struggles and offers considerable support for the stresses inherent in raising adolescents.

IV. Divorce/Remarriage

1. Anderson, H. W., & Anderson, G. S. (1981). *Mom and dad are divorced but I'm not: Parenting after divorce*. Chicago: Nelson-Hall.

   This book on parenting through the divorce process focuses on looking at children's perspectives and meeting their needs during divorce. Topics covered include custody, visitation, and how to talk to children about divorce.

2. Berman, C. (1986). *Making it as a stepparent: New roles, new rules*. New York: Harper & Row.

   This book is based on interviews with stepparents and covers a broad range of issues they face. It includes quotes from various professionals on how to handle stepparenting issues and addresses difficult issues in a sensitive, informative fashion.

3. Blau, M. (1994). *Families apart: Ten keys to successful co-parenting*. New York: Putnam Publishing Group.

   This book shows ex-spouses who are parents how to co-parent effectively. It provides parents with strategies for effective communication, conflict negotiation, and handling stressful and/or important events in their children's lives.

4. Burns, C. (1985). *Stepmotherhood: How to survive without feeling frustrated, left out, or wicked*. New York: Harper & Row.

   This book is based on interviews with stepmothers and is designed to reassure women who are just stepping into the role. It defines common problems, feelings, and situations faced by stepmothers and offers sound, practical advice for handling these problems.

5. Eckler, J. (1993). *Step-by-step parenting*. Cincinnati, OH: Betterway Books.

   This guide covers a large range of concerns experienced by parents living in a blended family. Topics covered include transition to stepparenting, long-term adjustment in blended families, choosing roles in the new family, special problems and situations, and handling developmental issues associated with divorce and remarriage.

6. Erickson, M. S., & Erickson, S. K. (1992). *The children's book: A communication workbook for separate parenting after divorce*. West Concord, MN: CPI Publishing.

   This workbook provides a structured forum for communication between parents who share joint custody of children. It focuses on alleviating family tension by providing a place for parents to update each other on their children's time spent in alternating households.

7. Gardner, R. A. (1991). *The parent's book about divorce*. New York: Digimedics.

   This book provides divorcing parents with information regarding the issues faced by their children. It also discusses the potential impact of divorce on development and provides sound advice for minimizing the negative impact of divorce on children's adjustment.

8. Marston, S. (1995). *The Divorced parent: Success strategies for raising happy children after separation*. New York: Pocket Books.

   This book dispels the myth that a single-parent home must be an unhappy one. It provides strategies for handling the stress of separation on a family and for raising well adjusted children while working on a new sense of self after divorce.

9. Mayer, G. S. (1994). *The divorced dad dilemma: A father's guide to understanding, grieving, & growing beyond the losses of divorce & to developing a deeper, ongoing relationship to his children*. Bouse, AZ: Desert City Press.

   This book for divorcing fathers provides sensitive and sound strategies for handling the transition from living in the home to parenting from outside the home.

10. Olsen, R. P., & Pia-Terry, C. D. (1984). *Help for remarried couples and families*. Valley Forge, PA: Judson.

    This book outlines issues commonly faced in blended families in a thoughtful manner that encourages readers to gain insight into their own situations. It also includes strategies for personalizing the advice presented and handling specific situations.

11. Paris, E. (1984). *Step-families: Making them work*. New York: Avon.

    This easy-to-read book provides accurate information about, as well as useful suggestions for, blended families. It covers a broad range of topics, including handling money, building relationships between stepparents and children, and coping with conflict in blended families.

12. Ricci, I. (1982). *Mom's house, dad's house: Making shared custody work*. New York: Collier Books.

    This book focuses on negotiating a working relationship between divorced parents so that they can effectively meet their children's needs. Topics covered include coping with stress, working through the divorce process, and handling legal issues.

13. Salk, L. (1978). *What every child would like his parents to know about divorce*. New York: Harper & Row.

    This book discusses how to handle all aspects of divorce in a way that meets children's needs. Topics covered include talking to children about divorce, custody, visitation, and the potential impact of divorce on their adjustment and behavior.

14. Savage, K., & Adams, P. (1988). *The good step-mother: A practical guide*. New York: Crown Books.

    This book covers a broad range of stepfamily issues and provides practical strategies for dealing with them. Although the book is written for stepmothers and their spouses, stepfathers will also find it helpful. Topics covered include handling money, coping with ex-wives, and dealing with the stages of stepfamily development.

15. Teyber, E. (1992). *Helping children cope with divorce*. New York: Free Press.

    This book provides practical suggestions for understanding and coping with the emotional impact of divorce on children. It focuses on easing transitions and minimizing the traumatic impact of divorce.

V. Children With Special Needs

1. Bain, L. (1991). *A parent's guide to attention deficit disorders*. New York: Dell Publishing.

   This short, simple guide provides parents with basic information about attention deficit disorders and their treatments. It is excellent for parents who are new to the information, but not for parents who have some experience or knowledge.

2. Baldwin, V. L., Fredericks, H. D. B., & Brodsky, G. (1973). *Isn't it time he outgrew this? or a training program for parents of retarded children*. Springfield, IL: Charles C. Thomas.

   This volume focuses on principles and techniques to develop self- and child-adaptive behavior with the retarded child. These principles focus on areas such as feeding, toilet-training, dressing, washing, and language development.

3. Beckman, P., & Beckman Boyes, G. (1993). *Deciphering the system: A guide for families of young children with disabilities*. Cambridge, MA: Brookline Books.

   This book is for families whose children with disabilities are under 6 years of age. It contains information from parents and professionals about parents' rights under recent legislation, the assessment process, how to work with multiple service providers, how to manage information, and how to obtain support from other parents. In addition, the book contains a glossary of professional jargon and an extensive list of resources.

4. Blackman, J. (Ed.). (1990). *Medical aspects of developmental disabilities in children birth to three*. Rockville, MD: Aspen Publishers.

   This book, written for early service providers, provides simple but thorough explanations of a range of medical conditions commonly seen in young children with disabilities. Because the book is written in easy-to-understand language, it is an excellent resource for parents who are beginning to learn about their young children's medical conditions.

5. Budd, L. (1993). *Living with the active alert child*. Seattle, WA: Parenting Press.

   This book provides an alternative perspective on active children who are often diagnosed as hyperactive or learning disabled. It offers tips for raising and enjoying active children and discusses problems commonly experienced by parents of active children.

6. Crook, W. (1991). *Help for the hyperactive child*. Jackson, TN: Professional Books.

   This guide is for parents of hyperactive children and/or children with attention deficits. It provides simple but helpful information on a variety of subjects, including diagnosis, treatment, changing diet, structuring the home environment, behavior modification, and seeking professional support.

7. Fine, J. (1984). *Afraid to ask: A book for families to share about cancer*. New York: Lothrop, Lee & Shepard.

   This book for parents and teenagers provides a broad range of information on cancer. Topics covered include the biology of cancer, preventing cancer, treatment, and the experience of dying. The book provides information, but contains little in the way of coping strategies for families facing the disease.

8. Kerns, L., & Lieberman, A. (1993). *Helping your depressed child*. Rocklin, CA: Prima Publishing.

    This guide addresses depression in children and adolescents. It includes sections on the definition of depression, signs of depression in children, behaviors associated with depression, assessment, treatment, hospitalization, suicide prevention, and family adjustment.

9. McCaffrey, F. D., & Fish, T. *Profiles of the other child: A sibling guide for parents*. [Pamphlet.] (1988). Columbus, OH: Nisonger Center Publications Department.

    This pamphlet discusses the role of nondisabled siblings in families raising a child with a disability. Topics covered include informing the nondisabled child, giving equal attention, sibling rivalry, and sibling involvement in specialized care. It provides suggestions for helping children to understand, accept, and become involved with their disabled siblings.

10. McCarthy, W., & Fegan, L. (1984). *Sex education and the intellectually handicapped*. Baltimore: Williams & Wilkins.

    This book guides parents of intellectually handicapped children through the process of sexually educating these children. It covers a wide range of topics, including societal attitudes toward the sexuality of handicapped persons, personal hygiene, birth control, masturbation, and sterilization, and provides suggestions for communicating this information. There is also a list of available resources for parents.

11. Moldow, D. G., & Martinson, I. M. (1984). *Home care for seriously ill children: A manual for parents*. Alexandria, VA: Children's Hospice International.

    This manual is for parents of seriously ill children who would like to care for their children at home. All the practical aspects of caring for seriously ill children are described and discussed, and an appendix of recommended readings is provided. The book also contains a section on coping with grief.

12. Moore, C. (1990). *A reader's guide for parents of children with mental, physical, or emotional disabilities*. Rockville, MD: Woodbine House.

    This comprehensive sourcebook for parents provides a wide range of resources for parents of special-needs children and for the children themselves, including support groups, books, directories, journals, magazines, and services.

13. Seljeskog, B. B., Moller, J., Starr, C., Johnson, S., Shapiro, B., & Huessner, R. (1988, 1991). *A parent's guide to spina bifida; A parent's guide to heart disorders; A parent's guide to cleft lip and palate; A parent's guide to cystic fibrosis*. Minneapolis, MN: University of Minnesota Press.

    This continuing series provides parents with a broad range of helpful information about childhood disorders and disabilities. Topics discussed include causes, medical concerns, family adjustment, future research, and developmental issues associated with each disorder.

14. Sussan, T. A. (1990). How to handle due process litigation effectively under the Education for All Handicapped Children Act of 1975. *International Journal of Reading, Writing, and Learning Disabilities*, 6(1), 63-70.

    This article tells parents how to prepare for and conduct due process hearings under Public Law 94-142. Key legislative terms are defined and discussed. Suggestions are given to minimize the cost of special education litigation.

15. Woodbine House. (1986, 1989, 1991, 1992). *The special needs collection: Babies with Down syndrome, Choices in deafness; Children with epilepsy; The language of toys: Teaching communication skills to special needs children; Children with autism; Negotiating the special education maze; Children with cerebral palsy; Children with Tourette syndrome.* Rockville, MD: Author.

This series of books, edited by various professionals in the field of developmental disabilities, is designed for parents of young children. Each guide provides a host of simple, readable information on the disability or disorder involved. Topics covered include medical concerns, developmental issues, family adjustment, and advocacy. Each guide also provides a useful resource list.

16. Zipper, I., Hinton, C., Weil, M., & Rounds, K. (1993). *Family centered coordination: A manual for parents.* Cambridge, MA: Brookline Books.

This manual provides guidelines for parents of young children with special needs, including information about early intervention and parents' rights. Technical terms are carefully defined and discussed, and a checklist helps parents test their understanding of the service system.

VI. Sexuality

1. Calderone, M. S., & Johnson, E. W. (1993). *The family book about sexuality* (Rev. ed.). New York: Bantam Books.

This book is a comprehensive and up-to-date encyclopedia of sexual information for parents and children. Topics covered include sexual anatomy, sexuality, birth control, and sexual decision-making.

2. Fagerstrom, G., & Hansson, G. (1982). *Our new baby: A picture story for parents and children.* Woodbury, NY: Barron's.

This book, appropriate for parents of children ages 3 to 10 years, tells the story of a family expecting a baby. Designed for parents to read with their children, the book uses cartoons to describe "how babies are made" (sexual intercourse) and the birth process.

3. Gordon, S., & Gordon, J. (1983). *Raising a child conservatively in a sexually permissive world.* New York: Simon & Schuster.

This book covers all areas of sexuality, with a focus on communication between parents and children. Topics covered include building self-esteem, what to tell children of various ages and how to tell them, and how to talk about sexually transmitted diseases.

4. Kaus, D. S., & Reed, R. D. (1985). *A.I.D.S.: Your child and the school.* Saratoga, CA: R & E Publishers.

This book addresses many of the concerns parents have regarding the presence of children with AIDS in schools. It clearly describes the transmission of AIDS and discusses the risks involved in sending children to school with children who have the disease. In addition, the book contains a four-page handout for children that defines AIDS, describes how the disease is transmitted, and provides children with simple precautions to take against getting the disease.

5. Leight, L. (1988). *The parent's guide to raising sexually healthy children*. New York: Rawson Associates.

   This book provides parents with a broad range of information regarding sexuality throughout childhood and adolescence. Topics covered include nudity, masturbation, birth control, fostering self-esteem, talking about physical development, and instilling sexual values in children. The book provides strategies for communicating information regarding sexuality to children, both verbally and nonverbally, and contains clear illustrations of male and female anatomy.

6. Martin, A. (1993). *The lesbian and gay parenting handbook*. New York: Harper Perennial.

   This book provides information and resource lists for lesbian and gay couples who are planning on having children. Topics covered include revealing sexual preference, handling the child's concerns, dealing with the extended family, and coping with the attitudes of individuals outside the family.

7. McCarthy, W., & Fegan, L. (1984). *Sex education and the intellectually handicapped*. Baltimore: Williams & Wilkins.

   This book guides parents of intellectually handicapped children through the process of sexually educating these children. It covers a wide range of topics, including societal attitudes toward the sexuality of handicapped persons, personal hygiene, birth control, masturbation, and sterilization, and provides suggestions for communicating this information. There is also a list of available resources for parents.

VII. Special Problems or Situations

A. Abuse Prevention/Coping With Abuse

1. Adams, C., & Fay, J. (1981). *No more secrets: Protecting your child from sexual assault*. San Luis Obispo, CA: Impact Books.

   This widely used book for parents provides information about and suggestions for teaching children about sexual assault and its prevention. It also includes a resource list of films, books, and curricula regarding the subject, as well as a list of Child Abuse and Neglect Resources Centers.

2. Adams, C., Fay, J., & Loreen-Martin, J. (1984). *No is not enough: Helping teenagers avoid sexual assault*. San Luis Obispo, CA: Impact Books.

   This book provides parents with the information they need to talk with teenagers about sexual assault. Topics covered include date rape, media messages about sexuality, teaching children not to assault others, and what to do if your child is assaulted. The focus of this book is education and prevention, with some helpful information for assault survivors.

3. Byerly, C. M. (1985). *The mother's book: How to survive the incest of your child*. Dubuque, IA: Kendall-Hunt.

   This book provides comprehensive information for mothers whose children have experienced incest. Topics covered include the dynamics of incest, disclosure, the impact of incest on children and the family, legal implications of incest, and recovery. The book also provides a list of readings and a directory of Rape Crisis Centers in the United States.

4. Freeman, L., Hart-Rossi, J., & Johnsen, K. (1983, 1984). *Personal safety series: It's MY body; The trouble with secrets; Protect your child from sexual abuse.* Seattle, WA: Parenting Press.

This series helps parents teach their preschool-aged children about personal safety. The series includes a simple book that teaches children about "good" and "bad" touches, a teaching guide for parents, and a book that distinguishes between good surprises and harmful secrets.

5. Hyder, M. O. (1987). *Sexual abuse: Let's talk about it.* Philadelphia: Westminster Press.

This book provides information about, guidelines for coping with, and resources for victims of sexual abuse. It is appropriate for parents and children of all ages and covers the problems of both victims and perpetrators. Topics include appropriate touches, sexual abuse, disclosure, recovery, and prevention.

6. Quinn, P. E. (1986). *Renegade saint: A story of hope by a child abuse survivor.* Nashville, TN: Abingdon.

This autobiographical book tells the story of a young adult attempting to stop the cycle of abuse as he comes to terms with his history of abuse and his abuse of his own children. The book provides information about the impact of abuse on children and encourages parents to get support as they cope with abuse issues in their own families.

7. Sanford, L. T. (1980). *The silent children: A parent's guide to the prevention of child sexual abuse.* New York: McGraw-Hill.

This book provides information about the theory and dynamics of child sexual abuse and includes suggestions for parents. Topics covered include talking to children about abuse, the dynamics of incest, and healthy family functioning as a preventive measure.

8. *What's a kid to do about child abuse?* [Pamphlet]. (1990). Ithaca, NY: Cornell University Distribution Center. (Available from Cornell University Distribution Center, 7 Research Park, Ithaca, NY, 14850)

This easy-to-read pamphlet provides comprehensive information about the definition, reporting, and prevention of child abuse. It is an excellent resource for family members who are concerned about the possible existence of abuse in their family and want to know what to do about it.

9. Wooden, K. (1986). *Child lures: A family guide for the prevention of youth exploitation.* Shelburne, VT: Wooden.

This publication provides a program for the prevention of child abduction and exploitation. The program discusses 10 lures commonly used to abduct children and provides strategies for teaching children how to resist these lures.

B. Adoption

1. Melina, L. R. (1986). *Raising adopted children.* New York: Harper & Row.

This simple guide covers a broad area of concerns experienced by adoptive parents. Topics include minority adoption, developmental issues associated with adoption, and family adjustments when adopting a child.

C. Conflict Resolution

1. Cloud, K. (1984). *Watermelons not war! A support book for parenting in the nuclear age.* Philadelphia: New Society.

   This book provides suggestions for parents who are attempting to instill the values of peace and nonviolence in their children. The focus is on ways that parents can balance their children's frequent exposure to violent, war-glorifying images with parenting techniques, in-home discussions, and family activities that present peaceful negotiation of conflict as an effective, everyday alternative to violence.

2. Faber, A., & Mazlish, E. (1992). *How to be the parent you always wanted to be.* Seattle, WA: Parenting Press.

   This guide provides a quick and easy method for improving parenting skills. It includes two audio tapes and a workbook and helps parents deal with their children's emotions, set limits, teach cooperation, and resolve conflicts.

3. McGinnis, K., & Oehlberg, B. (1988). *Starting out right: Nurturing young children as peacemakers.* Yorktown Heights, NY: Meyer Stone.

   This book sets forth simple, effective strategies for teaching peaceful conflict resolution to young children. The focus is on instilling nonviolent values in children from an early age so that they will grow up to question the use of violence and war as a means to conflict resolution.

4. Wichert, S. (1989). *Keeping the peace: Practicing cooperation and conflict resolution with preschoolers.* Philadelphia: New Society Publishers.

   Although this book about teaching conflict resolution to preschoolers is written for teachers, it contains a wealth of information that will also be useful to parents. Topics covered include building self-esteem, teaching children to find common goals, and helping youngsters develop independent negotiating skills. The book includes many exercises that parents can use at home to help their children resolve conflicts peacefully and with minimal adult intervention.

D. Death and Dying

1. Anderson, M. K. (1987). *Coping with sorrow on the loss of your pet.* Los Angeles: Peregrine.

   This general-audience book on coping with the loss of a pet contains a helpful chapter on how to support children. Topics covered include the grieving process, getting a new pet, and explaining the death of a pet to children.

2. Creel, M. J. (1987). *A little death.* New York: Vantage Press.

   This nonfictional book tells the story of the author's experience of her infant daughter's death. The story is divided into informational chapters and covers such topics as how to talk to siblings, how to support bereaved parents, and how to cope with the process of losing an infant.

3. Fine, J. (1984). *Afraid to ask: A book for families to share about cancer.* New York: Lothrop, Lee & Shepard.

   This book for parents and teenagers provides a broad range of information on cancer. Topics covered include the biology of cancer, preventing cancer, treatment, and the experience of dying. The book provides information, but contains little in the way of coping strategies for families facing the disease.

318

4. Fitzergald, H. (1992). *The grieving child: A parent's guide*. New York: Simon & Schuster.

    This book provides strategies for parents who are helping their children cope with the death of a loved one. Topics covered include visiting the seriously ill, using age-appropriate language when discussing death, bringing children to funerals, and recognizing signs of grieving in children.

5. Grollman, E. A. (1991). *Talking about death: A dialogue between parent and child*. Boston: Beacon Press.

    This book, for parents of children ages 2 to 9 years, is designed to help parents understand their children's concerns about death and respond to them appropriately. It features a read-aloud story for parents and children, which will facilitate discussion of a child's feelings and concerns about death.

6. Jarratt, C. J. (1994). *Helping children cope with separation and loss*. Boston: Harvard Common Press.

    This book offers ideas for helping children overcome the difficult feelings they experience during times of separation and loss. Topics covered include death, divorce, illness, moving, and going to foster care.

7. Kubler-Ross, E. (1983). *On children and death*. New York: MacMillan.

    This book, for parents whose children have died or who are terminally ill, discusses a wide range of topics associated with death and loss. Topics covered include the funeral, dealing with siblings, and coping with loss.

8. Lombardo, V. S., & Lombardo, E. F. (1986). *Kids grieve too!* Springfield, IL: Charles C. Thomas.

    This book will help parents support their children through the grieving process. Topics covered include how children of different ages think about and react to death and how to talk to them about death. The book also includes a list of support groups for grieving families and a list of books about death for children.

9. Mellonie, B., & Ingpen, R. (1987). *Lifetimes: The beautiful way to explain death to children*. New York: Bantam.

    This book teaches parents to explain death in simple and comforting terms to their children. It helps parents frame death as a natural part of life and provides color illustrations of people coping with the death of a loved one.

10. Schaefer, D., & Lyons, C. (1986). *How do we tell the children?* New York: Newmarket Press.

    This book provides guidance for parents who are trying to help their children understand and cope with death. It is divided into an informational section that discusses such topics as what children think about death, how to explain death, and how children respond to death; and a section outlining the information from the first section in tabbed, easy-to-find areas for discussions with children. The book also deals with each topic by age levels so that parents can tailor their actions to their children's developmental stages.

E. Discipline

1. Crary, E. (1990). *Pick up your socks...and other skills growing children need*. Seattle, WA: Parenting Press.

   This guide offers insight into and guidance for teaching responsibility to children. Topics covered include motivating children to do homework, setting consequences for unacceptable behavior, and getting children to do age-appropriate household chores.

2. Crary, E. (1993). *Without spanking or spoiling*. Seattle, WA: Parenting Press.

   This comprehensive guide contains a broad range of information on overcoming behavior problems. The book includes ideas, exercises, examples, and summary sheets for easy use.

3. Dinkmeyer, D., & McKay, G. (1989). *The parent's handbook: STEP: Systematic training for effective parenting*. Circle Pines, MN: American Guidance Service.

   This illustrated book presents principles of parenting that stress the use of logical consequences, communication, and open expression of emotions when raising children. It can help parents manage their children's behavior and cope with the feelings that their children arouse in them.

4. Faber, A., & Mazlish, E. (1980). *How to talk so kids will listen & listen so kids will talk*. Seattle, WA: Parenting Press.

   This easy-to-read book addresses communication skills for parents and provides realistic and simple ideas on communicating effectively with their children. Although the ideas are presented for use with older children, all concepts in the book are useful with all ages.

5. Fishel, E. (1994). *I swore I'd never do that: Recognizing family patterns and making wise parenting choices*. Berkeley, CA: Conari Press.

   This book explores the ways in which unresolved issues from a parent's childhood can prevent him or her from being the parent he or she wants to be. Topics covered include discipline, intimacy, and self-esteem.

6. Turecki, S., & Tonner, L. (1989). *The difficult child*. New York: Bantam.

   This book offers compassionate and practical advice to parents with hard-to-raise children. Topics covered include discipline, managing conflict, and getting emotional support.

7. Whitham, C. (1993). *Win the whining war and other skirmishes*. Seattle, WA: Parenting Press.

   This simple guide helps parents reduce obnoxious childhood behaviors. The author provides step-by-step strategies designed to reduce such behaviors as whining, tantrums, teasing, fighting, and interrupting.

F. Eating Disorders

1. Hollis, J. (1986). *Fat Is a family affair*. Center City, MN: Hazelden Foundation.

   This book explains how individuals and families use food to feel in control and protected from the need for love. It also shows how eating can become a substitute for true intimacy and emotional risk.

2. Siegel, M., Brisman, J., & Weinshel, M. (1988). *Surviving an eating disorder: New perspectives and strategies for family and friends*. New York: Harper & Row.

This book offers basic information about anorexia nervosa, bulimia nervosa, and compulsive overeating. Topics covered include behaviors typical of each disorder, underlying psychological issues, and family dynamics. Case examples are provided, and the book focuses on offering strategies for coping with a loved one who suffers from disordered eating.

G. Environment

1. *E for environment: An annotated bibliography of children's books with environmental themes*. (1992). New Providence, NJ: R. R. Bowker.

This book provides parents with a wide variety of resources for teaching their children about the environment through books.

H. Multicultural Issues

1. Comer, J. P., & Poussaint, A. F. (1975). Black child care. New York: Simon & Schuster.

This book focuses on the development of the black child through adolescence. Although the content is similar to that of other books on child care, the authors provide through examples and special sensitivity, a black perspective on child care.

2. Hopkins, S., & Winters, J. (1990). *Discover the world: Empowering children to value themselves, others, and the earth*. Philadelphia: New Society.

This book, for parents of children under age 14 years, provides a host of activities for learning to value other cultures and the environment. It contains information and activities to help children learn about conflict resolution, global cultural awareness, and the environment. Both parents and children can appreciate the extensive list of books about these subjects.

3. Hopson, D. P., & Hopson, D. S. (1993). *Raising the rainbow generation*. New York: Simon & Schuster.

This book provides stories and activities that celebrate a variety of cultures and will help parents teach their children to appreciate and respect cultural, ethnic, and racial groups of all kinds.

I. Only Children

1. Sifford, D. (1989). *The only child: Being one, loving one, understanding one, raising one*. New York: G. P. Putnam's Sons.

The advantages and disadvantages of being an only child are accurately described in this book for parents. Discussions include case studies and research citations; topics covered include raising an only child, spoiling, and gaining independence as an only child.

J. Psychotherapy

1. Annunziata, J., & Jacobson-Kram, P. (1994). *Solving your problems together: Family therapy for the whole family.* Washington, DC: American Psychological Association. (Available from APA Books, P.O. Box 2710, Hyattsville, Maryland 20784-0710)

   This illustrated book is designed for family members of all ages and introduces the idea of family therapy as a safe place where people can learn to solve family problems, improve communication, and handle stress. The book answers typical questions and feelings that arise when a family is considering family therapy. It is appropriate for all types of family therapy.

K. School

1. *Helping your child succeed in school.* [Booklet]. (1989). New York: Association of American Publishers. (Available from Association of American Publishers, School Division, 220 East 23rd Street, New York, NY 10010.)

   This booklet offers parents tips for encouraging a positive attitude toward school in their children, effectively helping with homework, and dealing with a variety of problem situations at school.

2. Kuepper, J. E. *Homework helpers: A guide for parents offering assistance.* (1987). Minneapolis, MN: Educational Media Corporation. (Available from Educational Media Corporation, P.O. Box 21311, Minneapolis, MN 55421.)

   This guide helps parents learn to motivate their children, teach them effective study skills, and help improve the quality of their homework. It also offers suggestions for dealing with problems surrounding homework, such as special projects, deadlines, and incomplete work.

3. Reichel, H. (1988). Getting the most from parent-teacher conferences. In *Perspectives on Dyslexia, 14*(2), 6-11.

   This article describes the fears, frustrations, and problems that parents often have when participating in parent-teacher conferences. It gives helpful suggestions for preparation and suggests a system for opening lines of communication with the school before the first conference is scheduled.

L. Sibling Rivalry

1. Crary, E. (1984). *Kids can cooperate.* Seattle, WA: Parenting Press.

   This simple, readable book gives parents tips on teaching children cooperation and conflict resolution.

2. Faber, A., & Mazlish, E. (1988). *Siblings without rivalry.* Seattle, WA: Parenting Press.

   This book provides simple yet effective ways to reduce antagonism between siblings. Strategies are illustrated with real-life examples, and specific skills are presented and described clearly.

3. Hendrickson, K. (1990). *Baby & I can play* and *fun with toddlers.* Seattle, WA: Parenting Press.

   This book offers parents of very young children tips on reducing sibling rivalry early in life. It provides ideas for helping children play with a young sibling and explains developmental phases in terms that children can understand.

M. Sleep Problems

1. Ferber, R. (1986). *Solve your child's sleep problems*. New York: Simon & Schuster.

   This resource for parents who are struggling with their children's sleep problems provides basic information about sleep and gives information about common childhood sleep disorders. Most importantly, the book offers detailed advice on handling these problems and an annotated bibliography of books about sleep for children.

2. Huntley, R. (1994). *The sleep book for tired parents*. Seattle, WA: Parenting Press.

   This book presents three helpful approaches to addressing sleep problems and helps parents choose which solution will work best for them.

N. Stress

1. Kersey, K. (Ed.). (1986). *Helping your child handle stress: The parent's guide to recognizing and solving childhood problems*. Washington, DC: Acropolis.

   This book presents a range of childhood problems—common and uncommon—from both child and adult perspectives. Problems are described, and advice is given on what to do and what not to do for each situation. In addition, the book helps parents decide when a problem needs professional attention.

2. *Stress and your child*. [Booklet.] (1987). South Deerfield, MA: Channing L. Bete.

   This booklet defines stress, discusses the emotional and physical effects of stress on children, and outlines the warning signs of stress in children. It also offers information about various sources of stress experienced by children and ways for parents to handle those sources and alleviate children's stress.

O. Toilet Training

1. Azrin, N. H., & Foxx, R. M. (1974). *Toilet training in less than a day*. New York: Simon & Schuster.

   This book provides step-by-step, intense training procedures for parents who are having difficulty toilet training their children.

2. Brooks, J. G. (1981). *No more diapers*. New York: Delacorte.

   This book for children contains an introduction for parents on how to toilet train them. It contains pleasant illustrations and encouragement for toddlers who are going through toilet training.

Resources for Children

I. Materials for Children Ages 8 Years and Younger

A. Abuse Prevention/Coping With Abuse

1. Bass, E., & Betz, M. (1985). *I like you to make jokes with me, but I don't want you to touch me*. Carrboro, NC: Lollipop Power.

    This book, written for preschoolers, tells the story of an interaction between a young girl and a man. Although the man is pleasant and much of their interaction is positive, the little girl is uncomfortable with some things that he does. The story helps children learn that they can set rules about interactions with adults so they feel comfortable and remain safe.

2. Caruso, K. R., & Pulcini, R. J. (1988). *Chris tells the truth*. Redding, CA: Northwest Psychological.

    This book, written for children ages 4 to 12 years, tells the story of a child who is sexually abused. The child, whose gender is not identified, goes through the legal and recovery process.

3. Davis, D. (1985). *Something is wrong at my house*. Seattle, WA: Parenting Press.

    This book, for ages 3 to 12 years, helps children to acknowledge their feelings about domestic violence in the home and to decide how to act on those feelings. The boy in the story explores several methods for coping with domestic violence and eventually finds outside help for his problem. The book also provides a list of resources for abused children.

4. Freeman, L. (1985). *Loving touches*. Seattle, WA: Parenting Press.

    This book, for children ages 3 to 8 years, shows positive ways to touch and be touched. The book encourages children to express their need for touch and to exercise their choice about who touches them and how.

5. Kehoe, P. (1994). *Something happened and I'm scared to tell*. Seattle, WA: Parenting Press.

    This book is written for children ages 3 to 7 who are suspected victims of abuse. It provides information about who to tell, how to talk about the experience, and how to rebuild their self-esteem.

6. Wachter, O. (1983). *No more secrets for me*. Boston: Little Brown.

    This book for school-aged children tells the stories of four children who suffered sexual abuse, stopped the abuse, and began the recovery process.

7. *You're in charge* and *What every kid should know about sexual abuse*. [Coloring and Activity Books.] (1986). South Deerfield, MA: Channing L. Bete.

    These coloring and activity books, designed for school-aged children, focus on the prevention of sexual abuse. *You're in Charge* teaches that children's bodies belong to them and presents guidelines for staying in charge of their bodies. *What Every Kid Should Know about Sexual Abuse* teaches children about sexual abuse, how to recognize potential abusers, and what to do if someone tries to abuse them.

B. Death/Dying/Coping With Loss

1. Doleski, T. (1986). *A present for Jessica*. Mahwah, NJ: Paulist Press.

   This book, written for children ages 10 years and under, tells the story of a young girl who loses her pet dog. The story presents the grieving process in easy-to-understand language and reinforces all the emotions that come from grieving and loss.

2. Kunz, R. B., & Swenson, J. H. (1986). *Feeling down: The way back up*. Minneapolis, MN: Dillon.

   This book, written for children ages 7 to 11 years, tells the story of a young boy whose sister has attempted suicide. It discusses what leads to suicide and how families can cope with losing someone to suicide.

3. Porter, B. A., & Abolafia, Y. (1985). *Harry's Mom*. New York: Greenwillow.

   This book, written for children ages 3 to 7 years, tells the story of a young boy whose mother has been dead since he was 1 year old. The boy attempts to get information about his mother from family members and begins to incorporate what he finds out about his mother into his own sense of identity.

4. Swenson, J. H., & Kunz, R. B. (1986). *Cancer: The whispered word*. Minneapolis, MN: Dillon.

   This story, written for children under the age of 10, tells the story of a young boy whose mother is suffering from breast cancer. In addition to describing the emotions that come up when a parent has cancer, the book provides medical information about cancer in language that children can understand.

C. Divorce/Remarriage

1. Brown, L. K., & Brown, M. (1993). *Dinosaurs divorce: A guide for changing families*. New York: Little, Brown.

   This picture book, for children ages 2 to 7 years, tells the story of a divorce. The book helps children and their families deal with the anxieties surrounding divorce and encourages children to express their fears and feelings.

2. Fassler, D., Lash, M., & Ives, S. B. *Changing families: A guide for kids and grown-ups* and *the divorce workbook: A guide for kids and families*. [Activity Books]. (1985, 1988). Burlington, VT: Waterfront Books.

   These books use an activity-based format to cover issues related to divorce, separation, and remarriage. Activities such as drawing and coloring are designed to involve children and parents in expressing feelings and learning to cope with divorce-related issues.

3. Gardner, R. A. (1982). *The boys' and girls' book about stepfamilies*. New York: Bantam.

   This book, appropriate for ages 6 to 12 years, covers most issues faced by children in stepfamilies. It provides sound advice for children in straightforward, practical terms, and may be useful for parents and teenagers as well.

4. Gardner, R. A. (1992). *The boys' and girls' book about divorce*. New York: Jason Aronson.

   This book, appropriate for ages 6 to 12 years, covers most issues faced by children whose parents are divorcing or divorced. It provides sound but sensitive advice for children about even the most painful issues associated with divorce.

5. Perry, P., & Lynch, M. (1978). *Mommy and Daddy are divorced*. New York: Dial.

   This book, written for children ages 3 to 7 years, discusses the emotions commonly experienced by children whose parents are divorcing and provides reassurance regarding the future.

D. Emotions

1. Conlin, S., & Friedman, L. (1989). *Ellie's day: The let's talk about feelings series*. Seattle, WA: Parenting Press.

   Written for ages 3 to 7 years, this series of books follows a young girl named Ellie through her daily activities and the different emotions she experiences. The books provide an excellent format for helping children begin to talk about and deal with their own emotions.

2. Crary, E. (1986-1993). *Dealing with feelings series: I'm furious; I'm excited; I'm scared; I'm mad; I'm frustrated; I'm proud*. Seattle, WA: Parenting Press.

   These books explore common feelings using an interactive format. Each story, about a character who is experiencing the emotion in the story's title, allows the reader to decide how the character will handle his or her emotions. The books are especially appropriate for ages 3 to 9 years.

3. Hazen, N. (1988). *Grown-ups cry too*. Carrboro, NC: Lollipop Power Books.

   This story depicts times and reasons that adults and/or children cry. The book is designed to help children ages 4 to 8 years learn that expressing feelings is both acceptable and necessary.

E. Multicultural Issues

1. Begaye, L. S., & Tracy, L. (1993). *Building a bridge*. Northland.

   This book, written for children ages 5 to 10 years, tells the story of a Navajo girl and an Anglo girl who avoid each other because they look so different from one another. As the girls work together on a school project, however, they learn that their different colors do not really matter.

2. Hamanaka, S. (1994). *All the colors of the earth*. New York: Morrow Junior Books.

   This book, written for children ages 3 to 8 years, tells the story of children from different cultures and the ways that they enjoy their loved ones and their lives. The story celebrates diversity and commonality.

3. Lacapa, K., & Lacapa, M. (1994). *Less than half, more than whole*. Flagstaff, AZ: Northland.

   This book, written for children ages 6 to 12 years, tells the story of a young Native American boy who suddenly notices that he looks different from his friends. The story will help children from all multicultural backgrounds think about the ways that they are different from their friends and about the specialness of their culture's differences.

4. Mendez, P. (1991). *The black snowman*. New York: Scholastic Books.

   This book, for children ages 5 to 10 years, tells the story of a young African American boy who feels bad because he is black. As his mother teaches him about his ancestors, however, the boy begins to feel proud about who he is.

5. Williams, M. L. (1994). *Let's celebrate our differences*. Deerfield Beach, FL: Health Communications.

   This book, for children ages 4 years and older, features color photographs of multiracial children living, working, and playing together. Its captions invite children to explore their differences and similarities with other cultures and to accept themselves and others.

F. Psychotherapy

1. Nemiroff, M. A., & Annunziata, J. (1990). *A child's first book about play therapy*. (Available from APA Books, P.O. Box 2710, Hyattsville, Maryland 20784-0710.)

   This illustrated book is designed for children ages 4 to 7 years. In simple language, the book talks about play therapy: what it is, what happens there, why children go, how children get better, and how therapy ends. The book answers typical questions and feelings that children have when they are referred for therapy.

G. Sexuality

1. Cole, J. (1985). *How you were born*. New York: William Morrow.

   This book, appropriate for children ages 5 years and older, provides simple, factual information about the birth process. It contains photographs of fetuses at different stages of development and drawings of many aspects of pregnancy, but does not discuss sexual intercourse.

2. Johnson, P. H., & Shiffman, L. (1988). *The boy toy*. Carrboro, NC: Lollipop Power Books.

   This book, appropriate for preschoolers and beginning readers, explores the issues of sexual stereotyping. It tells the story of a boy named Chad who is forced to give up his favorite doll when he begins school. The story ends on a positive note, however, and sexual stereotypes are challenged and corrected.

3. Waxman, S. (1989). *What is a girl? What is a boy?* New York: Harper & Row Junior Books.

   This book focuses on a discussion of sexual identity which is appropriate for preschool-aged children. It explains, with simple text and photographs, that external physical features do not really differentiate boys and girls, but that genitalia determine one's gender.

H. Sibling Rivalry

1. Alexander, M. (1977). *Nobody asked me if I wanted a baby sister*. New York: Dial.

   This story, written for children ages 2 to 3 years, focuses on the feelings of jealousy often experienced by toddlers with the arrival of a new baby. It also describes the special feelings that new babies eventually develop toward their older siblings.

2. Alexander, M. (1981). *When the new baby comes, I'm moving out*. New York: Dial.

This book, for preschool-aged children, discusses some of the emotions that arise when a family is expecting a new baby.

3. Cole, J., & Hammid, H. (1985). *The new baby at your house*. New York: William Morrow.

This book for preschool-aged children and their parents, provides information for parents on how to prepare children for the arrival of a new baby. It also contains a story, written for children, about the arrival of a new sibling.

4. *Jack and Jake*. (1986). Aliki, New York: Greenwillow.

This story, written for children ages 3 to 5 years, is about identical twins who are often confused for each other.

5. Rosenberg, M. B., & Anconar, G. (1985). *Being a twin: Having a twin*. New York: Lothrop, Lee & Shepard.

This book, written for children ages 6 to 10 years, provides factual information about what it is like to be a twin. It includes photographs of four sets of twins and emphasizes their unique characteristics.

I. Other Situations and Problems

1. Bernstein, J., & Fireside, B. (1991). *Special parents, special children*. Morton Grove, IL: Albert Whitman.

This book is appropriate for children ages 8 years and older. It consists of true stories about and photographs of children whose parents have a variety of disabilities.

2. Berry, J. (1984). *The teach me series*. Newark, NJ: Peter Pan Industries.

This series is aimed at helping young children learn self-care and prosocial behaviors. Each book explains appropriate and inappropriate behaviors regarding the topic discussed in that book and provides parents suggestions for reinforcing the information presented. Topics covered include toilet training, crying, getting dressed, bedtime, mealtime, and traveling.

3. Black, C. (1982). *My dad loves me, my dad has a disease*. Denver, CO: M. A. C. Publishing.

This book, written for children ages 2 to 11 years, presents writing and drawing exercises designed to help children with alcoholic parents express their difficult emotions.

4. Boritzer, E. (1990). *What is God?* Buffalo, NY: Firefly Books.

This book, written for children ages 5 years and older, discusses traditional and nontraditional views of God and religion. It teaches that God is a feeling of connectedness that people of all religions can experience.

5. Brett, D. (1988). *Annie stories: A special kind of storytelling*. New York: Workman.

This book contains stories about children who experience various stressors and common childhood problems. The stories can be adapted to a child's unique experience and contain suggestions for helping children master difficult events or feelings. Topics covered include nightmares, going to the hospital, death, and going to school.

6. Crary, E. (1982-1986). *A children's problem-solving book series: My name is not dummy; Mommy don't go; I can't wait; I'm lost; I want it; I want to play.* Seattle, WA: Parenting Press.

   This series of books, especially helpful for ages 4 to 7 years, is designed to help children learn to solve problems. They encourage children to think before they act, and offer a variety of ways to handle each problem situation. The interactive format allows children to decide what each character will do and to turn to the page describing the consequences of their decision.

7. Gilbert, S. (1983). *By yourself.* New York: Lothrop, Lee & Shepard.

   This book, for elementary school-aged children, provides practical information to make staying home alone easier and more fun. It discusses how children feel when left at home and gives suggestions for how to handle snacks, safety, activities, and a variety of other situations. The book also includes a section for parents.

8. Hastings, J. M., & Typpo, M. H. (1984). *An elephant in the living room: The children's book.* Center City, MN: Hazelden Foundation.

   This book, written for children ages 7 years and older, helps children learn about alcoholism. It provides information and writing/drawing exercises designed to help children with alcoholic relatives handle their difficult emotions.

9. Joose, B. (1991). *Mama, do you love me?* San Francisco: Chronicle Books.

   This book, for children ages 2 to 6 years, tells the story of a young girl testing the limits of her independence. Throughout the story, the girl's mother reassures her that a parent's love is unconditional and everlasting.

10. Keyworth, C. L., & Bracken, C. (1986). *New day.* New York: William Morrow.

    This book, written for children ages 2 to 4 years, tells the story of a child who is moving to a new place. The story is told in pictures with very little text and will allow for discussion of the individual child's experiences around moving.

11. Lifton, B. J., & Nivola, C. A. (1994). *Tell me a real adoption story.* New York: Alfred A. Knopf.

    This book, written for children ages 2 to 8 years, tells the story of a young girl who is adopted. When the girl asks for information about how she came into her adoptive family's life, her family tells her about her adoption and her birth family. The book focuses on honest communication and fostering a sense of trust.

12. Lindsay, J. W. (1982). *Did I have a daddy? A story about a single-parent child.* Buena Park, CA: Morning Glory Press.

    This book, appropriate for preschool-aged children, tells the story of a boy who has never known his father. It is designed to stimulate discussion and provides a model for coping sensitively but honestly with difficult emotions. The book also includes a section for parents on how to respond to their children's questions.

13. Livingston, C. (1993). *Why was I adopted?* (see below)

14. Mayle, P., & Robins, A. (1993). *Where did I come from?* (see below)

15. Mayle, P., & Robins, A. (1993). *What's happening to me* (Puberty)*?* (see below)

16. Stuart, S. L., & Robins, A. (1993). *Why do I have to wear glasses?* (see below)

17. Ciliotta, C., Livingston, C., & Wilson, D. (1993). *Why am I going to the hospital?* (see below)

18. Berman, C., & Wilson, D. (1993). *What am I doing in a stepfamily?* Secaucus, NJ: Carol Publishing Group.

    This series of books, written for school-aged children, covers a broad range of issues in honest but reassuring terms. The illustrations are colorful and humorous, and the books are reissued every year.

19. Long, L. (1984). *On my own: The kid's self-care book.* Washington, DC: Acropolis.

    This workbook, especially appropriate for ages 8 to 10 years, covers a variety of situations that children who spend part of their day alone might face. Topics covered include getting ready for school, fixing snacks, and visiting friends. The book provides easily understood instructions for dealing with these situations.

20. Meyer, L. D., & Peaker, D. (1986). *I take good care of us (a first aid coloring book)/I take good care of me (teaching fire, water, electrical, assault, and abduction safety).* Edmonds, WA: Charles Franklin.

    This book, written for children younger than 9 years of age, teaches about a broad range of safety and first aid issues. Each topic covered (fire safety, water safety, etc.) includes a cartoon for children to color.

21. Millman, D. (1991). *Secret of the peaceful warrior.* Tiburon, CA: H. J. Kramer.

    This book, written for children ages 5 to 11 years, tells the story of a young boy who is being harassed by the school bully. It teaches children how to resolve conflicts peacefully.

22. Scovel, K., & Hunter, T. (1992). *Joe's earthday birthday.* Seattle, WA: Parenting Press.

    This book is written for children 5 to 10 years of age. It tells the story of a young boy who creates a trash-free birthday party and presents ideas about conservation in simple and delightful terms.

23. Seattle, C., & Jeffers, S. (1993). *Brother Eagle, Sister Sky: A message from Chief Seattle.* New York: Puffin Books.

    This book reproduces a speech by Chief Seattle, a Native American chief who lived more than 100 years ago. His speech teaches children, ages 5 to 11 years, that the earth and every creature on it are sacred.

24. Stevenson, J. (1985). *That dreadful day.* New York: Greenwillow.

    This book tells the story of two children who listen to the story of their grandfather's first day at school. As they hear how their grandfather's day turned out, they begin to feel better about their upcoming first school day.

25. Zolotow, C., & Semont, M. (1989). *The quiet mother and the noisy little boy.* New York: Harper & Row.

    This story, written for children ages 5 and 6, tells about noise, quiet, and how too much of either can be bad.

II. Materials for Children Ages 8–13 Years

A. Abuse Prevention/Coping With Abuse

1. Caruso, K. R., & Pulcini, R. J. (1988). *Chris tells the truth*. Redding, CA: Northwest Psychological.

   This book, written for children ages 4 to 12 years, tells the story of a child who is sexually abused. The child, whose gender is not identified, goes through the legal and recovery process.

2. Davis, D. (1985). *Something is wrong at my house*. Seattle, WA: Parenting Press.

   This book, for ages 3 to 12 years, helps children to acknowledge their feelings about domestic violence in the home and to decide how to act on those feelings. The boy in the story explores several methods for coping with domestic violence and eventually finds outside help for his problem. The book also provides a list of resources for abused children.

3. Wachter, O. (1983). *No more secrets for me*. Boston: Little Brown.

   This book for school-aged children tells the stories of four children who suffered sexual abuse, stopped the abuse, and began the recovery process.

4. *You're in charge* and *What every kid should know about sexual abuse*. [Coloring and Activity Books.] (1986). South Deerfield, MA: Channing L. Bete.

   These coloring and activity books, designed for school-aged children, focus on the prevention of sexual abuse. *You're in Charge* teaches that children's bodies belong to them and presents guidelines for staying in charge of their bodies. *What Every Kid Should Know about Sexual Abuse* teaches children about sexual abuse, how to recognize potential abusers, and what to do if someone tries to abuse them.

B. Death/Dying/Coping With Loss

1. Doleski, T. (1986). *A present for Jessica*. Mahwah, NJ: Paulist Press.

   This book, written for children ages 10 years and under, tells the story of a young girl who loses her pet dog. The story presents the grieving process in easy-to-understand language and reinforces all the emotions that come from grieving and loss.

2. Kunz, R. B., & Swenson, J. H. (1986). *Feeling down: The way back up*. Minneapolis, MN: Dillon.

   This book, written for children ages 7 to 11 years, tells the story of a young boy whose sister has attempted suicide. It discusses what leads to suicide and how families can cope with losing someone to suicide.

3. Swenson, J. H., & Kunz, R. B. (1986). *Cancer: The whispered word*. Minneapolis, MN: Dillon.

   This story, written for children under the age of 10, tells the story of a young boy whose mother is suffering from breast cancer. In addition to describing the emotions that come up when a parent has cancer, the book provides medical information about cancer in language that children can understand.

C. Divorce/Remarriage

1. Fassler, D., Lash, M., & Ives, S. B. *Changing families: A guide for kids and grown-ups* and *the divorce workbook: A guide for kids and families.* [Activity Books]. (1985, 1988). Burlington, VT: Waterfront Books.

   These books use an activity-based format to cover issues related to divorce, separation, and remarriage. Activities such as drawing and coloring are designed to involve children and parents in expressing feelings and learning to cope with divorce-related issues.

2. Gardner, R. A. (1982). *The boys' and girls' book about stepfamilies.* New York: Bantam.

   This book, appropriate for ages 6 to 12 years, covers most issues faced by children in stepfamilies. It provides sound advice for children in straightforward, practical terms, and may be useful for parents and teenagers as well.

3. Gardner, R. A. (1992). *The boys' and girls' book about divorce.* New York: Jason Aronson.

   This book, appropriate for ages 6 to 12 years, covers most issues faced by children whose parents are divorcing or divorced. It provides sound but sensitive advice for children about even the most painful issues associated with divorce.

4. LeShan, E. (1986). *What's going to happen to me? When parents separate or divorce.* New York: MacMillan.

   This book is written for children ages 8 years and older whose parents are currently in the process of divorcing. It discusses common problems that arise for children during this process and provides strategies for handling them. Most importantly, the book helps children decide how to tell their parents how they are feeling in a constructive way.

5. Wood, P. A. (1977). *Win me and you lose.* Philadelphia: Westminster.

   This book, written for children ages 9 to 13 years, tells the story of a boy whose parents are fighting over custody of him. As the story progresses, the boy chooses to live with his father, and the two begin to build a closer relationship than they have had before. This is an excellent resource for children who have been through a custody battle and are currently living with a single parent.

D. Emotions

1. Crary, E. (1986-1993). *Dealing with feelings series: I'm furious; I'm excited; I'm scared; I'm mad; I'm frustrated; I'm proud.* Seattle, WA: Parenting Press.

   These books explore common feelings using an interactive format. Each story, about a character who is experiencing the emotion in the story's title, allows the reader to decide how the character will handle his or her emotions. The books are especially appropriate for ages 3 to 9 years.

2. Delis-Abrams, A. (1990). *ABC feelings.* [Coloring Books, Audiotape, Poster]. (Available from Adage Publications, P.O. Box 2377, Coeur d'Alene, Idaho 83816.)

   All components of this series are designed to teach children of all ages about their emotions and to stimulate conversation about different emotions that children feel.

E. Multicultural Issues

1. Begaye, L. S., & Tracy, L. (1993). *Building a bridge*. Northland.

   This book, written for children ages 5 to 10 years, tells the story of a Navajo girl and an Anglo girl who avoid each other because they look so different from one another. As the girls work together on a school project, however, they learn that their different colors do not really matter.

2. Lacapa, K., & Lacapa, M. (1994). *Less than half, more than whole*. Flagstaff, AZ: Northland.

   This book, written for children ages 6 to 12 years, tells the story of a young Native American boy who suddenly notices that he looks different from his friends. The story will help children from all multicultural backgrounds think about the ways that they are different from their friends and about the specialness of their culture's differences.

3. Mendez, P. (1991). *The black snowman*. New York: Scholastic Books.

   This book, for children ages 5 to 10 years, tells the story of a young African American boy who feels bad because he is black. As his mother teaches him about his ancestors, however, the boy begins to feel proud about who he is.

4. Wilkinson, B. (1987). *Not separate, not equal*. New York: Harper & Row.

   This novel, written for children ages 11 to 16 years, tells the story of a young African American girl growing up in the newly desegregated South. The novel sensitively presents the perspectives of African Americans who endured persecution and of Caucasian Americans who wanted to support equal rights but were frightened of speaking up. This book provides an historical perspective on some of the racial tensions still present in the United States.

5. Williams, M. L. (1994). *Let's celebrate our differences*. Deerfield Beach, FL: Health Communications.

   This book, for children ages 4 years and older, features color photographs of multiracial children living, working, and playing together. Its captions invite children to explore their differences and similarities with other cultures and to accept themselves and others.

F. Sexuality

1. *As boys grow up*. [Pamphlet.] (1987). South Deerfield, MA: Channing L. Bete.

   This pamphlet, written for boys who are between the ages of 9 and 13 years, provides information about such topics as sexual changes, intercourse, pregnancy, sexually transmitted diseases, and birth control in a straightforward, simple manner.

2. Cole, J. (1985). *How you were born*. New York: William Morrow.

   This book, appropriate for children ages 5 years and older, provides simple, factual information about the birth process. It contains photographs of fetuses at different stages of development and drawings of many aspects of pregnancy, but does not discuss sexual intercourse.

G. Other Situations and Problems

1. *About good health: A coloring and activities book*. (1988). South Deerfield, MA: Channing L. Bete.

   This book, written for third and fourth graders, presents information on eating, bathing, dental hygiene, exercise, and many other health-related topics. It presents exercises and activities that teach children ways that they can stay healthy.

2. Beaudry, J., & Ketchum, L. (1987). *Carla goes to court*. New York: Human Sciences.

   This story, written for school-aged children, tells the story of a young girl who witnesses a burglary and must go to court to testify about it. The book provides details about the entire legal process, and discusses different feelings children might experience when participating in that process.

3. Bernstein, J., & Fireside, B. (1991). *Special parents, special children*. Morton Grove, IL: Albert Whitman.

   This book is appropriate for children ages 8 years and older. It consists of true stories about and photographs of children whose parents have a variety of disabilities.

4. Black, C. (1982). *My dad loves me, my dad has a disease*. Denver, CO: M. A. C. Publishing.

   This book, written for children ages 2 to 11 years, presents writing and drawing exercises designed to help children with alcoholic parents express their difficult emotions.

5. Boritzer, E. (1990). *What is God?* Buffalo, NY: Firefly Books.

   This book, written for children ages 5 years and older, discusses traditional and nontraditional views of God and religion. It teaches that God is a feeling of connectedness that people of all religions can experience.

6. Dinner, S. H. (1989). *Nothing to be ashamed of: Growing up with mental illness*. New York: Lothrop, Lee & Shepard.

   This book, written for children ages 9 to 12 years, provides a wide range of information on mental illness. Each chapter covers a particular mental illness and presents information on the common symptoms, treatments, and overall impact of that illness. The book also discusses the feelings and difficulties that arise for families coping with mental illness.

7. Dolmetsch, P., & Shih, A. (Eds.). (1985). *The kid's book about single-parent families*. Garden City, NY: Doubleday.

   This book was written by children ages 11 to 15 years, and is appropriate for that age group. It focuses on understanding the feelings of children with single parents, but it also includes advice on how to handle issues faced by those children. The book also discusses some of the reasons for having one parent, including divorce, desertion, and death.

8. Hall, L., & Cohn, L. (1988). *Dear kids of alcoholics*. Carlsbad, CA: Gurze.

   This book is written for children, ages 8 to 17 years, who have an alcoholic parent. It tells the story of a young boy named Jason, whose father is an alcoholic. Jason explains the facts and feelings associated with alcoholism from a child's point of view.

9. Hastings, J. M., & Typpo, M. H. (1984). *An elephant in the living room: The children's book*. Center City, MN: Hazelden Foundation.

   This book, written for children ages 7 years and older, helps children learn about alcoholism. It provides information and writing/drawing exercises designed to help children with alcoholic relatives handle their difficult emotions.

10. Jordan, S., & Philbrook, D. (1986). *Good losers and gracious winners*. Cincinnati, OH: Standard.

    This book, written for children ages 10 to 13 years, tells the story of a boy who competes in his school spelling bee. The story focuses on the feelings that children who compete have and provides strategies for dealing with losing, winning, and respecting one's competitors.

11. Krementz, J. (1993). *How it feels series*. New York: Alfred A. Knopf.

    These books, written for adolescents, consist of interviews with real children 12 to 18 years of age who have experienced a specific problem or situation. The series includes books about the death of a parent, being adopted, adjusting to divorce, having a terminal illness, and having a disability.

12. Livingston, C. (1993). *Why was I adopted?* (see below)

13. Mayle, P., & Robins, A. (1993). *Where did I come from?* (see below)

14. Mayle, P., & Robins, A. (1993). *What's happening to me* (Puberty)*?* (see below)

15. Stuart, S. L., & Robins, A. (1993). *Why do I have to wear glasses?* (see below)

16. Ciliotta, C., Livingston, C., & Wilson, D. (1993). *Why am I going to the hospital?* (see below)

17. Berman, C., & Wilson, D. (1993). *What am I doing in a stepfamily?*
    Secaucus, NJ: Carol Publishing Group.
    This series of books, written for school-aged children, covers a broad range of issues in honest but reassuring terms. The illustrations are colorful and humorous, and the books are reissued every year.

18. Long, L. (1984). *On my own: The kid's self-care book*. Washington, DC: Acropolis.

    This workbook, especially appropriate for ages 8 to 10 years, covers a variety of situations that children who spend part of their day alone might face. Topics covered include getting ready for school, fixing snacks, and visiting friends. The book provides easily understood instructions for dealing with these situations.

19. Meyer, D., Vadasy, P., & Fewell, R. (1985). *Living with a brother or sister with special needs: A guide for sibs*. Seattle, WA: University of Washington Press.

    This informative book for adolescents provides a wide range of information, including a section on how it feels to have a sibling with special needs.

20. Millman, D. (1991). *Secret of the peaceful warrior*. Tiburon, CA: H. J. Kramer.

    This book, written for children ages 5 to 11 years, tells the story of a young boy who is being harassed by the school bully. It teaches children how to resolve conflicts peacefully.

21. Scovel, K., & Hunter, T. (1992). *Joe's earthday birthday*. Seattle, WA: Parenting Press.

    This book is written for children 5 to 10 years of age. It tells the story of a young boy who creates a trash-free birthday party and presents ideas about conservation in simple and delightful terms.

22. Seattle, C., & Jeffers, S. (1993). *Brother Eagle, Sister Sky: A message from Chief Seattle*. New York: Puffin Books.

    This book reproduces a speech by Chief Seattle, a Native American chief who lived more than 100 years ago. His speech teaches children, ages 5 to 11 years, that the earth and every creature on it are sacred.

III. Materials for Children Ages 13 Years and Older

A. Abuse Prevention/Coping With Abuse

1. Wachter, O. (1983). *No more secrets for me*. Boston: Little, Brown.

   This book for school-aged children tells the stories of four children who suffered sexual abuse, stopped the abuse, and began the recovery process.

B. Adolescence

1. Barr, L., & Monserrat, C. (1983). *Teenage pregnancy: A new beginning*. Albuquerque, NM: New Futures.

   This book describes the physical and emotional aspects of pregnancy in a clear, concrete style. It is thorough in its coverage of teenage pregnancy and related issues, but does not contain information about AIDS. It includes quotations from actual teenagers who are pregnant or who have had a child.

2. Cooney, P., Heller, N., & Heller, W. M. (1985). *The teenager's survival guide to moving*. New York: Atheneum.

   This book was written to help adolescents cope with the process of moving. It includes case examples, information, and practical advice for handling a move. Topics covered include dealing with stress, saying goodbye to old friends and making new friends, and transferring school transcripts and records.

3. Elchoness, M. (1986). *Why can't anyone hear me? A guide for surviving adolescence*. Supulveda, CA: Monroe.

   This fictional book tells the story of a character named Jamie who faces a variety of issues commonly encountered during adolescence. Each chapter covers a single topic and combines fiction, information, and advice. Topics covered include peer pressure, family relations, dating, and substance abuse.

4. Gilbert, S. (1981). *Trouble at home*. New York: Lothrop, Lee & Shepard.

   This book addresses a variety of adolescent concerns about family relations. It describes normal family functioning and provides a list of fictional and nonfictional reading for adolescents. Topics covered include divorce, domestic violence, substance abuse, and death.

5. Landau, E. (1986). *Different drummer: Homosexuality in America*. New York: Julian Messner.

   This is a resource for teenagers who are concerned about homosexuality. The book provides a broad range of information about homosexuality and includes interviews with young homosexuals and references to helping agencies. Topics covered include telling your parents, mental health, and AIDS.

6. Lindsay, J. W. (1984). *Teenage marriage: Coping with reality*. Buena Park, CA: Morning Glory.

   This book presents the realities of married life and encourages adolescents to think seriously about those realities when choosing to marry. Topics covered include sex, communication, financial decisions, having children, and domestic violence. The book includes interviews with married teenagers who are coping with these issues.

7. Madaras, L. (1984). *The "What's Happening to My Body?" book for boys and The "What's Happening to My Body?" book for girls*. New York: Newmarket Press.

These two illustrated companion books answer questions about changes during puberty which are commonly asked by adolescents. They provide basic information about puberty and sexuality in a matter-of-fact, readable way. Both books contain a section on pubertal changes in the opposite sex and include an extensive annotated bibliography of other books about sexuality for adolescents and children.

8. Packer, A. J. (1993). *Bringing up Parents: The teenager's handbook*. Minneapolis, MN: Free Spirit.

This book provides teenagers with strategies and techniques for building a healthy relationship with their parents. Topics covered include getting what you want, helping parents to trust, and being yourself.

9. Wallace, C. McD. (1983). *Should you shut your eyes when you kiss?* Boston: Little, Brown.

This humorous book, while spoofing adolescent life, manages to inform teens about family relations, drugs, dating, and education.

10. Wirth, C. G., & Bownman-Kruhm, M. (1987). *I hate school: How to hang in and when to drop out*. New York: Crowell.

This book is written for teens and preteens who are experiencing trouble in school. It uses a dialog format to address specific problems that cause teenagers to drop out of school and presents advice and information in an easy-to-read fashion.

C. Death/Dying/Coping With Loss

1. Grollman, E. A. (1993). *Straight talk about death for teenagers: How to cope with losing someone you love*. New York: Beacon.

This book discusses normal reactions to death, how grief affects other relationships, and how one can work through grief and live again. Its style is particularly appropriate for teenagers.

2. Naughton, J. (1989). *My brother stealing second*. New York: Harper & Row.

This book for teenagers tells the story of a 16-year-old boy whose brother dies in an automobile accident. The book focuses on the boy's attempts to function in school, in social relationships, and at home, as he struggles to come to terms with his brother's death.

D. Divorce/Remarriage

1. Getzoff, A., & McClenahan, C. (1984). *Stepkids: A survival guide for teenagers in step-families*. New York: Walker.

This well written, easy-to-read book takes a positive view of the difficulties faced by teenagers in stepfamilies. Topics covered include rebelling, adjusting to divorce, getting along with stepparents, parents in homosexual relationships, and getting professional support.

2. LeShan, E. (1986). *What's going to happen to me? When parents separate or divorce*. New York: MacMillan.

This book is written for children ages 8 years and older whose parents are currently in the process of divorcing. It discusses common problems that arise for children during this process and provides strategies for handling them. Most importantly, the book helps children decide how to tell their parents how they are feeling in a constructive way.

3. Wood, P. A. (1977). *Win me and you lose*. Philadelphia: Westminster.

This book, written for children ages 9 to 13 years, tells the story of a boy whose parents are fighting over custody of him. As the story progresses, the boy chooses to live with his father, and the two begin to build a closer relationship than they have had before. This is an excellent resource for children who have been through a custody battle and are currently living with a single parent.

E. Eating Disorders

1. Kubersky, R. (1992). *Everything you need to know about eating disorders*. New York: Rosen Publishing Group.

This book, for children ages 9 to 13 years, explains the causes and consequences of anorexia and bulimia. Topics covered include the pressure to be thin, how to keep healthy, and how to get help.

2. Landau, E. (1983). *Why are they starving themselves: Understanding anorexia nervosa and bulimia*. New York: Julian Messner.

This book provides a comprehensive overview of eating disorders. It includes factual information, personal interviews and real-life anecdotes and outlines types of help available. The book frankly discusses what to do if you have an eating disorder and is appropriate for a teenage audience.

3. Moer, B. (1991). *Coping with eating disorders*. (see below)

4. Kane, J. K. (1990). *Coping with diet fads*. (see below)

5. Bowen-Woodward, K. (1989). *Coping with a negative body-image*. (see below) New York: Rosen Publishing Group.

This series of books for teenagers and preteens contains important information about eating disorders, weight control, and the struggle for body acceptance. Each book provides practical information on the topic covered, as well as ways of getting help when eating, dieting, or body-image has gotten out of control.

F. Emotions

1. Delis-Abrams, A. (1990). *ABC feelings*. [Coloring Books, Audiotape, Poster]. (Available from Adage Publications, P.O. Box 2377, Coeur d'Alene, Idaho 83816.)

All components of this series are designed to teach children of all ages about their emotions and to stimulate conversation about different emotions that children feel.

2. Sieruta, P. D. (1989). *Heartbeats and other stories*. New York: Harper & Row.

This book of short stories will help adolescents come to terms with their own emotions regarding a variety of situations presented. The stories include such topics as disabilities, first love, and leaving home, focusing on the feelings teens typically experience in these situations.

G. Multicultural Issues

1. Wilkinson, B. (1987). *Not separate, not equal*. New York: Harper & Row.

   This novel, written for children ages 11 to 16 years, tells the story of a young African American girl growing up in the newly desegregated South. The novel sensitively presents the perspectives of African Americans who endured persecution and of Caucasian Americans who wanted to support equal rights but were frightened of speaking up. This book provides an historical perspective on some of the racial tensions still present in the United States.

2. Williams, M. L. (1994). *Let's celebrate our differences*. Deerfield Beach, FL: Health Communications.

   This book, for children ages 4 years and older, features color photographs of multiracial children living, working, and playing together. Its captions invite children to explore their differences and similarities with other cultures and to accept themselves and others.

H. Psychotherapy

1. Gilbert, S. (1989). *Get help: Solving the problems in your life*. New York: Morrow Junior Books.

   This resource book for adolescents provides information on agencies that provide assistance for common and unusual teen problems. It also gives suggestions on how to ask for assistance, what questions to ask when choosing professional help, and how to decide whether an agency is appropriate for the adolescent requesting help.

I. Sexuality

1. *As boys grow up*. [Pamphlet.] (1987). South Deerfield, MA: Channing L. Bete.

   This pamphlet, written for boys who are between the ages of 9 and 13 years, provides information about such topics as sexual changes, intercourse, pregnancy, sexually transmitted diseases, and birth control in a straightforward, simple manner.

2. Cole, J. (1985). *How you were born*. New York: William Morrow.

   This book, appropriate for children ages 5 years and older, provides simple, factual information about the birth process. It contains photographs of fetuses at different stages of development and drawings of many aspects of pregnancy, but does not discuss sexual intercourse.

3. Eager, G. B. (1989). *Love, dating and sex: What teens want to know*. Valdosta, GA: Mailbox Club.

   This book, for junior and senior high school students, provides information and illustrations about sexuality. Topics covered include love, infatuation, sexual desire, sexually transmitted diseases, and birth control. The book advocates abstinence, but discusses the pros and cons of having sex before marriage.

J. Other Situations and Problems

1. Beaudry, J., & Ketchum, L. (1987). *Carla goes to court.* New York: Human Sciences.

   This story, written for school-aged children, tells the story of a young girl who witnesses a burglary and must go to court to testify about it. The book provides details about the entire legal process, and discusses different feelings children might experience when participating in that process.

2. Bernstein, J., & Fireside, B. (1991). *Special parents, special children.* Morton Grove, IL: Albert Whitman.

   This book is appropriate for children ages 8 years and older. It consists of true stories about and photographs of children whose parents have a variety of disabilities.

3. Dolmetsch, P., & Shih, A. (Eds.). (1985). *The kid's book about single-parent families.* Garden City, NY: Doubleday.

   This book was written by children ages 11 to 15 years, and is appropriate for that age group. It focuses on understanding the feelings of children with single parents, but it also includes advice on how to handle issues faced by those children. The book also discusses some of the reasons for having one parent, including divorce, desertion, and death.

4. Gilbert, S. (1982). *How to live with a single parent.* New York: Lothrop, Lee & Shepard.

   This book is most appropriate for adolescents who live with a single parent. Topics covered include understanding parents' feelings, working out living arrangements, and keeping out of divorced parents' disagreements. The book provides advice for coping with the feelings aroused by these issues and for improving communication with parents.

5. Hall, L., & Cohn, L. (1988). *Dear kids of alcoholics.* Carlsbad, CA: Gurze.

   This book is written for children, ages 8 to 17 years, who have an alcoholic parent. It tells the story of a young boy named Jason, whose father is an alcoholic. Jason explains the facts and feelings associated with alcoholism from a child's point of view.

6. Hastings, J. M., & Typpo, M. H. (1984). *An elephant in the living room: The children's book.* Center City, MN: Hazelden Foundation.

   This book, written for children ages 7 years and older, helps children learn about alcoholism. It provides information and writing/drawing exercises designed to help children with alcoholic relatives handle their difficult emotions.

7. Jordan, S., & Philbrook, D. (1986). *Good losers and gracious winners.* Cincinnati, OH: Standard.

   This book, written for children ages 10 to 13 years, tells the story of a boy who competes in his school spelling bee. The story focuses on the feelings that children who compete have and provides strategies for dealing with losing, winning, and respecting one's competitors.

8. Krementz, J. (1993). *How it feels series.* New York: Alfred A. Knopf.

   These books, written for adolescents, consist of interviews with real children 12 to 18 years of age who have experienced a specific problem or situation. The series includes books about the death of a parent, being adopted, adjusting to divorce, having a terminal illness, and having a disability.

9. Meyer, D., Vadasy, P., & Fewell, R. (1985). *Living with a brother or sister with special needs: A guide for sibs.* Seattle, WA: University of Washington Press.

   This informative book for adolescents provides a wide range of information, including a section on how it feels to have a sibling with special needs.